Johann-Albrecht Meylahn

Trans-fictional Praxis

Studien zu Religion und Kultur
Studies of Religion and Culture

herausgegeben vom
edited by the

Institut für Religionssoziologie
der Humboldt-Universität zu Berlin

Prof. Dr. Wilhelm Gräb

Band 5

LIT

Johann-Albrecht Meylahn

Trans-fictional Praxis

A Christ-*poiēsis* of imagining non-colonial worlds
emerging from the shadows of global villages

LIT

Published with the support of the Alexander von Humboldt Foundation

This book is printed on acid-free paper.

Bibliographic information published by the Deutsche Nationalbibliothek
The Deutsche Nationalbibliothek lists this publication in the Deutsche
Nationalbibliografie; detailed bibliographic data are available on the Internet at
http://dnb.d-nb.de.

ISBN 978-3-643-91068-4 (pb)
ISBN 978-3-643-96068-9 (PDF)

A catalogue record for this book is available from the British Library.

© LIT VERLAG GmbH & Co. KG Wien,
Zweigniederlassung Zürich 2018
Klosbachstr. 107
CH-8032 Zürich
Tel. +41 (0) 44-251 75 05
E-Mail: zuerich@lit-verlag.ch   http://www.lit-verlag.ch
Distribution:
In the UK: Global Book Marketing, e-mail: mo@centralbooks.com
In North America: Independent Publishers Group, e-mail: orders@ipgbook.com
In Germany: LIT Verlag Fresnostr. 2, D-48159 Münster
Tel. +49 (0) 2 51-620 32 22, Fax +49 (0) 2 51-922 60 99, e-mail: vertrieb@lit-verlag.de
e-books are available at www.litwebshop.de

Table of Contents

Acknowledgement and Dedication

A book is always written by a community and therefore I need to acknowledge the community that was part of the writing of this book.

The space for research and writing was created by a grant from the Alexander von Humboldt Foundation, from whom I received a research fellowship for the years 2014–2016. The grant made it possible to have the time and the space to do all the reading, research and writing for this book.

I want to thank Professor Wilhelm Gräb, my host at the Humboldt University of Berlin, for his mentorship and encouragement and for the space to work. I had the privilege of offering two modules during my time at Humboldt University, and the lively discussion with students provided vital inspiration and energy to continue reading-writing.

My family, my wife Ronél and my son Joschka, sacrificed to create the necessary space for me to work, read and write, without which this book would never have been possible. Thank you.

Ronél has given so much of herself in support of my work. She spent days reading and re-reading the manuscript after listening to my thoughts, frustrations and inspirations and without her this book would never have appeared.

I dedicate this book to her. Thank you, Ronél!

I received the Alexander von Humboldt Fellowship for advanced scholars, which made the research and writing of this book possible.

The publication of this book was also made possible by the financial support of the Alexander von Humboldt Foundation.

I would like to extent my deepest gratitude to the Alexander von Humboldt Foundation for the amazing opportunities they create for research and collaboration.

1. Introduction

To have a body is to be embodied in a political world.

From where do you speak?, is a question that I learnt to ask from Paul Ricoeur, thanks to Richard Kearney (2010 pos 77 of 6156), who shared that this was the way in which Ricoeur began his lectures. This is perhaps a fair question with which to introduce a book and thereby also introduce myself, as its author. Where do I write from, where do I respond from, where do I think from, in other words, my embodiment, my incarnation, or my context?

Embodiment

Michael White argues that one needs to be aware of and more importantly be accountable for one's own embodiment, and specifically be conscious of the power and privilege that comes with one's embodiment.[1] To be embodied is never something neutral, but the body that I am is always political, at least this is what this

---

[1] I do not think that the point is to deny one's power or privilege, but rather to work with it and be responsible and accountable for the privilege that one's embodiment has given one. As Michael White argues:

The version of responsibility associated with this work is one that emphasizes accountability. It involves a commitment to establish therapy as a context in which we are accountable to those persons who seek our help; accountable for how we think, for what we do, and for the real effects or consequences of our interactions with those persons who seek our help.

This is not a context in which therapists can presume a position of neutrality, a context in which therapists can hold out a claim to a space that is free of the relations of power and of the biases associated with their location in the social world. This is not a context in which it is possible for therapists to entertain an "objective" position in this work; to transcend their ways of being and thinking that are informed by culture, class, race, and gender. Instead, it is a context of accountability that encourages . . .

Therapists to render visible certain aspects of their taken-for-granted ways of being and thinking, to expand their consciousness of their biases.

Therapists to acknowledge their location in the social world, and the privileges and the limits of understanding that are associated with this location.

Therapists to acknowledge the assumption and purposes that are associated with those metaphors that guide their work.

Persons to confront the limits of their therapist's understanding and to express their experience

book will argue. To have a body is to be embodied in a political world. In other words, the body that appears, always appears in a specific world, and in that world it has a particular place or status. The body has a political place (status or privilege), which is determined by amongst others: politics, culture, race, gender and economics. This is particularly important with regard to the *poiētics* of this book, as it is not a neutral objective account, but written from a specific privileged embodiment.

Concerning my embodiment: I have lived and worked most of my adult life in South Africa, although with numerous shorter and longer exposures to Europe. My undergraduate studies I completed at the University of KwaZulu Natal, and these years were very influential in my formation. I studied philosophy, theology and religion at the University of KwaZulu Natal. The theological focus at the School of Theology was predominantly contextual theology, with emphasis placed on Liberation Theology, Black Theology, African Theology, Feminist as well as Womanist Theologies. My postgraduate studies were predominantly influenced by post-structuralist philosophy, specifically from the French speaking world, and a turn towards narrative through the work of Ricoeur and narrative approaches to therapy. This might explain where I am writing from, but it has not given an indication as to why I am writing: to what or to whom am I responding? What called this book forth? This book will not be a response to that question, as it will not seek to determine nor understand that which called it forth, but it will seek to understand or interpret that thoughts, or thinking, for example, books are responses to that which called them forth.

Why am I writing this book? The easy answer is: I cannot but write. Perhaps this book is trying to understand exactly that: *I* cannot but write. To be an I is to write. I write therefore I am. Writing understood very broadly as any form of externalisation, even the externalisation of inner thoughts or consciousness.

I believe the *why* is important. The why also introduces the first part of the title of the book, trans-fictional praxis.

Was heisst Denken? (What calls thinking- forth?)

Some might argue that to be human is to be a *noetic* soul, at least since Aristotle, which I will interpret as: to ex-ist and to exist is to externalise.[2] To be, to be

---

of these limits.

Persons to honor the unique understandings and experiences of life that pertain to their location in the world of gender, race, class, culture.

Therapists to transgress the limits of their thought by stepping into alternative sites of culture. This notion of responsibility emphasizes responsibility for the real effects of our actions and interactions within the context of therapy itself (White 2011:63–64).

[2] These ideas I have taken from Stiegler (2014; 2015a; 2015b), and I will unpack them in more detail in the following paragraphs and chapters.

present, to appear, is to externalise through the creation of texts (tools, artefacts as well as written texts) and therefore I will refer to existence, that is to be (as ex-*text*-tiert or ex-*text*-ence), to externalise (ex-*text*-ualise). To be, to be present, is to have a body that is visible, in other words that appears, that is disclosed. A visible body that appears, that is disclosed, is a political text, as the visible body becomes visible as differentiated into gender, race, culture, age and economic status. It appears as a differentiated body, that is an identifiable body, which can be classified and categorised. A body appears, for example, as a white, male, educated and middle-class body, but whiteness and maleness are not characteristics of the Flesh or Life, but they are texts inscribed into or onto the flesh, and through this inscription the Flesh becomes visible as body and it is given a particular place within a world: a *Dasein* within a world.

To be human, noetic soul, is to respond to a Call – even if the Call is the Call of one's own Flesh, one's own Life, it is that which Calls thought forth, *was uns denken heisst* (Heidegger 1961). One is Called, for example, by one's own Flesh (Life) as a me called by the Call into the responsibility of being a responding I. An I who responds, perhaps with the words: 'Here I am!', and in this response, becomes a *Dasein* (subject) in a particular world.

To be human, a *Dasein in Mitsein*, is the praxis of thinking, which is externalisation (ex-*text*-ualisation). It is a praxis, namely *to do* things, even if the doing is just to be, but even just to be is to be out there (external), be visible, to appear, which only happens through ex-*text*-ualisation. This doing (praxis) thus includes things such as: to think, to create, to work, to be present: a *Dasein*. It is a work to be. To be is to work. The question is: who works? Is it the me co-working in its becoming an I, is it the Flesh co-working in becoming a body, or is the work done exclusively by others and thus determining the visible body as a docile body? There is Life, or there are lives who actively co-participate in their becoming visible as some*body*, although embodiment is always a collective process and to a large extent one is thrown into an embodiment one did not create, but there is a degree in which one can partake in the inscriptions and what is ascribed to one's Flesh as it becomes a body and a some*body*. It is this active participation in embodiment that makes one a noetic soul and therefore perhaps human. But what about the numerical majority of bodies who do not actively participate in their embodiment, but are docile bodies, primarily determined only by others? It is important to understand that to be is to work. To be is to write, but conscious that it is a privilege to work and thus to be, and that many are estranged from their work, and thus estranged from their being (ex-*text*-ence), as they did not co-write their text, but are determined by the Text of an other. Writing is always co-writing, but what if certain texts are so dominant that co-writing becomes impossible as it is supressed? I will come back to this question of those estranged from the labour of being, but first focus on the labour of being.

A *Dasein* is always to be in-a-world and the world is the con*text*, the social construction or rhizome as Deleuze and Guattari (2011:3–26) refer to it, the *Da* of the *Sein*. The *Dasein* (ex-*text*-ence) within-a-world (con*text*) engages with the things of her or his world, the phenomena, all that which is visible, which come into appearance within her or his world as something external, that is as something ex-*text*-ual.[3]

The Call that calls thought forth perhaps begins by calling forth the most existential thoughts or questions. A me is called and the me responds by thinking, and perhaps the first thoughts that come to mind are existential questions such as:

- Why am I here?
- Who am I?
- What am I?
- From what and to what am I?
- For what purpose am I here?

Or because there is something that Calls thought forth, the question could be: what is this something that calls or why is there something rather than nothing? Is one sure that there *is* something rather than nothing? What if the something that *is*, is purely contingent? It is perhaps contingent as the something that is; for it to be, it must be external and if it is external it is ex-*text*-ual. If it is external (ex-*text*-ual) then it could be a figment of the imagination, or rather figments of imaginations. But what if these fictions (figments of imaginations) are all there is – there is nothing outside of text (Derrida 1997:158)? If fictions are all there is, then these fictions are as real as it gets, there is nothing more real. But what inspires the imagination, or in Heidegger's terms, what calls thought forth? That which Calls is what truly *is*, but for it to be, it must become visible and appear in the external (ex-*text*-ual) world, and therefore it only *is in* the response, there is nothing outside of text, there is nothing that appears that is outside of text. Flesh appears only as differentiated body. Whatever *is* might be created out of nothing as in the idea of *creatio ex nihilo*, as figments of imagination or figments of creation (creativity), the absent-presence of fictions. Yet, there must be something that calls

---

3   The light into which things come in order to show themselves in their quality as phenomena is the light of the world. The World is not the set of things, of beings, but the horizon of light where things show themselves in their quality as phenomena (Henry 2003:14). To re-present anything to oneself, for consciousness is to place it before oneself (Henry 2003:15). In German "to represent" is *vor-stellen* which means to place (*stellen*) before (*vor*). "Ob-ject" designates that which is placed before, in such a way that it is the fact of being placed "before" that renders the object manifest (Henry 2003:15). Consciousness is nothing other than this manifestation that consists in the fact of being placed before. The fact of being placed before is equally well the fact of being placed outside: it is the "outside" as such. The "outside" as such is the world. We say "the truth of the world," but the expression "the truth of the world" is tautological. It is the world, it is the "outside," that is manifestation, consciousness, truth (Henry 2003:15). As things exists for us only if it shows itself to us as a phenomenon. And it shows itself to us only in that primordial "outsideness": that is the world (Henry 2003:15).

this figuration forth, that calls this creation forth, and that something has been named God in some traditions.

Andrew Root (2014) in his book Christo-praxis, returns to this idea of *creatio ex nihilo*. The creation of something out of nothing. What if this nothing is the founding basis of what there is, in the sense of *Sein zum Tode* (to be unto death)? It is only if one learns to love the nothing that one is truly free to be. Free to construct, *creatio ex nihilo*, the something that one is and then also to co-construct the world in which one co-exists with others.

Is it nothing, is it death? Or is "nothing" and/or "death" not a name given to something, in other words a determination of something? A name, and with the name an explanation of the absent-presence of that which called something forth. Therefore, it might be better to refer to it as less than nothing, as even nothing is already a thought, but so is less than nothing. Another name is the Real (Laruelle 2013:43) or Flesh or absolute Life (Henry 2003; 2012; 2015), the Body without Organs (Deleuze and Guattari 2011:43ff) or preindividual fund or ground (Stiegler 2015:53) or Heterogeneity (Laclau 2007:140f), or independent objective reality as Root (2014), in reference to critical realism, might refer to it. Different names given to that which remains foreclosed to thought, that which cannot be directly touched in the sense of truly known, comprehended, *Begriffen*. That which at best can only be caressed (see Levinas 1969:257–258). It is that which is outside of language's grasp and therefore outside of human thought, that which is outside of text, but according to Derrida (1997:158) there is nothing outside of text. Of course there is everything outside of text, but one does not have access to that besides through text: that which *is*, that which is visible, is external and therefore ex-*text*-ual. Henry (2003:10) argues that language cannot blaze a trail to either reality or truth.[4] Henry's critique of language argues that language is the negation of Reality and thus negation of Truth. This unreality is for Henry the truth of language (Henry 2003:10). Yet, it is this Other, Real, Flesh, Heterogeneity that arouses one's desire, that calls one forth as a thinking subject. It is more than an arousal of desire. It is in a certain sense the arch-intelligibility as Henry calls it.[5] It is an arch-intelligibility as it is prior to the intelligibility of ex-*text*-ence.

---

[4] Language passes as the means of communication par excellence, that is, as the means of communicating or transmitting the truth. But that is the greatest illusion, since the single truth that it can transmit is a truth that already exists, has already been revealed, reveals to itself by itself, independently of and prior to language (Henry 2003:10).

[5] "Arch- intelligibility" means that a mode of revelation comes into play that is different from the one by which the world becomes visible; and that, for this reason, what it reveals is made up of realities that are invisible in this world, and unnoticed by thought. The Prologue list them: Life, in which Arch-intelligibility consists; the Word of Life, in which this Arch-intelligibility of Life is fulfilled; and, finally, the flesh, in which the Word of Life becomes identical with each of the living beings that we are, we men and women. So an entirely new definition of human is formulated, which is as unknown to Greece as it is to modernity: *The definition of an invisible,*

It is the affectivity of the flesh, experiencing itself in suffering and joy (Henry 2015:58–59), which is for Henry the very condition for ex-*text*-ence. For example: the body cannot be without Flesh, and yet Flesh can never be visible but in body. Therefore, the Flesh is the very condition for the existence of the body, which is an ex-*text*-tence. Henry refuses to accept that all there is, is the social construction of reality, as there is more or something else, namely the living Flesh (Henry 2015:xi). He argues that Life reveals itself through flesh.[6] This revelation or self-revelation or auto-revelation of flesh or of Life is phenomenological, but in the sense that it denotes phenomenality itself, givenness itself (Henry 205:xii). It is the Call that solicits a response and in the response, that which called is determined as something that called (that solicited a response). One exists, one comes into existence through a desire aroused in one: an arousal, a solicitation, a Call, or an awakening to which one can only respond: *Here I am*. And in this response, "Here I am", the I comes into being. The I comes to *Dasein*, *Da* – there, but it's coming there is always in the here of the response. In the response of the me,[7] the me becomes the I of *Dasein*, an I of being-in-a-world, being as ex-*text*-ence. A desire aroused in one by the other. A desire to connect, a desire to touch (direct contact) or to be touched, a desire to become one, become whole, to be connected and have a place and identity within a greater whole. In this sense the praxis of being, the work of *Dasein* is a form of eroticism (see Bataille 1986). One is here (Here I am) because one is aroused, solicited, called, awakened by the Other, or the Flesh (me) is solicited to respond, and in the response the me becomes an I, and the Other is interpreted, is determined as the caller or the solicitor and is given a name, is given a determination. Or as Henry argues, that affectivity is the essence of life (Henry 2012 pos 450 of 2078), the Call is the essence of life. The solicitation, the affectivity, the eroticism is the *pathos* of life.

"To live" means to undergo experiencing oneself. The essence of life consists in the pure fact of undergoing experiencing oneself, and, the "world," is devoid of this. This very simple definition of God starting from the definition, which is itself very simple, of Life

---

    and at the same time carnal, human being, and invisible in so far as carnal (Henry 2015:18–19).

6   Life "reveals itself" in flesh in a way that no act of thought, philosophical or otherwise, can do, since it is only by being alive that we know, with an invisible certainty, what life is (Henry 2015:xi)

7   "Me," says the Self generated in the original Ipseity of Life, but it says it in the accusative (not nominative) case. That the singular Self speaks of itself in the first place and must use the accusative precisely translates the fact that it is engendered, not bringing itself into the condition that is its own, not experiencing itself as a Self, and not having this experience of self, except in the eternal self-affection of Life and of its original Ipseity. The "me" is engendered in the self-affecting of absolute Life and experiences itself passively against the background of the original Ipseity of Life, which gives the "me" to itself and makes of it what it is at every moment; therefore this "me" finds itself at the same time much more than what is designated as a "me" (Henry 2003:135–136).

as a pure "trial of oneself" (the most difficult is often the most simple, which also means that the most simple is often the most difficult) now gives us possession of the insight that will guide our investigation, which is precisely the Arch-intelligibility we are talking about. Yet no trial of oneself is possible if an Ipseity does not also happen within this trial, at the same time as it does and as its condition – thus, as consubstantial with it. "Ipseity" denotes the fact of being oneself, the fact of being a Self. To the extent that a real life is produced (and not the simple "idea" or a simple "concept" of life), and thus to the extent that Life's trial of itself a real trial, actually experienced and lived, and as such is inevitably singular, the Ipseity in which it occurs is itself, qua an actually lived Ipseity, a singular Ipseity. It is a singular and real Self, the Fist Living Self that Life generates, as how it is experienced and has revealed itself in this Self, which is thus is self-revelation, its Word. This is Johannine Arch-intelligibility: the very essence of absolute Life, the movement of its self-generation as its self-revelation in its Word – a Word within this movement, as the very mode whereby this movement comes about, and as old as it is. "In the beginning was the Word." From Johannine Arch-intelligibility the first law of Life follows: No Life is possible that dos not bear within it a first living Self, in which it undergoes experiencing itself and becomes a life (Henry 2015:19).

The Call (the Real), that which calls thinking forth, determines-in-the-last-instance (Laruelle 2012:315) the response (ex-*text*-ence), but only in the last instance and not directly or conclusively. It is not out of nothing that "life" is created, there is no *creatio ex nihilo*. Not even in the Genesis story was there a *creatio ex nihilo*, but a *creatio* out of chaos – the undefined (see Caputo 2006:75f). The nothing is in reference to the desire that is never completely fulfilled. The touch, the desire to comprehend, to be able to *ergreif* something in a*Begriff* is never perfect or final. It is therefore that Levinas speaks of a caress rather than a grip (Levinas 1969:257–258). The nothing is in reference to the cinders (see Derrida 2014) that one is, as ex-*text*-ence.

Or stated differently, in the response the Call is absent and only present as that which is named "the Call". It is present only in the name, but in the name the Call is absent. It is present in its absence, as it is present only as being part of a response based on a decision of how to call (Name or determine) the Other, the Call, when one responds: Here I am. In this response, Here I am, one determines or names that to which one is responding. There are different Names that have and are given to the Call, and each Name carries out a different world, together with different objects and subjects of that world in response to the Name. For example, if one names the Call "matter" and the world of physics or the natural scientific world appears; if one names the Call "God" and a world of faith appears where God might be understood as the creator of the world. Yet, likewise name the Call Life and Henry's philosophy of flesh begins. There are different responses to the Call, different names, different narratives, and thus different metaphysical systems, as different responses to a Call. As Derrida argues, there is always another voice, as the Call calls forth another response.[8]

Heidegger said: '*Der Mensch ist, sofern er als das* animal rationale*vorgestellt wird, das Physische in der Übersteigung des Physischen; kurz gesagt: im Wesen des Menschen* als animal rationale*versammelt sich das Hinüber von Physischen zum Nicht- und Überphysischen: der Mensch ist so das Meta-Physische selbst'* (Heidegger 1961:25). The human is the metaphysical.

One is often part of different metaphysical systems, for example one might drive to work, fly across the globe, talk on a cell-phone in the scientific world, but when it comes to other matters, such as moral issues, then one is part of a different world, a religious world perhaps. Sometimes these worlds (metaphysical systems) are in conflict with each other, and at other times they can co-exist harmoniously next to each other. Then again at other times they traverse and intersect with each other and create the plural world one exists in. It is because of this experience that the book refers to the praxis of being human in a pluralistic globe as a trans-metaphysical praxis, but for reasons that will become clearer later, I name it a trans-fictional praxis.

The Call is that which affects us, or as Heidegger says (1961:158) *Es ist das was uns angeht.* This affectivity is what calls thought forth. Heidegger in his book, *Was heisst Denken?* reflects on both meanings of that question, namely: what does it mean to think, and what calls forth thought? Thought responds to that which calls thought forth and in responding there appears a thinking being (*Dasein*), a noetic soul, as the being that ex-*text*-ualises – the being that thinks: I think, therefore I am. If I am it means I think. In that sense Descartes was completely right: it is in responding that the I appears (exists – I am), I am only exists in responding. I am, exists in the "Here I am!", and therefore it ex-*texts* in the response.

Called into a world carried out by thought

One ex-ists (*Ex*-text-*tiert*) within a time and space, which is probably the most basic definition of metaphysics (see Meylahn 2017a) – the time and space (place) of being. It is narrative that provides time and place for things. In other words, praxis happens within a context: a context that offers the praxis a particular time and place – a metaphysics, a narrative, which gives the praxis meaning and purpose. Yet, living in South Africa, and as in most parts of the global world, one lives in a pluralist world, or in pluri-verse worlds. In some contexts, the pluralism is felt more acutely as one is daily confronted with different races, languages, cultures, religious as well as worldviews. Living in a multi-racial, multi-cultural and multi-religious world one is confronted with different metaphysical systems, different

---

8   But the words "another voice" recall not only the complex multiplicity of people, the "call," they
     "ask for" another voice: "another voice, again, yet another voice." It is a desire, an order, a prayer
     or a promise, as you wish: "another voice, may it come soon now, again, another voice . . . ." An
     order or a promise, the desire of a prayer, I don't know, not yet (Derrida 2014:10).

narratives, therefore it is not strange to be confronted in a single day with modern so-called Western medicine and a few minutes later to be confronted with a more traditional belief system concerning healing and illness.

I said earlier that this book is a response – a response, as all responses are, to a Call, the Call of Life perhaps, and this response (this book) is trying to make sense not of that which calls, but of being (ex-*text*-ing) in this Call-response or Call-naming interaction.

In this response (book), I will attempt to offer a generalised interpretation of the praxis of *Dasein*, the labour of being, whilst using examples from my particular *Dasein* in South Africa. The implied readers of this praxis (writing of this book) are people similarly struggling to make sense of their existence (*Dasein*), but not only as individuals but also as collectives and therefore in the context of political – the political, understood as collective sense making and meaning creation. One does not make meaning in isolation, but always with others (*Mitsein*), in other words, meaning is a social construction. The construction of a people (*Mitsein*) and the construction of the social, in the social construction of meaning, is political and/or religious. This and/or will be unpacked in greater detail in the following chapters, but what is important to keep in mind is the construction of a "we" as a religious or political act. Laclau argues that the 'political operation par excellence is always going to be the construction of a people' (Laclau 2007:153). I will argue in a later chapter that this political (ideological task) can also be interpreted as a religious task depending on how one interprets religion.

It is this political or religious task of binding (*religare*) individuals together into a people that interests me. Therefore, a book about the praxis of *Dasein,* is and will always also be a religious and/or a political book.

Therefore, I am proposing in this book a trans-fictional approach to interpreting praxis. Trans- in a similar sense to how Dussel (2012) interprets a transmodern – where different metaphysical worlds traverse each other, different narratives, different responses, and thereby creating a transversal fictional space in a certain sense, or at least a sensitivity that one's own metaphysics, one's own narrative, one's own response is not universal, but particular to one's own con*text* and world.

The terms religious and political are used generically and without reference to any particular party-political or ideological affiliation, although texts are never neutral. In the same way, it is not specifically a particular religion that I am referring to, but religion as the belief that binds, although in a global world one cannot think, or be, ex-*text* without the Christian texts playing a dominant role (see Meylahn 2017b) in the ex-*text*-ualisation. In the global world, the Christian texts plays a dominant role in thinking. This will be unpacked in more detail later.

Therefore, the question might be asked: Is this a Christian book? Is it a book written for Christians, and theologians in particular? Perhaps it is, but that depends on how one interprets Christianity.

If Christianity is interpreted as a metaphysical system, as a religion amongst other metaphysical systems, then this book is not Christian. If the Christ-message, the Christ narrative of Jesus' incarnation, His Crucifixion and Resurrection, is interpreted as a metaphor (fiction) that can serve as hermeneutical key to interpret this praxis of *Dasein*, the labour of being, then perhaps it would be a Christian book. If the Christ-event is interpreted as a metaphor that "reveals", or allows something to appear, of what it means to be human: the human condition or the praxis of humanity, then perhaps this book is Christian. It is perhaps Christian in the sense that it offers a way of interpreting metaphysics, interpreting religion and of being liberated momentarily, through Christ, through Grace and Faith alone, from metaphysical systems. In that sense, the Christ narrative offers a truth and a way towards the kingdom, as Jesus says in the Gospel of John chapter 14:6, but where Truth is not understood as *adequatio*, or as perfect correlation or representation, but as a way, as a praxis revealing not truth, or reality, or the way things truly are; truth as liberation and the *way* towards an impossible kingdom always still to come, a kingdom insisting or insurrecting (resurrecting) on the edges or in the shadows of the kingdoms of this world.

This book called into which world?

This book is a response to a Call, and in its response it becomes part of a particular world. To position, or embody this book, I will shortly introduce this book in conversation with three other recent books, namely Root's (2014) *Christo-Praxis*, Rollins' (2006) *How (not) to speak about God* and Kearney's (2010) *Anatheism*. This book is in conversation with numerous other books as well, but these three books are recent books that address both the philosophical world as well as the theological, and in the case of Root, specifically practical theology.

Root would probably see himself as being mainline evangelical and writing for that specific audience. Rollins describes his book as part of the emerging movement and Kearney is a philosopher of religion. All three books describe a dissatisfaction with contemporary Western theology and/or philosophy. Kearney wants to move beyond the atheism-theism divide and both Root and Rollins are frustrated with the God-talk in churches, both the fundamentalist God-talk as well as the liberal theological reduction of Christianity to ethics. Specifically, Kearney and Rollins try to think theology by taking the fathers of suspicion seriously, and thereby bring an element of doubt into the centre of their theology, in for example Rollins' a/theology (Rollins 2006:21 & 25), which could be brought into conversation with Kearney's Anatheism. I have responded to Kearney in a previous study (see Meylahn 2017c), and therefore will not go into too much detail here, but rather focus on Rollins and Root to position this book. Both Rollins and Kearney find the resources for their own ideas in the mystical tradition – Rollins mainly Christian mysticism, whilst Kearney also includes other mystical traditions that are not specifically Christian. Rollins interprets God as being hyper-present (Rollins 2006:23) and hypernymity[9] (Rollins 2006:24). In reference to Samuel Beckett, Rollins (2006:42) argues that language has to be torn, ripped so as to express that which is beyond language. One must rip language (one must rip open the Name given to the Call, and thereby expose the Response, the Name, the social construction to its limitations) to discover something of the Call that called a response (thinking) forth. This idea of the inadequacy of language is taken up in most mystical traditions and mystical God-talk. If I would need to position myself spiritually, this would be the tradition I would be most comfortable in. Yet, this book is written for people living in a global world, with various different religions and cultures, in a trans-cultural and trans-religious context, namely a trans-metaphysical world, and therefore the need for a trans-fictional praxis, rather than choosing one thought-system, even if that one is mystical or hospitable to others.

Rollins, although proposing an a/theology, goes on to develop a mystical theology, where he describes God with the help of various theologians and mystics (Rollins 2006:26–30) so as to develop a theology where God is described as hyper-presence and hypernymous. It is not that Rollins says nothing about God, as he says a lot, and thereby develops a Name for God, maybe a mystical non-name, but a name all the same. Such a non-name name is contrasted with *the* Name given to the Call (that which is beyond language), and giving the Call *the* Name is interpreted as creating an idol. Therefore, the non-name name is interpreted with the help of the idea of an icon, but how different is a non-name name from a name, as it remains a determination, as not-determining of that which called it forth? The difference between an idol (a strong name) and a non-name name is only a matter of degree, but the general thrust is the same. In an idol the Call is captured and solidified, in mystical theology the Call is embraced in an open net, or is embraced in an open hospitable non-name name, where new names can be added continuously. In other words, whatever it is named, even a non-name-name, it remains a response from the called to the Call, seeking to determine the Call, even if it is determined as not determined.

Rollins pleads for an Icon (see Rollins 2006:31f) to think about God. An idol is a determination of God, an icon is something through which God calls one, addresses one, without returning the address. I find in the idea of an icon, in contrast

---

[9]   In this way the God who is testified to in the Judeo-Christian tradition saturates our understanding with blinding presence. This type pf transcendent-immanence can be described as 'hypernymity'. While anonymity offers too little information for our understanding to grasp (like a figure on television who has been veiled in darkness so as to protect their identity), hypernymity gives us far too much information. Instead of being limited by the poverty of absence we are short-circuited by the excess of presence. The anonymous and the hypernymous both resist reduction to complete understanding, but for very different reasons (Rollins 2006:24).

to an idol, something very precious to think about thinking. The icon becomes a space in which to respond without determining. The Call calls and through an icon, as response, one seeks not to determine the Call, but to be continuously addressed (called) by the Call. The icon offers a response that does not seek to determine, but to be continuously called.

One could argue that an Idol, even if it is crossed out (deconstructed), is still legible. Even a destroyed idol remains a name given to the Call. In that sense, a mystical idol, or destroyed idol, is created and although it might be a beautiful idol that certainly offers an alternative to the fundamentalist idols that are plaguing the world, it still is an idol, a slightly more sophisticated idol, but an idol all the same. In other words, there is a response to the Call, even if that response is a humble, tentative, hospitable response, it is still a response and in that sense a Name, or maybe a name (without capital letters) or even a name, but even a crossed-out name remains a name, as it remains legible. A name can either say what something is or it can say what something is not, but it still says something about (seeks to determine) that which calls-a-name-forth. The icon in that sense is different, as it creates a space for responding without determining (naming).

Both icons and idols are what they are not in themselves, but in the way they are used. But if an icon is used to make relatively clear statements about what or who God is (or about what God is not), or relatively clear statements about the way of believing correctly (orthopraxis), then it becomes a name: a determination. Rollins argues not for a correct belief, but by reading orthodoxy backwards, as one would read a Hebrew word, it would read not as right belief, but believing in the right way (Rollins 2006:66). This is what Rollins suggests: not the right belief (orthodoxy), but believing in the right way: a correct praxis of believing (orthopraxis).

This is probably very close to the praxis that is developed in this book. A praxis of being faithful to the Call, without being faithful to the belief of the Name. The difference between trans-fictional praxis and Rollin's orthopraxis is the normative element, of believing to have the correct praxis.

Does reading orthodoxy from right to left, really change the idea that one knows what is correct? One can be so convinced that one has the one and only Name for the Call, but one can also be fundamentally convinced that one has the right way of responding to the Call, the icon becomes the right way of responding. The difference between the Right Name and the Right Way of Responding will be marginal, as one would still have a basis to judge others, who are then believed to have the wrong Name or who are doing things the wrong way, for example the other, the "they", can be classified as idol worshipers and only "we" are the ones who believe correctly. The trans-fictional praxis of this book will not accuse anyone of idol-worship, but rather accept that to be (to exist) is to worship an idol, that is to worship (believe) that which one created (the Name) and gave to that which called the name forth (the Call). There is no being (existence), there is no labour of being that does not worship an idol, that is, believe in the Name that carried out the world in which one ex-*texts*. Therefore, trans-fictional praxis will not attempt to save the world from idol-worship, as no work (theory or praxis) can save us from the labour of being, but Christ alone (*sola Christus*). It is in-Christ that one is saved – not from this labour (which continues), but from the belief that drives this labour, which is the belief that justifies and legitimises the labour, and therefore one is saved by grace alone, saved from the belief in the labour of belief.

As long as one is still stipulating a right way, a correct way, and thereby determining what is right, or determining a sense of what is good, one is being determined by a belief. To place it into the Genesis (Gen. 2–3) story, one would have eaten of the tree of knowledge of good and evil and believe that one knows what is right and what is wrong. The Genesis story tells the story of Adam and Eve who ate from the tree of knowledge, and it was this act that got them expelled from God's presence: paradise.

What is the difference between a fundamentalist statement about God and a mystical contemplation about God? Just because the one is clear and the other is more subtle or hidden does not change that they both offer a "correct" understanding or "more correct", maybe even more "politically correct" determination of who God is or who God is not, or a correct way of believing, whichever way the correct is understood. It gives either a clear indication of what is believed to be good or right, or it indicates into that direction, and therefore serves as a basis to justify oneself and judge others. This knowledge gives one the ability to pronounce something good as well as the opposite, condemn something as being wrong, evil or inappropriate or politically incorrect.

Many people would argue that one needs a normative element in thought, by which one can judge one's own thoughts (self-justification) as well as the thoughts of others. I would agree that to be, to exist (ex-text), one needs to differentiate and differentiate on the basis of some knowledge. The problem in a plural globe is that there are different knowledges and therefore different beliefs as to what is good and what is wrong.

Is there a true democracy of thoughts,[10] a true democracy of interpretations, a true democracy of metaphysical systems, of fictions, or are certain thoughts, metaphysical systems, interpretations still more superior than others, perhaps because they are closer to the truth, or more correct than others, or more acceptable than others? If so, who decides what is more acceptable, and according to whose norms would one decide what is "more acceptable"? Would one use Habermas' validity claims, as does Browning (1991:70)? Are these validity claims not part

---

[10] Ó Maoilearca basing his thoughts on the work of François Laruelle and specifically his argument for a democracy of thought (Laruelle 2013 pos 1344 of 7408), argues that all thoughts are equal (see Ó Maoilearca 2015).

and parcel of . . . , in the sense of being emplotted within a certain metaphysical system, namely a Western metaphysical world?

Once one tries to move away from orthodoxy towards orthopraxis, away from a correct belief towards the correct way of believing, the correct praxis of a believer, as Rollins suggests, how different is such a correct praxis from his critique of liberal theologies and their immanent ethics (Rollins 2006:2)? Rollins describes God in mystical terms and then he moves towards an ethic of love, which is based not on the naming of God, but is founded on certain biblical verses and the teaching of Jesus. The praxis that is suggested is a praxis of love – which is not connected to God and the naming or hypernymity of God. What has God as hyperpresence and hypernymity got to do with an ethics of love, based on the teaching of Jesus? One could have developed an ethics of love without worrying about naming God. In that sense, Rollins has not moved beyond what he accuses the liberal theological tradition of, namely: immanent ethics. One could have developed numerous ethical systems from the teachings of Jesus, and in the past there have been numerous different ethical systems developed and interpreted as being Christian. Each of these ethical systems based its ethics on their interpretations of specific chosen scriptural texts. What makes love stand out? Is it not the primary, secondary and tertiary retentions and protentions of Rollins as well as of his audience that make this choice inevitable? In other words, love is chosen, as love fits neatly within a certain metaphysical system, within a certain narrative.

Root reflects on the tradition of Practical Theology from the time of Schleiermacher and he follows this tradition, mainly from a Western (North America) perspective to, amongst others, Browning (1991). According to Root, this tradition has focussed too much on human agency whereby leaving little or even no room for divine agency.[11] 'Divine action is actually lost in the hermeneutical operations of constructing practical wisdom within communities of ethical action' (Root 204:57). Root argues that for him, reality is more than these human constructs and that 'practice and action themselves may exist outside of human constructs (Root 2014:58). He hopes to gain access to divine action by interpreting the 'revelatory realism of God's action in concrete, lived experience' (Root 2014:59).

I agree with Root and Rollins, that to reduce everything to social construction is unsatisfactory. Root, in his Christo-praxis, tries to move beyond social-construction via his interpretation of critical realism, where he gives this real, or the experience of the real, a Christian interpretation via protestant interpretation of central Christian ideas such as: *ex nihilo*, and a *theologia crucis*. In this way, he wants to move beyond descriptive theology's collapsing of divine action into

---

[11] . . . Christopraxis perspective is highly hermeneutical as it also seeks a fusion of horizons. But for Browning, this fusion happens only at the critical correlational level (at the level of placing distinct traditions or fields of thought in discourse); this keeps the horizons bound almost fully in the realm of human agency (Root 2014:57).

human praxis and thereby losing the experience of God's coming to humanity (see Root 2014:59). The place, which Root believes where one can do this, is in the experience of finitude or the experience of our wounds. This experience of finitude, or an experience of the wounds, opens the cultural (social construction) to the religious (Root 2014:64). In other words, similar to Rollins, there where social-construction is wounded, or fails, or shows cracks, there something of the divine, the Call is *believed* to become visible. Yet, for it to become visible it needs to ex-*text*. In other words, there where language (culture) reaches its limits, there is the possibility for the religious. The religious is thus to be found on the edge, or over the edge of human reason (human response). The divine is to be found beyond the Name, outside the Name. In this sense, the divine is not found in the dependent objective reality, but it is sought in the independent objective reality, taking critical realism's terms into account.

Rollins (2006), and the emergent movement in general, are frustrated with the orthodoxy vs heresy dualism. Dogmatic formulations of correct belief frustrate them and therefore they try to move towards an orthopraxis. Rather than correct belief, they propose a correct way of believing. Root and Rollins also do not side with the more liberal theological ideas where Christianity has been reduced to an immanent ethical system, without any talk about God as such. Root turns towards critical realism as mentioned above, and Rollins turns to orthopraxis – 'The reversal from 'right belief' to 'believing in the right way' (Rollins 2006:3). This book is probably well situated between these two views, although critically situated with regards to both of these views. With Root and Rollins, the book agrees that the Call, which is beyond language, is important, and with Rollins, I fully support the move towards praxis away from dogma. The Call is important, but not because the Call is a good name with which to save the name God, but because the Call is a way to refer to that which calls-thought-forth,[12] but without determining it as something or someone. The Call refers to that (whatever that is) which calls thought forth.

For Rollins, faith is the experience, the experience of God[13] in the Real, or the experience of God in the experience of finitude, or the experience of wounds (the impossible) in Root's terms, and theology would then have the task of interpreting these experiences. To interpret the experience of faith one uses the Jewish-Christian historical texts, which provide the metaphors and narratives with which

---

[12] This idea I will unpack in depth in the next chapters.

[13] For Christians testify to having been caught up in and engulfed by that which utterly transcends them. In short, the experience that gives birth to faith, at its most luminous, is analogous to the experience of an infant feeling the embrace and tender kiss of its mother. On the other hand, theology could be provisionally described as that which attempts to come to grips with this life-giving experience, to desire the source from which everything is suspended and from which our faith is born (Rollins 2006:1).

to give meaning and explanation to these experiences. Thus, the faith experience is emplotted into a Jewish-Christian *muthos*. The experience of being grabbed, solicited, affected, caressed, called, awoken is emplotted into a Christian narrative, using Christian metaphors. There is not just one Christian tradition or metaphor, as there are very different and diverse Christian traditions, for example, Rollins and Kearney have focussed specifically on the mystical traditions, whilst Root focussed on the Protestant tradition. Root and Rollins can use these Christian metaphors and even re-interpret them because they live in a context that is strongly influenced by the Christian texts, but what if one lives in a context where other texts play a dominant role? In a context of different metaphysical systems, often conflicting metaphysical systems, re-interpreting Christian metaphors and thereby saving Christianity would not necessarily make sense. If this experience of faith is interpreted theologically within the Christian narrative how does one engage other traditions that have interpreted a similar experience of the Other differently, be it within a different religion or with the use of scientific or secular metaphors? Rollins, Root and Kearney and numerous others determine the Call through the use of Christian-Jewish or mystical metaphors and names, and thereby in a certain sense save Christianity. This book will in the later chapters also turn to a Christ-*poiēsis*, but not in an attempt to save Christianity.

In this book, such use of the Christian-Jewish text, as a metaphysical system seeking to determine the Call, will be equated with any other attempt to determine the Call.

It does not matter which theology or which philosophy, as they all seek to determine the Call, name the Call. Only a non-philosophy or a non-theology as Laruelle (see 2012; 2013a; 2013b) suggests seeks to not determine the Call, but understands all philosophy and religion as determined in the last instance by the Call.

Why name this experience of being called God?

This experience of the Real, the Call, which Rollins interprets as hyper-presence or hypernymity, could also have been interpreted differently. Hyper-presence could also be interpreted as there being nothing outside of text (Derrida 1997:158) and that one is always already in the midst of things, one is present, present to the extent of being caught or intertwined in the rhizome (Deleuze & Guattari 2011) which one cannot escape – hyper-presence. One is present in a hyper-presence of texts. Hyper-presence can thus also be interpreted as the rhizome, as the infinite chain of texts that one is always within. This experience can also be described as hyper-presence, hyper or radical immanence, and for some that experience might be named "God", but for others it could be the Rhizome or the Text within Contexts or the infinite chains of signifiers. Rollins decides or he responds to this Call by naming (calling) this solicitation an experience of faith, which he then continues to give a mystical theological interpretation. Root on the other hand takes the experience of being, or more specifically the experience of nothing, the impossible, the void, the experience that there is no beginning and no end, no final meaning or purpose, as *creatio ex nihilo* as well as interpreting this experience of the impossible (finitude or the wound) through a *theologia crucis*.[14]

How does one interpret these experiences in communities where there are people who interpret differently – where people or neighbouring communities interpret otherwise? That is the focus of this book: it is about interpreting otherwise – trans-interpretation, trans-narrative, trans-metaphysical and trans-fictional. It is about being in that transversal space where these different narratives, metaphysical systems, fictions traverse each other.

Both Root and Rollins acknowledge the experience of faith as an experience of the Real, the experience of heterogeneity, the experience of the Other, and give that experience a Christian theological interpretation – Root with the *theologia Crucis* and *Creatio ex nihilo* and Rollins with using various mystical theologians to describe the experience in terms of hyper-presence and hypernymity. They both emplot the experience of faith into a specific metaphysical system (using the secondary and tertiary retentions and protentions) of the communities of which they are part: Western Christian communities. These interpretations (theology) could be and will be in conflict with other interpretations of "similar" and very different experiences of the Real, as how something is experienced is already determined by the primary and secondary protentions and retentions. I do not want to revert to a religious or metaphysical pluralism with the belief that all religions essentially speak about the same experience, or speak about the same Thing, but just different interpretations thereof. I would not want to make such a determination of the Real, but rather argue that thought is called forth, and it is called forth by a variety of possible things which exist only once thought has responded, as then they ex-text. So, what Calls is something foreclosed to thought and this book is not one more attempt at trying to determine what calls thought forth, but focuses on the different responses that are called forth and therefore is a trans-fictional praxis.

In this book, I would like to interpret the Christ-narrative, firstly consciously as narrative, and secondly as narrative outside of different metaphysical interpre-

---

14 Jesus is "where" he is in ministry and where he is in ministry is places of death (cross as revelation) bringing forth life (resurrection and reconciliation)... This death-to-life, life-out-of-death paradigm is simultaneously an epistemological structure embedded in an ontological reality. It is the logic of God's ministry; it is a lens, even a pattern, that allows events to be discerned as God's own action. But this pattern as epistemological structure rests in an ontological reality; to epistemologically discern God's ministry is to encounter God's ontological being (Root 2014:104).

tations (outside of theology or any other ideology or ontology or onto-theo-logy).
A conscious fiction about fictions, which could help individuals and communities
to be (to ex-*text*) in a trans-fictional space, and therein lies for me the praxis of
love, but without calling it an orthopraxis. To love humans who are doomed to
idolatry, who are doomed to metaphysical systems, who are doomed to ideology
or religion or theology and all the positive and negative consequences thereof.

Root living in North America and Rollins coming from Ireland, are writing
from, in and for a context that is predominantly Christian, or one should rather say,
predominantly influenced by the Christian Texts. Living in South Africa, which
is also statistically a Christian country, but after the birth of a secular democracy
other voices and other metaphysical systems are regaining their voices, and specifically the call for decolonial thinking, one is challenged to question the dominant
role of Christianity. Thus, one is daily confronted and challenged to question the
dominant metaphysical systems, to perhaps hear the call of other narratives, other
religions and other metaphysical systems.

There is another important reason to seek a trans-fictional praxis, and that
is that the world today has never before in its history seen so many people on the
move – migration. People from other cultures and religious backgrounds are moving into spaces, and through their entry into these spaces, the dominant metaphysical system of those spaces are being challenged. One response to these challenges
is the rise of fundamentalism in various traditional religions as well as the rise in
fundamentalist atheism and even fundamentalist secularism. How does one move
beyond the clash of fundamentalisms, how does one interpret in a trans-cultural
and trans-religious world? A trans-fictional praxis is the suggestion of this book.
In this sense, it is a trans-metaphysical praxis, or a trans-narrative praxis and not
a Christo-praxis nor an ortho-praxis, yet the book suggests a Christ-*poiēsis*. As it
is a *poiētics* inspired by the narrative of Christ in that transversal space between
metaphysical systems, between narratives, that is between fictions, therefore a
trans-fictional praxis as Christ-*poiēsis*.

Christ-*poiēsis* is not to give the Real, or the Call, a Christian interpretation, but
to think through the Christian narrative. To think the labour of being through the
Christ-event, and thus create the possibility of a Christ-*poiēsis*, where the labour
becomes the work of *poiēsis*, which it always was, but unconsciously so – a conscious *poeisis*, as the labour of being, through the Christ-event, and therefore I
refer to it as Christ-*poiēsis*.

The Christ-event is interpreted as a hermeneutic fiction, with which to interpret the labour of being, so as to insurrect the various interpretations that are
believed to be true, or good or correct, including the Christian interpretation. In a
certain sense it is a Christ-*poiētic* insurrection (resurrection), and specifically an
insurrection of Christianity, or Christendom, where Christianity is interpreted as
a universal and imperialist religion, and likewise an insurrection of any religion

that offers a correct dogma (orthodoxy) or that offers a correct way of believing (orthopraxis), but without Christ-*poiēsis* offering a correct anything. It is the freedom to be, without ever being free, but a freedom to labour: to labour the labour of being, which is *poiēsis*. *poiēsis* is a work, a writing, a text, a response, but without belief in its sufficiency as a response, and therefore *poiēsis* is the creation of literature (fiction), without any claim or belief to be a sufficient presentation or representation of the Real, or the Call as that which called the labour of being forth.

The approach of this book is non-idol or non-ideological or non-religious or non-theological and non-philosophical, but where *non* is not interpreted as being against ideology, or against theology, or religion or philosophy, but where each of these are recognised as absolutely necessary and inescapable, as they are a necessary part of what it means to be human, but they are all interpreted as being insufficient, and therefore as various fictions. They are interpreted in Laruelle's (2012; 2013a; 2013b) sense of the *non* of non-philosophy. They are each necessary but insufficient, but without suggesting an alternative that proposes to be sufficient, but rather accepting this human condition and offering a praxis that takes this condition seriously, and that invites people to actively participate in this condition, especially those who have been estranged from this labour of being by dominant and hegemonic metaphysical systems that reduced them to being docile bodies.

A Christ-*poiēsis* as an insurrection of philosophy, theology, ideology and religion, not because of a different understanding of God or of *the* Truth, or the correct or the good or the right understanding of either God or non-God. A Christ-*poiēsis* as an attempt to move beyond any correct or right or good or best way, because as soon as there is a right way or correct way there is the possibility to justify oneself, judge others and therefore exclusion. Any human determination of what is right, correct, best and or good becomes the determination of God, and there is sin (separation from God through determination of God), as one has eaten from the tree of knowledge of good and evil. How is one liberated from that desire to know what is Good or God, how does one pray to God to rid one of God, as Meister Eckhard prayed? Maybe by being in Christ and in Christ alone, seeking *imitatio* and *participatio Christi*, participating in his incarnation and crucifixion and in that alone, without any additions added to Christ. A radical interpretation of *sola Christus*, which includes without Christology – Christology is Christ and a logos, but *sola Christus* is without any additions even the addition of a logos which creates and determines a Christology. When one is in *sola Christus* one is left with nothing but love, not love as a practice, not love as a law, but alone love: the pathos of affectivity, or the pathos of the caress without a name with which to touch.

What about God? Well, Jesus once said that if we want to know God, we should know him, for God is in him, as he is in God (John 14:7). In other words, God is not to be sought outside of Christ and even more pertinent not outside of Christ crucified, for we shall find not God, but the devil, Luther (see Althaus 1983:33) once claimed. There is no Father beyond Christ, there is no God beyond Christ. Is that still a God or is it the death of God as the transcendental becomes immanent, incarnate in flesh? The incarnation can be understood as the death of God, as God (the Transcendent) has made His dwelling amongst humans, God becomes immanent (see Meylahn 2013:315–21).

In an immanent understanding of the incarnation, Christ would become the incarnation of an idea, whatever idea it is, but it is the binding idea or binding principle of what is believed to be good and right and or true. Yet, the story of Christ does not end with the incarnation, as there is the crucifixion and resurrection. The idea that is incarnated is also the idea that is crucified – the incarnation, or the incarnated one, is crucified. Thus, whatever is incarnated has died. Whatever idea is incarnated, it is crucified, but crucified by what? It is crucified by the dominant hegemonic powers of the world in which the idea was incarnated. The resurrection would need to be interpreted in the light of the previous two moments of the Christ-event, as an insurrection (resurrection) of the incarnated one. These ideas will be unpacked in the later chapters in the development of a Christ-*poiēsis*.

For now, it is important to interpret the incarnation, crucifixion and resurrection as Christ-event, as a radical insurrection of any Naming (determining) of the Call. The Call is believed to be incarnated in some or other idea. The idea in turn identifies, differentiates and classifies (determines and names) the Call. This determining (incarnation) is crucified and the resurrection is interpreted as insurrection. It is an insurrection of any, and all, thoughts, thus an insurrection of theism and atheism, an insurrection of theology and atheology, as well as an insurrection of anatheism. The crucifixion of the incarnation allows for an insurrection (resurrection) of that which was believed to be incarnated in the first place. The Call is incarnated in thought, but this incarnated thought is crucified, and thus the Call insurrects as resurrection.

The question this book asks is perhaps: is there a way to be a follower of Christ (disciple) without a metaphysical system or without a meta-narrative, without Naming the Call? How to be a follower of Christ, not a follower of an idol, not a follower of an ideology or a theology, but a follower of Christ and Christ alone, in a non-theological or non-philosophical sense, or as Paul (1 Cor. 2:2) says, I bring you only Christ, and him crucified. What does this mean? This is the passion that inspired and inspires this book.

I agree with Root in his reference to Bonhoeffer, that 'discipleship is not primarily about practices but first and foremost about following Jesus (it may be secondarily about *imitatio Christi*, seen for instance in *Life Together*). And this following is about participation (*participatio Christi*), not through practice but through death (*theologia crucis*) (Root 2014:73).

Can there be a community of followers of Christ? Can there be a community of non-theologians, non-philosophers? This question will be unpacked in a later chapter.

Publication houses want to know in which subject field a book is written and for which subject field it is written. Well, as this book is about Life and as Henry (2015:21) argued about his book, it could be a philosophical book, a phenomenological book, or a theological book. It is about Life, but Life is ex-*text*-ualised in *Dasein* within various worlds. The book is about this praxis of ex-*text*-ence in various worlds and therefore it is indeed about all three fields: philosophy, phenomenology and theology.

It is a book about a praxis of being human, the labour of being, through making sense and creating meaning, and the important role religion plays in this praxis, as it binds meaning and sense into a world. The world of which the human authorship eventually is forgotten, as it ascribes that authorship to God or some or other Idea: whatever Name is given to that which called-forth-thought. In that sense, this praxis of being, the labour of being, is a religious praxis and a theological praxis, as thinking is responding by naming (determining) the Call, and as this name (logos) binds (*religare*) a world together, the very world the Name (logos) carries out. Therefore, this book is a theological praxis as it is a metaphysical praxis, but it seeks to move towards a trans-metaphysical (fictional) praxis.

In that sense, this book being about praxis and theology is a practical theological book, but it certainly is not a traditional theological or a traditional practical theological book.

Trans-fictional Praxis and Practical Theology

The turn towards praxis in practical theology has certainly played an important role in the thinking of this book. Practical theology has gone through a major metamorphosis over the last few decades, since Schleiermacher placed practical theology as the crown of the theological disciplines. I will not repeat the whole history of the development of the subject field, but focus on the field as it has impacted my own context and *Dasein*, and respond to the question, why this book is not a typical practical theological book? The practical theology that I was exposed to, can be summarised into two categories: firstly, the Western practical theology that has been determined by the cultural-linguistic turn and the focus on hermeneutics, and secondly, the various traditions of transformative praxis as liberation, for example, Black, African, Feminist and Womanist theologies.

The question of why this book is different has to do with the frustrations I have with these traditions.

The cultural-linguistic turn in practical theology, as Root emphasised, is problematic as it places all focus and emphasis on the human construction and human action and leaves very little room for God's action, God's praxis. Root *responds* to this emphasis on the human by turning to critical realism (see Root 2014:189ff). For Root, there must be more than social construction (dependent objective reality), namely the Real (independent objective reality), and theology cannot be reduced to only the dependent objective reality. Root reflects on the experiences, the evangelical experiences, that people have of the more-than-dependent-objective-reality. He acknowledges that the Real cannot be known perfectly and completely, and if it is known it is always known only in the dependent objective reality, but he also denies that there is an unbridgeable gap between the Real and social construction. He turns to *critical* realism in the tradition of Roy Bhaskar, Margaret Archer, and Andrew Collier (Root 2014: 191). In other words, it is not a naïve realism, but critical realism. For Root, God acts in the realm of the Real, beyond the possibility of the socially constructed. In other words, God acts in the impossible of what is determined as being possible in the various social constructions. People have experiences of the impossible, that is, they have experiences of that which does not make sense in the realm of what is determined as possible in the dependent objective reality. These experiences indicate in the direction of the independent objective reality. These experiences Root interprets firstly as God's actions, because these experiences can be interpreted through theological metaphors such as *creatio ex nihilo* and a theology of the cross: therefore, what he offers is a Christo-praxis, as a praxis of interpretation.

Another development in practical theology is the turn towards lived religion (see Failing and Heimbrock 1998; Ganzevoort 2009; 2013; Gräb 2000; 2002; 2005; 2012 Grözinger & Pfleiderer 2002). In broad strokes this turn to lived religion can be interpreted as a turn towards lived religious experiences, outside of traditional religious forms and determinations. The turn to lived religion is partly inspired by Schleiermacher's interpretation of religion, or Otto's interpretation of the sacred, which is outside of traditional Names and traditions of institutional religion. Again, experiences that indicate that there is more to life than dependent objective reality. Here these experiences are interpreted as experiences of the sacred or feelings of there being something more, or a feeling of absolute dependence. Experiences and/or feelings of the more than dependent objective reality (social construction of reality), are experiences and feelings of the more than what reason can capture. To place it into the context of the first sections of this chapter, there are experiences of something that Calls (calls thinking forth), and that this something is more than, or other than, the traditional (institutional) Names that have been given to or that tried to capture (comprehend) the Call. This more than or other than has been given the name living God in certain interpretations, for example Root as well as Rollins with his idea of hyper-presence and hypernymity.

An experience of that which is believed to be more than or other than what reason can capture often leads to a mystical turn in theology.

My response to this religious and/or mystical turn I have unpacked in another article (Meylahn 2016) and do not wish to repeat here. I would prefer to remain within the text, within the response, rather than speculating about that which is beyond the text, whilst agreeing with Root, that focussing purely on the human construct (texts) has its limitations, but speculations about the Real also does not really offer an alternative, irrespective if one calls it critical or not.

Likewise, my frustration with the various forms of liberation theologies, I found expressed in an article by Küster on Intercultural Theology,[15] that many of these theologies have taken the idea of the Other, incorporating numerous of the ideas of post-structuralism and often relying on Levinas' radical ethics, to develop their response, but reducing the Other to their particular political agenda, thereby in their response giving the Other a particular identity – a racial, sexual, social-economic, cultural or gender identity. In this sense, the universalism of Levinas' Ethics is made particular which is necessary in the formation of identities and in the formation of the people as Laclau would argue (2007), and therefore there is a contextual historical and political necessity for such movements, but it also has its limitations. Through these movements an alternative ontology is created, which as I have just argued, is vitally important for the development of identities, yet the alternative ontology is the same as the previous ontology. It may be more just as it is more inclusive than the previous ontology from which certain groups were excluded, but new exclusions are bound to follow (see also Laclau criticism of Fanon 2007:151). This is for me too much of the same, in other words, there is too much of a repetition of the same, an eternal return. Then again, such repetition might be unavoidable.

Yet, both these traditions focus on that which insists, Calls. In the first tradition, there is the experience of the more than and other than in individual experiences. In the second tradition, the focus is on the other of the political-social-and-economic reason or a system that needs to be transformed. Yet, both traditions give specific names and/or interpretations to that which is experienced as more than or other than, and therefore they determine the Call.

The excluded, the more than or other than needs to be taken into consideration, but is there a way to take it into consideration without determining it?

---

[15] Bei der Rezeption kontextueller Theologie lassen sich im Wesentlichen drei Modelle unterscheiden, (1.) die konservative evangelikale Gegenposition, (2.) die eurozentrisch westliche Position und (3.) das Projekt einer interkulturellen Theologie ... . In den Kreisen akademischer Theologie wird in Allgemeinen eine eurozentrische-westliche Position gegenüber den Dritte-Welt-Theologien vertreten. Ihre Kritik wird schnell unter Reproduktionsverdacht gestellt, sie wiederhole nur was die westliche Theologie schon längst an Selbstkritik geleistet habe (Küster 2005:184).

Stiegler (2014) focusses on those excluded and interprets them as the minority. In Stiegler's sense the minority are all those who are excluded, in the sense that they are those who do not have access to the progress and fruits of the "developed" world, as well as the minority interpreted as those who have been reduced to consumers, and therefore are no longer individuals, but purely *dividuals*; those excluded from power, from the fruits of development, as well as estranged from production (estranged from ex-text-tualisation) and in that sense proletarian. The minority can be interpreted as those who are estranged from the labour of being and do not co-write their bodies, but are reduced to being docile bodies of a system they did not co-create; those deprived from individuating themselves through externalisation, because they exist only as determined, as docile bodies, and not determining individuals. Populism often is thought in connection with groups of the population that experience this exclusion, that feel that they have been reduced to being docile bodies who are determined by the Other, the State or the Market or whoever or whatever is interpreted as Other. In this interpretation populism is a protest of the excluded. Yet, populism has also been used to offer an explanation as to why Trump won the presidential election in the USA, or why the Brexit vote passed and why there is a rise of populist movements throughout Europe and the world and the tremendous support that populist thought, including theology, is receiving globally and in South Africa.

Therefore, there is a need to re-think practical theology to be able to respond to the minority, but without determining them, as is often the danger in various forms of liberation theologies, but the politically correct theologies of liberal theology do not respond to needs of the minority either.

I would love to write a book in ordinary language in Wittgenstein's sense, not the language of politically correct leftists in Žižek's (2017) terms, nor the conservative traditional theology nor in the language of a new kind of universal lived religion, as the religion of a post-secular globe (dominantly determined by Western thought), but if anything, I would love to write about a praxis of Flesh as Henry (2015) might argue. I am fully aware that the moment I start writing, the Flesh will have disappeared, and all I will be left with is the text and the bodies the text wrote into ex-*text*-ence. In other words, I would love to write a book about the Call, that which is other than or more than the closed systems (political, religious, ideological and economic) or any closed thought-systems. The problem is, the moment I write about the Call (what calls thought forth), I will have determined the Call, named the Call. I want to write a book that does not determine the Call, but that is determined by the Call, that is continuously in a stance of being called to respond, called into responsibility, but without determining the Call in return. Determined by that which is other than, and more than the closed political, economic, cultural systems that have divided the earth, as well as the closed systems of thought (metaphysics) that determine and define everything that is and thereby create docile bodies. In that sense, I wish it was possible to write in the naked words[16] of the Call, the ordinary naked language of the Call, but that seems impossible as it would end history.

This is my desire, which is also the calling of this book, to respond to this Call in ordinary language about flesh. To write a book about *Flesh*. But I know that is not possible, so what I can write about is about *writing*, which is about responding to the Call: naming the Call, determining the Call, and the different names that are given and therefore a trans-fictional praxis, with a special focus on those who are excluded from this labour of being. Those who are not privileged enough to co-determine, but are determined.

I sometimes cannot help but wonder if Žižek is not right when he argues that the leftist rhetoric does not actually want to change the world, but they enjoy the arguments (Žižek 2017:11). In his book, *The courage of hopelessness,* he responds to the leftist with their rhetoric, but not really wanting to change the world, and maybe that is what is necessary: the courage to be hopeless, or to recognise the meaninglessness of all. However, such courage would again be a metaphysical courage based on a metaphysical interpretation, a belief that there is no meaning and thereby determine the Call, as a Call that called forth nihilism. Trans-fictional praxis engages with the fictions of hopelessness, but likewise it needs to engage with the most naïve fictions of hopefulness.

This can only be done, if one no longer thinks from the meta-discourses towards Flesh, or from the Name to the Call, but allows oneself to see all these meta-discourses (metaphysical systems) to be determined by the Call (in that they are called forth by the Call), determined by Flesh, determined by Life or the Real, but determined only in the last instance and not in a reciprocal relationship, or as a direct and final representation.

To respond by taking up Heidegger's (1961) challenge and to try and think the most thought-worthy, but not to try and think "that" which calls, as that is what all thought does, but to think thought from the stance of that which Calls it forth. To think thought from the stance of the Call. This stance with the Call that calls thinking forth might perhaps bring one inevitably into solidarity with those, the minority, whose determined bodies have been determined by others and therefore cry out (call out) for a response where they are allowed to co-write.

An attempt to think the most thought-worthy is to try and think from the stance of the Call, but without giving it a particular Name and thereby determining it as Life or Flesh as Henry (2003; 2012; 2015) has done. The problem is to think

---

[16] The idea of naked words, I take from Derrida's (2008) book, *The animal that therefore I am,* where he writes, 'In the beginning, I would like to entrust myself to words, were it possible, would be naked' … I would like to choose words that are, to begin with, naked, quite simply, words from the heart (2008:15).

about the Call, that which calls thought forth, to think the *Bedenklichste*, the most thought-worthy, it has to exist and to exist it has to ex-text.

It is only in naming, externalising it (ex-*text*-ualising) that it can appear in the world so that it can be thought. Henry tried to think the *Bedenklichste*, by attempting to remain in the immanence of Flesh (Life) without the externalisation, or what others try to do when they speak of immanence or carnal hermeneutics, but to do that he had to name it Flesh or Life. Only as Flesh and Life could he think the most thought-worthy, that which calls thought forth. It is impossible to do otherwise, as any attempt to think or even not-think "it", is an externalisation (ex-*text*-ualisation). The trans-fictional praxis this book proposes is an incarnational praxis in the sense that it seeks to think from the Call – the Call that calls thought forth and in thought becomes incarnate in the world as an idea, as a Name; to think from the Call, but without determining the Call in any way, besides as that which calls thought forth. Like Henry there are those who have tried to think from the Call, from that which calls thought forth, but to be able to think they have given the Call a name. Another attempt to think from the Call is the idea of carnal hermeneutics, but if anything, it could only be thought of as *meaningless* carnality. Meaningless Flesh or meaningless Life (meaningless Call), but in the literal sense of the word *meaningless* as it does not have meaning, as meaning is what it calls forth, and it is in the response, in thinking, that meaning is given to Flesh, to Life, meaning is given to the Call, in that the Call is determined as Flesh, or is determined as Life, or as God. Stated differently, to think carnality (Flesh or Life), the Body without Organs, are all attempts to think the Call, but they have given the Call a name, even if Life, Flesh, Carnality, Body without Organs are names given to something before meaning is ascribed to it. The stance of Flesh before it becomes body, the me before it responds as I, but without any attempt to determine that which calls thought forth, and therefore I do not determine it as Flesh, Body without Organs, Life, but only as Call, which refers to that which calls thought forth. This Call could be anything, but what it is will only be determined in the response, that is, it will be determined in what it calls forth, namely thinking. Not meaninglessness as a meta-discourse of some or other variant of nihilism – where meaninglessness is still too meaningful. The meaninglessness of carnality in the literal sense of the word meaningless, where meaningless does not become a meaningful metaphysics, but is a presupposed state prior to the creation of meaning. As Derrida (2008:15) argues '... to go back in time, back to an earlier moment still, to a time before that time. And to speak starting from that point in time, so long ago, as one says, a time that for me becomes fabulous or mythical'. A time before time, without being in time, that which is, Calls, and in the response it is *placed in time*, and thanks to time it finds a place. The response to the Call is always a response in a *Zeit-Spiel-Raum* (see Heidegger 1965:214 and Caputo 1993:30), therefore one can say that the response is metaphysical. Before that, there is a state of meaning-

lessness that is *meaningfully* prescribed and ascribed to a presupposed state prior
to meaning and the way to do this, is as Derrida argues, mythical and/or religious.
In this book, the meaningless state is ascribed to the Call prior to the response,
that is prior to any Name given to the Call. Thereby, not meaning that the Call
has no meaning, but it has no meaning for *me* until *I*, as part of a *we*, ascribe
meaning to it. It is to this "point" prior to names and meaning that Schleiermacher
also directs the gaze of those who seek to understand what religion is.[17] Similar
to Derrida's naked words, one needs to become naked of meaning, to gaze to that
point where religion, as Schleiermacher understands it, will not reveal itself, but
where it might be. Maybe even that point is the place where the last God will wink
(beckon) to us, as Heidegger once claimed, the *Ortschaft* where this *Last God* is
to be thought is *in* and *as* the Event. '*In der Wesung der Wahrheit des Seyns, im
Ereignis und als Ereignis, verbirgt der letzte Gott*' (Heidegger 1989:24). Event interpreted as does Hofstadter in his translation of Heidegger (1971), as *disclosure
of appropriation* (Hofstadter 1971:xxi). The event of language, of meaning, is the
disclosure of appropriation, something is disclosed (appears) to the same degree
that it is appropriated (named, given meaning).

Any attempt to think the Call will always place the Call within either a
metaphsyical system (orthodoxy) or the metaphysics of an ethics (orthopraxis),
which is the frustration that both Root and Rollins respond to. Yet, this frustration
is not new, as it was already the frustration that Schleiermacher responded to.[18]

This book will not offer another Name for the Call, it will not seek to name or
understand the Call, it will not attempt to argue that the Call is a good name for
God, but will view all names given to the Call, all determinations of the Call as
different, yet equally responses to the Call. Each name given to the Call, carries
out a different world (metaphysical system) and likewise there will be different

---

[17] Ihr werdet wissen, wie der alte Simonides durch immer wiederholtes und verlängertes Zögern
      denjenigen zur Ruhe verwies, der ihn mit der Frage belästigt hatte: was wohl die Götter sein.
      Ich möchte bei der weit größeren und mehr umfassenden, "was die Religion ist, gern mit einer
      ähnlichen Zögerung anfangen. .... . Eure Blicke unverwandt auf den Punk hinrichten möget,
      den wir suchen, und Euch alle andern Gedanken indes gänzlich entschlagen. Ist es doch die
      erste Forderung derer, welche nur gemeine Geister beschwören, daß der Zuschauer, der ihre
      Erscheinung sehen und in ihre Geheimnisse eingeweiht werden will, sich durch Enthaltsamkeit
      von irdischen Dingen und durch heilige Stille vorbereitet, und dann, ohne sich durch den An-
      blick fremder Gegenstände zu zerstreuen, mit ungeteilten Sinnen auf den Ort hinschaue, wo die
      Erscheinung sich zeigen soll (Schleiermacher 2001:41).

[18] Stellet Euch auf den höchsten Standpunkt der Metaphysik und der Moral, so werdet ihr finden,
      daß beide mit der Religion denselben Gegenstand haben, nämlich das Universum und das Ver-
      hältnis des Menschen zu ihm. Diese Gleichheit ist von lange her ein Grund zu mancherlei Verir-
      rungen gewesen; daher ist Metaphysik und Moral in Menge in die Religion eingedrungen, und
      manches, was der Religion angehört, hat sich unter einer unschicklichen Form in die Meta-
      physik, oder die Moral versteckt. Werdet ihr deswegen glauben, daß sie mit einer von beiden
      einerlei sei (Schleiermacher 2001:43)?

ethical systems of thought. The Call can be named (determined) differently and the praxis this book focusses on is the praxis of being amongst all these different names and therefore I refer to it as a trans-fictional praxis.

This book is about praxis, the praxis of responding to the Call and in responding giving meaning to the Call by determining it, or naming it. This praxis is individual, but it is always also collective or social and therefore political. It is collective in the sense that the meaning ascribed to the Call collects (binds-*religare*) a world into ex-*text*-ence. The name that is given to the Call, calls a world into ex-*text*-ence – a world that offers a home (a place and a time) for numerous things just as all these collected things carry out a world (see Heidegger 1971:200). Therefore, the praxis of responding is political and/or religious as it binds people and things into a world and into a collective (*polis*). Yet, some people are excluded from this praxis, and a trans-fictional praxis will seek to include as many as possible in this praxis.

In that sense this book could be a practical theology, but it could also be in the field of public or political theology, as it brings politics and religion together in the praxis of responding, and responding is the praxis of *Dasein* in *Mitsein,* or stated differently, the praxis of embodied *Dasein*. However, not in the classic sense of practical theology or public theology, which is traditionally interpreted as bringing together in dialogue or conversation the Text (Biblical text – story of God) and the context (lives of individuals, families or communities and/or congregations).

Another common trait of both practical and public theology is the focus on ethics in the sense that public and practical theology want to change something in the world, they want transformation based on some normative idea of what is good or right or just. They want to change something, change the world, heal a community or individuals or families, transform society, provide answers to problems.[19] Each of these theologians, and many more that I have not mentioned,[20]

---

[19] The following list of books in Practical Theology is not an exhaustive list, but books that have become part of my tertiary retentions and protentions with regard to Practical theology. Don Browning *A Fundamental Practical Theology* (1991); Richard Osmer's *Practical Theology: An Introduction* (2008); Charles Gerkin's (1984), *The Living Human Document: Re-Visioning Pastoral counselling in a hermeneutical mode,* (1991); *Prophetic Pastoral Practice* and (1997) he wrote *An Introduction to Pastoral Care*; Elaine Graham wrote her book in 1996 *Transforming Practice: Pastoral Theology in an Age of Uncertainty*; Riet Bon-Storm in 1989 wrote *Hoe gaat het met jou? Pastoraat als kommen tot verstaan*; Barbara Rumscheidt wrote in 1998 wrote *No Room for Grace: Pastoral Theology and Dehumanization in the Global Economy*; Gerben Heitink wrote in 1999 (or the translation) *Practical Theology: History, Theory, Action Domains*; Bonnie J Miller-McLemore edited *The Wiley-Blackwell Companion to Practical Theology* (2012) and in 2014 Andrew Root wrote his *Christo-praxis*.

[20] This list most certainly is not exhaustive and numerous important books in the field of Practical Theology have been left out, specifically those not written in the dominant global language, English. Books written in Spanish or Portuguese from Latin America are not featured here, and the main reason is that these books are not that accessible to an English reader. The list is

have a normative and/or, on the basis of the normative, a transformative element. It might even be argued that it is essential for any practical or public theology to have a normative (Osmer 2008) or transformative (Graham 1996) moment, based on an interpretation of the "Will of God" (historical theology). Some will argue that it is not practical or public theology if it does not have a normative element. Osmer (2008) argues that the normative is one of the four essential tasks of practical theology. Based on the interpretation of what is believed to be normative, change or transformation or healing or wholeness can be evoked. Transformation or healing or change happens by bringing the normative texts (historical theology – a correct interpretation of the biblical texts as well as the texts of tradition) into a fusion of horizons (systematic theology) with a correct analysis of the context (descriptive theology) (see Browning 1991). The problem field needs to be described and understood in the first step of descriptive theology or in response to Osmer's (2008:4) first two questions: What is going on?, and Why is it going on? Once the context, the individual, the family or the community context has been analysed or described, that is, the problem identified, determined, classified and understood, it can then be brought into conversation with historical theology (the Bible as well as the Tradition), which will guide (normative) the remedial action. The remedial action will be a fusion of horizons between historical and descriptive theology interpreted as systematic theology and/or ethics, which will then need to be developed in the final moment of praxis. The basic hermeneutic cycle or spiral of practical or public theology is that the answers of Osmer's first two questions (what is going on and why is it going on) are brought into conversation with the answer from the third and fourth question (What ought to be going on? and How might we respond? (Osmer 2008:4), which then leads to a transformed practice.

In any serious theological context, the Bible is not just applied to the problem, but the historical gap between the context of the Bible and the world today needs to be taken into consideration. Therefore, the Bible needs to be interpreted before it can be brought into conversation with descriptive theology, which accentuates the importance of New and Old Testament scholarship. Once both the context as well as the Bible have been studied and "correctly" interpreted they can be brought together in conversation with the hope of a fusion of horizons, this would then be the task of systematic theology (ethics). This fusion of horizons will offer a unique outcome and thus offer healing or transformation or reconciliation or wholeness, depending on what the problem was that was identified in the first place.

For practical and/or public theology there should be a fusion of horizons between biblical texts, together with the texts of the theological tradition, interpreted "correctly", and the "correct" analysis or description of the problem field, with the

---

primarily to indicate theoretical activity over the past 3–4 decades as well as specifically books that have influenced *my* thinking.

help of the latest theories in the social, political and economic as well as biological, bio-chemical and psychological, or any other relevant sciences.

Practical theology can be understood as this hermeneutic praxis of bringing these two together: God's Word and the context, or Text and context. Or understood as bringing the four tasks (Descriptive–Empirical, Interpretive, Normative and Pragmatic) of practical theological interpretation together (Osmer 2008:11). Bon-Storm argues that the Pastor is also a product of socialisation and lives within a certain cultural/value context, which she calls the 2nd hermeneutical circle. The first hermeneutical circle is the cultural world of the ancient texts. Where these two circles meet, there is the point X, which is where the hermeneutical adventure of theology (see Bon-Storm 1989:21) begins.

What unites all these books is their hermeneutical approach to practical theology, as Root argued, that the main skill of a practical theologian is hermeneutics.[21]

Root argues that the task of practical theology is to interpret the concrete and empirical (context) of God's becoming.[22] I would argue the task of trans-fictional praxis is to interpret the incarnation of the Call (the determination of the Call) in the concrete and empirical of different metaphysical systems, different narratives, that is different fictions.

Shifts in interpreting Praxis

Praxis can no longer just be understood as the application of theory, but the shifts in human consciousness and practices need to be taken into consideration.

Likewise, practical and public theology can no longer be interpreted as the application of biblical truths onto a context, but most recent books in practical and public theology have taken the shifts in human cultural consciousness and practices into consideration.[23] The role of narrative with regards to our thinking, our understanding of self, other and world has become ever more important. Linbeck argued, as quoted in Gerkin (1997:105f), that there are three shifts in the approaches to theology: propositional, experiential-expressivist and cultural-linguistic.

As practices are motivated by the normative element, and specifically the practices of practical theology, these shifts have had a specific impact on how one

---

[21] So just as the New Testament scholar exegetes the Greek text, so the practical theologian's primary hermeneutical objective is to discern the movements of God's ministry (as mission), confessing God's ministry is God's being as becoming (Root 2014:99).

[22] Practical theology is not concrete and lived because it is empirical, but because it seeks to discern (hermeneutically) the concrete and lived reality of God's becoming in ministry (Root 2014:99).

[23] To speak of paradigm shifts in pastoral care practice implies that there have been shifts in human cultural consciousness and practices that present pastoral practitioners with an altered context for their ministries (Gerkin 1997:97).

views the helping professions –practices which have as their aim to help people reach or fulfil a norm. In such a normative context, helping in the sense of
therapy and/or counselling, or helping in the sense of community transformation
and/or community development, is understood as analysing on the basis of some
or other understanding of what the norm is or what is perceived to be normal, and
on the basis of that analysis, develop remedial action. With regards to community and specifically community transformation, or as it was called, development,
there has been a shift. A move away from expertise coming from outside, mainly
from the Modern West "reaching" out and helping the *under*-developed (those
below the norm) and "lacking" other, to a more inclusive approach where the local knowledges are taken into consideration. Yet, also in the individual context of
counselling, in the past there was an expert and a patient (somebody experiencing
a lack or a need) and the idea is to transfer the expertise from the expert to the
patient, who is most often seen as being rather passive, as she or he firstly is determined (diagnosed by the expert) and secondly passively receives the *pharmakon*
(the medicine) that the expert or the professional prescribes.

The shifts in the normative and helping practices can be interpreted with the
help of cybernetics.

In first order cybernetics, helpers view families or communities as machines.
In this view, helpers, therapists and/or community workers ("developers" or activists) are seen to be separate from their patients or community and able to control or manipulate and thereby fix the incorrect or problematic workings of the
machine. A separate and objective expert can objectively analyse the problem,
which is seen as a deviation from a norm, and on the basis of the correct analysis or reading, proposes how it can be fixed. Thus, therapists would diagnose
problems in an individual psyche, system theorist would identify and diagnose
problems in families, organisations and/or communities. They could intervene in
individual psyche, family or community, as they had the ability to make objective and detached assessments (analysis) of what is wrong, and then decide on the
correct solution to fix problems, in a way analogous to the way a mechanic fixes
a malfunctioning engine (see Freedman & Combs 1996:3). The patients, those
who are ill (abnormal), were completely passive, as they were passive recipients
of external wisdom and got very little credit (Freedman & Combs 1996:6) for the
"healing" or "transformation" that might have happened.

Second Order Cybernetics is a model that tried to move away from the expert
(professional) – patient model towards a less control-orientated model, a model
that did not place the therapist outside of, or above, the system (either the psychic
system of the individual or the family system or the socio-economic-political sys-

tem of the community).[24] For example, Graham focusses in her *Transformative Practice* on a critical reading of late capitalism together with a feminist reading of current Western world, thereby clearly indicating the problem and analysing the problem field, fully conscious of her own position within the context. Yet, what remained even in the second order cybernetics was the idea that there is something that needs to be fixed. There is always a problem that firstly needs to be "correctly" identified, as a "correct" analysis must be made, so that a "correct" cure can be found, in other words, the normative plays a vital role. There are numerous approaches to identifying different problems and likewise there are a variety of explanations (therapies) to the same identified problems. Yet, the basic dialectic remains in place: identify the problem (thesis), an expert knows the solution (anti-thesis) and the problem is solved (synthesis).

In a highly simplified version, one could argue that a problem, in its different interpretations, is necessary so as to offer Jesus, in the different interpretations, as the answer. This pattern is not confined to theology, it seems to be a general pattern. Problems are identified and then a specific idea is sold as the only, or best solution to the problem. I do not want to belittle the various analyses of problems, as they are highly insightful and very useful and certainly help one in interpreting numerous phenomena today. Depending on one's own context and narrative there are certain analyses that speak more to one than others. I for example, find myself within Bernhard Stiegler's analysis and description of much of the human condition with his concept of symbolic misery[25] as well as the idea of general proletarianization[26] of the people, who are estranged from their symbolic labour, or are deprived of being noetic souls. I will be making use of his analysis or de-

---

[24] A therapist was, like it or not, part of the very system undergoing therapy, and therefore incapable of detached objectivity (Freedman & Combs 1996:5).

[25] By symbolic misery I mean, therefore, the loss of individuation which results from the *loss of participation* in the *production of symbols*. Symbols here being as much the fruits of intellectual life (concepts, ideas, theorems, knowledge) as of sensible life (arts, knowhow, mores). And I believe that the present state of generalized loss of individuation can only lead to a symbolic collapse, or the collapse of desire – in other words to the decomposition of the social as such: to total war (Stiegler 2014:10).

[26] Today these technologies are integrated into a single digital technical system, to which all modes of human knowledge are delegated (delegated, that is, to the machines and the apparatuses that are linked in with it), allowing for the control of both production and consumption. But this delegation is commensurate with a social organization which, as it structurally opposes consumption and production, leads to a generalized proletarianization: like the producer, the consumer is here deprived of all knowledge. And this is what Leroi-Gourhan considers to be *incompatible* with the *possibility of sensing*. Because the one who senses as a noetic soul gives sense to his sensations: he cannot *receive* and gather (*legein*) the sensible except to the extent that he is able to give it a sense, and not only from himself, but give it a sense for others – to give back to others the sense that he receives (Stiegler 2015a:26) … 'Control societies' refers to social organization characterized by a loss of individuation as a loss of aesthetic participation and a generalized proletarianization (Stiegler 2015a:48).

scription as his ideas resonate with my own embodiment and therefore help me to make sense of numerous contemporary phenomena.

Each book, set of ideas, presents a clear explanation of the problem so as to present their ideas, their ideal or their theory, their idol or their good, as *the* answer.

In this book, my approach will seek to move away from such an approach: To identify the problem and then present Jesus saviour–kingdom on earth dialectic, in the sense that I do not want to solve any problems or heal any illnesses or ailments, nor do I want to offer a specific transformative praxis. What I am looking for is a way to move beyond good and evil, that is a praxis without a normative element and in that sense a trans-fictional praxis, where the different metaphysical systems (fictions) are all seen to be equally responses to a Call.

This book will not offer any norm concerning what is normal, right or correct or even good, and neither will it offer norms by which to judge what is bad, wrong or evil. But it is also not a sociological book that only offers analysis or explanations or description of phenomena or the human condition. It is a trans-fictional praxis, which is also a Christ-*poiēsis*, and thus offers an ethical modality to this praxis without it becoming a normative ethics.

To illustrate what I mean by Christ-*poiēsis* I will shortly unpack my interpretation of the Genesis story of the Fall, and why I want to move beyond good and evil in this praxis which I describe as a Christ-*poiēsis*.

The traditional interpretation of the "fall of humanity" is that in the Garden of Eden, Eve was tempted by the snake to eat from the forbidden fruit. She could not resist the temptation and ate the fruit, whilst also giving Adam to eat. The forbidden fruit according to the text (Gen. 3: 5) is the fruit of the tree of knowledge, the knowledge of good and evil. When God discovered that they had eaten the fruit of this tree, they were expelled from paradise. Thus, the consequence of sin (this knowledge of good and evil) is separation from God or expulsion from paradise.

If sin is interpreted as separation then it would make sense that salvation is the healing of that separation. Salvation is then a return to paradise or a return to the kingdom of God, a return to the harmony that existed between humanity and God – a healed, reconciled relationship.

What if the desire to get back into paradise is the problem? What if the wish to return to the original union, the original wholeness and connectedness is the problem, because that desire can only be fulfilled if one identifies the cause of the believed original separation? What caused the fall of humanity in the Genesis story, or what caused the original separation?

Humanity, interpreted as a noetic soul, is a separated being, as to be human is to be externalised (ex-*text*-ualised). In psychological or psychoanalytical perspective this is called birth. Or from a more philosophical-existential perspective it is to be, namely to exist – to ex-*text*-tiert (ex-*text*-ence) and to be conscious thereof is to be separated. One cannot reach the Body without Organs (Deleuze & Guattari 2011:43f), but one always already exists on it, but to exist is to be conscious of a differentiated body into clearly defined strata and organs. What if to be (exist which is to ex-*text*) and to return are mutually exclusive, as to be is to ex-*text*, and the text is marked by différance, it is born of dif-ference (*Austrag*)?[27] The text cannot reach the Real, nor be the Real, the text can never fully comprehend the Other, not even the self (Flesh). The texts that one exists in (ex-*text*-ence), which is unavoidable, but necessary, could be called sin – or the fall of humanity into exteriority (ex-*text*-ence). Is it the fall of humanity or is it the calling into responsibility, called to respond, called to be an ex-*text*-ence? This response, to think, to be in language, can be identified as the great sin (separation). This is how it is often interpreted, that language (response) is interpreted as illusion, as language is interpreted as negating reality (Henry 2003:10) or the illusion of the thinking ego that makes itself the foundation of all (Henry 2012 pos 1618 of 2078) language as the illusion of ideology as Laclau (2014:13) argues. In other words, language is the great sin (separation). Language responds and names the Call, but in that naming the Call, it simultaneously reduces the Call to a Name, which can be interpreted as idolatry. In that sense responding would be sin. That means to be is sin: separated as an ex-*text*-ence.

Rollins speaks of God as hyper-present. If paradise, the "original" pre-birth connectedness, is interpreted (named or determines) as the Body without Organs, as the Real, as that which *is* prior to it existing (ex-texting), or as that from which all that appears comes, then that "*is*" is certainly hyper-present and hypernymity (more than words). But why call that which is more than words, God? In a certain sense, everything that is, is more than its name, or is always more than the word that tries to capture it. Take the beach as example, I can be aware of the beach with the word beach, but the beach is always much more than the word *beach*. I can write a poem about the sand between my toes, the wind, and the sound of the waves, but the beach will always be much more than any names or words that try to capture the experience on the beach. The beach as such is also hypernymity, and it is hyper-present, which brings me to what Derrida said, that every other is wholly other (*tout autre est tout autre*) (Derrida 1995:76). The beach, the forest, my son is hypernymity and hyper-present, as there is always more of him or to it than what I can be conscious of in a name or a concept: a determination. Even I myself am hyper-present as there is more to *me* than what *I* am conscious of. There is always more than what ex-*text*-tiert. It is this remainder or excess, which haunts all texts. This excess or remainder are the ghosts that haunt the texts or names. If every other is wholly other, it would not make sense to keep the name God, as the name for the Other; on the other hand, in this way the name God is

---

[27] These ideas will be further explored and unpacked in the next chapters.

saved, and only the name is saved in both senses of the word saved. It is saved in the sense that it can still be used and it is saved from idolatry. Derrida argues that the name God could be saved for this endless desertification of language.[28] The name God is retained, but what does it mean? Does it mean anything, or is it only a name that is saved and thereby theology is saved as well? Save the name God from what or for what? Save the name God from idolatry? Yes, indeed keeping the name safe from idolatry. Save but the name, only the name remains. Only the name remains as one possible fiction amongst numerous other fictions, to give meaning and sense to experiences. As Root (2014) argues, to give meaning and sense in the subjective reality of experiences that point into the direction of an independent objective reality, but off course these meanings and sense making is only possible through the primary, secondary and tertiary retentions and protentions of what critical realism refers to as dependent objective reality. Root wants to create space for the evangelical subject's experience (2014:205) of God or the divine. Is the name God saved for such experiences in or of independent object reality? He gives numerous examples of such subjective experiences, where individuals testify and witness to their experiences of the divine, mainly through the metaphors of *creatio ex nihilo* and *theologia crucis* (Root 2014:35ff). The name is saved for one possible truth, amongst numerous other possible truths, that create a specific reality (both truth and reality with small letters). This is the passion of this book, these multiple truths, this trans-fictional experience, which is then developed into a trans-fictional praxis. In this sense, it is not only the name "God" that is saved, but also the name of Truth, if one takes Rollins' (2006:55f) differentiation between Truth and truth into consideration.[29]

There are different realities (worlds), created by different truths (different metaphysical systems) and one of these worlds could be the Christian world amongst others. If this is the case, then conversion between truths and their realities is possible. It is possible to discover a new truth or a different truth, and with these new truths a new or different reality is opened, or carried out.

For example, it is possible to convert from a psychoanalytic truth to an evolutionary biological truth and then later to a Christian truth, and each truth will open a new reality, carry out a new world. Yet conversion does not transform a

---

[28] "God" "is" the name of this bottomless collapse, of this endless desertification of language (Derrida 1995:55–56).

[29] At this point I would like to make a distinction between the idea of Truth and truth. The first, which is distinguished by the use of a capital letter, refers to the subject matter of theology and metaphysics and refers to what some philosophers have called the 'Real'. Here the word 'Real' refers to the ultimate source of everything that is. To possess some knowledge of the Truth means that one rationally accepts some propositions that accurately describe what this Real is like. ... ... In contrast to Truth, the term 'truth' can be said to relate to statements of fact concerning reality. Unlike the Real, 'reality' is a term that refers to the world as we experience it (Rollins 2006:55).

truth into *the* Truth, even if it is seen as *the* Truth for that particular individual or community. The testimony of an evolutionary biologist converting to Christianity does not say anything about the Real or the Call, but it says a lot about the primary, secondary and tertiary retentions and protentions of the individual who converted.

In this book, all these realities carried out by different truths, are equal in the sense that they are all equally called forth, by that which Called them forth. For Root these different truths and realities are not equal. As some realities are better than others, he would like to keep a sense of what is normative (Root 2014:251ff). I do not want to save the name God for one possible reality, I accept that there are possible realities that are called into being through the metaphors of the Christian-Jewish texts, just as there are other realities that are called into ex-*text*-ence through various names given, also the names of other gods. Nor do I want to save God through the mystical tradition like Rollins and Kearney, or even Caputo (2013) with his *Insistence of God,* but rather stand with Derrida, by agreeing with him that every other is wholly Other. God can be replaced with any other Other. The Call, that which calls thought forth, that which calls faithful thought forth, can be called by many different names. Thereby I am not arguing that the Call *is* plural or multiple, because plural and multiple would also again only be names given to that which called thought forth. Nor am I saying that it is the same Call that calls all these different names forth, and that therefore all these names refer to the same Call. Different things call, my flesh can call, the other can call, the material world can call, God can call. By Call I refer to all that which calls thought forth, and different things call thought forth.

For a trans-fictional praxis, there are different worlds carried out by their different truths, for example the natural world carried out by the truth or the laws of nature as discovered by science, or the psychoanalytic world, or evolutionary world, or all the different worlds carried out by the different religions. Different worlds, as different responses to all the different things that called thought forth. The Call refers to none of these things specifically, but to the Calling that calls thought forth.

Henry wants to save the name God differently, he does not want to save the name God for some or other metaphysical principle or truth, but he argues that God is Life, absolute Life (2003:564), or that God is the Real. Root argued that the place to seek God or to find God is in the Real (independent objective reality), similar to Caputo (2013) with his *Insistence of God*, where God is interpreted as that insistent calling. Now Henry argues that one does not and cannot know God, but that one experiences that the biblical texts are true.[30] Yet, such an experience,

---

[30] The extraordinary agreement established between the word that Christ speaks to humans in their own language and the one which generates all of us in our hearts and speaks our own birth to us, causes and intense emotion in those who recognize it. It is this emotion that the two disciples feel when, overcome by the death and the crucifixion of the one in whom they had placed their

for example, the burning sensation of the heart, one can experience with other texts as well, where alternative names are given to the Call. One can experience this burning in the heart when one reads Caputo's (2007) *What would Jesus deconstruct* or Karl Barth or Paul Tillich for that matter. Thus, the Truth of Christ, as Life, or as Justice, or as Love, etcetera shows that this Truth becomes incarnate in various truths (Life, Justice, Love, Grace, Faith), which each can cause a burning sensation in the heart and be experienced as a true interpretation of *Dasein* in-the-world. But the same could be true for non-Christian texts as well as the texts of novels, or even popular songs, or movies. The burning sensation has maybe less to do with Truth, than with a specific aspect of the collective protentions and retentions that have carried out the world in which one is a *Dasein*; one's primary protentions and retentions resonant (*Erkling*) with aspects, sometimes hidden aspects, of the collective protentions and retentions that have carried out a world in which one is. This resonance, or *Erklingen* of the primary with the secondary and tertiary retentions and protentions, could be experienced as a burning sensation in the heart or the revelation of a truth, which is experienced as: "it makes perfect sense!", "or everything became crystal clear!" Such clarity or perfect sense has less to do with the Real and everything to do with the primary and secondary retentions and protentions that resonate with the secondary and tertiary retentions and protentions of the text which one is confronted with, which can be a biblical text or a Bruce Springsteen song. Now it is interesting that the biblical text so often makes perfect sense, for example one can read the Genesis story in conversation with postmodern or post-structuralist thought. Is that interesting or is it to be expected, without that expectation meaning anything with regards to Truth or the Real? It is to be expected as the Bible is dominantly part of the tertiary retentions and protentions of Western thought. Thus, Western thought resonates in the Bible and the Bible resonates in Western thought.

Theology as saving the name God – *fides quaerens intellectum*

Theology has often been understood as faith seeking reason (understanding), which was St. Anselm of Canterbury's (1033–1109) motto, or the basis for his theistic proofs. A reason, *intellectum*, a reasonable response is sought to explain, make sense, of experiences. Reason wants to make things clear and visible, which includes making sense of that which is believed to be invisible. Making sense is to make things appear, even if they appear as invisible, but whatever is made sense of, appears within a certain light (*Lichtung*) and therefore is believed to be evident: "it is as clear as daylight". This is probably the most common understanding of Western reason (understanding), to use a quote from Henry (2015:18):

An intelligibility of that sort pertains to thought, and to its capacity to make visible everything that, in some way spread out before its gaze, constitutes the

---

hope, they walk along sadly toward the town of Emmaus (Henry 2012 pos 1935 of 2078).

visible universe – a collection of things that we can really see and that we call "true," rational", and "evident," to the extent that we can actually see them.

If theology subscribes to this reason, this intelligibility, if it wants to understand it's subject matter within the light (logos) of this *intellectum*, then God needs to appear in this *Lichtung*, even if God appears in this *Lichtung* as invisible or beyond comprehension. But is this the only Logos, the only *Lichtung* in which and through which to think God?

Is faith seeking reason the only way to understand theology's task? Could it not be as Henry argues with regards to phenomenology (2015:21), that it should be turned around? There needs to be a reversal, and not faith seeking reason, but faith embracing itself against reason, which would be a totally different intelligibility as Henry proposes.

From the Prologue of John another type of intelligibility emerges, an Arch-intelligibility that properly overturns these ways of thinking. "Arch- intelligibility" means that a mode of revelation comes into play that is different from the one by which the world becomes visible; and that, for this reason, what it reveals is made up of realities that are invisible in this world, and unnoticed by thought. The Prologue list them: Life, in which Arch- intelligibility consists; the Word of Life, in which this Arch- intelligibility of Life is fulfilled; and, finally, the flesh, in which the Word of Life becomes identical with each of the living beings that we are, we men and women. So an entirely new definition of human is formulated, which is as unknown to Greece as it is to modernity: *The definition of an invisible, and at the same time carnal, human being, and invisible in so far as carnal* (Henry 2015:18–19).

This Arch-intelligibility refers, as Henry (2015:19) argues, to what philosophy calls absolute reality or what critical realism would maybe refer to as independent objective reality. This absolute reality is what religion names God (Henry 2015:19), or as George Bataille refers to this Real as the Sacred (see James, 1997:3–15). What if theology is not about finding reason to defend and save God, but if it is about losing reason, sacrificing reason, sacrificing the thing, the Name, the Name that allows things to appear within the *Lichtung* of reason? As James (1997:12) argues in reference to Bataille, 'Likewise our notions of "God" (a thing) all too often becomes screens which prevent us from experiencing the sacred: they must themselves be sacrificed (crucified) (but if we see "nothing" as an object, a thing, not even this is true)'. In this sense the sacred *is* nothing, as it cannot exist, because it should not ex-*text*. The danger is of this nothing becoming a something, in other words if "nothing" becomes a definition or a determination of the Sacred, of the Call. Faith seeking reason in the traditional sense, is about seeing God as a thing within a *Lichtung* and thereby destroying the sacred. For Bataille this thing needs to be sacrificed. 'And the moment of sacrifice (including the sacrifice of language in poetry and the sacrifice of selfhood in eroticism) is essentially that point at which knowledge slips into non-knowledge (*non-savoir*)' (James 1997:12).

Faith embracing itself in its own self-revelation (auto-revelation) is what Henry suggests. Should the Jewish-Christian scriptures be seen as emplotments into a specific reason, emplotment into a specific narrative, placing things into the *Lichtung* of a specific Logos (*Muthos*)? Or could the scriptures be seen as narratives revealing themselves, revealing a truth that cannot be known, nor appear in any kind of externalization, as no *ex-text-ence*? In other words, a truth that does not exist, as it has no ex-*text*-ence, but which can only be known, as Henry argues, in the burning of the heart in reference to the Emmaus disciples, when Christ as Truth was revealed to them (see Henry 2012 pos 1935 of 2048) – a truth that is immanent to itself, never external, never ex-*text*-ualised. Are the Christian texts unique with regards to this self-revelation, as Henry argues (2012)? Would it be important that the Christian texts are unique in this regard? Would it make Christianity unique, or could one say the same of other religious texts? Although these are important questions, I will not further explore this theme, as this book is not a comparative study of religions and their sacred texts. In this book, I will follow a different route, as in the following chapters I will further explore Henry's arguments and develop them into what I call Christ-*poiēsis*, as a trans-fictional praxis, but which is not a theology of religions.

I believe the Jewish-Christian Text is important to take into consideration, not because of its uniqueness, but for a very different reason, namely the dominant role they play in the carrying out of the Western worlds. There are two primary reasons why I argue that the Christian text is important for a trans-fictional praxis: the first is geo-political and the second is hermeneutical.

Geo-political

Taking Deleuze' and Guattari's argument of the abstract machine of the West (see Deleuze and Guattari 2011:168), or the Face of Christ (see Deleuze and Guattari 2011:167–191),[31] into consideration, one could say that thinking in the Global village is thinking through this Face. 'It was under the sign of the cross that people learned to steer the face and processes of facialization in all directions' (Deleuze & Guattari 2011:179).

Or as Walter Mignolo[32] argues, that anyone in the global world with a secondary education has been influenced and impacted by Western thought. The

---

[31] Christianity is a particular important case of a mixed semiotic, with its signifying imperial combination together with its postsignifying Jewish subjectivity. It transforms both the ideal signifying system and the postsignifying passional system. It invents a new assemblage (Deleuze & Guattari 2011:125).

[32] See Walter Mignolo where he argues '... that Western knowledge has been spread globally and, therefore, it is in all of us who went through at least secondary education.' (Gaztambide-

globe has been influenced and impacted by Western thought, and therefore one could say that the dominant way of thinking (responding) in the globe is according to the Face of Christ, as it is in the light of the Face of Christ that the global village appears. Mark Taylor argues, 'with the rise of globalization, it is not exaggeration to say that no society or culture has been untouched by this originally Western movement' (Taylor 2007 pos 65 of 6286). This Western movement cannot be separated from Christianity and more specifically, Taylor argues, from Protestantism.[33]

He argues, 'It is undeniable that, for better and for worse, the world as we know it would not have come about without Protestantism' (Taylor 2007 pos 71 of 6286).

If this is the dominant carried out globe then it would not help to try and ignore the Face of Christ, neither should one resign to the Face of Christ, but rather, and that is my suggestion, to think *through* the Face of Christ.

A theological or Christological hermeneutic

Such a hermeneutic is linked to the first, as a way of thinking *through* Christ. The two inspirations for such a Christ-centered hermeneutic came from Michel Henry and François Laruelle. Both Henry and Laruelle do not offer a theology or a Christology, where a specific logos carries out a particular Christian world, on the contrary, in their thought, Christianity is not seen as a religion that binds a world together, but the Christ-event is seen as a fiction (see Laruelle 2015b) about the fictional nature of our worlds. A fiction (words of the world) that tells the story of itself – a self-revelation (the word of Life) (Henry 2012).

This book is not about saving God, or theology, but in the same vein, some could argue that it is about saving Christ, or saving the name Christ, and thereby keeping safe the name Christ. This could perhaps be a valid argument, and my response would be that my wish is not to save Christ, but rather to argue that Christ is already there in the global world and therefore the need – not to save Christ, but to think through Christ. Not in an independent objective reality sense, to use the terms of critical realism, but Christ is there in the dependent objective reality, as the Face of Christ is the abstract machine of the West (Deleuze & Guattari 2011:167ff). In other words, not seeking Christ in the independent objective reality as does Root, but knowing Christ, as Abstract machine to be there in the dependent objective reality of the West, as the Face of Christ.

Christ is already there, because Western thought is created through this abstract machine, and in a global world, Western thought has a universal reach, as

---

Fernández 2014:201).

[33] Modernity as well as postmodernity is inseparably bound up with Protestantism (Taylor 2007 pos 65 of 6286).

anyone exposed to primary or secondary education has been exposed to Western thought.

I am not trying to save the name Christ but to think *through* Christ and *in* Christ. I find myself more at home in the work of Henry, who does not want to develop a Christian phenomenology of life, but rather finds in the Christian texts words that can express what philosophy cannot (Henry 2012 pos 174 of 2078). The Christian texts offer metaphors to express that which is most thought-worthy, but which is also impossible to think.

What is necessary is a new way of thinking from the flesh, from the Real and maybe the Christian texts can help in exploring this way of thinking. The Christian Text helps Henry think Life, but he named it Life and thus determined it, and also determined the Christian Text. One must think through the Christ-event to think that which Calls such names as Life forth.

Now, if flesh – and, first of all, coming in flesh, Incarnation – were grasped by the first Christian thinkers as a mode of manifestation of the Word of God, and if we suspect that the flesh's mode of manifestation and the Word's mode of manifestation could indeed be the same, as modes of Life's manifestation and revelation, then a systematic elucidation, a science of this revelation as such, is needed (Henry 2015:20).

A science of this revelation is what Laruelle offers with his science of Christ (Laruelle 2010).

Henry argues that such a science already exists (Henry 2015:20). It is called phenomenology. These ideas will be further explored in the coming chapters.

A Science of Christ and not a theology of religions

Transversal rationality or postfoundational approach allows Christianity to join the conversation with its specific epistemology (theology), its specific interpreta-tion (dependent objective reality) of the independent objective reality, and thus Christianity becomes one of the conversational partners (see Van Huyssteen 2006:23). In this book, Christianity is not just one of the conversational partners, it is not just one epistemology or metaphysics amongst others, nor is it *the* meta-physics, but I will interpret it as offering *a* narrative of that which metaphysics and epistemologies (philosophy) cannot express. In Henry's thought, the idea of incarnation is not just one possible metaphysical idea, but it is 'a more fundamen-tal principle of *intelligibility*, all the while depending upon that intelligibility for its own' (Henry 2012 pos 207 of 2078 emphasis added). This science of Christ therefore cannot be developed into a theology of religions or a theology of meta-physics, but offers a more fundamental principle of intelligibility, as it offers a *way* to think thinking. It offers a *way* to think the intelligibility of intelligibility and therefore it is not a truth in the popular sense, but a way and as way a truth and a life (see John 14:6).

Back to the Genesis story, let us presume that the story (fiction) does not want to capture any Real, but wants to offer a narrative with which to make sense of the human condition – a narrative that tells the story of being human, where being human is interpreted as a being who wants to capture the Real, that is make sense and create meaning of Life. What if Genesis tells the story of humanity's need to seek reason, *fides quaerens intellectum*? In the beginning, God created the world and with the world humans – all things that are, came from and are in God. But God, the creator of all this, is more than all that is created. The created world is differentiated by his creating Word. For God spoke (Word) and through the speaking, things were differentiated as well as humans, but with one difference: these humans were created in His image. The humans also had the ability to speak, like God, and therefore were given the task to name all the things created by God's calling them into existence (ex-*text*-ence). The human task was to name the text of ex-*text*-ence. They were given the task to differentiate by naming the things that God had called into ex-*text*-ence. In other words, the task to name the things that were differentiated by God's Word (Call) from the chaos (the undifferentiated mass). They happily did that, but perhaps they also had the desire to pronounce their naming good, right or correct, just like God pronounced his creation (differentiation) good. How else would one ever know if an elephant is truly an elephant rather than something else, unless one knows that one's name is a good name or the correct name? It was maybe this desire, to know if one's names are good and therefore correct, which the snake (the devil) exploited. Humans wanted to be like God by being able to judge what is good and what is evil, but to be able to judge, one needs to be separate and thus the separation (sin) happened through the desire to be able to judge what is good, right and correct from what is evil, wrong and incorrect. To be able with certainty (knowing it is right) to enumerate and identify all things (ontology) one needs a *logy* – a logos. On the basis of this logos one can differentiate, identify and count the things that make up a world. To develop an ontology there needs to be a logos. In physics for example, to be able to identify and differentiate physical things, they need to appear, and they appear within a certain time and place, a certain world. A certain *Lichtung* is necessary for things to appear, and this clearing is created by a light (logos): a physical world appears in the world of physics with its laws (logos) and theories. A physical, scientific world, which was different from what was called the mythological and religious world of the Middle Ages, began to appear in the light of the *Aufklärung*, the light of the Enlightenment. The placing of things into time and space is metaphysics (or narrative) – the logos that gives meaning and sense to the *onta* of a particular onto*logy*. To be able with certainty to differentiate and identify, one needs metaphysics (narrative): a world into which things are called and where the things called carry out a world (see Heidegger 1971:200). It is this logos that creates the world – that speaks and a world appears, just like God's creation.

Probably numerous Old Testament scholars and New Testament scholars would ask, on what historical evidence do I base such an interpretation? What historical, cultural, linguistic evidence do I have for such an interpretation? My response is that such arguments presuppose that there is a correct reading, a true reading, but such a correct or accurate reading is only possible through eating of the tree of knowledge. I do not propose a correct or true reading, only *a* reading, where the storyline offers metaphors which help me make sense of my ex-*text*-ence. This might offer one fiction where the idea of original sin comes from and why one is born into original sin. Yes, indeed to be born is to be born into ex-*text*-ence, born separated and differentiated. Thus sin, separation, is to be: to exist (ex-*text*). This separation is what makes humans human, that it is noetic souls who individuate into subjects by ex-*text*-ualising.

Why would one want to heal ex-*text*-ence? Or transform it? There is no return to paradise, only via the destruction of creation (ex-*text*-ualisation). In the end of the world one could return to paradise, the Body without Organs or the Real, and be one with the Call, but only through destruction of creation: ex-*text*-ence. The biblical story has provided numerous metaphors to think thinking, or maybe to think thinking in a world that has been strongly influenced by the Bible and so it comes "naturally" to think along these lines. To think about thinking cannot happen in the abstract but is embodied. My embodiment and all the thinkers I have referred to in this chapter have been influenced directly or indirectly by the Jewish-Christian texts, which is part of the tertiary retentions of this embodiment. Therefore, it will always be a question: does thinking about thought today help in interpreting the Bible in a particular way, or does the Bible's stories influence (consciously or subconsciously) the way one thinks about thinking today? All I can think (respond) is that there is a resonance between for example my primary and secondary reflections on for example the human condition and the tertiary retentions and protentions of my embodiment, which include the Bible.

If I interpret the Bible in this book the interpretation needs to be understood in this mutual *Erklingen*, and I am thereby not making any truth claims either way.

This is a possible interpretation of the human condition, or the condition of creation – differentiated through text (Word). Differentiated through thinking (noetic soul). Thus, humanity's "problem" is not that they do not think, but *that* they think. If one remains with the idea of wanting to return, then the greatest enemy is thought, the greatest enemy is that which makes humanity human – to think, to be co-creators, co-differentiators, and as differentiators expand the rhizome, continually creating the worlds in which humans live.

In this book, sin (separation or differentiation) will not be seen as the problem to be overcome, but the very condition of our ex-*text*-ence. Thus, I will not try and present Jesus as the answer (solution) to sin, or as the saviour in that sense, but sin (separation-differentiation) will be interpreted as a given: an unavoidable given as it is absolutely necessary to one's ex-*text*-ence, but it simultaneously makes ex-*text*-ence insufficient, which some have interpreted as a lack, which in turn "causes" desire. This lack or fault can then in turn be interpreted as sin, which needs to be overcome.

In this book, I will not separate the Real from the Ideal or place social construction against realism, neither materialism against idealism, but see all these polarities as One, which would then avoid the lack idea and therefore also the sin as lack idea. One exists in the texts (various fictions) that are all absolutely necessary as without them one would not exist (ex-*text*), but they are insufficient as they remain but fictions, yet determined in the last instance by the Real, the Call. The idea of them being *but fictions* is not a degradation of fictions, because fictions are all there is: all that ex-*texts*. They are necessary but insufficient, insufficient because none of these fictions grabs (*begreifen* comprehends) and thereby captures the Real in a *Begriff*, but they are all fictions of a real, not the Real, but determined in the last instance by the Real. These fictions are absolutely dependent on the Real, or rather on the Call, as that which called them forth, just as an ego, an I, is absolutely dependent on there being a me. For there to be any meaning or sense, there has to be Life, that calls meaning forth, but without that Life being captured or determined in the meaning called forth. Each fiction carries out (*Austrag*) a world, a real world in which humans and numerous other things ex-*text*: a whole ontology, governed by the logos that carried out this world. Thus, the fictions create a world of meaning and sense in which one ex-*texts*, but these worlds with their fictions (logoi) are insufficient, not because somewhere there is a sufficient narrative or Logos, but because of différance. These fictions are not in opposition to the Real or Life, but are responses to the Call, and therefore they are determined in the last instance by Life or the Real, as that which Called them to respond. It is for this reason that I prefer to speak of the Call rather than Life or the Real, as these are for me already responses (determinations) of that which called them forth.

These fictions are totally dependent on Life or the Real for their existence, and thus I will try to move away from the opposition between social construction and the Real or Life, or the opposition between Call and response (Name), because it is the Call that calls a response forth and therefore determines the response in the last instance. The response (for example, dependent objective reality) is always in response to that which called thinking forth (independent objective reality).

The Old Testament God is interesting as this God forbids to be named. One should not make representations or descriptions of God, neither physical nor cognitive. In a certain sense theology is forbidden – YHWH is unpronounceable for a reason. According to numerous traditions, for example Schleiermacher, Barth, or Tillich, and including the mystics, it is unpronounceable because God is the ground, the all, and yet beyond names. Yet, in a certain sense YHWH is beyond names just as the beach is beyond the name "beach" (every other is wholly Other). I would like to interpret the Old Testament prohibitions on naming YHWH differently, as I am reading the Old Testament as a narrative that offers metaphors to help make sense – a mutual *Erklingen*. The prohibition was not so much to protect (save) YHWH, but to protect humanity – to protect humanity from perpetuating the sin with the *belief* that they have discovered the right, correct and only good name or direct access to what is, to what is Real, that which Called them. The belief to have found the right name for that which Calls to respond, in for example naming, determining that which Called naming forth. The Call that perhaps would later call Abram onto the journey of faith to become Abraham, or Moses to liberate his people.

In this book, I will not offer an explanation as to what *is*. In the same sense, I will not offer an explanation as to why people voted for Trump or Brexit or why certain things are going wrong in South Africa, as by doing so I would be perpetuating the sin. My focus in this book is not what is wrong, but I will focus on those who *believe* they know what is wrong, and why it is wrong so that they can offer a solution. In that sense, it is a non-practical theology as it does not follow Osmer's (2008) four tasks (what is wrong, why is it wrong, what should happen and how can this happen). I will not join the chorus of all those who know what is wrong and why it is wrong (through description or analysis), but focus specifically on those who *believe* they know what is and why it is wrong and who offer their particular solution, either their Jesus as the answer or some or other idea, theory, or concept as *the* answer.

Rollins in his book, tells an "old anecdote"[34] about a mystic, an evangelical and a fundamentalist who all three die and end up going to heaven.

I will use the metaphors of this anecdote to describe three possible ways to approaching Truth, or the belief to have given the Call its true Name. Or three approaches to knowledge of good and evil, which was the gift [*Gift*[35]] of the tree

---

[34] There is an old anecdote in which a mystic, an evangelical pastor and a fundamentalist preacher die on the same day and awake to find themselves by the pearly gates. Upon reaching the gates they are promptly greeted by Peter, who informs them that before entering heaven they must be interviewed by Jesus concerning the state of their doctrine. The first to be called forward is the mystic, who is quietly ushered into a room. Five hours later the mystic reappears with a smile, saying, 'I thought I had got it all wrong.' Then Peter signals to the evangelical pastor, who stands up and enters the room. After a full day has passed the pastor reappears with a frown and says to himself, 'How could I have been so foolish!' Finally, Peter asks the fundamentalist to follow him. The fundamentalist picks up his well-worn Bible and walks into the room. A few days pass with no sign of the preacher, then finally the door swings open and Jesus himself appears, exclaiming, 'How could I have got it all so wrong!' (Rollins 2006:20)

[35] *Gift* is German for poison.

in the Garden of Eden. I am not thereby giving any phenomenological description or analysis concerning mystics, evangelicals or fundamentalists. The mystic, evangelical and fundamentalist are not only in reference to religious truths, but all forms of knowledge of what is good, correct or truthful.

The first is the mystic, humble, doubting her answers, in the full knowledge that human knowledge is fallible and finite, and God or Reality or Life is infinite. The second (evangelical) and third (fundamentalist) both believe that they have the answer, the first in a sense where conversion remains possible and the latter in a strong sense ruling out any possibility of conversion.

In a trans-fictional praxis, the focus is on the mystic and the evangelical, those who seek answers and *believe* in their answers, they know what is right and good either as orthodoxy or orthopraxis, but are open to the idea that they could be converted.

It is for this reason that the book will reflect on how one comes to such knowledge and conviction (belief) that one is right (orthodoxy) and knows what is good, or what is the correct thing to do (orthopraxis). Practical theologians tend to present what is right, the answer, that which they believe is necessary for justice, for example. In other words, there is an element of a crusade for what is right, just and good, or a messiah complex, because they know how to save the world. In that sense, this book will be different, it will not join the chorus of answers that seek to save the world, but it will focus on the desire of wanting to save the world. This desire of wanting to save the world, will be interpreted as the desire to eat of the tree of knowledge of good and evil and how this knowledge is generically part of ex-*text*-ence, specifically the ex-*text*-ence of a collective gathered together into a *polis* or a community or congregation, as the disciples of this knowledge (belief) of what is good or of what or who the devil (enemy) is.

The book will ask the question if it is possible to be a disciple of Christ, without any form of normativity and consequently judgement of who is or who is not a good disciple. Is it possible to ex-*text* as a disciple without any knowledge of the good? Is it possible to ex-*text* as a disciple as part of a group, a congregation or a community without any knowledge of the good or clear knowledge of the devil or the enemy?

Yet, the book will not just offer descriptions as if it was a sociological book, describing the human condition, as it will seek to engage the worlds, but from a trans-fictional perspective and a non-normative perspective of a Christ-*poiēsis*, where ethics is not based on any knowledge of good and evil, but ethics is a modality of a stance or a posture of a trans-fictional praxis.

Is liberation possible without normativity? Is liberation possible without transformation? Is liberation possible or even desirable? Liberation interpreted as a radical sense of freedom, without normativity, without judgement and without a sense of what is good and what is evil, or rather a liberation from the desire to eat the fruit of the tree of knowledge. Is freedom possible? Or are the broken chains not immediately replaced by temporary invisible chains, which only become visible in time? Thus, in this book it will not be liberation that is sought, but insurrection as resurrection, but this will be discussed in detail in the later chapters.

The narrative approach to therapy (Freedman & Combs 1996; White and Epston 1990; White 2011), engages individuals and communities beyond normativity, by seeking together with their clients preferred realities. What is preferred is decided in community, with the subjects and the dependent objective reality of those subjects together with the other subjects of that specific world, rather than trying to heal or transform the reality according to some or other norm[36]external to these worlds in which the subjects live.

This book will seek to understand trans-fictional praxis, to understand human praxis in the transversal space between various metaphysical systems – systems that are viewed as being equal, as they are equally called forth, and in that sense a democracy of thought. A democracy of metaphysical systems, a democracy of fictions, where there is no normative standard outside of metaphysics, outside of fiction, whereby to judge these different systems, as any standard or norm would be part of another metaphysical system seeking hegemonic control over the other systems. For one system to establish itself as norm above the others it would have to establish itself as hegemonic system, to dominate the others. If there is no normativity, it could be argued that a trans-fictional praxis would be stuck in relativism. This is true, and therefore the turn to a Christ-*poiēsis*, as an ethical modality. A Christ-*poiēsis* reveals something of the human condition within metaphysical systems, and calls for imitation (*imitatio Christi*) as a radical liberation, but not a liberation from one system into another (conversion), but liberation in the sense of understanding the necessity but insufficiency of metaphysical systems, and thus proposing an insurrection as resurrection within these systems. It would be a liberation through understanding, a stance, and therefore without normativity. Root, in his turn to critical realism, presents Christianity as *one* possible way of interpreting experiences of the real (independent objective reality). In this book, the Christ-narrative will not be presented as one possible way of interpreting experiences of the Real, but it will be interpreted as a fiction for interpreting the multiple experiences of the Call and the different necessary but insufficient Names given to the Call. For Root, Christianity in a sense enters the transversal space of differing metaphysical systems, where these systems are in a competition with

---

[36] Where a modernist worldview would invite us to close down options and work methodically to identity a universally applicable interpretation, we invite ourselves to celebrate diversity (Freedman & Combs 1996:33). Instead of looking for an essential self, we work with people to bring forth various experiences of self and to distinguish which of those selves they prefer in which contexts. We then work to assist them in living out narratives that support the growth and development of these 'preferred selves' (Freedman & Combs 1996:35).

each other. Within this trans-metaphysical space one could argue, according to Root, that there are better interpretations, namely interpretations that make more sense and therefore conversion is possible (see Root 2014:203). In that sense, he keeps alive the idea that there is a truth, as truth is that which is real.[37] In this book, truth will be interpreted in the sense that for a particular subject a particular interpretation is real and makes sense, but the making sense has more to do with the secondary and tertiary retentions and protentions than with Reality. The Christ narrative, Chris-*poiēsis,* is not there to offer a truth, but to offer a truth as a way of being liberated from the various necessary but insufficient truths, without establishing a new truth, but Christ alone as a way. A Christ-*poiēsis* without norms, an *imitatio Christi,* a *participatio Christi* without normativity, without eating from that tree of knowledge of good and evil. The incarnation of Jesus into the world was not about judgement based on the knowledge of what is right and wrong. On the contrary, he was very critical about judging people, as he argued that one would be judged by the same measure that one judges others (Matt. 7:1–5). For example, the parable of the farm workers wanting so eagerly to weed out the weeds, yet Jesus scolded them saying that they should leave the weeds with the corn (Matt. 13:24–30). The desire to weed out the weeds is very deep within humanity. Did Jesus weed out the weeds? No, he did not come to judge, but associated with the least of the brothers and sisters (Matt. 25:31–46), he associated with those who were outside or on the margins of the law, outside the logos (light of glory) of the particular ontology: all those who had experienced the weeding of the law-makers and law-keepers. Did Jesus associate with the least, because they are the truth and are right? No, that would only be another ontology, a different ontology, but an ontology all the same. It would then be a matter of conversion from one metaphysical system to another, or a revolution from one metaphysics to another. This association with the least of the brothers and sisters, might be because of another reason, maybe because those outside or on the margins of a given law, given ontology, are where the hyperpresence is, the Other is, that which is beyond a given ontology, the Real, the Call or in Rollins terms, the hypernymity – God. By associating with those on the margins or outside and giving them a voice, the current ontology is deconstructed and opened to include the previously excluded and thereby justice is served, if justice is understood as giving voice and place to the previously voiceless and place-less. Justice is thus a by-product of His incarnation. Jesus also says that there will always be the poor amongst you (John 12:8), so it is not about a particular marginal and ostracised, but it is about enlarging the

---

[37] If we claim that there is no reality but only competing experiential epistemologies, then truth is an impossibility. But if there is a real world that exists beyond the human mind, if there is a shared objective reality (like oxygen, matter, and finitude), then there is the humble and always contested but nevertheless possible ability to say something true, for to say something true is to say something that is real (Root 2014:203).

hegemonic ontology, opening the ontology for those excluded, democratizing the
ontology to include more voices. It is not as if Truth is now found amongst the
marginal. It is only another narrative (fiction) that is found there, but that fiction
also needs to be heard in the great democracy of fictions. Just as love is not a new
law (see Henry 2003:186), but a consequence of liberation from metaphysics,
liberation from the knowledge of good and evil, as now enemies, as those who
question my existence are the ones who open my ex-*text*-ence to the Call.

It is not a particular ideal of justice that Jesus followed, but it is justice that
happened because he associated with the least of the brothers and sisters. It is not
in a specific marginal that justice lies, as the poor will always be with you, but
justice lies in that which is excluded. In that sense one could come back to the
idea of God – God who is hyper-present, hypernymity, then God is to be found
amongst those excluded from any ontology, from any world, from any metaphysical system. God is that which is excluded, cannot be named, God is the wholly
Other, God is the Call who called these systems forth. God is the Other of any
Same (system), but every other is wholly Other. By giving voice and place to the
place-less and voiceless a *more* just ontology is created, but not a *just* ontology.
There will never be a just ontology as justice is always something that is still to
come as there will always be poor amongst you, just as democracy is always still
to come.

The local context

In this book, I will make use of various examples from my context, South Africa,
to illustrate and describe how individuals and communities ex-*text* (come into
existence) via some or other knowledge of the good – this knowledge of the good
that binds (*religare*) into a *Mitsein*, a being together in a *polis*, and in that sense
the praxis is religious and/or political.

What is the story of the context? Is there *the* story of the context? No, there
are a plurality of stories of the context as it depends on who you ask. The South
African context can be described with totally different and conflicting stories.

Most of the books in practical theology since the late 1980's, have taken the
contemporary philosophical, social-political and cultural context into consideration and they have responded to the various turns and developments in Western modernity towards what some have called postmodernity, specifically from a
cultural-linguistic perspective.

What is missing in these books is the divided world, the majority who are
excluded from the benefits of all these cultural artefacts, as well as those who
might benefit, but who are reduced to consumers. The book will therefore not
repeat these developments, but will take these developments for granted, but try
to respond *from*, *with* and *in* the shadows of global villages, taking the subsistence

of those in the cracks, the excluded, into consideration, not speaking *for* them nor believing myself to be speaking *with* them, but taking their existence (ex-*text*-ence) and their cry (*text*) into consideration, or rather the cry of their non-ex-*text*-ence. Spivak (2010) asks: Can the subaltern speak? No, the subaltern cannot speak, at least not in the language that carries out a particular world in which the subaltern is excluded or marginalised, or reduced to a docile body, but they haunt the worlds that excluded them – an insistent haunting that does not give the world rest but disturbs it.

In the title it says Global villages in the plural as *the* Global Village as such does not exist, but is experienced differently in different contexts.

The book is motivated by my subjective and particular experiences, but written in conversation with the implied global audience.

Written in the particular context of South Africa, which is a highly-divided society, if one takes the Gini Coefficient into consideration, a context in which I teach future community workers and pastors who will be serving in very diverse contexts. A certain percentage of those that I teach will be serving typical middle-to-upper-class congregations that are not that different and certainly similar to middle-to-upper-class congregations throughout the Western world, but an ever-growing number of students come from and will return to very poor communities, working in informal settlements or rural communities without the privileges and resources that typical middle class and or upper class congregations might have. In these communities, there are very few of the typical resources that characterise Western modernity, and the indigenous resources, local knowledges, have to a large extent been destroyed by colonialism and exploitation, or have been patronised into a marginal and shadowy existence. All these books mentioned above were written to a large extent from and for the middle-to-upper class Western contexts. This book is also written from a context of privilege, and the readers, because they are reading and or studying, could also be interpreted as being privileged, but it is written in response to the needs of practitioners who will be working in different and diverse contexts, but specifically from a context of those on or in the margins or the periphery of power, that is in the shadows, amongst the minority.

The book is motivated by the challenge of South Africa, but taking the global context into consideration. The specific context I am referring to is the current movement of people from the South to the North, from the East to the West, what some have termed a migrant crisis. This movement of bodies around the globe will not leave middle-to-upper-class communities untouched in the USA or in Europe, as these bodies are insisting to enter spaces and these new bodies will transform those spaces, and with their bodies they challenge the ontology, the languages (epistemologies) as well as the politics and religion of the host communities, therefore, the metaphysics will be challenged. This is currently a major global phenomenon and therefore the need for a trans-fictional approach, trans-metaphysical, where the different metaphysical systems are respected, appreciated and given equal space to be heard, but they are seen as fictions. It does not matter if it is the migrant crisis in Europe, the Black lives matter in the USA or the call for de-colonial thinking and Africanisation as part of the #FeesMustFall movement in South Africa, the hegemony of a singular metaphysics or a singular interpretation of modernity is over, even if that interpretation is a post-modern interpretation of that singular modernity, and therefore the need for a trans-fictional praxis.

The world has changed and with the world the subjects in and of the world have changed, in the sense that we are beginning to think about ourselves as embodied in a specific context. 'We are animals who are embodied, encountering our world through our emotive experiences (and practices), not primarily our rational-instrumental minds' (Root 2014:258). Root wants to bring in the emotive experiences, and I in the previous section wanted to bring in not only emotions, but also the embodied conditions of subsistence.

The feminist critique made us very aware of the patriarchal point of view. The views of liberation theology as well as de-colonial thinking or trans-fictional thinking makes one very aware of certain epistemological privileges based on race or cultural or epistemological position. Trans-fictional praxis creates a space where these privileged epistemologies, metaphysical systems are not only opened to patronisingly include other voices, but where hegemonic epistemologies and metaphysical systems are questioned, not because they are wrong, but because, like all others, they are necessary, but insufficient, that is, they are fictions, like all other Names given to the Call, and no fiction has priority over another. The only "thing" that has priority is the Call that calls fictions (thought) forth and therefore determines all thoughts (fictions), but only in the last instance.

Frustration with the cultural-linguistic approach to Practical Theology or with regards to practices and therefore praxis

I agree with Root in the sense that I also experience tremendous frustration with the cultural-linguistic approach to practices, and specifically practical theology. Not by what it includes, but why what it excludes. I find myself maybe more at home in Dussel's approach between realism and idealism (Dussel 1985:106–108). Dussel speaks of the other,[38] which has great similarities with Henry (2003; 2012;

---

[38] In face-to-face proximity, in the nonspatial timelessness of immediacy, in closeness to the other, with the other, in the child's suckling, in the lover's kiss, in the toast of compatriots celebrating a liberation victory, or in the dance of happiness, there are no words; silence or music reigns. It is the dense silence of plenitude where words originate. In the origin of words there is the other, who "speaks" by presence (not as substance, *ousia*, but as self-revelation, *parousia*). Pro-

2015) with what he calls absolute Life or Flesh.

What unites most of the books on practical theology is that they are written from within the system as Dussel would argue – as practical theologies inside the system, inside the totality of Western capitalism (Dussel 2003:135f). Although they might be critical of the system they seem to accept that the system is here to stay. When doing theology from the periphery, for example Africa, where numerous theories of developmentalism have "failed", and it is no longer a matter of tweaking the system here and there until it "works" for the majority of the people living or rather suffering in Africa, it becomes a question of viewing the system from the point of view of the majority suffering in Africa. Dussel unpacks this development in many European scholars, of being critical and yet eventually resigning to the dominant system as an unchangeable given, by reflecting on the development in the thought of Niebuhr, Tillich and even Thielicke. All three began in the 1920's to be highly critical of capitalism and then in their later work "resigned" to the fact-of-capitalism and sought to propose moral guidelines for Christians within the system (see Dussel 2003:135–137), making Christianity capitalist with a human-face.

As Dussel argues, the 'European-North American theology has begun to give importance to the '"paradigm of language," to the theory of communicative action' (Dussel 2003:149). Just as towards the end of the decade of the 1960s, theology of liberation had to delimit itself from the theology of hope inspired by Ernst Bloch as well as the political theology inspired by the Frankfurt school, so today Dussel argues, liberation needs to delimit itself from communicative action (Dussel 2003:149–150), as such a theology or philosophy is not sufficient.

Root in a sense also sought to move beyond communicative action or the linguistic turn, with his turn towards critical realism. Others have turned towards the economic and social conditions of subsistence or embodiment. In the turn towards subsistence, there are the polish thinkers who have turned towards labour as the centre of their theological reflection (see Dussel 2003:148). In Europe, even in Eastern Europe, the question of labour is the question of alienation from the product of labour, but in Latin America and likewise in Africa it is not only a question

---

tosemiotics is an ineffable "say-ing"; it does not say something; it does not say anything! It exposes itself in proximity. It is the epiphany of sincerity. It is not truth but veracity, fidelity, the *veritas prima*: a stripping, a nakedness before the other, a silent responsibility before the one about whom nothing can be said because one is there entirely, next to the other (Dussel 1985:117–118).

The other – the poor; the oppressed; the Latin American, African, or Asiatic; the violated woman; the alienated child – advances in defiance, pleasing, provoking from beyond (*symbolon*) the world. The other in his or her bodiliness is the first word (*dabar* in Hebrew, meaning both "word" and "thing"), the significant identically signified, the historical and exterior content, the biographical metaphor, nakedness as self-revelation; the other is veracity more than truth (Dussel 1985:122).

of alienation from the product of one's labour, but an alienation from the bread, basic food that is produced, and thereby the conditions of subsistence which are undermined. Thus, these theologies, even if they are critical of the linguistic turn, fail to transcend the 'abstract solipsism produced by the regime of capital or the destruction of rural community experience' (Dussel 2003:149). A movement inspired by the work of Paulo Freire, the so-called grass-roots movement, sought to go beyond the situation of abstract solipsism produced by the regime of capital gain, both in the urban margins as well as in the systematic destruction of rural community experiences (see Dussel 2003:150). In these communities, unique experiences were found that were beyond the hegemony of the dominant paradigm. In a later chapter I will challenge Dussel's ideas of the possibility of grass-roots, or of any group being in touch with something more basic, more fundamental than the various abstractions. Yet, it remains a unique voice, an alternative voice, as these voices are heard outside the hegemonic communities of the dominant communication, where these voices are not heard or even silenced and systematically excluded. I will come back to this in a later chapter, but creating space for these alternative voices, alternative epistemologies and alternative metaphysics is essential to the trans-fictional praxis of this book, so that no single metaphysics or epistemology dominates, as no fiction has priority.

Trans-fictional praxis with a bias for the fictions from the periphery or with-in the shadows and cracks of the dominant metaphysics

The un-thought of most of the recent books on practical theology or pastoral care, for example, the books by Gerkin, Graham, Osmer, Rumscheidt, Bon-Storm, Browning, Root is what de-colonial thought criticises, namely that these "post"-modern approaches, or "post"-structuralist approaches to practical theology, although they challenge many of the nostrums of modernity, challenge the dominant discourses of modernity from a very privileged locality or position (embodiment). This is probably also the reason why I appreciate these books so much, they speak to me, they address me in my current socio-economic-cultural, political and historical embodiment. But that is exactly the problem: my embodiment is the embodiment of a very small minority. A small privileged minority, who, as Bernard Stiegler argues, have had and have 'access to human works that Kant said were the fruits of the spirit' (Stiegler 2014:79). Those who have access to such human works and who appreciate such works is becoming a tiny minority (Stiegler 2014:79). Stiegler describes the life of this minority with words that make it sound so normal, and thereby creating an awareness regarding that which sounds so normal to many working in academia, namely that such normality is only true for a very small minority.

We, who make up this tiny minority, we live in privileged, if not very privileged urban milieu: in districts that still look like towns, where we sometimes visit restaurants worthy of the name, where our children go to schools in which it is still just about possible to learn something, even if this is becoming increasingly difficult, where we can visit theatres and cinemas showing a variety of films, where we can wander in streets with shopkeepers selling quality goods. But we know NOTHING, for the most part, of the conditions in which our fellow citizens live, which have often become detestable, if not unbearable (Stiegler 2014:79–80).

This book that you are reading is no different, it is a book written from and for the tiny minority, but it is different in the sense that it tries to keep the vast majority in mind [if that is possible to keep the other in mind, as the Other by definition is always outside of mind]. The majority is kept in mind, not in the language the book uses, neither in the references to the great human works that are the fruit of the contemporary Spirit, admittedly strongly influenced by "Western" thought [although I would like to challenge the idea of there being such a thing as "Western" thought, and rather highlight transversal nature of thought], but in the sense that the majority haunts this language. The book will not seek to interpret this haunting or determine it, or silence it, but seek a stance with that which Calls, a stance with all that which haunts, in the sense of Derrida's *hauntology*,[39] but without the *logos* of a hauntology, that is without determining the ghosts that haunt, or determining the Call that calls a response forth.

Many of the recent books on practical theology, at least those that are easily available on the dominant Western market, and by implication, their practical theology, are written for congregations, made up of people living in industrialized countries who are able to feed themselves, dress themselves and find somewhere to live (even if an ever increasing and evermore IMPOSING number, right next to us, sometimes outside the building where we live, do not really have access to these perks of civilization)' (Stiegler 2014:80). Although these critical post-modern and post-structuralist books are written for a small group of these living in privilege, those that Stiegler calls a majority[40] in comparison to the large minority, are no longer individuals, but dividuals. I am not arguing that this book is any different. I do not think that any book is written *for* or *with* the "vast majority". The vast majority are not only the poor, but it includes, in Stiegler's terms, ever growing numbers of the shrinking middle class, those people who are 'seeing their living conditions degrade to the point where they themselves are physically

---

[39] *Hauntology* is a concept coined by Derrida (1994) in his book *Spectres of Marx*. Derrida argues: 'Haunting belongs to the structure of every hegemony' (Derrida 1994:46).

[40] Stiegler use of the terms, "majority" and "minority" is in reference to Kant understanding of sovereign politics, where majority are the mature, those who are *Mündig as an exit from Unmündigkeit*. The minority would then in this Kantian interpretation be seen as the *Unmündig* or immature (Stiegler 2015b:2).

and morally degraded – stuffed with bad food, dazed, to a point that it is hard to imagine, by always more demeaning culture industries' (Stiegler 2014:80). This book will probably also only be read by the privileged, but with the hope that it will enable those who choose to work amongst the minority (although being the numerical majority of the worlds' population) with some tools, without the tools being answers. A stance with the minority, whilst addressing (calling) the dominant discourses of this globe (to responsibility). In a previous study (Meylahn 2010a & 2010b), I tried to bring these two worlds together, referring to the insiders and the marginalised or excluded, those who are excluded from privileges of "Western" civilization, and in a sense this book is a continuation of that project. My embodiment in South Africa, one of the globe's most divided countries into the haves and the have-nots, probably is the reason why this is a concern to me, as I am teaching future community workers and pastors, some of whom will serve typical middle-class congregations, but an ever-growing number will serve in communities who do not have access to the privileges mentioned above.

In the study mentioned above (Meylahn 2010a & 2010b), I indicated that the struggle of the excluded is linked to the struggles of the included. One of the major challenges of the current economic system is that there are very few included. Some argue that only 1% are truly the included, but between the excluded one could interpret there to be different classes of exclusion – those that are excluded to the extent that they do not have access to any of the perks of "industrialized" society (medical aid, education, insurance, pensions, etcetera) and therefore live on the margins, literally on and off the rubbish dumps of the cities, or those who do not live in industrial countries, as Stiegler describes them: 'As for the inhabitants of the planet who do not live in industrial countries – in the overwhelming majority of cases, they are reduced to a state of unspeakable misery, the colossal, immeasurable scale of which is in all likelihood without precedent in the history of humanity' (Stiegler 2014:79). But even those who are connected, via education, medical aid, insurance funds and pension schemes are forced to carry out their professional tasks, tasks that have become ever more thankless, and stripped of all meaning for those who carry them out. Even those who are connected to the system, their labour is '– as far removed from any meaning as it is possible to be – tasks with generally extremely trivial purposes, paying the working population enough to enable the adoption of increasingly standardized consumer behaviours' (Stiegler 2014:79). Consumption is believed to be the only freedom and identity left (see Meylahn 2010c) for the consumer, but it brings not the promised truth, identity or freedom; it brings no life to the consumer with the result and ever more abyssal feeling of frustration results, and the only solution offered to that feeling is more frenetic intensification of consumption (Stiegler 2014:79)

In such a divided context, it is impossible to address a book to a reader who one presumes is part of "universal humanity" and who will work (practice) in a community of such abstract humans.[41]

The socio-economic realities of the world have changed and these realities of the majority of the world's population need to be taken into consideration. On the level of subsistence, there were people struggling to make a living, the conditions have changed or have taken on proportions as never before in the history of humanity. This embodiment, this subsistence, or the social-economic conditions of subsistence, needs to be taken into consideration. Likewise, the paradigm shifts, how Western humanity thinks about itself and the world that have taken place over the last century also needs to be taken into consideration. How does one do that? One way of doing that is becoming conscious that my privileged constructions of thought are haunted, constantly and insistently haunted by all that it excludes.

Trans-fictional and non-colonial

One dominant interpretation of our globe at present is that the globe is facing a major economic, political and ecological crisis. This narrative also argues that this crisis is the result of humanity, as the earth, according to this interpretation, has entered the age of the Anthropocene (see Meylahn 2014c). In that sense the crisis is self-inflicted, that is, it is a consequence of the dominant thought, the dominant metaphysics.

Within this interpretation one can argue that this dominant view of the world (metaphysics) is bringing the earth close to collective suicide. This dominant world-view that is dominating the globe needs to be challenged, not as in the cold war with an equally strong anti-capitalist Marxist view for example, but rather with various pluri-verse world-views that challenge this dominant view locally.[42] Challenge it, not because it is wrong and because one has the right view, but because it is dominant and thus excludes other views.

It is in the local challenge of the dominant metaphysics that one becomes aware of the role of decolonial thought, as my own locality is a locality that is

---

[41] It became common at the end of the twentieth century to speak of humanity as though those making up this we were all, more or less, in an equal condition. This so-called equality points to an absolute fiction, and the growth of inequality in living conditions is such that the groups making up different communities and social groups often have very little in common (Stiegler 2014:79).

[42] To maintain cosmopolitan ideals we (all those who engage in this project) have to decolonize cosmopolitanism which means moving toward a de-colonial cosmopolitan order no longer modelled on the law of nature discovered by science. Decolonial cosmopolitanism shall be the becoming of a pluri-versal world order built upon and dwelling on the global borders of modernity/coloniality (Mignolo 2011:22).

suffering and wounded by colonialism, and therefore in this specific context a decolonial trans-fictional approach is called for.

Trans-fictional decolonial praxis reads bodies within their languages, but does not limit the reading of these bodies to the dominant languages. Instead of limiting the reading of the bodies within the dominant language, it challenges these dominant languages, breaking these languages open for what they exclude, what they marginalize and ostracize. Therefore, offering alternatives, even if those alternatives might be labelled folly within the dominant discourses. They are labelled folly because they offer hope for the impossible within those confining languages, and this hope breaks open those confining languages determining the possible for the impossible. One could argue with Badiou (2009) for the need to create space for truth events, where new languages are created and with the new language new bodies, new worlds come to view, worlds that might be liberated from the dominant, mainly Western Modern colonial views of reality.

It is a trans-fictional interpretation and not an anti-modern or anti-metaphysical, and therefore the modern is not rejected, nor the metaphysical, for how could one do that? Thinking in a global world is deeply influenced by modernity and therefore, what is called for, is not an anti-modern attitude that seeks to return to something pre-modern with various forms of nostalgia, but rather to incorporate the critical thought of modernity, to think beyond the geography of modernity, by allowing non-Eurocentric, non-USA-centric voices to be heard.

What trans-fictional and decolonial thought is, is impossible to pin down to a singular concept or idea for the very reason that it is in close proximity to post-modernism and poststructuralism, and therefore has moved beyond giving precise and exact definitions and explanations of concepts.

Trans-fictional and decolonial thinking are also not the same thing, as trans-fictional is a broader concept with a broader focus, whereas decolonial focusses specifically on the colonial element in modern thinking. Yet, both address those aspects of modernity that are colonial, dominant, patriarchal and connected to global capitalism.

What is the challenge? The challenge is that modernity has influenced all who think and write in the academic paradigm. All who have been to Western schools and learnt Western grammar, literature, and science, have been trained in the Western epistemological paradigms, as Walter Mignolo in Gaztambide-Fernández' (2014: 201) interview argues.

It is therefore necessary to introduce new concepts, like Fanon's sociogenesis (1967), which focuses on sense experiences[43] that are conscious of individual's

---

[43] I am who I am because of the gaze of the other, and that other, is a White other (Fanon 1967). Sociogenesis is a decolonial concept that evidences the colonial wound; the type of experience Fanon is describing in the experience of the racialized subject, the wounded subject, because racialization is always a classification and a ranking, and that classification is not embedded in

and communities' geo-political embodiment.[44] 'De-colonial options have one aspect in common with de-westernizing arguments: the definitive rejection of 'being told' from the epistemic privileges of the zero point what 'we' are, what our ranking is in relation to the ideal of humanitas and what we have to do to be recognized as such' (Mignolo 2009:3).

Heidegger interprets the call for thinking as that which affects us. *Es ist das was uns angeht* (Heidegger 1961:158). Trans-fictional praxis therefore is to be aware that thinking is always the thinking of a geo-political-historical body within a specific *Lichtung* into which one is called by thinking. One is Called, and responds as geo-political-historical being (ex-*text*-ence), by thinking (responding) in a specific geo-political-historical place where the thinking I is given place and identity.

Thinking is a response to all *was uns angeht* – all that which affects one, and in responding (thinking) one orders a world by *making* meaning of this world, and how one understands one's place in this world. Yet, because one is aware of the Call, which calls thinking forth and that the thinking called forth is always thinking within a world of language, one also has the ability to transform one's place, one's world, and create new worlds.

Trans-fictional praxis is thinking – thinking in a geo-political context as well as understanding oneself as embodied within a particular geo-political-historical context.

"nature" but is man-made. And the wounded subject is not necessarily the poor or the subaltern, but it could be you or me. The colonial wound cuts across social classes, and it is both racial and patriarchal (Gaztambide Fernández 2014:201). But it is necessary also to work with existing ones in order to de-naturalize them, or, if you wish, to decolonize them. Once you accept this fact, you work from given concepts and look behind and under them. You work by analectic negation. That is not the dialect negation of thesis, antithesis, synthesis, but the geo- and body-political negation. The analectic negation comes from memories, sensibilities, skills, knowledge, that were "there" before the imperial contact with European education. Once European education intervened, whatever creation and conceptualization of creativity was there became trapped in the category of, for example, art and folklore. The analectic negation tells you first that art and folklore are two Western concepts, not two differentiated ontologies. Once you accept this, you can use the label philosopher or artist for an Aymara amauta; or you can call amauta a Western philosopher or artist, such thinking doesn't need permission the IEF (International Epistemic Fund); creativity doesn't need to get in debt with the IAF (International Artistic Fund) (Gaztambide-Fernández 2014:202).

[44] Geo-politics of knowledge goes hand in hand with geo-politics of knowing. Who and when, why and where is knowledge generated (rather than produced, like cars or cell phones)? Asking these questions means to shift the attention from the enunciated to the enunciation. And by so doing, turning Descartes's dictum inside out: rather than assuming that thinking comes before being, one assumes instead that it is a racially marked body in a geo-historical marked space that feels the urge to get the call to speak, to articulate, in whatever semiotic system, the urge that makes of living organisms' human' beings (Mignolo 2009:2).

What has been called white privilege, certainly is a privilege, but it is not a privilege that should disqualify one, but rather a privilege that should be used to serve, as Enrique Dussel argues regarding those who are not poor, but have chosen to stand with the poor. In this book, I will rather choose the generic victim than the poor, but that will be explained in a later chapter.

I do not want to get involved in the battle of thoughts, as all thoughts are equal (see Ó Maoilearca 2015) in the light of Laruelle's democracy of thought (see Laruelle 2013 pos 1344 of 7408), and therefore it would not make sense for me to present one more thought (opinion) on specific local or global matters, which of course I would only do, if I had the absolute conviction that my thoughts would be the final and the only true *present*ation of the facts of a *matter*. I, or rather my thoughts, would be the truth, the final in-depth critical analysis and therefore making me the only legitimate advocate of this "reality".

There are more than enough advocates out there already, *present*ing and re*present*ing their clients, truths, metaphysics and thus worlds. The public space, the agora, which is today the media together with social networks, has become the court of law, where these different advocates (various intellectuals) battle it out, probably believing that they are fighting for the soul of something, in "truth", maybe it is all about one's own soul, one's noetic soul which needs to externalise one's thoughts to ex-ist (ex-*text*): to be, to individuate (see Stiegler 2015a:32).

Therefore, I will not give my opinion, although I cannot deny that this book as a book is as all texts are, an externalization (ex-*text*-tualisation) and/or technics. In that sense, it is individuation, a battle for my own soul, but with the hope that once one understands how and why thoughts are created, one can find a praxis that moves beyond the battle for souls. The battle of the soul seems to always be the battle between God and Satan at least within Western secondary and tertiary re-tentions. I would like to move beyond the battle between God and Satan – beyond good and evil, without that beyond becoming the new good.

In this introductory chapter I tried to answer the question: where do I speak from? And in answering I have touched on numerous topics. It will be impossible to respond to each in detail, but the hope is that in the following chapters the connection between these various themes will become clearer as a trans-fictional praxis, a Christ-*poiēsis* develops, where non-colonial worlds emerge or insurrect from the shadows of global villages.

That which called this book forth, will not and could not be said in this book, but will haunt the pages of this book. The hope that inspired me to continue writing, in full knowledge that the text is but cinders (see Derrida 2014), is that the haunting might continue in all the tombs we create, and maybe tombs are necessary for ghosts to haunt us. If this book has any worth, its worth lies in what it does not say, namely in the ghosts that haunt it, perhaps the Holy Ghost that called it into being.

2. Incarnation: The appearance of the self, the world and the other

The praxis of sense-making is a political and/or ideological and religious praxis.

In the previous chapter I touched on numerous ideas with the promise that some of these will be unpacked in more detail in the chapters that follow, yet this unpacking will be interwoven with examples from my embodiment and through this embodiment *my* interpretation of *my* South African context.

I teach at a university and certain events of the past years have had an impact on my life as an academic, and it is with this embodiment within a tertiary educational institution, that I shortly describe certain events, each of which calls for interpretation so as to be made sense of, and whilst making sense integrating them into a greater narrative of meaning. What I offer, as way of illustration, is a sense making of these events, and not a sense. The purpose is to offer a reflection on the process of sense *making*, rather than focus on the sense that is made. The sense that is made is to illustrate the process of sense making and therefore I do not present the sense made as *the* sense that I want others to accept or even share. The focus on sense making rather than offering this sense to others, is because I will argue that sense making is integral to an interpretation of what it means to be human. In these illustrations of *my* sense making, my embodiment needs to be kept in mind, as a privileged embodiment, as I described in the beginning of the previous chapter.

I emphasise the word *making*, as it is about *making* sense (*creating* sense) and not about discovering or finding sense, but I will unpack these ideas in this chapter.

My embodiment in the South African university context in the years 2015–2017

Towards the end of 2015 #FeesMustFall student protests disrupted numerous South African tertiary institutions. These protests continued into 2016 with numerous other hashtags from #AfrikaansMustFall to #StopOutsourcing and #RhodesMustFall. Student protests are not unique to South Africa, as perhaps other student protest in India and Turkey as well as other parts of the world, might have certain similarities with these local protests, yet keeping in mind that there are always important contextual differences. In following some of these hashtags (movements) on social media it is interesting to see how global movements are brought into conversation with these local movements. For example, the #Black-LivesMatter movement in the USA is certainly impacting many of the discourses in South Africa, as on the social media local and global posts intermingle and inter-interpret each other creating *glocal* discourses.

Part of sense-*making*, which is part of the construction of meaning, is to typify and/or classify, which is what I already started doing in the previous paragraphs, as I typified these protests by classifying them and claiming them to be 'similar to' other student protests in other parts of the world. Even the most basic experiences, the experiences of emotions, are made sense of by typifying and classifying them as either sad emotions or happy emotions, and thereby grouping them into identifiable clusters: sad emotions or happy emotions. Not only are experiences classified, but one also emplots them/it into a greater narrative with a time-line, which might explain the cause or effect of these experiences. To make sense of these protests and hashtags in South Africa, I classified and grouped them under the theme of social justice (race, exclusion, white privilege, colonialism, decolonialism), but they are also about democracy, as some students feel excluded from the different dominant discourses, and feel their voice is not heard. By doing this I have already started with the sense making of these events. Others have classified and typified these events and experiences very differently. This difference in classification, I will argue, is because of different primary, secondary and tertiary retentions and protentions of the one seeking to make sense. In other words, certain remembered experiences in my personal past (primary retentions), as well as texts that I have read in the past and communities of which I am part of (secondary retentions), together with the theories, norms and values (tertiary retentions) that have developed in my specific embodiment, all have influenced how I typify and classify these events and experiences. Also, my expectations and interpretation of the future (protentions, including primary, secondary and tertiary) will impact how these events are classified and typified. Different primary, secondary and tertiary retentions and protentions will classify and typify these events differently.

I mention this context because, as I stated in the beginning, I believe that a book (as a text and as an externalisation – ex-*text*-ualisation) is a response, and maybe this book is a response consciously and/or unconsciously to these events. In that sense, I understand this book as my response to these themes of justice and democracy, but the focus of this book is offering an interpretation of *a* praxis of *Dasein* within a *Mitsein* and the binding (*religare*) role of religion and politics in sense-*making* and the *creation* of meaning, which I interpret as being part of what it means to be human. To be (*Dasein*) is a praxis, as to exist is to externalise (ex-text-ualise) or to be ex-*text*-ualised by and/or in a *context*. A context that is shared with others and other things, therefore a *Mitsein*. The context into which one is thrown, or in which one finds oneself, one's embodiment, is created by the different things and people that make up this context, and it is the context that gives all these things their specific place (see Heidegger 1971:203ff). What binds (*religare*) the things together into a world? For Heidegger it is the speaking of language, but which Word, which Logos creates the *Lichtung* in which all the different things appear, which in turn carries out the world (*Lichtung*)? In this chapter, it will be argued that this Word that binds (*religare*) is a political (ideological) and/or religious Word. Or that this Word has a political and or religious task, of binding things and people together into a comprehensive whole.

A response to...

I have already mentioned the various student protests to which I am consciously and unconsciously responding, however these protests are not isolated but are intertwined with global events, and therefore one could describe them as glocal. My global context, or rather the global context that directly, for various reasons which has to do with my personal narrative, has an impact on *my life,* are the events happening in the United Kingdom with Brexit, the United States of America with the election of Donald Trump and the elections in the year 2017 in many European countries, first the Netherlands, then France and later Germany, where those labelled populists did not get the desired majority, but certainly have established themselves as serious political contenders, which indicates a clear shift to what has been classified as the "right". These are events from a small part of the global world, but a part that directly or indirectly has an impact on the way *I* interpret the world and therefore these events call for a response from *me*: how I *make* sense of them and integrate them into a narrative of meaning. Somebody else, whose narrative is different from mine, might have a very different interpretation of the global world, a world that focusses on different countries from those that have had an impact on my life-story, and therefore my view of the world. I did not mention Russia, China, India or Latin America, as these countries are not part of my personal narrative, but somebody whose narrative has been influenced by these countries, might have a very different view. This needs to be kept in mind, as it offers multi-polar views of the globe and not a singular view of the globe. The dominant media outlets encourage such a singular Western view of the world.

    In South Africa, the 2016 local government elections [in my interpretation] were a blow to the African National Congress in the urban areas and later that year the Public Protector's report was released on State Capture, which also had an impact on the local politics. In 2017 emails were leaked that seemed to support the State Capture report. The year 2016 was also the year in which the Dutch Reformed Church of South Africa did an about turn regarding the LGBTI community and reversed their very inclusive 2015 decision, which was made at their general synod.

So much has happened, both locally and globally, and one seeks to try and comprehend and interpret these global events and how they are related not only to each other, but also to local events – events which one could argue from a certain perspective, that have shocked the modern West, and could be emplotted into a narrative, which tells the story of deeper problems within modern Western understanding of democracy, modern (liberal) Western identity, etcetera. If these interpretations are brought together, a new dominant narrative of crisis emerges, which might help to make sense of other events, as they become events of crisis in the dominant narrative. The question is, how useful are these emerging narratives of crisis? I am referring to, for example a crisis in Western democracy, a crisis in the liberal Western identity, and/or a crisis in global capitalism.

One possible way to make meaning of these events is to connect these different events into a comprehensive whole, in other words to emplot them into such a narrative of crisis in Western democracy and/or global capitalism. Yet, there are numerous other possibilities of making meaning and sense of these events. Any event can be emplotted into a variety of different narratives, again depending on the primary, secondary and tertiary retentions and protentions available to the individual and/or community seeking to make sense.

As already alluded to above, somebody from a different context, or even the same context but with a different personal and/or community narrative, will emplot these events differently.

What makes meaning and sense different?

The way events are classified, which depends on the way they are integrated (emplotted) into a greater narrative. Narrative gives events a specific context (place) and time. For example, the rise of populism can be emplotted into a narrative of a crisis in Western democracy and global capitalism, or it can be emplotted into a narrative of migration and the influx of foreigners. The narrative places the event into a certain context and explains cause and effect, that is, places it into a time sequence. It places events into a *Zeit-Spiel-Raum* (Heidegger 1965:214 & Caputo 1993:30) where time and place create the narrative context for the event, which gives it its sense and meaning. In the previous chapter I argued that the basic description of metaphysics is to offer time and space to things and events.

The differences in interpretation of these events is because they are placed into different metaphysical systems.[1] A different metaphysics opens a different ontology, because a different *logic* (light) provides a different place (*Lichtung*) for different objects (things, experiences, and events) to become visible or to become visible differently, as they are connected to different cause and effect sequences (time), and such differences change everything.[2] The Logos and the *onta* (things) that become visible in that Logos (ontology) are intimately connected, the *onta* that appear, are visible, carry out the *Lichtung,* and the *Lichtung* offers each of these visible things (*onta*) their specific place. If something else appears, previously invisible, it challenges the ontology, and a new logos needs to *be carried out* so as to give the new things that appeared place and time. The question of Europe, is in this sense an ontological question. Who or what is part of Europe and what kind of Europe is carried out by the inclusion or the exclusion of certain people?

There is not just a single narrative that can give meaning to these events, there is not just one narrative that can link these events into a cause and effect sequence within a specific ontology, and therefore one finds oneself in a trans-narrative context, or what I call a trans-fictional context. Any of these events, the protests in South Africa, the elections in the USA and the UK, are emplotted into different narratives, and one is confronted with various attempts at sense-making and meaning creation. One reads various newspapers, and each paper tries to give *the* sense and offer *the* meaning of these events. One is left in a context of various narratives, various metaphysical systems vying for readers [profit] to accept their narrative, their truth, and thus competing, accusing the other narratives of being fake news. This is a highly frustrating context, because if one is not directly involved, and reads or sees the news from a distance, it is difficult to know which news outlets to trust. For some individuals within strongly bound communities involved in the events, everything is crystal clear, and they can't believe why others cannot see it – for them the writing is clearly on the wall. People cannot comprehend why so many voted for Trump or for Brexit or for the new right parties in Europe, or continue to support Zuma. But the other side feels exactly the same, and can't believe why people cannot see that what is necessary is a strong nationalist party that looks after the needs of the people.

Each of these narratives, each of these ontologies, each of these metaphysical systems, are part of the collective meaning *making* of a particular *Mitsein,* and in that sense, they are part of creating a community – binding (*religare*) a community together. Therefore, the praxis of sense-making is a political and/or ideological and religious praxis. Sense-*making* is not only a matter of emplotting

---

things (experiences, objects, people and events) into a particular *Lichtung* (clearing) in which they appear, whilst connecting them into a cause and effect sequence (time or narrative), but by *giving* meaning to things within a particular narrative, a political or religious community is created through binding (*religare*) all those together who find (create) meaning through the same or similar narratives.

Meaning-*making* is political[3] and religious, as it binds people together into a collective as well as providing the collective with an ultimate meaning, and therefore it is a religious praxis, as it provides that community with their ultimate reference for sense making.

There are various such narratives, but these narratives are more than just narratives, as they have this binding role as well, by offering ultimate meaning and thereby constructing a people. These narratives do not only carry out a world, they also carry out a people, a nation or a congregation, and therefore I will refer to these narratives as metaphysical: metaphysical as that which gives time and place to things and binds people into a world and with the world a specific worldview. Metaphysical in the sense that it creates the *Lichtung* or world in which things find their place, whilst that particular world is carried out by all the things that appear in that particular Light (*Lichtung*) (see Heidegger 1971:203ff), as there is not only one metaphysics, but a plurality of metaphysical systems which are not necessarily in conflict with each other, but intersect or traverse each other. I will refer to this intersection or traversing of metaphysical narratives as trans-fictional. It is a trans-fictional praxis in which the individual seeks to make sense of her or his world; it is a trans-fictional praxis in which the individual seeks to create her or his world in conversation with others (*Mitsein*), and thereby through sense-making within a collective, become an individual *in* a particular world and *of* a particular collective.

Back to the #FeesMustFall as an illustration of this religious-political sense-making and meaning creation. Every member of the university community needed in some way to emplot these protests, these happenings into a narrative that offered meaning and sense to them. The different staff members and students emplotted these events differently, but as I said above this is not only done individually, but collectively, by binding those with similar narratives together, and thereby the university community was politicised, and divided into various "political" camps.

I will not offer an interpretation of these protests, which would only be *my* emplotment of this event, namely how *I* tried to make sense of this event by emplotting it into a narrative, and thereby identifying myself with a certain grouping on campus. The purpose of this illustration is not to interpret or to offer a *correct* interpretation of the events, as that would be impossible, but it is solely to

---

[3]   Political understood in Laclau's sense: the political operation *par excellence* is always going to be the construction of a 'people' (Laclau 2007:153).

illustrate the process of *making* sense individually and collectively, and thereby individuating oneself into a group and therefore the birth of a community, which is always a political act, a political-religious praxis.

#FeesMustFall

#FeesMustFall together with #AfrikaansMustFall as well as #RhodesMustFall are various student movements on the various South African university campuses. In my sense *making* of these events, I have interpreted them as being different expressions of the call for *Free, Decolonial, Decommodified, Quality Education*. For example, the statue of Cecil John Rhodes on the Campus of the University of Cape Town was symbolic for the need for decolonial education, and therefore the need for the statue, and all that the statue stands for, to fall. The same with #Afrikaans-MustFall, Afrikaans, having been the language of the Apartheid government and the Nationalists, needed to fall, but not only because of the political past, but also because of the inherent inequality or Afrikaans privilege, as Afrikaans is the only other South African language that is used as a medium of instruction in education from primary to tertiary level. For me, this means that most South Africans are taught in their second or third language and not in their mother tongue, which gives the Afrikaans students an unfair advantage, as they are the only students taught in their mother tongue.

In my interpretations (making meaning and emplotting into a greater narrative), these movements are different expressions of anger and frustration amongst the student body, mainly black student body, about how little has changed since the end of Apartheid with regards to the lives of the majority of black people. A reason needs to be found for this lack of change. There are different possible reasons, for example, white monopoly capital, lack of transformation, and/or corruption. The next step of sense-making is to ask, who is to blame for the identified problem, for example white monopoly capital, corruption and lack of transformation? For some, the blame is sought in democracy and constitutionalism. In a sense, it is anger at the failure of democracy and constitutionalism to change the lives of the majority. In that sense, this movement links up with Brexit and the USA presidential election, in the sense that a large portion of the constituency feel excluded and not taken seriously by the democratic processes. I do not want to equate the struggle of the students with Trump supporters, as the content of their grievances are certainly very different. Yet, there is a similarity in the feeling of being excluded, one's voice is not heard and the "system just does what it wants." The similarity lies with the feeling of not being heard, and of not being taken into consideration, which is *a* possible definition of populism.[4]

---

[4] Margaret Canovan asserts that the two features universally present in populism are the appeal to the people and anti-elitism (Laclau 2007:7).

All these events, in my interpretation, pose the question whether democracy and constitutionalism can truly bring about justice? The South African constitution is, according to some interpreters, the most advanced constitution in the *Western* world, and enshrines all the values of Western equality and democracy, that is, it enshrines all the laudable *Western* values and rights that have been hard fought for over the past centuries in the West. Yet, it seems to be failing the people, the very people it is supposed to serve.

On the other hand, the democracies in the heartland of Western Democracy (USA, UK, France, Germany) are clearly showing cracks, at least that is how some interpret the latest events in the USA, UK and Europe.

In this book, these global events will be in the background, but the focus will be on the local events concerning the #FeesMustFall movement, in the hope that such a glocal focus might be useful in thinking about all these other events as well. In *my interpretation*, it is a local event of a global (Western) phenomena, namely the crisis in Western values and democracy.

Over the past two years, I have tried to listen to the #FeesMustFall students by attending some of their meetings, as well as their meetings with academic staff and/or church leaders. I have also listened to them in smaller groups, and tried to listen to individuals in one-on-one conversations with the students. In 2016, I facilitated a meeting with the different groups from amongst the theology students, where we created a space to listen to each other. The request to be listened to runs like a common thread throughout this movement at the University of Pretoria, as the students feel that they are not being listened to, or that they are not being heard.

I was part of the process of the drafting of a statement in response to the protests of the students. I read with great interest and appreciation the various drafts and the comments made by the various drafters of the statement. I am specifically referring to *A Call for Critical Engagement – Study Document*.[5] I did not comment myself nor did I write any aspect of the statement, but attended most of the drafting meetings and listened to the discussions concerning the drafting of the statement. I did not sign the statement – not because of an aloofness or lack of solidarity with regards to any movement or groups within the broader movement, but because I wanted to listen rather than individuate myself into a particular collective through externalisation (ex-*text*-ualisation) in a statement (text). In a sense, I was exploring the possibility of a trans-fictional praxis, without clearly individuating myself within one of the narratives.

---

[5]   https://docs.google.com/document/d/1zIAKtKhIPDy9WYMY3BCmNwR5UHnwQD6kKK
      GH7TCvkFg/pub

Before the draft of *A Call for Critical Engagement*, there was the statement by the four deans and/or acting deans of the four theological faculties[6] in South Africa. Besides these two statements, there have been numerous other statements, for example by concerned academics, "progressive" academics, concerned parents, and the various memoranda from the students and statements from other student groupings, press releases from the various managements together with numerous newspaper articles and posts on social media. One was literally surrounded by statements, memoranda, articles, posts, tweets, and discussions on WhatsApp chats, interspersed with the odd video clip of what happened somewhere on one of the South African campuses. It is in this context of texts upon texts that one tries to make sense of what is happening, and in the process of making sense individuating oneself within a collective, which stands in relation to the various interpretations of what is *believed* to be happening in South Africa. Therefore, one could speak of one's political and/or religious individuation into some or other collective, which has a certain view of the world (worldview), a certain metaphysics (where things and people are in a particular time and space). In such divided contexts one is often called to take a stand, in other words individuate oneself, by becoming part of, or identifying with a certain collective, by making a public statement (ex-*text*-ualise) or endorsing or signing a statement.

Any student or staff member that enters the South African university context is confronted with these various collectives called together via the different metaphysical systems that *give* meaning and purpose to "reality". No matter how political or apolitical the student or staff member see themselves, they enter this plurality of narratives and consciously or unconsciously choose to individuate themselves into one or more of them. This is a trans-fictional experience of multiple narratives and trying to *figure* out which one, one *believes*.

It is about making meaning of what is happening, and through making meaning to be individuated into a certain collective.

These events have certainly affected most South Africans and therefore one is trying to make sense, either from the position of watching these events from the distance of newspaper articles or being involved in various ways. It is probably the most human thing to do, when confronted with a phenomenon or an event like these different hashtags, and the varied responses to them, to try and make sense of them, by trying to emplot these happenings into some or other narrative. By emplotting them into a narrative gives meaning to these events or phenomena, and it does this by relating the happening to a remembered past (retentions) and by trying (successfully or less successfully) to integrate it into some form of projection into the future (protention), and thereby it becomes an event that is part of

---

6   http://www.up.ac.za/en/faculty-of-theology/news/post_2367794-press-statement-deans-of-theology

some or other narrative with a time line of past-present-future. It is between the remembered past and anticipated future that one makes sense of happenings that become events and phenomena, as sense is created between past experiences (re-tentions including political, social and economic theories) and hopes and/or fears concerning the future (protentions).

One cannot avoid these hashtags, as they affect us all. The "movement" shut down numerous universities in 2016, which has had a tremendous impact on the future – the future of thousands of students, as well as the future of the country. It is probably this tremendous impact on the future that made this event so emotional for many.

In a similar way, following numerous friends on social media, people in the USA are trying to make sense of the Trump election or in the UK trying to make sense of BREXIT. There are the personal comments and views on social media, but also "critical analyses" posted from "respected" newspapers, who in turn are accused of spreading "fake news" by other media outlets.

One could say that one is currently living in a world bombarded by various texts, narratives, which compete with each other in emplotting major events. This context of news and fake news concerning any event, makes it very difficult to form opinions, or to "know what is actually going on". As I am writing this, the major news event is the crisis with North Korea and the USA, as well as the no confidence vote in South Africa. The media outlets and newspapers all offer their interpretation of these events, and one is left in this trans-fictional space or trans-political space, where these different and conflicting narratives literally traverse your computer screen, and in this transversal space one tries to *figure* out where one stands, which translates into the question: who or what do I *believe*? Which of these narratives does one believe is telling the "truth"? This question, which is a fundamental or existential question of existing (ex-*text*-ing), is maybe the wrong question, as none of these narratives are true, but one or more resonates with one's personal retentions and protentions and therefore is experienced as being true. An *experience of truth* that can be so powerful, as it is described in the Gospel as a burning sensation in the heart, like with the Emmaus disciples (Luke 24:13–35). Such powerful experiences of truth can lead to conversion from one metaphysical system to another. In that sense there *is* truth, as an experience of truth. Conversion is not understood as conversion to truth, but conversion as embracing a different epistemological *conception* of what is real on the basis of encountering a part of experienced reality differently. This is how Polanyi also views the paradigm shifts in science (see Root 2014:203). Truth is thus this burning sensation that a certain narrative (a certain fiction) provides one with better sense and meaning in the context of one's past meanings and projections into the future. Things that did not make sense, begin to make sense, as a different Logos provides a "better" *Lichtung* for that which didn't make sense, as it could not meaningfully appear.

This is experienced as truth. Lies are experienced when one hears a story, reads a commentary or analysis of events, and there is no resonance or even a dissonance between the text and one's own narrative, and therefore it is experienced as lies, false or fake news. Truth and lies therefore have very little to do with what is "actually out there" (wherever "out there" is), nor does it have to do with what "actually" happened, but it has to do with this resonance between one's own narrative and the narrative of the other (newspaper or commentary). This harmonious resonance is then experienced as truth, as it is like a burning sensation in the heart. This burning sensation is a powerful feeling and a wonderful feeling and as things fall into place, everything begins to make sense. It is for this reason that conversations take place, as sometimes other narratives provide better time-places for things. I will come back to this resonance later in the chapter.

In this book, I will not engage in the "truth" and/or "factuality" and/or "correct or incorrect analysis" of the different statements or newspaper articles, as I believe that the media statements, various statements of academics, as well as statements and comments on social media have certainly done that more than sufficiently. All these opinions, the opinions of the different statements and articles, are presented with so much conviction, that is, the *belief* that they are proclaiming the final truth on the matter by *presenting* the facts: their text presents (represents) the matters as they *are*. They are right, as that is exactly what texts do. Texts (language) *believe* itself to be presenting things as they *are*, that is as they exist, but forgetting that things exist only to the extent that they ex-*text*. Things exist in as far as they are externalised, that is, in as far as they appear, and they appear, are disclosed, in as far as they are appropriated. This disclosure of appropriation is the speaking of language (see Hofstadter 1971b:*xxi* in Heidegger 1971), or the event (*Ereignis*) of Language. Thus, things exist in language (texts) or as texts, therefore they ex-*text*. Thus, texts do indeed present things as they are (exist), for they only *are in* or *as* those texts (ex-*text*).

The problem arises if there are different texts, offering different versions of existence, or different interpretations of existence (ex-*text*-ence). There will necessarily always be different texts in which things ex-*text* differently, as things are disclosed differently depending on different appropriations. The appropriations are different because of different primary, secondary and tertiary retentions and protentions of the individual as part of her or his particular community or collective.

The different narratives are thus in competition with each other, also wishing to convince (convert) readers. Therefore, the truth is *present*ed with the necessary rhetorical skill to convince the readers of the said truth. Amid all these texts one is left with numerous opposing truths, each growing in meaning, substance, support and conviction, all of which is not helpful at all. I do not think that one more text trying to explain the "truth" or *present* the "facts" or offer a "critical analysis" of the matter is necessary or helpful.

My interest in this book, is twofold.

Firstly, in response to the question why one creates these texts, convinced that we (the collective one identifies with) know the truth of the *matter*, or that we *present* the facts or that we are offering an in-depth critical analysis of the situation.

Secondly, in response to the question what one hopes to achieve by such a creation, or drafting of such texts. Thus, why is it so important to create such texts and secondly how do we create these texts, or how are these texts created?

Heidegger (1961) asked the question, *Was Heißt Denken?* What is called thinking? This question has, as so often with Heidegger, a double meaning. What *is* this *thing* called thinking and secondly and more importantly, what calls thinking forth? For him it is that which calls thought forth (*was uns Denken heisst*) that is the most thought-worthy, das *Bedenklichste* as it is also the*Fragwürdigste* (most questionable). That which calls thinking-forth is the most questionable (that needs to be questioned) as well as being a worthy question.

The human is believed to be a thinking being, the human is a sense-making being, and I say this without wanting to exclude animals and plants, but I cannot speak *for* them, but only *about* them, and whatever I say about them, it will be me saying it, and not them speaking for themselves. Therefore, it does not really matter if I a*scribe* thinking to them or not, it will always only be my a*scrip*tion, and if they actually think or not will only be or not be (exist or not exist) *in* my or our a*scrip*tion (text) about them.

To be human means to make sense and one appears (is disclosed) as human in and through sense-making. The flesh appears (is disclosed) as body through the a*scrip*tion and in*scrip*tion of meaning and sense onto the flesh, and only the body appears as in*scrib*ed flesh. Would that mean that people who for whatever reason cannot speak or communicate (to whom it has been a*scrib*ed that they cannot think), are not human? Again, I cannot speak for them, and as they cannot speak for themselves, meaning is ascribed to them. Different meanings are ascribed to them, as they appear (are disclosed) within a particular appropriation. As already mentioned in the first chapter, there are people and groups of people who only appear in somebody else's appropriation, in other words, they are docile bodies who are determined by others. To an extent everyone is determined by others, but part of being a noetic soul is to partake in this determination, is to partake in this writing ascribed and inscribed on the Flesh (Body without Organs) making it a body. Part of the focus of this book is to create a trans-fictional space for more self-inscription.

To ask such a question, when is somebody human, is very human, and maybe it is only a *thinking-questioning* human that would ask such questions regarding the role of thinking in the being of being human.

Therefore, I will agree with Nancy, when he argues that we need to rethink humanity, 'We don't need more humanism or more democracy: we need to begin by questioning anew the entire thought of "man," returning it to the workshop' (Nancy 2013:5). The human needs to be returned to the work-shop, as many of the presumptions about being (existing) and about thinking have never been thought. They have never been questioned and thus they are the most questionable, they have never been thought and therefore the most thought-worthy.

Making sense – creating meaning: Embodiment

I gave this chapter the title, *Incarnation*, to be incarnate, to be embodied, to be given a body, a body that one hopefully also co-gives oneself. That in a sense, is the question: To what extent does one co-give the body to oneself and how much of the body is imposed by others? It is never a matter of pure self-inscription, as inscribing always happens in and through community, and yet it is important that one *co*-writes one's body and *co*-writes the world in which this body ex-*texts*. Maybe the degree of co-writing might be a new interpretation of the Enlightenment's *Mündigkeit*. One is a majority, a *Mündige* subject, if one co-writes one's body and the world in which the body ex-*texts*.

As the focus of this chapter is incarnation, embodiment (and embodiment is never something abstract, but personal), this chapter will probably be the most personal, where I write in the first person.

My interpretation of incarnation has been influenced by Michel Henry's (2015) philosophy of Flesh, which he interprets in the light of the incarnation, and thereby develops a philosophy of Christianity (Henry 2003). Henry's starting point for philosophy and likewise for theology is Life and/or Flesh, as he wants to think from the Incarnation, from Life. Said differently in the context of the introductory chapter, he wants to think the Call, that which calls thought forth, but he thinks it as Life (Flesh), as for him it is Life that calls thought forth. In other words, he names (determines) the Call (that which calls thought forth) Life (Flesh). My Flesh, naked (undetermined) flesh, breathing and [existing] calls to be thought. Existential questions, as mentioned in the first chapter, come to mind. What am I? What is this Flesh? Why is this Flesh? Is there Flesh?

Henry wants to think from that which calls thinking forth (*was uns denken heisst*), but which cannot be captured in thought, and is therefore the most questionable and most thought-worthy. That which calls thinking forth, but cannot be *begriffen* in a *Begriff*, in other words, that which escapes conceptualisation and/or comprehension – he calls Life.

What does thought think? Why does it think what it thinks? Who thinks and
by thinking becomes a who that thinks? Perhaps even a who, who only becomes
a who, because she or he or it thinks that [she] or [he] or [it] is thinking.

What does thought think and why does it think, and what is thinking?

Thought responds to a Call that calls thinking forth. In other words, something
makes one think, or inspires thought, even if that something is raw, naked, breathing Flesh (or Life) that one is and that calls to be thought, and in being thought
appears as Life and/or Flesh that exists (ex-*texts*). This second part of the above
sentence Henry did not think. Yes, one can agree with him that Flesh (naked Life)
calls thinking forth, but to say that one has already thought Flesh, naked Life,
one has already made a determination as to what calls thought forth. One could
argue that Deleuze and Guattari argue that it is the Body without Organs that calls
thinking forth, the thinking that in turn stratifies this Body without Organs – inscribing it with meaning. Yet, Deleuze and Guattari (2011:149ff) were aware that
one must first make this Body without Organs. In other words, one must first think
it, before it becomes that which calls thought forth. 'At any rate, you have one (or
several). It's not so much that it pre-exists or comes ready made, you make one,
you can't desire without making one, and it awaits you; … ' (Deleuze & Guattari
2011:149). Naked Life, Flesh or BwO[7] pre-exists in the sense that it is there before being thought and yet it has to be made to be thought, it has to be determined,
named (Life, Flesh, BwO), and then it awaits to be thought. It is this "has to be
made" that Henry did not think. It is so difficult to think this, and therefore the
most thoughtworthy, but also the most questionable.

Thought thinks because it is called to think (*heisst uns denken*) by that which
calls it to think, but thought never *is* that which calls it to think. Thought *is* never
the Call, but always only the response to the Call. Thinking, in response to the
Call, decides to name whatever it is that called it forth, Life or BwO, for example,
and by calling it Life, it determines what Life is, it develop "facts" about life, but
whatever it does, it never captures conclusively that which Called these thoughts
forth, but that which Called withdraws from thought.

One can bring these ideas into conversation with Critical Realism. Where independent objective reality calls dependent objective reality forth, but what is not
thought in critical realism is that independent objective reality is just a possible
determination of that which calls dependent objective reality (thought) forth.

Thinking is convinced that it has finally caught that which called it forth, and
in that sense, it *believes* itself to be a true reflection, true representation, or presentation of that which called it forth.

Yet, all of these attempts to think that which calls thought forth and thought's
belief that it has captured (determined) that which called it forth, is based on a

---

[7]   This is the abbreviation that Deleuze and Guattari (2011) use for the Body without Organs.

decision. The decision, to use Deleuze and Guattari's words, to make the BwO, or to make that which is *believed* to have called thought forth, and which in turn awaits the thought that it called forth.

This decision (*making* of that which is believed to have called thought forth) is very important, as this decision (the creation of that which is believed to have called thought forth) is also the decision that determines the kind of world the thinker and her or his community live in.

It is a philosophical and or religious decision that carries out a certain world. For Henry, his decision to make Life that which calls thought forth, carries out a phenomenology-of-flesh-world. If one decides to make that which calls thought forth, independent objective reality, then a critical-realist-world is carried out.

Any philosophy or theology (thinking) is a response to that which called it forth, and only *in* thought is that which called-thought-forth thought (named or determined). For example, that which called thought forth is determined as Life in Henry or it is determined as independent objective reality in critical realism. Depending on how the Call (that-which-called-thought-forth) is determined there will be a different world that is carried out by the determining thought or thought-system. Therefore, a critical realist world is different to an idealist's world as well as a realist's world. Once that which called-thought-forth is named or determined, *It* is no longer that which calls forth thought, but it *is* a thought, and that which called it forth, withdraws from it. The most thought-worthy has been reduced to a singular thought, for example: Life, critical realism's independent objective reality, etcetera.

Now, one could come to the conclusion that if there are different determinations that all *believe* themselves to be *the* determinations of that which called-thought-forth, then that which called-thought-forth must be plural or multiple, for example as Badiou (2009) argues. Or it *is* heterogeneous (Laclau 2007:140) or hypernymity (Rollins 2006:24) or Other (Levinas 1969; 1981). Such a conclusion would still not be thinking the most thought-worthy, as each of these (multiple, hypernymity, Other) are again just determinations of that which called these determinations forth. Again each of these will be a decision to make that which is believed to pre-exist thought, as it is made as multiple, hypernymity, or Other.

Each one of these determinations are different names (thoughts, responses) given to that which is most thought-worthy and which calls thought forth, that which calls for a response. I am not criticising these names, they are good names, many of these names have caused a burning sensation in my heart, as they offered a "truth", a "true" re-presentation of the Real, the Call, but truth only in the sense that they made absolute sense *to me* with my specific primary, secondary and tertiary retentions and protentions. A burning sensation which I interpret as a harmonious *Erklingen* (resonance) of my primary, secondary and tertiary retentions and protentions in the secondary and tertiary retentions and protentions of these theories (determinations of that which calls-thought-forth). The way some-thing appears, is disclosed, appears only to the extent that it can be appropriated (see Hofstadter 1971b:*xxi*). It appears as truth if there is an *Erklingen,* a resonance between the text in which it is disclosed (appears) and the texts in which it is ap-propriated in my world. In other words, the newspaper articles that make sense of events for me are those articles that disclose certain events in a text that finds resonance in my embodiment (ex-*text*-tence) and therefore the "ah ha" experience or the burning sensation in the heart.

François Laruelle's (2013a; 2013b) non-philosophy might help in understand-ing this force-of-thought. He refers to that which calls thought forth as the Real. That which calls thought forth *is* the force-of-thought, which is called forth by the Real. Laruelle turns the direction of thought around. It is no longer the symbol, writing, thought that aims at the real-One in the manner of it being an object, the reality out there, etcetera. It is the other way around, as words do not transcend towards the real-One, but from it towards philosophical objects 'without however being a question of an auto-positional transcendence, divided and refolded. The symbols as "lived-without-life", "given-without-givenness", etc., are symbols *for* philosophy but not symbols *of* philosophy and still less knowledge *of the* Real' (Laruelle 2013b pos 4913 of 7408). In other words, philosophy is called forth by that which calls-thinking-forth, and it responds in the belief that it can and/or has determined that which calls.

In other words, by returning humanity to the workshop, one turns everything on its head. It is no longer thought (reason) aiming at objective reality, but it is the Real that Calls[8] and by calling thought forth determines thought in the last instance. Thought responds to the Call by believing that it has determined that which called it forth, but these determinations have been and can be very different and therefore different worlds, different metaphysical systems emerge.

There is a uni-direction from Real (Call) towards philosophy without a re-turn. A uni-direction from the Call (*was uns denken heisst*) to thought without a return. Thus, the Call determines thought in the last instance, but thought only insufficiently determines that which called it forth, as it has to make that which it believes pre-exists its thought, so that that which it made can await it and receive its thoughts (determinations). Thoughts, philosophies, metaphysical systems are thus different fictions or creations (philosophical fictions) who made that which they believe pre-exists their thoughts, so as to await their determining thoughts.

Thus, symbols, words, thoughts find their cause in the Call, but their operatory destination is not the Real, their intention is not the Real, but philosophy (Laruelle 2013b pos 4913 of 7408). '. . . Real, which is thus never the *object* or the referent

---

8   I will write Call with a capital letter to express something of its foreclosure to thought and yet
     it determining of thought in the last instance.

of the symbol' (Laruelle 2013b pos 4913 of 7408). Humanity and/or philosophy stands in the force-of-thought interpreted as Heidegger does, to be in the (*Zug*) pull of that which withdraws[9] – to think is to be in the pull of the Call, the *Zug* of that which Calls-thought-forth, but withdraws from thought.

To be human for Heidegger is to be in this force-of-thought, or in this pull-of-that-which-calls-thought-forth, and *in* this call-response humanity *is*.[10] The human *is* only as a noetic soul. The human exists only as noetic soul, in that it ex-*texts*, stands in this *Zug* of thought: the *Zug* of that which Calls and yet withdraws from that which it called forth. Therefore, this sign (response), this ex-*text*-ence, which humanity *is*, is an empty sign, Heidegger argues.[11]

To argue that thought, to be human, is an empty sign, would be a too final response, as an empty sign would be one possible response, because what philosophy or thought (the response) points to is not nothing, but to that which Calls, and by naming the Call X (that which it created as pre-existing its thoughts so as to await its thought) it points to itself. In that sense, and only in that sense, is it an empty sign, or a self-referencing sign. Laruelle argues, as quoted above, that the operatory destination of thought is not the Real, but philosophy. This Heidegger refers to as the *Sichentziehen* of that which Calls, so the reference of philosophy is that which it named, that which it created to pre-exist its thought so as to receive its thought. Let us say, the Call calls forth a response and *in* the response that which called-forth is named Life, or is determined as Life, as for example Henry does. Then his philosophy of Life, or rather his philosophy of Flesh (Henry 2015) does not point to that which Called-it-forth, but his whole philosophy points, explains, theorises Life, as it is a philosophy of Life. But Life is not the Call, but only that which the Call called forth and in response was named (determined) as Life. Thus, philosophy thinks itself, but does not think that which Called it forth. It has never thought the most thought-worthy, but not because of a lack of attempting to think it. It will never think it, but always only think itself.

This impossibility to think the most thought-worthy is not something to disturb one, nor is it something that needs to be done, it should not become the Holy Grail of philosophy, that one day it will think the most thought-worthy. But per-

---

[9] Wenn wir in den Zug des Entziehens gelangen, sind wir – nur ganz anders als die Zugvögel – auf dem Zug zu dem, was uns anzieht, indem es sich entzieht. Sind wir als die so Angezogenen auf dem Zuge zu dem uns Ziehenden, dann ist unser Wesen schon durch dieses »auf dem Zuge zu ... « geprägt (Heidegger 1961:5–6).

[10] *Als* der dahin Zeigende *ist* der Mensch der Zeigende. Der Mensch ist hierbei jedoch nicht zunächst Mensch und dann noch außerdem und gelegentlich ein Zeigender, sondern: gezogen in das Sichtenziehende, auf dem Zug in dieses und somit zeigend in den Entzug, *ist* der Mensch allererst Mensch. Sein Wesen beruht darin, ein solcher Zeigender zu sein (Heidegger 1961:6).

[11] Weil dieses Zeichen jedoch in das Sicht*entz*iehen zeigt, deutet es nicht so sehr auf das, was sich da ent-zieht, als vielmehr in das Sichtenziehen. Das Zeichen bleibt ohne Deutung (Heidegger 1961:6).

haps it should be accepted, and the task of thinking should not be to try and think the most thought-worthy, but to think in a context of different fictions: to think as a trans-fictional praxis.

As trans-fictional praxis, it will reflect on the relationship between language (decision/response) and reality (the Real as that which Calls thought forth) with the idea of a call-and-response, and it is within this call-response that both the world and the individual come into being: ex-*text*. It is in the call-response that both world and individual within a collective exist (ex-text). This idea of the Call has a lot in common with Laruelle's idea of the Real or man-in-man.[12]

Henry thinks this Call, the Real, by naming it Life. For Henry, this Life is the primary Word, the arch-phenomenon, the arch-intelligibility.[13] What makes

---

[12] The Real no longer puts up with these categories, it cannot be said in terms of World History, or Truth. In order to exists, It must step out of itself. But by definition the Real is unable to step outside of itself, unlike Being which leaves itself if only to show itself to itself. But the Real does not reveal itself to itself from the exterior of itself, and the intellectuals will find themselves definitively amidst finitude, without any possible glimpse [*survol*] of victims. It is a point of immanence, and yet ... This is a bad definition because a point of immanence is something one can project into space and turn into a transcendent thing, something like the Neoplatonic One. We could say that it is a consistent interiority, but interiority is also a term to rework because one kind of interiority is imagined under a psychological form. You can see that as soon as I give definition it is a failure. We have to refuse the temptation or appearance of definition. Man-in-Man is not a psychological subject or a political subject. This is the presupposed, the condition, which negatively determines or determines in-the-last-instance a subject for all the games of giving definitions and predicates that drives [*font mouvoir*] philosophy. I can't say it or unsay it any other way (Laruelle 2015a:37–38).

[13] "Arch- intelligibility" means that a mode of revelation comes into play that is different from the one by which the world becomes visible; and that, for this reason, what it reveals is made up of realities that are invisible in this world, and unnoticed by thought. The Prologue list them: Life, in which Arch-intelligibility consists; the Word of Life, in which this Arch-intelligibility of Life is fulfilled; and, finally, the flesh, in which the Word of Life becomes identical with each of the living beings that we are, we men and women. So an entirely new definition of human is formulated, which is as unknown to Greece as it is to modernity: *The definition of an invisible, and at the same time carnal, human being, and invisible in so far as carnal* (Henry 2015:18–19). Arch-intelligibility concerns reality, and, even more importantly, absolute reality, as philosophy calls it, and what religion names God – the God that according to John is life (Henry 2015:19). Arch-intelligibility denotes an Intelligibility of another order, fundamentally foreign to the one that has just been in question, and which does indeed come about before it: before the vision of things, before the vision of Archetypes according to which things are constructed, before every vision, before the transcendental event from which every vision gains its possibility, before the coming outside of the "outside itself" of the horizon of visibility of every conceivable visible, before the appearance of the world – before its creation (Henry 2015:86). So Arch-intelligibility really means an Intelligibility that precedes all contemplation, and every opening of a "space" to which a vision can be open. An Intelligibility that, as it reveals itself to itself before thought and independently of it, owes it nothing, but owes revealing itself to itself only to itself. An Arch-intelligibility that is an Auto-intelligibility, a self-revelation in this radical sense: Life (Henry 2015:87). Thus Arch-intelligibility does not only come before every conceivable intelligibility, it founds intelligibility and makes it possible: What is intelligible, comprehensible, and capable of

Henry's thought interesting and important for this book is that he thinks this Call as Life, but he does this with the help of the Christ narrative. He does not think Christ philosophically, which would be typical of most apologetic theologies, but thinks philosophy with the help of the Christ-event. In other words, the –logy of his theology or Christology is not taken from philosophy, but is used to interpret philosophy, or rather to think what philosophy cannot think.

What can philosophy not think? In the previous paragraphs, it was the most thought-worthy that philosophy cannot think. Now Henry argues that the Christ-event can help one to think that which philosophy can't, namely the most thought-worthy.

Henry turns to Christ to interpret and understand philosophy and/or phenomenology (Henry 2003; 2015). In other words, Henry does not use philosophy to interpret Christianity, but the other way around – Christianity helps in understanding the human condition and therefore his interpretation of Christianity offers a phenomenology of phenomenology. I will later return to Henry when reflecting on a Christ-*poiēsis* developed in this book. Henry interprets, names, or makes the Call, Flesh (Life) as that which awaits the thinking of philosophy, and the Christ-event does not help philosophy think, but helps to think the thinking of philosophy. I will do the same with Christ-*poiēsis*, with one important difference: not naming the Call Life or Flesh. In other words, not making a BwO to pre-exist and await *my* philosophy, and thereby neither determining the Call nor determining Christ as Life or Truth, or as Love, but Christ radically or nakedly alone (without determination): *sola Christus*.

For Henry, the Word that becomes Flesh, or God that becomes Flesh, is none other than Absolute Life, the Arch-intelligibility becoming flesh. This Arch-intelligibility is forgotten and yet without it one could not individuate (ex-*text*). Before one thinks and makes sense, one has to be alive, one has to have life, but a life that one has not created or given to oneself, but which one has received. It is because of this received Life, this received Flesh, that there is phenomenology and in that sense Life or Flesh is the primal phenomenology. In other words, there is this Arch-Intelligibility that is the primary phenomenon, the me (flesh) called, to which the me can only respond: Here *I* am. It is in the calling of a "me", that the I of 'here-I-am' can be born. What is this *me* that is called before it is born as an *I*, as a subject within a world, but without this conception of *before* being understood in the sense of sequential time? To translate this into the language of Deleuze and Guattari's BwO, the me (bleeding, breathing me of flesh) is *believed* to pre-exist and await the thinking or conscious I, or the response. For there to be

being grasped by us is what we can see without knowing what we see. Before that Intelligibility to which modernity limits its knowledge, comes the Arch-intelligibility in which absolute Life is revealed to itself, and in this way, every life, every modality of life and every conceivable living (Henry 2015:90).

an I think, there has to be a me of flesh and blood that breathes, that is, that is alive.

It is a me that is firstly and primarily alive, has life, breathes and exists. It has life and breath, which it did not give to itself, but which it received as a gift: the gift of life and/or the gift of breath. This Life is for Henry the arch-revelation, the phenomenality of phenomena.[14] It is this Life (existence), Flesh that makes phenomenology possible. Without this Flesh, this Life, there would be no phenomenology. There should be something that calls thinking forth, especially the thinking of a thinking subject, and that something is *believed* to be Life (Flesh), the Flesh of the thinking subject, which is *believed* to pre-exist and to await the thinking subject (I or ego), as the "material" foundation of the thinking subject. The basic idea of any materialism or realism, is that the "material" ground, or the real is the basis, that is, it is that which calls thought forth. Yet, materialism or realism forgets that this material ground or real basis is first made to pre-exist and to await thought in thought. Is this an argument for idealism? No, it is not, as both idealism and materialism or realism are called forth by that which withdraws from thought.

Humans respond to Life and in this response the me (Flesh) is individuated as an existence (an I or an ego), a phenomenon, but always as an ex-*text*-ence within a world: *Dasein* in-a-world. Life for Henry, is the arch-intelligibility, that which Calls, as Heidegger (1961) would say, which calls thinking forth. Henry believes to have determined that which calls thinking forth, he has determined it as Life, forgetting that he made Life as that which pre-exists thinking (arch-intelligibility), awaiting thought, and all this happened *in* his thought. Something always must be *made* the arch-intelligibly, to pre-exist human intelligibility to receive human intelligibility *in* human intelligibility.

The impossibility of thinking the most thought-worthy.

The impossibility has to do with the "fact" that thinking creates that which it thinks about. In other words, thinking *is* never that which it thinks about, but it is thought (language). That which thinking thinks about is that which called thinking forth, but which withdraws from thinking. Derrida's concept of différance and/or the *pharmakon* helps in understanding this difference and deferment between thought and that which thought thinks about.

That which calls thinking forth, cannot be captured in thought, for the simple reason that thought (language) is not what called it forth, but thought is a *pharmakon*, (Derrida 1981:67ff) both gift and *Gift* (poison) (see Derrida 1981:99).

Yet, what is important to remember, is that whatever is, and all that is, is because it appears, and it appears in a disclosing appropriation: the speaking of

---

[14] "Life," for Henry, is "phenomenological." By this he does not mean that life is one thing among others, appearing in world alongside other phenomena. Rather, life is phenomenological 'in the sense that it denotes phenomenality itself, givenness itself' (Henry 2015:xii).

language (Heidegger 1971). There is nothing outside of text (Derrida 1997:158). But this nothing should not disturb one, because even this nothing appears in text. Therefore, nothing is lost, and everything still is, it just is in text, but then again so am I, as my Flesh and the earth exist in ex-*text*-ence. Nothing has really changed, as the world still is, it has not disappeared into a book or a fantasy. But one thing has changed: our confidence in thinking has changed, or our belief in thinking has changed. Not that one can do without thinking, but thinking's ability to finally and conclusively determine things has changed.

This is not a fantasy world, only a fiction, a fiction called forth by the Call and the Call, that which calls thinking(fictions) forth, is Real.

It is *in* this calling forth of thought, in the response which is always in language, for example the response "Here I am", that one becomes an individual that exists and therefore I write it as ex-*texts*, as it is in texts (response – language) that one exists. This ex-*text*-ence is real, as real as it gets.

For Henry this being in language, is where everything is lost,[15] like the empty sign for Heidegger. Thought is the dependent objective reality of social construction, the texts that create, language that carries out the world in which one lives. Thought (the response to the Call) is the logos, the Light in which the world and phenomena appear, yet the primary or original phenomenality of the phenomena is forgotten: that which called phenomenology forth is not thought.

These worlds that one lives in are metaphysical creations, based on a certain logos, which carry out these worlds (see Heidegger 1971:202–203). The logos is the decision (the particular name given to the Call – the particular determination of the Call, or the making of that which is believed to call thought forth), the response to the primary Call. Henry names this Call "Life", which is for him (according to his determination) the primary Call of the *Word* as the Arch-intelligibility. In the response one gives to this Word, this Call, this Life (independent objective reality) a name, and calls it: the Other, Life, Real, independent objective reality, etcetera. Through responding the I and the we are born into the exterior of the world[16] as a *Dasein*, a being there-in-the-world, namely as existence [ex-*text*-ence], but always as a *Mitsein* that is with other people and things, namely all that which populates that particular world. A world is carried out by all that which becomes

---

[15] The poverty of language, which comes along to contradict and annihilate the purpose with which one usually defines language's essence, does not pertain only to the decisive fact that it does not constitute in itself and through itself our access to reality, that is not itself a producer of truth. A more radical reflection, to be developed below, will show that language is the negation of this reality, of any conceivable reality – unless one exempts that pallid reality that pertains to language as a system of significations and that finds itself in principle to be an unreality. This fundamental unreality is precisely the truth of language (Henry 2003:10).

[16] To be born, we have seen, means to come into appearing. Because appearance is double, there are two ways of coming into it: In the "outside itself" of the world, and in the pathos of life (Henry 2015:130).

visible (phenomenological) in the *Lichtung* of that particular decision (name given
to the Call), Logos. All that becomes visible in the *Lichtung* carries out a world
and the world grants to all the things that become visible a particular time-place
(Heidegger 1971:203ff). Yet, this world is not perceived to be carried out by the
decision, the Logos, the Light of the *Lichtung*, but is *believed* to be the way things
truly are. This belief is the basis of the principle of sufficient philosophy (see
Laruelle 1999:287). A belief that is necessary for a world to be carried out, or a
world to grant things their particular time-space. It is also this belief that Laclau
calls the illusion par excellence of ideology (Laclau 2014:17). I would like to
reflect on this idea that one has captured reality, the way the world truly is, with the
thought of Berger and Geertz regarding their interpretation of the role of religion
in the social construction of reality, and thereby link the principle of sufficient
philosophy (Laruelle) to ideology (the political) (Laclau) and religion (Berger and
Geertz).

This *belief* that the carried out world is the real world is for Berger[17] and
Geertz[18] the role of religion. The *dependent* objective reality is perceived to be
the independent objective reality because of the reifying role of religion. In other
words, the Logos that allows the world to appear in its *Lichtung* is interpreted as
religion, as the appeared world is not viewed as a social construction, but as the
real world. This *belief* that the world one lives in *to be* the real world is the work
of religion or the work of ideology, Laclau (2014) would say, or is based on the
principle of sufficient philosophy.

Taking the above into consideration, one could argue that religion is to be
found on both ends of the critical realist's spectrum of reality. It is found in the
independent objective reality, where Root[19] for example, places God. It is not only
Root who places God there, Bataille (see James 1997:8) argues that that which
is beyond language (dependent objective reality, beyond social construction), that
which is the most thought-worthy, *is* Sacred (Separated) and thus divine. Heidegger (1989:24) argues that it is in the *Ereignis* (the Event) or the truth of Being that
the last God beckons to us. In other words, there from where the world is carried
out (*Austrag*), the last God beckons (*winkt*) to one. I would argue that most mystical religious traditions that speak of the divine as being beyond language, as does

---

[17] Berger interprets religion as follows: Finally there are the highly theoretical constructions by
which the nomos of a society is legitimated in toto and in which all less-than-total legitimations
are theoretically integrated in an all-embracing *Weltanschauung*. This last level may be described by saying that here the nomos of a society attains theoretical self-consciousness (Berger
1967:32).

[18] According to Geertz (1993:90), religion is: (1) a system of symbols which acts to (2) establish
powerful, pervasive, and long-lasting moods and motivations in men by (3) formulating conceptions of a general order of existence and (4) clothing these conceptions with such an aura of
factuality that (5) the moods and motivations seem uniquely realistic.

[19] ... the independent objective reality that is God (Root 2014:217).

Rollins, Kearney, and Caputo, would place religion, God, the divine there. Henry interprets this as Life, and interprets absolute Life in the light of the God of the Old and New Testaments.

In the context of the above paragraphs I would not call it independent *objective* reality, as does critical realism, but would turn it around, the uni-direction that Laruelle speaks of, and therefore argue that the independent objective reality is very subjective, as this independent reality, this Real, the Call, this Other, this hypernymity (Rollins 2006:24), is what Heidegger would say, is *was uns angeht*. In other words, it is very *subjective*, it is probably that which is most subjective of all, as it is what affects one,[20] that which calls one, which calls to a me before that me becomes an I or an ego. It is the most subjective, or a radical immanence, that affects the me, calls the me, before the me responds as the *I think therefore I am*, of the I in the response: "Here I am".

The moment the I responds it responds within the transcendental illusion of the ego that Henry (2003:141–142) speaks of, the transcendental illusion of the ego that forgets the me and thereby enters the world as an I.[21]

It is the subjective experience of a Call to which the me responds and in the response is individuated into an individual (I or ego) as part of a community. Root (2014:217) also argues that 'independent objective reality is experienced as subjective reality that is lived out in dependent objective realities in the church and world'. A Call to which one can only respond: Here I am. My *Dasein* (my being here or being there) is dependent on this *was mich angeht – was mich Denken heisst*.[22] Many have tried to think that which calls thinking forth, as Deleuze and Guattari would say by *making* a BwO, which will await and receive their thinking. One must *make* an arch-intelligibility (in reference to Henry) to understand thinking. One must make that which is believed to call thinking forth, and this *made* has been *made* (named-determined) as different things: Life, Real, independent objective reality. Others have interpreted that which is beyond language, and yet which calls language forth as the Sacred (Bataille[23]), God (Root (2014),

---

[20] Life undergoes experiencing itself in pathos; it is an originary and pure Affectivity, an Affectivity that we call transcendental because it is indeed what makes possible experiencing undergoing itself without distance, in the inexorable submission and the insurmountable passivity of a passion (Henry 2015:61). Life's self-revelation takes place in Affectivity and as Affectivity. *Originary Affectivity is the phenomenological material of the self-revelation that constitutes life's essence* (Henry 2015:61–62).

[21] Forgetful of its "me", the ego is concerned with the world (Henry 2003:142).

[22] Wenn wir demnach die Frage »Was heißt Denken?« so hören, daß wir fragen: was ist es, das uns daraufhin anspricht, daß wir denken?, dann fragen wir nach dem, was unserem Wesen das Denken anbefiehlt und so unser Wesen selbst in das Denken gelangen läßt, um es darin zu bergen (Heidegger 1961:83).

[23] The profane (homogeneous) world is the world of work, project, utility, tools, morality, and so on. It is a servile world: a world of "things." Humanity, as it exists within the restricted economy occupies a place in the profane world: it defers current satisfaction in favour of accumulating

Other or Stranger (Levinas 1969; 1981; Kearney 2010 and Caputo 2006; 2013) and as that which insists (Caputo 2013). That which insists, affects, calls, is transformed into a consistency through thought, the moment the Call is given a name, and is thereby determined as something real. It is determined as something real, which is believed to pre-exist and awaiting thoughts determination, forgetting that thought has already determined it as a pre-existing something; believed to be a pre-existing arch-intelligibility, that calls thought forth. Through this giving of a name (determination of the Call), the me in giving a name, in responding, becomes an I, an ego, a subject in-a-world. This naming always also has another religious meaning, as it is the naming of the ultimate reality, a naming of that which ultimately affects us. The world, which is created in response and as the response to the Call, in which the called becomes a *Dasein* in a *Mitsein* needs to be bound together into a comprehensive whole. It is bound together into a comprehensive whole by a particular Light (Logos) or a Good (God) that creates and binds all into the *Lichtung* or*polis*. It is religion which binds (*religare*) the dependent objective reality into a comprehensive whole, in other words religion as that which legitimises, justifies and eventually reifies this reality, so much so, that it is believed to be *the* independent *objective* reality that is found (discovered) as it is either created by God or governed by the laws of nature (physics). In other words, religion plays an important role in legitimising and reifying dependent objective reality so that the dependent reality is believed to be *the* independent objective reality. The social construction of a reality has these three moments, namely: typification, institutionalisation, and legitimation and this whole process is encompassed by the forth term reification (Berger & Luckmann 1976). What Berger & Luckmann refer to as religion, Laclau[24] (2014) interprets as ideology. I will return to Laclau's interpretation of ideology later in this chapter.

Humans are humans because they respond to the Call, and they respond by making, naming, determining, identifying, classifying, stratifying and typifying.

---

excess wealth. The sacred (heterogeneous) realm, on the other hand, is made up of all that threatens to reveal the profane world for what it really is – a sham. It is the excluded element which defines and lends meaning to the profane world. But because the sacred threatens to transgress and violate the stable order of the restricted economy it must, of necessity, be deemed taboo: its violent, lacerating forces are too volatile to be domesticated within everyday life. So the sacred realm is generally ostracized to the boundaries of language and experience. All that is not easily reducible to language, all that cannot be fully grasped by reason, belongs to the sacred realm (James 1997:8)

[24] Laclau says: 'There is ideology whenever a particular content shows itself as more than itself' (Laclau 2014:17), which is humanity's only access to meaning, namely via metaphor – a part for the whole. Yet, the part can never be the whole and therefore closure is impossible, yet it is necessary for the construction of meaning. 'the operation of closure is impossible but at the same time necessary – impossible because of the constitutive dislocation lying at the heart of any structural arrangement; necessary because, without that fictitious fixing of meaning, there would not be meaning at all' (Laclau 2014:16).

All that appears, appears because it is identified, named, stratified, and so the Body without Organs is transformed into various strata by typification and classification (see Deleuze & Guattari 2011:134). All that which appears, appears because it has been classified into categories, for example: into animate objects and inanimate objects, plants, animals, humans, etcetera. It is language (naming) that makes the ongoing process of objectification of ones unfolding experience possible (see Berger & Luckmann 1976:53). It is in language that the I and the world begin to exist – ex-*text*-ence.

As already alluded to above, typification can be described as the process through which humans sort their perceptions into types or classes (see Freedman & Combs 1996:24). Institutionalization would then be interpreted as the process through which institutions arise around sets of typifications: the institution of motherhood, the institution of law, as well as the different disciplines and sub-disciplines of various subjects (Philosophy, Theology, Physics, etcetera). Institutionalization helps families and societies maintain and disseminate hard-won knowledge and thereby control that knowledge. The institutions also legitimate knowledge, and once legitimated 'institutions are now experienced as possessing a reality of their own, a reality that confronts the individual as an external and coercive fact' (Freedman & Combs 1996:25). Experts from reputable institutions are called in to establish the "facts" and once the experts have spoken all doubt is supposed to disappear, because everyone knows [believes] they know.

These three moments are all part of what Berger and Luckmann call reification, where humanity is capable of forgetting their 'own authorship of the human world' (Freedman & Combs 1996:25).

Humans forget their authorship of the world and a*scribe* this authorship to something else: God, evolution, big bang, laws of physics, etcetera. It does not really matter if it is *believed* to be God or evolution, or the laws of physics, as it is a*scrib*ed to something other than human thinking, as something that pre-exists thought, calls thinking forth, and receives thinking, but forgetting that all this happens *in* thought and *as* thought.

Thus, God or the Sacred is a name that is *given* to that which calls thought forth, yet this given name is also the name of that which is believed to be the Good, or the Logos, or the Physics, or Evolution. In other words, the determined name given to that which called thinking forth, is believed to be ultimate meaning and/or ultimate reference, which legitimises and binds the whole world together into a whole, so much so that the human authorship of the world is forgotten. In other words that which Calls is given the name which binds all together into a comprehensive Logic, by giving ultimate meaning and sense to all that appears within its light (*Lichtung*).

The social construction (human authorship) is forgotten and the world is believed to be the way nature (evolution) or God created it, or it is exactly as science discovers it: a world bound together by the laws *of* nature, where the laws of physics (human thinking) are a*scrib*ed to nature.

The moment there is thought, there is a*scrip*tion. The logos is ascribed to the Call. Deleuze and Guattari argue that a beneficent God is fabricated to explain the reality of the earth, Geology.[25] This Geo*logy* is made up of numerous strata. Each of these strata is a judgment (legitimisation) of God. 'The strata are judgments of God; stratification in general is the entire system of the judgment of God (but earth, or the body without organs, constantly eludes that judgement, flees and becomes destratified, decoded, deterritorialized)' (Deleuze & Guattari 2011:40).

In other words, humanity cannot escape this legitimating, judging and reifying God, as Badiou argues: 'In both cases, a secularized or sublimated God operates in the background, the overexistent broker of being. One may call Him Life, or like Spinoza, Substance or Consciousness. We're always dealing with Him, this underlying infinite whose terrestrial writing is death' (Badiou 2009:268). The moment there is this binding (*religare*) through a*scrip*tion there is religion – the binding force, binding all the strata created on the plane of consistency together into a comprehensible whole.

It is in thought that both the ego and the world exist, as Heidegger says about humans: *Der Mensch ist, sofern er als das animal rationale vorgestellt wird, das Physische in der Übersteigung des Physischen; kurz gesagt: im Wesen des Menschen als animal rationale versammelt sich das Hinüber von Physischen zum Nicht- und Überphysischen: der Mensch ist so das Meta-Physische selbst* (Heidegger 1961:25). The human is the metaphysical, the human is the light in which the world appears as well as the self, as a *Dasein* in the world.[26]

Darum ist es ratsam, die eigentliche Frage sogleich um einiges deutlicher zu entfalten. Sie lautet:» Was heißt uns denken?« Was ruft uns daraufhin an, daß wir denken und so als Denkende diejenigen sind, die wir sind?

Was uns auf solche Weise in das Denken ruft, vermag dies wohl nur insofern, als das Rufende selber und von sich aus das Denken braucht. Was uns in das Denken ruft und so unser Wesen in das Denken befiehlt, d.h. birgt, braucht das Denken, insofern das uns Rufende seinem Wesen nach selbst bedacht sein möchte. Was uns denken heißt, verlangt von sich her, daß es durch das Denken in seinem eigenen Wesen bedient, gepflegt, behütet sei. Was uns denken heißt, gibt uns zu denken (Heidegger 1961:85).

Was uns denken heisst will gedacht werden 'das uns Rufende seinem Wesen nach selbst bedacht sein möchte'. According to Heidegger, the Call wants to be thought (*in seinem eigenen Wesen bedient, gepflegt und behütet sei*), wants to be named, as only in being named does it exist.

---

[25]   It is to fabricate a beneficent God to explain geological movements (Deleuze & Guattari 2011:3).

[26]   Das Licht kommt aus dem Denken selbst und nur aus ihn (Heidegger 1961:10).

The Call and the Name-given-to-the-Call as the ultimate meaning of the world
that is carried out in that meaning thus belong together in the different thought-
systems. That which is beyond the physical (that which is disclosingly appropriated to be beyond the physical) is also that which gives the physical its place and
time, in other words the metaphysical. But as Badiou quoted above argued, the
only terrestrial *writing* (ascription) of the Call, as that which gives and/or is believed to be the ultimate meaning (Logos/Light) of the world, is death (Badiou
2009:268). Once that which Calls-thought-forth is thought, is named or determined (terrestrial writing) it has died the death of the letter, as St. Paul says that
the Letter can only kill (2 Cor. 3:6). The letter, writing, the *pharmakon* is both
that which is called forth: the gift of thought, but in the same breath also the *Gift*
(poison) that kills (see Derrida 1981:99).

The Call calls forth a Name, but the Name does not determine the Call, but
the Name is determined by the Call in the last instance. The Call is the primal,
the Arch-Call, arch-intelligibility that Calls thought-forth and it calls for a Name,
at least that is how Heidegger interprets the "desire" of the Call (*verlangt von
sich her, daß es durch das Denken in seinem eigenen Wesen bedient, gepflegt,
behütet sei*). Through the Name-in-human-thought it in turn carries out a reality.
Stated differently the Name-in-human-thought (Logos/Light) creates the *Lichtung*
in which the world appears and so the world that appears is believed to be created
by that which the Name names, and the human origin of the Name is forgotten.

In thought (philosophy, theology, physics) there is a Name given to ultimate
reality as that which Calls-thought-forth. Thus, there is the Call and the Name,
which in most thought-systems are *believed* to be the same. It is necessary that
they are believed to be the same, as the Name names (determines) the Call. The
Call called the Name forth, and thus it must [it is believed] be the right, true and
correct Name for the Call (that which calls thinking forth). The Call exists (ex-
texts) only in the Name (text) and yet the Name is not the Call, but only that which
is called-forth by the Call. In my faith tradition, or in my secondary and tertiary
retentions, it is with Abraham and later with Moses that this Link between Call
and Name is questioned, where the desire of the Call is not to be named and thus
the Link is broken and replaced by a law that forbids naming the Call.

The link between the Call and the Names (or the Gods-of-human-thought)
is broken, this broken link is also what is explored in postmodern and post-
structuralist thought, which might explain why there is a return to religion and
specifically the Abrahamic religions in postmodernity and post-structuralism.
Specifically, there is a turn towards the mystical or negative theological traditions,
as well as radical theology (or God is dead) traditions, as the Name is indeed dead
as Badiou argues. But just because the name is death, that does not prevent the
Call from calling names forth. The name is death, terrestrial writing is death, but
that says nothing about the Call, which calls those dead names forth.

This faith tradition brings about a clash between followers of the Call (without Name) and followers of the Name and in a certain sense two religions: Religion$_1$ (on the side of the Call, with a law against Naming – idolatry) and Religion$_2$ (on the side of the Name). One could interpret these two religions as the priestly (Religion$_2$) and the prophetic (Religion$_1$). Or the difference that the cultured despisers make between religion and religiosity, where religiosity is that which sanctions religion.[27] One could argue in the tradition of Schleiermacher that Religion$_1$ is generic to humanity.[28] The feeling of absolute dependence, the affectivity that Henry (2015:61–62) speaks about, is generic to humanity; humanity is called by the Call. Or as Heidegger argues, humanity stands in this *Zug* (Call or Pull) and that is generic – *believed* to be unavoidable. All these names, "feeling of absolute dependence", affectivity, Life, Flesh would be religious in that generic sense, without any reference to something supernatural or spiritual or Transcendent with a capital T, but with reference to, one could say, that which is radically immanent such as Life, Flesh and breath. These radically immanent experiences of that which affects us, such as Life, Flesh and breath can be linked to the God who should not be named, as has been done in the work of Henry and others. Schleiermacher argued that one needs to empty one's mind (Schleiermacher 2001:41) to gaze towards the point where Religion would become visible, that which I interpret as the Call. He argues that to understand that which he calls religion, and that I refer to as the Call, is not to understand it through reason (metaphysics) nor through action or practice (ethics). In other words, not in terms of orthodoxy or orthopraxis, but to open oneself towards an auto-appearing and auto-revelation of that which Calls (for Schleiermacher religion) to reveal itself,[29] in Henry's (2015:29) terms: an auto-appearing. The Call calls forth a response, it calls-thought-forth, as it is the most thought-worthy, but it appears in thought through a Name, the event of language, as disclosure of appropriation. In other words, it only appears, is disclosed to the degree that it is appropriated into a Logos, which in turn creates a *Zeit-Spiel-Raum*, the specific metaphysics of that world that is carried out and in which it appears. Schleiermacher wants to focus the cultured despisers' attention to that place where religion auto-appears without being appropriated via the retentions (*alten Erinnerungen verführt*) or protentions

---

[27] Dieses Gemisch von Meinungen über das höchste Wesen oder die Welt und von Geboten für ein menschliches Leben (oder gar für zwei) nennt Ihr Religion und den Instinkt, der jene Meinungen such, nebst den dunklen Ahndungen, welche die eigentliche letzte Sanktion dieser Gebote sind, nennt ihr Religiosität (Schleiermacher 2001:45).

[28] Wessel Stoker (2000) in his article asks the question if humans are by nature religious in reference to Schleiermacher.

[29] ... und voll Verlangen, das Dargestellte aus sich selbst zu verstehen, weder von altern Erinnerungen verführt noch von vorgefaßten Ahndungen bestochen wird, kann ich hoffen, daß Ihr meine Erscheinung, wo nicht liebgewinne, doch wenigstens Euch über Ihre Gestalt mit mir einigen und sie für ein himmlisches Wesen erkennen werdet (Schleiermacher 2001:42).

(*vorgefaßten Ahndungen*) (see Schleiermacher 2001:42). It cannot appear under any name or *Bildung*,[30] but it is that which is prior to names, as it is that which calls names forth. Religion$_2$ is that which the cultured despisers wage war against (Schleiermacher 2001:46), but this Religion$_2$ is only a shadow, Schleiermacher argues.[31] Religion$_2$ is the terrestrial writing of death of Religion$_1$. Religion$_2$ is haunted by Religion$_1$, as Religion$_2$ is that which is called forth by Religion$_1$. Schleiermacher therefore wants to liberate Religion$_2$ via Religion$_1$ (Schleiermacher 2001:47).

There would not be much history if the link between Name and Call was a perfect link, or if the one was a perfect representation or presentation of the other, but because the link is broken the Call persists and insists to be named, even if it insists via forbidding any naming and so enters a prophetic and messianic element that drives history: the different epochs of naming, or the different sendings of Being (*Seingeschicke*), where each epoch, as well as each thought-system (philosophy, theology, physics) is characterised by a new Name given to the Call. Deconstruction is driven by this insistent Call, as that which calls in the Names (Derrida & Caputo 1997; Caputo 2007), that which haunts names. Deconstruction can be argued is faithfulness to the Call in the Names, and thus continuously opening the names to the Call, which insists, and therefore it has this messianic element, but without Messiah. A Call that is always only heard in a Name, but which is not the Name, but opens the Name for what is still to come: future names, future responses.

Yet, to "name" the Call "the-One-who-should-not-be-Named [I am sorry that this sound too much like Voldemort in Harry Potter], is still a Naming. In other words, the non-name, or the name crucified (sacrificed as Bataille would argue) is still a name, even if it is a name to save the name "God" or "Call" from naming (idolatry).

But instead of creating the traditional opposition between Name or Religion$_2$ and Call or Religion$_1$ or between reality and the Real, I would like to follow Laruelle (2013b pos 4913 of 7408) and interpret this relationship-non-relationship

---

[30] Ich wollte, ich könnte sie Euch unter irgendeiner wohlbekannten Bildung verstellen, damit Ihr sogleich ihrer Züge, ihre Ganges, ihrer Manieren Euch erinnern und ausrufen möchtet, daß Ihr sie hier oder dort im Leben so gesehen habt. Aber ich würde Euch betrügen; den so unverkleidet, wie sie dem Beschwörer erscheint, wird sie unter den Menschen nicht angetroffen und hat sich in ihrer eigentümlichen Gestalt wohl lange nicht erblicken lassen (Schleiermacher 2001:42).

[31] Ihr mögt die Religion nicht, davon sind wir schon neulich ausgegangen; aber indem Ihr einen ehrlichen Krieg gegen sie führt, der doch nicht ganz ohne Anstrengungen ist, wollt Ihr doch nicht gegen einen Schatten gefochten haben, wie dieser, mit dem wir uns herumschlagen haben; sie muß doch etwas Denkbares, wovon sich ein Begriff aufstellen läßt, über den man reden und streiten kann, und ich finde es sehr unrecht, wenn Ihr selbst aus so disparaten Dingen etwas Unhaltbares zusammennähet, das Religion nennt und dann so viel unnütze Umstände damit macht (Schleiermacher 2001:46–47).

as a unidirectional flow or as Heidegger might argue, a *Zug* (pull), where thought, the response, (real and Religion₂) are seen as a response called forth by the Call, and thereby determined in the last instance by the Call. This response to the Call is always dual, rather than a duel between thought and what is believed Real. It is dual as it has a double function.

Firstly, it names (creates) that which is believed to pre-exist thought, but which Calls thought forth.

Secondly, that which it made to pre-exist thought, yet calling thought forth, is believed to await and to receive the thoughts it calls forth.

There is no duel, but a dualysation according to Laruelle (see Laruelle 2013b pos 4717 of 7408).

There are two moments of thought, where thought names or creates the Call as something that calls, and in naming creates a link or non-link (non-name, or name) between the Call and the Name based on some philosophical decision as to how such a link is possible, for example: idealism, realism, critical realism or nihilism or theism, atheism, anatheism or a-theism.

Philosophy or theology both Names and decides what the link is whilst also explaining the link between language (the Name) and the Real (the Call), whilst the Call remains foreclosed to thought, or withdraws from thought, and one is left with terrestrial writing, which is death. The Real as Call (*Zug*) determines thought (Name–response) in the last instance, but without the Name (response) determining the Call. The Call (Real) being foreclosed to thought is no characteristic or essence of the Call, it is not a hidden God or a *Deus absconditus*, but it is a characteristic of naming, the terrestrial writing (the *pharmakon*), which is as Badiou says: death.

Religion₂ can be interpreted as the God of philosophers, the metaphysical God, or in Feuerbach's terms as the God humans project into the heavens, created in human-likeness. That would leave one with Religion₁ or God₁ as the "true living God", or as the God who calls, and who called Abraham, as in the Abrahamic traditions. But one would need to remember that God₁, even if naming is forbidden, is also just a Name (Not to be Named) given to the Call, a non-name, a sacrificed or crucified name, given to that which is most thought-worthy and which calls thought-forth. These two Gods, the Named and the Named, have often been in conflict with each other. In the Kairos document these two were interpreted as state religion (Named) and prophetic faith (Not-Named). One could interpret the prophetic and the priestly tradition as a battle between these two (Named and Not-Named), but both remain responses to the Call. It is this reason, as mentioned earlier, which brings post-structuralist and postmodern thought in close proximity to the Not-Named (mystical) response. In this tradition, following Bataille, one could argue that the one notion of God, the Named, needs to be sacrificed[32] or crucified so as to have access to the Sacred (the Call) (see James 1997). Religion$_1$ or the Divine$_1$ trying to give a name to the Call without Naming it, is often interpreted in its messianic, mystical and prophetic dimensions, whilst Religion$_2$ on the priestly side (the Name) is that which stabilises and gives ultimate meaning and purpose to our metaphysically carried out worlds: it is that which if *believed* gives the world its believed non-human origin.

I am not arguing that one is living in a human constructed world, neither am I arguing that one is not, but what I am arguing is that the Name, the ultimate meaning and Logos of the world is *but a name,* whilst the *Bedenklichste,* that *was uns denken heisst,* remains to be thought. *Ein Abgrund ruft den anderen in sich hinein* – Deep calls to deep (Ps. 42:7). There is the Call which calls thought forth and yet withdraws from thought and then there is thought which is the terrestrial writing and therefore death. Withdrawal and death could be seen facing each other. Or they could be seen as uni-directional, as one *Abgrund* calls the other into itself.

Johannes Tauler speaks of the *unio mystica 'als die Vereinigung des geschaffenen Abgrunds des Menschen mit dem göttlichen, ungeschaffenen Abgrund* (Heo 2015:54). The Call, the most thought-worthy, which withdraws from thought (*göttlichen ungeschaffenen Abgrund*), calls to the human constructed abyss (the endless desertification of language) (Derrida 1995:55–56). It does not call to, as if opposite, but the withdrawal calls the endless desertification of language forth.

Root (2014), as discussed in the previous chapter, argues that it would be wrong to conclude that everything is social construction (endless desertification of language). In a certain sense, I would agree, as the Call is Real, and as a Real Call to thought, it is the most thought-worthy. It is for this reason, of it being Real, that Henry argues it should be Life, as without Life thought (social construction) would not be possible. It is that which most intimately affects us, like breath, but it appears (disclosingly appropriated) only in thought, as it calls thought forth. The Call is Real and it is real *in* thought, but it is real in the thought which it (the Call) called forth.

The conflict between the priestly and the prophetic have characterised much of the history of the three monotheisms, where the priestly or Religion$_2$ is often interpreted as an idol. Thus, the moment the Call is named, for example God or Life, it is no longer the Call, but it becomes *the* THING of the carried out world, the ultimate meaning of the carried out world. Bataille argues, that the only way to reach the sacred is through sacrifice (crucifixion) of the THING (see James 1997).

---

[32]   … our notions of "God" (a thing) all too often becomes screens which prevent us from experiencing the sacred: they must themselves be sacrificed (crucified) (see James 1997:12). The sacred, the Other, the Real, Life 'is not the "real" – it cannot be captured. This is important: once the "sacred" is objictified in language and consciousness, it becomes a thing, and is therefore no longer sacred (James 1997:11).

The Thing is the Name given to the Sacred (the Call), the Name given to the most thought-worthy. Rollins (2006), as other post-metaphysical thinkers, tries to develop a thought (response) that takes Religion$_1$, the Call which is beyond Names, into consideration. Rollins (2006) for example develops the idea of an icon rather than an idol. In my interpretation, an icon would be a response, and therefore it is still a Name, but a name which tries to capture something of the Not-to-be-Named, as it does not create an image of God but it allows the Call to continue to call through the Name (not-named-name) icon. Likewise, with Kearney's (2010) hospitality which tries to keep the doors of our responses (Names) open to the continuous insistence of the Call: the stranger knocking at the door, and Caputo (2013), interpreting Religion$_1$ as insistence that is persistent, but refuses to become a consistence (Name). I would find myself very much at home in all these open or hospitable responses, who refuse to create idols (Religion$_2$). These hospitable responses that continually remain open for justice and democracy still to come, certainly bring a burning sensation to my heart within the context of my primary, secondary and tertiary retentions and protentions. Then there are also numerous immanent interpretations of the Call without any reference to religious texts, where the Call is named Flesh or the material conditions of existence, for example in various Marxist or materialist interpretations (see Laruelle 2015d).

Yet, they still Name – even if that name is written in humble small letters of a non-name, or even a name crossed out, or under erasure, it is still a name. A name under erasure is still a name, as it is legible, in other words it still is written (see Derrida 1997:23). Do these post-metaphysical thinkers (theologians-philosophers) really move beyond philosophy in Laruelle's sense (2012; 2013a; 2013b)? Do they not make a decision as to how the Non-Name, Name is linked or not linked to the Call? They have given new names, creative names, hospitable names, maybe even better names, preferred names, erased names, even some immanent names, but they still have given a name, made a choice (decided), and therefore offer a theory of the link or non-link between the Real and Thought, the Call and Name [Non-Name], they continue the duel, the war against the Call or against the Real. Thus, even immanent names in naming transcend that which is named, or stated differently, leaves that which Calls-names-forth transcendent to the name given.

According to some postmetaphysical thinkers, the name (determination) is interpreted more as an action (praxis) than a noun, for example as the praxis of offering hospitality, or as an icon rather than Idol, or justice and democracy always still to come, and they believe that these links (names, determinations) are better or that these names (non-names) are good in the sense of being more just and therefore they offer a certain orthopraxis, the praxis of hospitality or of justice, as opposed to orthodoxy of traditional metaphysics (Religion$_2$). It is not that their thought is flawed. Who would be in a position to judge? But it is and remains thought that is a response, a Name [Not-Named and/or Name]. As a response, these attempts to not-name are equal to all other responses and no better, which leaves us with a radical democracy of thought,[33] where all thoughts are equal, in the sense that they are equally responses to that which called them forth, and there is no hierarchy in the form of an orthodoxy or an orthopraxis. Thought, whichever or whatever thought, is a response, a Name or non-name given, and therefore it remains a determination of the Call, as that which calls thought forth. The Call, as soon as it is named, or determined, or made as something that pre-exists thought so as to receive thought, is written in the terrestrial language of death; language (writing) which is always both a beautiful gift to humanity, the gift of a world to live in, but simultaneously a *Gift* (poison). One cannot not respond to the Call, and therefore the response is necessary, but the response, as Name, Not-Named or Name, is and remains insufficient as the Name, Not-Named or Name does not capture the Call (*es begreift den Ruf nicht in einen Begriff*).

One is left with various Names, in other words various philosophical decisions that are all equal, as in equally determined by the Call in the last instance.

Nancy (2013:6) argues that nothing, nobody replies to our word any longer, nothing and nobody replies to our response any longer. Not that there ever was a response, but one believed that there was, when the Name was believed to be firmly linked to the Call. If nothing responds then this could lead to nihilism, one would stare into an abyss. But nihilism is still too meaningful, as nihilism is also a Name or Name. It is a response that believes there to be nothing that responds to the name, but thereby it names it Nothing, or make nothing as that which pre-exists thought, calling thought forth. Nothing responds to the Name, and yet as Nancy says, everything resonates with the address that we are. Humans and the world are the response to an address,[34] a Call and the response is an address to that which called it forth, although nothing answers to that response, which resonates with an address, resonates with a Call that called it forth.

Yet, this response to the address of which the whole world and humanity resonates, resonates predominantly with these two traditions: the prophetic Religion₁

---

[33] It is in this manner, through a translation of philosophical decisions or through solely transcendental equivalents of their respective identity, that a democracy that is not simple transcendental appearance can be introduced into philosophy and between philosophies in place of their conflictual and hierarchical multiplicity (Laruelle 2013b pos 4970 of 7408).

[34] Nothing, nobody replies to our word any longer. It is possible that mankind has always known this and always more or less skirted around any admission of it – this skirting around being the figuration of the gods – but that now mankind has come to the point of declaring that nothing and nobody is responding, and yet that everything and everyone resonates with this address that we are. This address that we all are, in which we have our equality (nobody being able to lay claim to a great response), our liberty (nobody being able to claim a monopoly on the word), our fraternity (all of us being before the same absence of the "father"), and our justice (everyone being able to expect of everyone that his address be picked up, but not responded to) (Nancy 2013:6).

(Not-Named and Name) and priestly Religion₂ (Named), interpreted with or without the name God. I have used the term God, but there are numerous traditions that do not interpret the Call nor the ultimate response with the term God, but have found other names, philosophical names, names from the sciences, or as stated earlier, immanent names or materialist names etcetera.

The world and humanity resonate with these responses, which can be divided, typified and classified into these three possibilities:

1. The response can clearly and full of conviction believe to be able to Name the Call (identify that which pre-exists thought and calls thought forth);
2. The response can clearly and full of conviction believe the Call cannot be named;
3. The response can clearly and full of conviction believe that it is impossible to decide between name and non-name: an undecidability.

Western history is characterised by these three responses: the priestly tradition, the prophetic tradition and then later the agnostic tradition. Or theism against atheism and then the undecidability of anatheism.

Deleuze & Guattari focus specifically on the two responses and interpret them as the priestly (Greek) and Prophetic (Jewish) sign regimes, which for them combine in Christianity to create the Face of Christ.[35] For Deleuze and Guattari, the Face of Christ is the abstract machine of the West. Nancy echoes this idea of Deleuze & Guattari, when he argues that Christ is at the centre of both enclo-

---

[35] See the chapter, 'Year Zero: Faciality' in Deleuze & Guattari 2011:167–191. It is in the Face of Christ that the two sign regimes, signifying and post-signifying regime come together. 'Of course, we have already seen that signifiance and subjectification are semiotic systems that are entirely distinct in their principles and have different regimes (circular irradiation versus segmentary linearity) and different apparatus of power (despotic generalized slavery versus authoritarian contract-proceeding). Neither begins with Christ, or the White Man as Christian universal: there are Indian, African, and Asiatic despotic formations of signifiance; the authoritarian process of subjectification appears most purely in the destiny of the Jewish people. But however different these semiotics are they still form a de facto *mix*, and it is at the level of this mixture that they assert their imperialism, in other words, their common endeavor to crush all other semiotics. There is no signifiance that does not harbor the seeds of subjectivity; there is no subjectification that does not drag with it remnants of signifier. ... If it is possible to assign the faciality machine a date – the year zero of Christ and the historical development of the White Man – it is because that is when the mixture ceased to be a splicing or an intertwining, becoming a total interpenetration in which each element suffuses the other like drops of red-black wine in white water. Our semiotic of modern White Men, the semiotic of capitalism, has attained this state of mixture in which signifiance and subjectification effectively interpenetrate. Thus it is in this semiotic that faciality, or the white wall/black hole systems, assumes its full scope. We must, however, assess the states of mixture and the varying proportions of the elements. Whether in the Christian or pre-Christian state, one element may dominate another, one may be more or less powerful than the other. We are thus led to define limit-faces, which are different from both the facial units and the degrees of divergence previously defined (Deleuze & Guattari 2011:182).

sure and disenclosure[36] of metaphysics. If Christ is the combination of the Named and Not-Named, and all the possibilities in-between, then he is at the centre of both enclosure of metaphysics as well as the disenclosure of metaphysics, therefore it makes sense that Christ is the abstract machine of Western thought. The Face of Christ is the abstract machine of Western thought, as Christ (the different variations of Name and Not-Name) is at the centre of all possible responses to the Call, as well as the undecidability between the two. You can either Name the Call or choose to Not-Name the Call or remain undecided, there do not seem to be any other possibilities. Whichever you choose, you will find in the narrative of Christ support for your choice, or stated differently: the Face of Christ will always already be in your choice. You will find Christ in your choice. Whatever metaphysical system carries out a world, as either Named or Not-Named or Name, materialist or idealist, based on immanence or transcendence, Christ will be there, irrespective if the Name given is God or Christ or any other name. Of-course only those whose primary or secondary and/or tertiary retentions and protentions have been influenced by the Christ-narrative, and because of colonialism and the reach of Western media, this is basically the whole globe.

Why is Christ always already there in these responses? There is no metaphysical or religious reason for this, but Henry I believe already begins to point into the direction of understanding this, as the Christ narrative, for him, offers a phenomenology of phenomenology and Laruelle develops this into a science of Christ (Laruelle 2010) and later Christo-fiction (Laruelle 2015c) which will lead me to a Christ-*poiēsis* of this book. As one *Abgrund* calls to another, so one Text resonates in another. The Christian Text (Bible) is fundamentally part of the retentions of Western thought and thus it resonates in Western thought.

Could this be the reason why the Christ narrative makes so much sense and has been interpreted as the truth of various metaphysical systems? If one takes the *Wirkungsgeschichte* of the Christ narrative into consideration, Christ can be interpreted as the incarnation of the Truth (Name/non-name) of the different Epochs or sending of Being (*Seinsgeschick*), but likewise Christ can be interpreted as the revolutionary, Non-Truth of every epoch (the Not-Named). It does not matter in which metaphysical system one finds oneself, one can read it as the Christ-narrative, and experience the burning sensation in the heart as did the Emmaus disciples, as Christ gives meaning and truth to whichever signs or non-signs are given in response to the Call. Therefore, it is not strange to read Kearney's books, Caputo, or Barth or Henry, or any other theologian for that matter and experience them as making sense, "telling or revealing the truth", as they will make sense and Christ will be the sense that is believed to be found: Christ is the revelation

---

[36] Christianity is at the heart of the dis-enclosure just as it is at the centre of the enclosure [*clôture*] (Nancy 2008:10).

of truth, the truth of that epoch of Being, the Truth of that Name, or the prophetic un-truth that exposes the un-truth of the Name. If one takes Deleuze and Guattari's view seriously, that the Face of Christ is the abstract machine of the West, then any Western metaphysical system can be interpreted with the help of the Christ narrative, as it is the Christ narrative which functions as the machine that creates or produces these Western metaphysical systems. Or stated differently, the Christ-narrative is an appropriate metaphor for understanding and interpreting the abstract machine that produces (carries out) the Western worlds.

In these worlds, Christ will be interpreted as the one who reveals the truth of whatever epoch of Being or metaphysical system (enclosure), of whatever Name, Not-Named and Name. Yet, he will also reveal the prophetic truth of the disenclosure of whatever epoch of Being or metaphysical enclosure.

It is always Christ, but it is never Christ alone (*sola Christus*), as it is always Christ as the incarnation of the Name or Non-Name given to the Call.

Christ is never *sola Christus*, but always the revelation (incarnation) of a Name, Not-Named or Name. Christ is the revelation (incarnation) of either God_2 the ultimate good, or God of the theistic theological traditions, as He becomes the incarnation of the ultimate Good or meaning of a metaphysical enclosure. Or Christ is the revelation of God_1 as the messianic disturbance, and/or prophetic disruption, as disenclosure of the enclosure. Christ as revelation or incarnation of God_1 is the opening of the kingdom for the other, the stranger, the marginal and in that sense Christ is interpreted as justice, hospitality and above all love. Never Christ alone, but always Christ as the revelation or incarnation of either $Religion_1$ or $Religion_2$. Most post-metaphysical theologians and thinkers or radical theologians (in the sense of God is dead theology) would agree that being the incarnation of $Religion_2$ (Name) is no longer possible in a post-metaphysical world. Yet, how different is $Religion_2$ from any other interpretation of the Call in the form of $Religion_1$ (Not-Named and Name)? Should any thinking concerning the Call not be passed over in silence, but is not even that silence a response (Non-Name or Non-Language of not speaking)? The moment that the Call is thought even in the most radical and post-metaphysical terms like hospitality, Other, justice, democracy to come, or love of enemies, the Call is still thought, and therefore falls under the curse of thought: that it is an illusion as Henry argues.[37]

Henry's interpretation of Christ moves probably closest to *sola Christus*, where Christ reveals nothing other than the human condition (2003:9). In other words, for Henry, Christ is the revelation of revelation, Christ is the phenomenology of phenomenology.[38] In this sense, Henry's Christ reveals nothing but himself:

---

[37] Therefore, the first cause of people's forgetting their condition as Sons is the transcendental illusion of the ego (Henry 2003:140).

[38] Christianity is nothing other, truly, than the awe-inspiring and meticulous theory of this givenness of God's self-revelation shared with man. Where can we see something like the phenome-

an auto-revelation and yet Christ reveals the human condition, reveals Life, reveals the phenomenality of phenomenology.

Christ reveals nothing but himself: *Sola Christus*. Nothing but himself as the truth, the way and the life (John 14:6). He does not reveal Life, or the phenomenality of phenomenology or the human condition as all these would again be a Name given to the Call, which Christ would be the incarnation and revelation of. Christ reveals himself as the way, not the way to justice, to democracy, to love, but just the way, which is truth and life. Justice, democracy and love will perhaps be the consequences of this way, but not its content. This will be unpacked in more detail later.

One would need to take a step back and interpret Christ generically or rather scientifically as Laruelle (2010) does. In other words, Christ is not the incarnation of a *specific* Word, but He is the incarnation of *the* Word, which is the Call, the primal phenomenology, as Henry (2003:25) argues above, *but* without giving that primal phenomenology a particular meaning, a particular Name, as Henry does, by naming the Call: Life. He is the generic incarnation of the Call, and depending on what one decides to name the Call, he will be the incarnation thereof. In that sense, the Christ-event (incarnation-crucifixion and resurrection) becomes the abstract machine of the West. Whatever is *made* to be that which pre-exists thinking, and yet calls thinking forth so as to receive thinking as the object of thought, is incarnated in thought. Or thought is believed to be the incarnation thereof.

The Word, which is the Call, is that which calls-forth-thought, it is a Call, it is something that affects one and demands a response, it demands a Name. In other words, it is the primal phenomenon of phenomenality, but without ever being captured by phenomenality as a phenomenon.

That is where Henry made the "mistake";[39] he responded to the Call by giving the Call a particular Name: Life. Is this not the unavoidable "mistake" that theology or Christology will always make, the ideological illusion in Laclau's sense (2014:18ff)?

There is a Call that has been Named numerous things throughout Western history and therefore the Call could be described as a floating (empty[40]) signifier (see Laclau 2014:20). This Call is interpreted differently, given a different name, in different contexts of philosophy, theology, in idealism and in materialism, etcetera. As already argued above, these different interpretations are all equivalent, as equally called forth.

---

nalization of pure phenomenality as its immediate and original self-phenomenalization of pure phenomenality as its immediate and original self-phenomenalization, as the self-revelation of what we are presumptively calling "God"? (Henry 2003:25).

[39] Mistake in the literal and unavoidable sense of it being human to err.

[40] Floating a term and emptying it are thus two sides of the same discursive operation (Laclau 2014:21).

If one focusses on theology and names the Call God, God is a floating signifier, as God could be interpreted as Creator, Judge, Father etcetera. Likewise, with
Christ who could be interpreted as Love, Life, Justice or God, and the theologian
would find numerous biblical quotes to substantiate such an interpretation. All
these different interpretations are thus equivalent in their differences. A theologian or a theology is born, is individuated, the moment one of these equivalences
is chosen to represent (incarnate) the whole of God or the whole of Christ (for
example Christ *is* love), or this or that being *the* interpretation of Christ or God
or Messiah. Philosophy or theology or ideology, or in short thought, is born the
moment a part is chosen to represent the whole. Thought is born the moment one
Name becomes *the* Name. Once one Name is chosen to be *the* Name of God, theology and with theology a theologian is born. It is born through the dialectic of
incarnation and deformation, Laclau (2014:18ff) argues, where the chosen Name
incarnates the whole. A part is believed to be the incarnation of the whole, which
in turn deforms the part and the whole, as it cancels all the other names that could
have been used.

This is probably the necessary, but unavoidable "mistake" that all theologians
make in the process of becoming theologians. They become theologians through
the theological dialectic (incarnation and deformation), where a part is taken for
the whole. The question is, will this book also be a theology, philosophy and
therefore an ideology, or is it possible to avoid this "mistake"? If it is human to
err then this mistake is unavoidable. This mistake cannot be avoided as it is a
necessary mistake for humanity to be. It is the necessary mistake for something to
exist, as it exists only to the extent that it ex-*texts*.

The Call is given a meaning, by being given a Name in the various philosophical or theological decisions, but these decisions are human made and the worlds
that follow from these decisions are human made constructions. In a generic interpretation of the Christ-event, Christ is the incarnation of the Call, but without the
Call being identified, named or determined or made into something or someone
specific.

The Call that calls thought forth is believed to be incarnate in the thought
called forth. Yet, this incarnate Call is crucified, in Laclau's language deformed,
and it does not matter if it is the incarnation of the prophetic or of the priestly,
it is deformed, crucified, as the Call withdraws from thought, or thought is the
terrestrial (incarnated) writing, which is death. The resurrection is the resurrection
in Henry's language of Flesh, that is, resurrection of that which Called thought
forth. It is the resurrection of the Call, which is the insurrection in all thought. In
this generic sense, the Christ-event, Christ-fiction is the fiction of thought, and it
is also the truth of thought.

In that sense Christ is the truth, but the truth as the way (John 14:6) of thought
and therefore of existence (ex-text-ence), life. It is the way of Christ that is im-

portant: incarnation, crucifixion and resurrection, and not that which Christ is *believed* to be in the different theological and philosophical traditions, for example Christ is named to be the incarnation of Life, or the incarnation of the theistic creator God, or the incarnation of the absolute dependence, incarnation of ultimate meaning, etcetera. All these different contents given to Christ are all part of humanity's response to the primal Call and therefore contingent to the I and the collective the I is part of in her or his thinking. *I think therefore I am*, the I is born in thinking, in responding, but prior to the thinking I, there was or is a me called by, amongst other things, its own flesh, its own breath, which it did not give to itself, but which it received. The me is called to thinking, and in thinking becomes an I in a world.

These various metaphysical constructions are important for the trans-fictional praxis and this also explains the choice for a Christ-*poiēsis* – as it is not a particular Word that is incarnated, but it is the incarnated Word; the Poetic Word that creates what it says, in reference to Heidegger (1971:208) and his thoughts on poetry being pure language. Henry[41] also reflects upon poetry as being the purest form of language. Therefore, the choice of the term Christ-*poiēsis* rather than praxis, as praxis can still too easily be transformed into orthopraxis, whilst *poiēsis* remains open. Whatever the decision to Name the Word, it will carry out the world that comes into view, in which Christ will be incarnate and crucified. Laruelle (2015c) speaks of Christo-fiction. What is important to remember is that the Christ who is incarnated, is the incarnation of the Call, the Word (without any specific decision, Name, as to what that Word means or is) as this Word which Henry refers to as Arch-intelligibility, is that (whatever that is, it is foreclosed to thought, as it withdraws from thought[42]) *was uns Denken Heisst* and therefore it is *prior* to any thought and thought-system. He is incarnate in whatever world is created by thought's (philosophy or theology) response to Naming of this Arch-Word or Call. The meaning that is given to Christ is not important, as there will be different meanings in the different thought-worlds (metaphysical systems or theologies or Christologies); what is important is the narrative of the Christ-event: the incarnation of whatever one names the Word (Call) and what happens to that incarnation in the world, namely crucifixion.

---

[41] The way ordinary language has of standing alongside reality, and of going at the same pace, is what hides the abyss that separates them. Poetic language unveils this abyss, because unlike everyday language, what is speaks of is never there (Henry 2015:43). For Henry, in reference to Heidegger, poetic words call into absence and thereby make present in absence. 'They are present in the sense that, born from the speech of the poet, they appear, but they are absent in the sense that, *though appearing, they are deprived of reality*' (Henry 2015:43).

[42] Auf dem Zuge zu dem Sichentziehenden, weisen wir selber auf dieses Sichentziehende. Wir sind wir, indem wir dahin weisen; nicht nachträglich und nicht nebenbei, sondern: dieses » auf dem Zuge zu ... « ist in sich ein wesenhaftes und darum ständiges Weisen auf das Sichentziehende. »Auf dem Zuge zu ... « sagt schon: zeigend auf das Sichentziehende (Heidegger 1961:6).

What happens to the incarnate Word in the world that is constructed on the basis of Naming the Word (Call)? For example, Christ is believed to be the incarnation of the Law of God, Will of God, etcetera. In the narrative, as re-presented in the Gospels, there are certain important characteristics that are integral to the telling of the story of this incarnate Word. The story of the Incarnate Word, the Christ-event, is in one tradition different from the incarnation that Laclau speaks about. For Laclau the incarnation is the incarnation of one of the equivalences as representative of the whole, and the choice of incarnation has everything to do with power. This could be interpreted as the priestly incarnation. Priestly theology is the theology of control and of power, where their choice of equivalence becomes the incarnation of the whole.

Yet, the Gospel stories can be interpreted differently to the priestly interpretation, for example in the Gospel of John it states that Christ is the incarnation of the Word, but the world (darkness) did not accept this Word. This statement is made axiomatically. It is not the incarnation of an equivalence to represent the whole reflecting the interests of the powerful, but it is an incarnation that the world did not accept (John 1:10–11), contrary to the world and those of power in the world. In this tradition, prophetic tradition, a very different story of incarnation is told in the Gospels.

The Word becomes flesh in a stable, not in a palace of power, for example. In the world, created and maintained by the incarnation, controlled by the political and religious powers of the time, there is no room for this Word that has become flesh, and therefore it is born in a stable, on the margins. The stable being a place for animals and therefore is not really a place for humans to live, and thus one could say that the Word becomes incarnate in the non-human margins of the human constructed world. The story in the Gospels continue with Jesus and his family fleeing because of political persecution, and living his childhood years as a refugee in Egypt. Again, his childhood is characterised by not really being welcomed, but as refugee, existing on the outskirts of the human political and religious world, where political and religious powers determine who is welcome and who is not. Once back in the country of his birth, his ministry tended to focus and associate with the least of the brothers and sisters. He identifies, incarnates completely with the least of the brothers and sisters in Matthew 25. He associates and proclaims that the kingdom is all about welcoming those that are not *normally* welcomed, and through this proclaiming he claims that this is the Word of God, the Will of God.

In the context of the above paragraphs, one can interpret this ministry as if Christ is sacrificing (questioning, disenclosing) Religion$_2$ in the name of the Call or Religion$_1$, by opening the world of Religion$_2$ to all that which Religion$_2$ ostracised and excludes. Such actions and such preaching will most certainly get one into trouble with the political and religious authorities, who are tasked to both protect the God of Religion$_2$ as well as the political world that such a God carries out. As such questioning does not only challenge the powers, it fundamentally challenges the construction (institution, legitimation and reification) of this world: it destroys the world. In that sense, Christ's actions make him the ultimate criminal in Benjamin's sense (see Meylahn 2014b). He was in trouble with both the political and religious authorities who had the task of protecting and upholding the world: the priests, those responsible for the religion as the *religare* of the world, as well as the Roman authorities, those responsible for the binding together into the Roman *polis* guided by the principle of *Pax Romana*. In other words, Christ's incarnation got him into trouble with political and religious powers of his time. The incarnation of the Call gets one into trouble with Religion$_2$. His incarnation got him into trouble with that which Bataille argues, needs to be sacrificed (crucified) so as to reach the Sacred.

Why the association with the marginal and ostracised? Is it because the marginal and the ostracised have or are the truth? This is a thought that one often finds in various liberation movements, where the oppressed are seen as the truth of the world. Yet, as long as one works with the idea that one can establish the truth of the world, the wheel of history repeats as it continues to turn and nothing really changes. The prophetic tradition often interprets the incarnation in the light of this believed truth. In that sense the prophetic and the priestly tradition become each other and the generic Christ-fiction reveals the truth of both priestly and prophetic theology.

No. it is because those living on the margins, or in the cracks on the edge or even over the edge of the system of the Name, are there where the Call came from. The Call, *was uns denken heisst*, withdraws from thinking, withdraws from the Name (Religion$_2$). In that sense, one can argue that whatever it is that Calls, it is the other of that called forth, over the edge of thought, thus those on the margin or in the cracks of the Name and the world carried out by the Name, do not reveal the Call, but they reveal the insufficiency of the Name, they reveal the death of terrestrial writing. In that sense they are important, as they are the occasion to think the death in terrestrial writing, but they are no closer to the Call than any other Name. The moment one makes them the truth of the Call, one has become a priest.

This focus on the cracks and marginal would be classical liberation theology, or critical theory challenging ideology. Yet the "mistake" is made once again, by identifying the Non-Name or Not-Naming that discloses the Name as the new Name and as name it has its own cracks, shadows and marginal.

That is, if God is the name given to that which is believed beyond or prior to our thought-worlds, the pre-existence, beyond the dependent objective reality in the independent reality, then not the Word of God is best heard in the cracks, shadows and the margins of the dependent objective reality, the World, the social construction, but the margins, shadows and cracks reveal the truth of the Name, the truth of the dependent objective reality: that it is insufficient. Not because the Truth is found there, or that these cracks are the Truth, or that a specific crack reveals the Call, but the crack is where the "true" light gets in, which does not make the crack or the shadow the truth, but rather *the exposure of the illusion* of the world. They are just the cracks, the shadows, which expose the vulnerability and insufficiency, the ideological illusion of human constructions. The cracks expose the principle of sufficient philosophy,[43] the principles of sufficient theology, the principles of sufficient thought, exposing all these to be fictions, illusions, but not because somewhere else there are non-fictions and truth to be found, but exposing thought as fictitious.

Why does the association with the marginal get Christ into trouble? It gets him into trouble with the priests and the political authorities exactly because it exposes the cracks of the Name and the world that is carried out in the Light of that Name.

The consequence of Christ's ministry is crucifixion, which is the unavoidable consequence of the Call incarnated in the human world, in contrast to a chosen Name being incarnated.

It is an either/or situation, either the Call exposes the illusion of the world (deconstruction) or the world crucifies the Call and thereby protects itself.

Revolutions and reformations have happened in the past because of the Call becoming incarnate in specific people, as Badiou would say – subjects of truth or faithful subjects (Badiou 2009:62ff), but who in response have each Named the Call something different to the previous Names and thereby challenged the previous system, and so the wheel of history turns in an eternal return of the same, or in the context of this chapter the eternal return of the Name.

Is it possible to move beyond Naming and live as those called by the Call, but without naming and without non-naming becoming a new Name (law)? In other words, to live in the *Zug* of that which calls thinking-forth, but without Naming it or not-naming it? Stated differently, is it possible to follow Christ and Christ alone, or in Paul's words, to know (name nothing), but Christ alone and him crucified (1 Cor. 2:2)? Such faithfulness, such faithful subjects, would not be faithful to a Truth as in Badiou, but faithful to the Call, and in this faithfulness be liberated from the illusions of Names and the worlds carried out in those Names. Could this

---

[43] Principle of Sufficient Philosophy is a concept that I found in François Laruelle, 'We shall call 'philosophy', beyond any given doctrine's claim to this title, any thought, explicitly 'philosophical' or not, that postulates that it holds within itself its ultimate validity for itself and consequently for the Real – and thus its radical non-subordination to the latter. This postulation is more precisely the Principle of Sufficient Philosophy' (Laruelle, 2012:190). This is its fundamental auto-position, which can also be called its auto-factualization or auto-fetishization – all of which we label as the *Principle of Sufficient Philosophy* (PSP) (Laruelle 2013a:12).

liberation through the crucifixion of Names and Naming be a resurrection into Life as Henry argues, or resurrection of the Call? In that way, the resurrection would be an insurrection – the resurrection as insurrection of Names, even non-names, and names in a faithfulness to the Call only; a resurrection as an insurrection in faithfulness to the Call, to the Word, the Calling Word and therefore resurrection into *poiēsis*. Resurrection into the Call, and the insistent calling to be poets of worlds, like the last transformation into the child in Nietzsche's (2000) Zarathustra, liberated from the camel and the lion (see also Meylahn 2014c). This would be a transformation into the free poetic play of the child, playing between all the fictions: trans-fictional play (praxis).

This is the way of Christ: incarnation of the Word (the Call) in the world can only lead to crucifixion. The temptation is to reduce this way of Christ to a particular group (the poor, the workers, women etcetera) or to reduce this way to a particular principle (justice, hospitality, democracy, liberation) or to reduce it to any particular thought or idea (Name) and thereby close the door to the plurality or heterogeneity of the Call, or as Rollins would say a reduction of the hypernymity to a singular Name or idea.

To try and translate the above paragraphs into something more practical I will try to follow a similar thought-path, but this time in conversation with other authors, other Names, as well as the #FeesMustFall movement.

Back to the story of #FeesMustFall, but different Names

Most of the advocates (intellectuals) presenting the different "facts" or "analyses" of an event like #FeesMustFall are convinced that they get their facts from actual Life, that they are on the ground with the students, or on the ground with the managements of the different universities, or they *believe* they are in touch with the economic reality or economic facts. It is human to *believe* oneself to be responding, and accurately at that, to the Call, or the Real. It is human to *believe* oneself to have correctly Named the Call and one can prove that one has the correct Name, as everything in the world makes perfect sense as everything has its correct place (time-place) and it would not, if the Name was not correct. If everything fits and makes sense then it must be the Real thing.

But of course everything does make sense in the world, because that very world is carried out by the Name. It is in the light of that Name that things appear and find their time-place within the *Lichtung* of the Name. A different Name will carry out a different world and that is why there is conflict. The conflict is often severe, as one cannot believe that the other does not see the truth, which is as clear as daylight. That the truth is as clear as daylight has everything to do with reification of the world, in other words it has to do with the binding logos that binds the world together, by creating the *Lichtung* in which all the things appear and have their proper time-place.

To argue that one is in touch with the grass-roots, which seems to mean that one is on the ground, or has reached the *founding* ground of a specific group that one associates with, is the illusion of the ideology that Laclau (2014:13) refers to, or the transcendental illusion of the ego that Henry[44] (2003:141) refers to. If the I forgets the me in the transcendental illusion of the ego, how could another I remember the me of someone else, especially if the other I, who is remembering, is a convinced academic, who has forgotten his own me, but *believes* (according to the principle of sufficient philosophy or sociology or psychology, or critical political theory) to remember the me of the other?

On the basis of the principle of sufficient philosophy (Laruelle 2012:190) the academic or activist is *convinced* that she or he is the true and only representative of the independent object reality, and that between their thoughts and reality there is a direct reciprocity, but this is the illusion of ideology par excellence (Laclau 2014:13), as well as the transcendental illusion of the ego (the I forgetting it's me). This belief is a necessary *belief* for the carrying out of any world that makes sense; this *belief* (conviction) is, as argued above, the reifying work of religion. There are numerous examples from history, and the great paradigm shifts or history of reformations and revolutions, in a certain sense the story of history, is driven by power of this belief. This might be the reason why some speak of the living God of history, as history is driven, revolutions are fought, in the name of believed truths, the belief that every new truth that is *discovered* is a step closer to the Call or the Real, or a step closer to the Truth, but in the process forgetting that truths are not discovered, but created. Every revolution is motivated and driven by this belief. The belief that now (amongst the activists or revolutionaries), for the first time, the true interests of the Real world will be served. The belief to be on the ground, to have reached *the* Ground, seems to want to argue that one is in touch with naked Life, naked Reality of, for example, the Life of the students, or the Life of the Management, or the Life of the economy – one is in touch with

---

[44]   Therefore, the first cause of people's forgetting their condition as Sons is the transcendental illusion of the ego. But this first cause immediately leads to the second. The ego's transcendental illusion is not totally illusory, in fact. In carries a portion of "reality" and "truth", which we have to deal with – simply because it is essential. The gift by which Life (self-giving) gives the ego to itself is in reality one with it. Once given to itself, the ego is really in possession of itself and of each of these powers, able to exercise them: it is really free. In making the ego a living person, Life has not made a pseudo-person. It does not take back with one hand what it has given with the other. ... Only that phenomenological status of absolute Life explains the ego's transcendental illusion. It is only because, naturally invisible, radically immanent, and never exposing itself in the world's "outside," this Life holds itself entirely within that the ego is ignorant of it, even when it exercises the power life gives it and attributes this power to itself (Henry 2003:141–142).

the Real. Laclau argues that such a belief is the ideological illusion par excel-lence.[45] Such belief is possible because of the reifying role of religion: the belief that the way I or we see the world is the real world. Religion is the belief that the dependent objective reality *is* the independent objective reality.[46] It is the ide-ological illusion par excellence when one believes that one hears the "true" cry of the Real world, or is in touch with the real suffering, or has identified the true wound. This is a necessary belief through which the believer is individuated into the group that shares this belief. The ego is only an ego through the transcendental illusion (Henry 2003:141–142). There is no such thing as an ego, or an I, without this transcendental illusion. The ego exists because it ex-*texts* – the text in which the me that is Called is forgotten. The text in which the ego exists as part of a collective by forgetting it's me cannot silence the insistence of the Call. The ego in its collective cannot silence the insistence of the Call that calls the me into re-sponsibility. This responsibility only an I (ego) can fulfil, but because it is the I (ego) that is fulfilling the responsibility to respond, the response is never complete or conclusive, and thus the responsibility to respond to the Call is never lifted. The I (ego) and its collective are haunted by the responsibility of the me, are haunted by that which Calls a thinking (I think therefore I am) I forth. It is the me that is called, but always the I that responds in the Here I am.

Because this responsibility is never fulfilled in the individual it is also never fulfilled in the collective either – the Call remains. The Call haunts all that is, that is all that ex-*texts*.

Individuals and/or groups respond to the Call, yet the only way they can re-spond is as I (egos), under the transcendental illusion or the ideological illusion. They respond because they hear the Call, but their response is only possible in the *belief* that they are truthfully or correctly responding to the Call.

It is this belief that they are responding to the Call and unlike the status quo, are truly in touch with the Real; the belief that they alone are in touch with the real suffering of the people. They believe themselves to be in solidarity with whatever

---

[45]   … any notion of an extra-discursive viewpoint is the ideological illusion par excellence (Laclau 2014:13).

[46]   Reification is the apprehension of human phenomena as if they were things, that is, in non-human or possibly supra-human terms (Berger & Luckmann 1976:106). Another way of saying this is that reification is the apprehension of the products of human activity *as if* they were something other than human products – such as facts of nature, results of cosmic laws, or mani-festations of divine will. Reification implies that man is capable of forgetting his own authorship of the human world, and, further, that the dialectic between man, the producer, and his products is lost to consciousness. The reified world is, by definition, a dehumanized world. It is experi-enced by man as a strange facticity, an *opus alienum* over which he has no control rather than as the *opus proprium* of his own productive activity (Berger & Luckmann 1976:106). In other words, reification can be described as an extreme step in the process of objectivation, whereby the objectivated world loses its comprehensibility as a human enterprise and becomes fixated as a non-human, non-humanizable, inert facticity (Berger & Luckmann 1976:106).

they re*present* or whatever they make *present*, forgetting that they are *making* whoever or whatever present. Whatever is made present, that is to exist, to be heard, to be seen, to be individuated as an individual (subject) or individuated as a group (identity politics), exists because they ex-*text* on the basis of the transcendental or ideological illusion. Can one develop a philosophy of Flesh? Can one develop a response that does not forget the me? Henry certainly tried and in a certain sense so did Marx. They both tried to think from Flesh, from Life, from the material conditions, from the level of subsistence, and yet that which Calls forth thought, is not Life, Flesh, materiality or matter, because whatever it is, must first be named, or made to pre-exist and receive thought. Whatever is, for it to be it must ex-text. For something to appear (to be disclosed) it must be appropriated and this disclosing appropriation is the speaking of language. Therefore Life, Flesh, materiality, or materialism – the moment they exist, they ex-text, that is they are already a response, and no longer that which Called thinking forth. Life, Flesh, materiality, matter are Names and therefore thoughts, and as a thought it makes *present*, it is only a re*present*ation of that which called it forth' and therefore it is the response and not the Call. It is not "Life", but a response and in the response that-which-called is named Life. The I is never the me, but a forgotten me. It is the response in that it makes a pre-existence and gives it a Name, and by giving a Name it becomes a *presence* (ex-*text*-ence) in the world, something that can be talked about, crafting the idea and with the idea determining what it means to be present. They believe that this presence, which they made but forgetting that they made it, is the starting point, forgetting that they created, crafted that starting point. They missed the starting point, because their naming of the starting point is already only a response to something that called-forth their response, their thoughts. Therefore, there is no starting point, no ground, no foundation, as one is always already in the rhizome of responding within the history or tradition of that particular response. There is no origin or no *arkhē* as everything has always already begun (Bennington 1993:19) and one is always already in the text, the moment one thinks one is already an ex-*text*-ence in a world.

This call-response one cannot escape and maybe it is this call-response that is the most *Bedenklichste* (Heidegger 1961), that which needs to be thought. I do not hereby want to emphasise the divide or correlation or non-correlation between thought and matter or the old divide between flesh and soul, but rather see this as One: as a response-called-forth-and-thus-named-whilst-believed-to-pre-exist-thought.

In practical theology this has been one of the major questions: where does theology start? Does it start with the flesh, context or with the Bible? What is the starting point or the place of annunciation? In the context of the above paragraphs, and taking Derrida (in Bennington 1993:19) into consideration, there is no starting point, as one is always already in the text, in a world, because the moment one is, one ex-*texts*. But this insight has not prevented people from believing that they can identify a starting point, and various starting points have been offered: Life, practice, lived experience with the turn in recent years also to lived religion (Failing and Heimbrock 1998; Ganzevoort 2009; 2013; Gräb 2000; 2002; 2005; 2012 Grözinger & Pfleiderer 2002).

As mentioned in the previous chapter, there is a certain frustration with the focus on social construction as it ignores the Call completely and only focusses on Naming. Dussel (2003), in his response to social construction, or in his words in response to theories of communicative action, tries not to focus on Life or the Real, but his focus is on what I would call subsistence, namely the economic conditions of life, fully conscious that these economic conditions of life are also embodied in a communicative community, in other words, a social construction: an economic social construction.

But what we are dealing with now – the result of an exigency that is imposed upon us by the reality in Latin America (as well as in Asia and Africa) – is that a person is not not language but also essentially and above all a living being – not merely as an irrational animal, but also a living being always human. The logic of life becomes present in every moment of a human being. His own rationality, language, spirituality, and so on are moments of his own human life. These are functions of life. For this reason, before the person is part of a community of communication (and subjected to the same communicative action), he is already a priori a member of a community of life; and because of his being a part of it, there is a community of communication serving as a function of the community of life. It is this fundamental human level that we will call "the economic base," not as a "system" in Habermasian fashion (as a *Wirtschaftswissenschaft*) but as a practical and essential constitutive relational moment of human life in which are established the primary practical "relations," the production of the objects of life, their distribution, the exchange, and consumption for human life (Dussel 2003:153).

Dussel's idea of a "community of life" are not that far removed from Henry's Life, the naked Life, but naked Life is firstly already a name (a response) and secondly this naked Life is embodied in an economic base, which is not a given, but a construction. Thereby, I am not denying the immense suffering of large parts of the globe's population, but this suffering is the suffering of political-economic bodies. In other words, the suffering is a consequence of political-economic embodiment. It is because of the political-economic texts that there is economic and political suffering, as certain bodies are determined to suffer by the economic-geo-political Text, and therefore, these bodies are estranged from their co-writing of their bodies.

Yes, indeed one is always born, embodied, into a specific world. It is in a world into which the Body without Organs, always already appears (comes to presence – ex-*texts*) as stratified, in*scrib*ed. The Body without Organs, or Life, or the me, cannot but appear in a economic-political world, as a racial body, sexual body,

cultural-educational body and an economic-political body. These are the levels, or
as I will argue stratifications (in*scrip*tions) that Dussel argues are always already
present: political, sexual and educational (see Dussel 2003:22–24). Flesh appears
in the world as body, as a political, sexual and educational body. The question is
not if Flesh can appear, but the question is to what extent the I co-writes that body,
or is the body a determination of the Other: a docile body?

The moment there is any appearance of Life – it is already a stratified life, a
politicized life. Human life appears as political life, sexual life and educational
life. It never appears as raw naked Life. How does this stratification happen? How
is the Body without Organs[47] transformed into a body with organs? That might be
the wrong question, as the body only ever appears as stratified, so there is no time
before it was stratified. If it appears, it appears as stratified. There is no appearance
of an un-stratified flesh, or un-inscribed flesh. Thereby I am not saying that there
is no such thing as Life or Body without Organs; I am only saying that it does
not exist (ex-*text*), because to be (to exist) is to be disclosed as to be appropriated,
that is in the *Ereignis* of language. That which calls thinking forth (the Call) does
not exist, it ex-texts only in the Name (response) as that which called thinking
forth. The Call, that which calls thinking forth, withdraws from thinking. It is no
wonder that God, the God of the religions of the Book, winks to one in the *Ereignis*
of language, as the one who Calls. It seems as if God, like the Call in the mystical
or negative theological tradition, only exists in the non-Name, saved but in the
non-Name, safe in the Name (see Derrida 1995). The Call calls thinking forth, but
withdraws from thinking, as it wants to be thought and be saved by thought, but
likewise it is saved from thought by withdrawing from that which it called forth.

These questions are related to the question: What does it mean to be human, as
discussed in the first half of this chapter? Is there a way out of social construction?
Is there a way out of the world? No, there is not, there is no outside text (Derrida
1997:158), because all that appears can only appear in a world. But there is not
only one stratification, there is not only one world, but pluri-verse worlds.

For Dussel there are dominant stratifications and these dominant stratifications are Western stratifications, as each body that appears, appears predominately
within a Western ontology. This coincides with the ideas of Deleuze and Guattari,
who argue that the stratifications are created by the abstract machine of the West.
There is no escaping these stratifications, just as there is no escaping the Abstract
machine of the West. Dussel is right in questioning this Western ontology, or West-

---

[47] You never reach the Body without Organs, you can't reach it, you are forever attaining it, it is
a limit. People ask, So what is this BwO? – But you're already on it, scurrying like vermin,
groping like a blind person, or running like a lunatic: desert traveller and nomad of the steppes.
On it we sleep, live our waking lives, fight – fight and are fought – seek our place, experience
untold happiness and fabulous defeats; on it we penetrate and are penetrated; on it we love
(Deleuze & Guattari 2011:150).

ern stratification and thereby inclusion into the Rhizome, but does his metaphysics really escape the Rhizome, the Western Ontology? Dussel's philosophy of liberation is very much akin to a theology of liberation based on the work of Levinas with this ethics as first philosophy, in other words a prophetic sign regime. The prophetic sign regime, Deleuze and Guattari argue, is part of the Abstract machine of the West. This is also what Nancy (2008:10) argues, that both the enclosure and the dis-enclosure is Christian, and therefore Western.

Dussel refers to this life as the ontological life and turns towards metaphysics as that which transcends this ontological life (Dussel 2003:4). He specifically turns towards Levinas and his idea of the Other to transcend the "closed" ontology of Being. In a previous study (Meylahn 2013) I reflected on various possibilities of postmetaphysical thought bringing Heidegger, Levinas and Derrida into conversation, and in that study, I challenged the idea that Levinas' Other offers a way out of metaphysics, as what he offers is an ethical metaphysics which remains a closed or rather enclosed *clôture* system. Yet, Dussel seems to find in Levinas the opening, the disenclosure of the system. I would argue that the Other only becomes the new Good, the new God, the new Name or even Non-Name of a different system, and the wheel of history repeats itself. There is *was uns denken heisst*, which in the first half of this chapter I referred to as that which calls-thought-forth, namely the Call. And this Call has been named other things as well, such as: Life, Other, Real. The only way to think that which *is*, namely that which calls-forth-thought, is to Name it. Outside of the name nothing appears and nothing is, beside that which called the name forth, but it does not appear without a name. It cannot be appropriated without being disclosed and it cannot be disclosed without being appropriated, in other words, it exists only in the event of language. It exists (ex-*texts*) only in the speaking of language and therefore Henry's reference to this Call as Word is perhaps very appropriate.

Dussel interprets the poor as the Other of the system and I will take up his thoughts again later when I turn to the generic victim, rather than the poor.

What is thinking? – making meaning and through making meaning individuating oneself within a collective

In a modernist and positivist world, there is a clear distinction between the objective world and the subjective (mental-rational) mind of humans. The link between these two, mind and world, is reason (language). Language is *believed* to be a reliable and accurate link to the real. This view was challenged, and the world is no longer the objective reality out there, but the socially (collectively) constructed world that humans share through their shared language. Language is no longer seen as the link but as an interactive process, not a passive receiving or transmitting of pre-existing truths (see Freedman & Combs 1996:28). Language does not reflect the world, but determines the world[48] or it carries the world out into ex-*text*-ence. Words are not connected to 'outside' reality, but words are connected to word-contexts, such as sentences and paragraphs and books and it is in and through these word-contexts that their meaning is established (Freedman & Combs 1996:29). Meaning is not found, but meaning is made, it is collectively made in and through language. There are lived experiences (see White & Epston 1990:9), but lived experiences need to be interpreted and in that sense is made and meaning is created. Yet, this process of meaning creation is always a collective process in which the I is individuated into a collective, and therefore one could argue that meaning creation or sense making is a political (ideological) or religious praxis.

Ricoeur (1984:31ff) argues that sense making or meaning creation happens through a process of emplotment into narrative. In other words, one makes sense of happenings, phenomena by emplotting them into a narrative with a past, present and future. Stiegler (2014:45f; 2015a:31ff; 2015b:103) adds to this sense-making, or meaning-making by arguing that it is not just a matter of making sense, but it is in sense-making that the human becomes human, that is a noetic soul.[49] One becomes human, becomes an identifiable person (an I or ego), by making sense, making meaning, and by making sense becoming someone who has a certain opinion about him/herself and the world. In response to the Call, the me called becomes the I who names the Call, and in Naming becomes an ego in the world, a *Dasein* in the very world carried out by the Name given to the Call.

In naming (responding/thinking) one becomes an individual, one is individuated and becomes an existence: an ex-*text*-ence. Sense-making, meaning-making is thus individuation, psychic individuation in relation to collective and technical individuation. These processes of individuation (psychic, collective and technical) are always intertwined and cannot be understood nor do they occur in isolation, as psychic individuation happens in collectives through technical individuation of that collective.

---

[48] Our language tells us how to see the world and what to see in it. It does not mirror nature; language creates the nature we know (Freedman & Combs 1996:29).

[49] When it appears in act, the sensed only appears as *idios*, which is to say, in its singularity: which supports and catalyzes the singularity of the one sensing, along with the singularity of what becomes, as it circulates in the social sphere, as it realizes, that is, psychic individuation through its participation in collective individuation – the *sense* of the sensed. The sensible thus wrest itself away from sensibility as it realizes the noetic act. The sensible which induces a *reaction* in the sensitive soul engenders an *action* in the noetic soul – and this action, which increases the possibilities of sense and the sensible, is an apprenticeship. *Tekhnēsis* is what makes apprenticeship possible: it is the heart of this *organology of total movement* that is the noetic soul. The noetic soul, which can always remain at the level of sensitivity, may also appear reactive when faced with the sensible, producing only a potential noetic sensible (Stiegler 2015a:32–33).

In other words, I am not only trying to make sense of #FeesMustFall, but in the process of making sense I am also individuating myself in relation to some or other collective, which I do via the technics or externalisation (ex-*text*-ualisation) of that collective, for example through the statement that I co-draft, or which has been drafted and I sign or endorse. I sign or endorse that which resonates with my embodiment (primary, secondary and tertiary retentions and protentions). Such an endorsement or signature individuates me as part of a collective, which has been externalised in a statement (technics) and thus begins or continues the path of grammatisation of that collective. In Berger and Luckmann's (1976) terms the path of institutionalisation, legitimisation and eventually reification.

I am firstly trying to make individual sense (psychic individuation), fully conscious that individual sense can never be separated from collective and technical sense. In other words, I make individual sense in conversation with a collective; one is often involved in more than one collective and therefore in relation to the different collectives and their technics (texts). Meaning changes slightly or dramatically according to the collective one might be part of, which explains how people can have totally different views at home and at the workplace, for example. These different worlds also explain why sometimes totally opposing ethical standards might even apply in these two worlds (work and home). For example, a person could be a very professional biologist working within the paradigm of evolution, and yet at home hold onto a set of values that would be more at home in a creationist view of the world.

Meaning is made in this exchange between the psychic (individual) and the collective through the various exteriorisations, that is *technics*, that are available to the individual as part of a specific collective. For example, in the home collective, the technics available to one might be religious traditions, whilst in the work collective the technics available might be scientific paradigms, or economic theories and more importantly the dictates of the market and the outcomes expected. These collectives already have numerous secondary retentions and protentions that the individual engages with in the process of her or his individuation within that collective, as well as tertiary retentions (documents, books, traditions, cultural-religious and technical artefacts, statistics, profits and losses). Gerkin (1991:53) argues that 'Prior to moral and even practical reasoning there is a more fundamental and intuitive process'. The first of these more intuitive processes Gerkin calls the imagistic, which can be described as a deep recall to primary stories that have shaped the images of collective life. This could be compared to primary and secondary protentions and retentions.

The secondary protentions and retentions are part of the culture or context in which one lives. These are the dominant narratives which will specify the norms of that collective and what the collective believes to be normal – the customary beliefs and behaviours (see Freedman & Combs 1996:32). The culture (secondary and tertiary protentions and retentions) that one belongs to will influence one to ascribe certain meanings to particular events and life-events and treat other events as meaningless (Freedman & Combs 1996:32). It is the primary, secondary and tertiary retentions and protentions, the narratives in which one lives, that allow certain things (events, phenomena, people) to appear within the world that these narratives carried out, whilst other things remain invisible or concealed.

What drives this process of psychic, collective and technical individuation? Or what prompts it? In the light of the beginning of the chapter: what Calls? What calls thinking forth or who or what Calls one into this process of individuation? What is this Call that can be interpreted as the *Zug des Denkens* (the pull of thought)? What Calls forth thought and with thought the individuation of the individual: the I or ego? One is prompted, Called, into this process of individuation, one is called into this *Zug* (pull) by the most thought-worthy, that which Calls forth thought. Whatever *is* that calls to be thought, is what Calls. It is because of this *is* that Calls thought forth that Henry describes it as Arch-intelligibility or the Word.

Stated differently, there is something insisting, maybe like Caputo's (2013) God is insisting, that insists to be thought, but that cannot *be* thought, as it withdraws from thought. In other words, it will never *be* thought, as it will always *be* the other of thought as that which called thought forth, and in that sense it is foreclosed to thought.

Many names have been given to this that Calls thought forth, for example: the Real, some call it God, it is that which in a sense is more real than anything that exists (ex-*texts*) and which insists to be thought. There is something insisting on the level of subsistence: Flesh, Life, the Real. One could say an insistent existence, but in thought it always ex-*texts*. And yet this insistence is closer to one than anything else, even closer and more immanent than thought that thinks and therefore *is*. It is as immanent as suffering or joy. It is an affectivity that affects one directly (see Henry 2015:58).

Something is insisting on the level of subsistence in South Africa and particularly amongst the students, but not only amongst the students. One could say there "is" a *persistent insistence* that disturbs, haunts (deconstructs), the various exteriorisations and grammatisations that are engramming the South African story. This story, be it the story of the New South Africa, or the Rainbow Nation, or the Constitutional Democracy, is being challenged, deconstructed by a persistent insistence: a suffering. An insistence that becomes so persistent that it cannot be ignored any longer: the exteriorisations (ex-*text*-ualisations) of the past (retentions and protentions) of the various collectives (economic, democratic, constitutional, cultural, traditional, social etcetera) are inadequate to make sense of this persistent insistence. Or the dominant story is exposed as being inadequate, or even as having failed the South African "reality". An insistence that haunts, disturbs, disrupts and will persist till it gets the attention that it deserves. It is an insistence that one might call the repressed, or the ghosts of what has been murdered by exclusion or marginalisation, or the voices that have been silenced by the dominant grammatisations, which have shaped and determined the various South African collectives. Once these grammatisations are disrupted, the protentions and retentions are no longer able to project a future, thus creating uncertainty and in some cases, hopelessness. The insistence disrupts the dominant grammatisations so that the future becomes uncertain and the past is questioned. Perhaps this is one way of interpreting what is currently happening, where there are voices questioning the recent past of the New South Africa. For example, questioning the negotiations of the Convention for a Democratic South Africa (CODESA), as well as the role of President Mandela – for some Mandela is interpreted as a sell-out and CODESA is interpreted as selling the people of South Africa to the highest bidder. The suffering that insists, challenges and questions the dominant grammatisations and the ability of those grammatisations (for example, the Rainbow Nation) to give meaning to the past and hope for the future.

Whatever it is, it insists and this insistence is persistent, which then demands to be taken notice of, and it is taken notice of by being individuated, that is, given a Name, identified, separated, differentiated, typified and classified. Together with the individuation of that which insists, the naming of the Call, the naming individual or collective, is also individuated and in the process an individual is individuated into a collective – a collective that is bound together by this particular individuation of the insistence, bound together by this particular Naming of the Call.

The insistence is individuated (Named) and by naming the individual is individuated into a collective and thus becomes part of the grammatisation of that collective, as she or he accepts the grammatisation of that collective as "the way the world truly is". The insistence (Call) can be individuated differently and thus creating different individuals and diverse collectives. One could argue that currently the various grammatisations of the various collectives (for example liberal democracy, capitalism socialism and Marxism to name a few) are showing cracks and can no longer contain (capture) the insistence in these consistencies. The insistence persists and various different individuals and new collectives are created in responding to this insistence, but by individuating this insistence differently, giving it a different consistence. These different collectives will then clash with each other, as they each claim to be the correct or truthful individuation of the insistence. Each collective believes they have found the correct and only Name for that which Calls: they know the true reason for the suffering.

An insistence is individuated, whilst also individuating individuals and collectives via the process of psychic, collective and technical retentions and protentions, to individuate a collective into a *polis*: a political body (see Stiegler

2014:2). This political body is the outcome of this process of individuation via primary, secondary and tertiary retentions and protentions, and therefore it is to be expected that the various South African political parties are circling, like birds of prey, around these hashtags seeking to score party political points from this political individuation, as collective individuation is always political (see Laclau 2007).

Such an insistence through its persistence eventually needs to be made sense of. It goes through the process of psychic, collective and technical individuation, and it emerges as, for example something individuated or singularized as the #FeesMustFall. That which insists through its persistence is individuated differently in different individuals and in different contexts (collectives), and is then consequently also externalised (ex-*text*-ualised) differently. This becomes clear as the movement is different on the various campuses, as different con*texts* (different student collectives) are *responding* to this insistence differently. They are *responding* to that which Calls (insistence), and because they are different collectives, with different secondary and tertiary retentions and protentions, their response is different. In other words, there is no singular *response* to that which Calls forth thought (*was uns Denken heisst*), but depending on the primary, secondary, tertiary retentions and protentions the thought thought, or externalised (ex-*text*-ualised) will differ, for example, in the style of the protest or the wording of the statements.

Once there is a response, there will soon be responses to the response so that one would never know what was the first response, and it would not make much sense to speak of a first response, but only an infinite chain of responses, as all there is are responses, there is nothing outside text (responses) (see Derrida 1997:158).

One response to the #FeesMustFall is the #KeepUniversityOpen, who seem to be arguing that they are responding to the same Call. The same Call to which the different collectives *believe* themselves to be responding is for example, the *belief* that they are all responding to the call for free, decolonised, de-commodified and quality education, but responding differently to this call. They are responding differently to a response: because the Call, the suffering, the insistence has already been Named: *a-call-for-free,-decolonised,-decommodified-and-quality-education*. They are not responding to the Call in the sense that the "call for free, decolonised, de-commodified and quality education" is already a collective externalised [ex-*text*-ualised] in the response, which named the call, a call for free, decolonised, decommodified and quality education.

There is an insistence, or there are cracks in the grammatisations of the past, but this insistence and these cracks are interpreted differently in the varied responses. There might also be numerous different cracks, but what is important for the construction of a people, the individuation of an individual within a particular collective, is to choose one of the equivalences, and interpret this particular chosen equivalence as *the* incarnation of the whole. For example, a particular equivalence is chosen, as it is believed to be the incarnation of the healing of society, or as *the* reason for suffering. One equivalence is chosen as *the* reason for suffering, or one equivalence is chosen as *the* solution. This one equivalence is then interpreted as *the pharmakon*, the medicine, that will heal the differences or problems, or as *the* reason for suffering. This idea of making a part the incarnation of the whole is what Laclau describes as the role of ideology.[50]

For example, there is a Call, an insistence, let's say suffering amongst the student body. This suffering could be caused by numerous different things, and these different things might all be equally valid and therefore equivalences, but one of these is then chosen to represent all the different problems and challenges. Onto this particular equivalence, name, idea, or response, the dream of the fullness of the collective is projected. This is the work of ideology, Laclau (2014:17) argues. For example, the belief that tertiary education will solve all, or at least many of the challenges if only it is decolonised, de-commodified and offers quality free education. But closure or wholeness is impossible, and being impossible it cannot have content on its own, but needs to project its "content" onto an object different from itself. This object will assume the role of incarnating the closure of an ideological horizon, but will in the process of incarnating the closure be deformed (see Laclau 2014:17). Whatever it is that is identified to incarnate the whole is deformed by what Laclau (2014:18) calls equivalence, which is not identity. In other words, there are always other words or terms which can replace each other, and more importantly, which can be enumerated and thereby become floating signifiers, to give meaning to the empty signifier (Laclau 2014:20): the absence of fullness. Democracy or justice are such empty signifiers and are loaded with floating signifiers that can be enumerated to indicate the direction of the empty signifier. At times a singular floating signifier is chosen as *the* Signifier and not as empty signifier, but as full signifier. Onto this particular signifier is incarnated the full meaning of the empty signifier and thereby it is distorted, and that is for Laclau the dual working of ideology. These two moments or movements are mutually dependent and as such form the two movements of ideological dialectic: incarnation and deformation (see also Meylahn 2017d).

These movements could be about numerous things that all point into the direction of the empty signifiers, for example justice or democracy, but the moment one of these signifiers (reasons why there is no justice or democracy, or what would bring about justice or democracy) is chosen and it is loaded with the full-meaning of the empty signifier, one is dealing with ideology. One cannot avoid ideology, as

---

[50] The ideological effect is the belief that there is a 'particular social arrangement that can bring about the closure and transparency of the community'. ... There is ideology whenever a particular content shows itself as more than itself (Laclau 2014:17).

it is necessary in the creation of meaning, the individuating of the self and binding together into a political collective, but it is insufficient,[51] as it is deformed.

Thus, for example, white privilege could be chosen as the object that stands in the way of full democracy or full justice. Whatever is chosen is always *partly* correct, but it is only a part that must then represent (incarnate) the whole. Yet, it cannot incarnate the whole as it is only a part and therefore is deformed. Yet, again it is a necessary deformation in the individuation of a self into a collective, and thus the creation of the political.

In the past, the various critical schools would argue that ideological distortion brings about a false consciousness and that people need to be liberated from false consciousness (see Laclau 2014:13). The classic Marxist view of ideology from *Das Kapital,* was '*Sie wissen das nicht, aber sie tun es*' – 'they do not know it, but they are doing it' (Žižek 2008:24). It was this false or naïve consciousness that one needed to be liberated from. In the Frankfurt School this idea developed into seeing 'how reality itself cannot reproduce itself without this co-called ideological mystification' (Žižek 2008:25). Just as Laclau argues that one cannot be liberated from ideology, just as one cannot be liberated from religion or the political, it is part and parcel of the process of individuation and collective individuation through sense-making and meaning-creation. The necessity of ideology was discussed in Peter Sloterdijk's book *Critique of Cynical Reason*, where he argues that today the dominant functioning of ideology is cynicism. In other words, Marx's view is translated: 'they know very well what they are doing, but still, they are doing it' (Žižek 2008:25).

Following Laclau, ideology is necessary, but keeping in mind that it is insufficient or impossible. What can be done with ideology is to open it up to the other equivalences, the differences, and thereby open its meaning up. The body of an individual or the body of a collective is a *co*-writing process. The problem is not that it is a writing process, the problem is that voices are silenced and excluded from the process, thus the problem is hegemony. The problem is when co-writing becomes a singular text that determines everything. This is a problem when sojourning with individuals, when an individual is reduced to a singular text (which would be ideological deformation according to Laclau). It is problematic if an individual becomes the victim of a singular text, for example the dominant text of an illness or of a problem, and the individual becomes the problem (is determined as the problem or illness), and thereby becomes a docile body to the narrative of

---

[51] In that case what we are dealing with is, *the presence of an absence, and the ideological operation par excellence consists of attributing that impossible role of closure to a particular content that is radically incommensurable with it.* In other terms: the operation of closure is impossible but at the same time necessary – impossible because of the constitutive dislocation lying at the heart of any structural arrangement; necessary because, without that fictitious fixing of meaning, there would not be meaning at all (Laclau 2014:16–17).

the problem. Likewise, in marriages or families there are dominant texts, that exclude or silence other texts (voices), and that is problematic, as certain members of the family will be docile bodies in that dominant narrative. In society, there are dominant texts that reduce individuals and communities to being docile bodies and that is a problem. It is not a problem that one only exists in a text. The problem is if one does not co-write that text, or when texts are reduced to singular dominant narratives, although keeping in mind that singular texts, singular names are necessary to individuate. The question is, Who all is included in choosing the singular narrative?

A university is a privileged space, but I would like to unpack this privilege as responsibility rather than interpreting it as an exclusion, in the sense that to have a variety of secondary and tertiary retentions has everything to do with privilege. It is a privilege to be exposed to a variety of collectives, to be exposed to a large variety of secondary and tertiary retentions, through the availability of technology. It is also true that such privilege has to do with the economic-social "reality" on the level of subsistence. Yet, it is and should be the privileged space of any university, as uni-versal education, where one is exposed to the universe or pluri-verse of tertiary retentions from various parts of the globe. The greater the diversity of tertiary and secondary retentions that are available the more diverse responses become possible.

The university as uni-versal education, should be the place where there are no dominant hegemonic narratives, but an universe of narratives, thus empowering individuals and collectives to *co*-write their selves and their worlds.

Is that not part of the call for decolonial education, to not reduce tertiary retentions to singular grammatisations, but to open grammatisations to the variety of moderns, as Dussel (2012 & 2013) argues for a transmodern perspective, where modernity is not reduced to a singular narrative. Or as this book is arguing for a trans-fictional praxis, which would indeed be the call for universal education of a university.

The call for decolonial education, is a call for opening education up to a variety of tertiary retentions, that are no longer reduced by a singular dominant and dominating grammatisation, i.e. a singular view of Western modernity. Decolonial education asks to be exposed to the trans-modern: a pluri-verse of secondary and tertiary retentions, and indeed that is what education should be in the global world.

My primary retentions and primary protentions determine my attitude to this movement and its externalisation in texts and actions (protests) as texts. These primary retentions and protentions are already shaped and formed by secondary retentions and protentions of the various collectives I am part of (academic-world, church, students, etcetera), which in turn are influenced and determined by the tertiary retentions and protentions of those collectives, and obviously the books (tertiary retentions) that have influenced my thinking, which in turn is influencing the writing of this book. One responds in this dual sense of both making sense whilst individuating oneself. These two cannot be separated, as it is not about making objective sense and then individuating oneself, but one is individuated in the creation of sense and the making of meaning within a collective. I am trying to make sense and the only material that I have with which to make sense, craft sense, are the conversations between these three levels of retentions and protentions.

If one would unpack that, I try to make sense through that which *I have heard* in the various meetings, what *I read-write*[52] in the texts that are available (for example: various statements made by various managements of universities, by the #FeesMustFall movement, by various concerned academics, media articles), and by reading some sources that have influenced this movement, namely the tertiary retentions that are providing the metaphors and grammar of this movement, eg. Fanon, Biko and others, as well as other books that have influenced my thinking over the years, and lastly *to listen to* (read) the process of drafting the statement, *A call for critical engagement.*

It is in this context of numerous externalisations, grammatisations, which is a con*text* of texts (technics), that I try to make sense and through making sense, individuate myself.

It is a con*text* of *texts* (primary, secondary and tertiary retentions and protentions), therefore I am never on the ground, never directly in-touch with the insistence, as I can never hear the *Call* itself, but only and always already the different *responses-to-the-Call*, Names given to the Call. It is only once the Call has been named that it is possible to consciously hear the Call, but it then speaks not in its own voice, but in the voice of the Name given to it. It is just as one does not only read a text, but also writes the text that one is reading.

What I hear is not the Call, but a [hearing-of-a-call] *in* my response that names the Call, for example a possible name is: the pain of the students. To hear the Call it must be audible, to see something it must be visible (appear), and it appears and is audible only to the extent that it is disclosed and it is disclosed only to the extent that it is appropriated. The Call, if it can be identified as Call, has already been responded to (it has been disclosed because it has been appropriated), and in the various responses it has been given different names, for example in the past, it has been called the transcendental, the subconscious, the repressed, the material economic conditions, the structural necessity, the colonial wound, etcetera. Yet, even with these names, I am not in touch with the insistence, but only in-touch with a particular naming thereof, in-touch with a particular response (disclosing appropriation), which is dependent on the psychic, collective and technical individuation through primary, secondary and tertiary retentions and protentions of

---

[52] One never only reads texts, one is also writing the texts that one is reading.

the collectives in which these names, externalisations and later grammatisations, were given, and the Call determined.

The moment meaning is created, the Call has been given a Name (disclosingly appropriated) *in* a response. It often feels as if a Truth has been discovered and it is a wonderful feeling: a burning sensation in the heart or enlightened experience as so much makes sense, as past and future fall into place. The moment meaning is created and one believes one has discovered a truth, it is an enlightened feeling of believing one is "in-touch" with the Real, to have access to the Truth, because it is the moment of making sense and thus one truly feels in-touch with "truth" or with the "facts". It is that burning sensation in the heart, that the Emmaus disciples also felt, but this sensation has more to do with the secondary and tertiary retentions and protentions than with the insistence, the Call, or Truth or the Real. One feels enlightened because sense has been created of the insistence, and together with the sense I have been individuated into a particular collective, where I feel at home in the carried-out-world, as it all makes perfect sense. To feel at home in the carried out world is indeed a powerful feeling. If somebody challenges this sense, it feels as if they are challenging my ex-istence (ex-*text*-ance), and they do indeed challenge my ex-*text*-ence, and my whole world with it, because they challenge my individuation – the way that I have co-externalised myself within a collective via the secondary and tertiary retentions and protentions of that collective. It feels as if they are challenging my Flesh, my Life or my actual being, but what they are challenging is my *Dasein*-in-a-world: my ex-*text*-ence in a con*text*. As one has forgotten the human authorship of this world, it feels as if reality has been taken from one. From social construction, we know that at the level of reification (Berger & Luckmann 1976:106) the externalisation becomes so real that one is convinced that there is nothing more real and that my world is the way the reality truly is.

I am never on the ground. Although the flesh of my feet might be on the earth, my humanity, as noetic soul, is always in a world. So, although I might be amongst the students, I am not on the ground *with* them, but nor are they, as what I hear is what *I hear* and not the Call. It is because one is not on the ground and never will be, which is maybe what drives the frustration, as all one has is oneself (my *Dasein*) in one's world (*Mitsein*), carried out by one's social-political-economic con*text*. The words uttered by the other's mouth are words I have co-placed there. I have never read a single text, as I have only co-authored texts that I thought I was reading. I am not on the ground even if I might be "with" the students. All I can ever be, is part of the process: psychic, collective and technical individuation and the grammatisation of an insistence, crafting *a* response to the Call. In other words, not in solidarity with the insistence, but only in solidarity with a particular individuation or singularisation, as an externalisation and eventually a grammatisation or abstraction thereof, or a response to the insistence that through the psychic, collective and technical individuation becomes a consistence, as something constituted through the process of these three levels of retention and protention (primary, secondary and tertiary). The insistence then might be constituted as black pain, with its opposite white privilege, or constituted as criminal with the opposite rational sober judgement.

Yet, black pain or white privilege do not exist, they consist, as likewise the criminal element and rational sober judgement do not exist, but only consist. Two opposing consistencies that are part of two dominant narratives, two dominant grammatisations, are now at war with each other. This is a necessary process of individuation into a collective and one cannot avoid it. It is for this reason that Chantal Mouffe calls for agonism rather than antagonism (Mouffe 2013:7). The reason why there will always be antagonism is the ideological necessity of incarnation and deformation, and consequently different ideologies. 'It is because of the existence of a form of negativity that cannot be overcome dialectically that full objectivity can never be reached and that antagonisms is an ever present possibility' (Mouffe 2013:xi). The negativity that the whole cannot be reduced or incarnated in a part, or the negativity that the Call can never be heard, as only the Name-given-to-the-Call can be heard. These thoughts will be further explored in the next chapter.

The various statements, memoranda, discussions, conversations, tweets, updates are all part of the process of grammatisation of this insistence into a particular consistence. It is the response that determines the meaning of the insistence, gives it a Name. As more and more collectives seek to make sense, create meaning, dominant grammatisations start to take shape and eventually there are two or more dominant grammatisations that gather collectives around them. How to judge between these two dominant grammatisations? That there will be dominant interpretations (Names-given-to-the-Call) is unavoidable, the moment there is order it is of a hegemonic nature.[53] Is one of them truer, or more factual, or is one better, in the sense of being more critical, or offering a more critical analysis of the reality? No, each one of them is true or factual relative to their primary, secondary and tertiary retentions and protentions, in other words relative to their collectives. How to decide what is right, what is ethical, will depend on one's collective. This leaves one in a state of relativism. The ethic which I will develop in a later chapter, which is an ethical modality rather than a worked-out ethics, is an ethic of a *stance* with the Call, but as one cannot stand with the Call, the excluded, those in the shadows of any dominant Text will be the occasion or the place of the stance:

---

[53] Society is permeated by contingency and any order is of a hegemonic nature, i.e. it is always the expression of power relations. In the field of politics, this means that the search for a consensus without exclusion and the hope for a perfectly reconciled and harmonious society have to be abandoned. As a result, the emancipatory ideal cannot be formulated in terms of a realization of any form of 'communism' (Mouffe 2013:xi).

an ethical stance of the shadows, or an ethic of the persistent insistence, which might offer a way beyond such relativism. The dominant grammatisation of the university as they currently are, excludes numerous voices (realities), realities of poor students, other epistemologies, and therefore there is this call for free and decolonial education. In that sense, this call is justified and being justified has received much support, even from university managements. And yet, once the excluded insistence or the insistent shadow is given a particular name, a name which might be historically and contextually justified, but once named, grammatised, it tends to repeat the same mistakes that the movement was challenging, by creating a new dominant narrative, grammatisation, that excludes.

The decolonial insistence always becomes a colonial consistence

One could argue that any determination of an insistence, determination of the Real, is colonial. As I (we) determine the insistence as pain, I colonise the insistence, force it to submit to my/our abstract idea, black pain within the greater abstraction (discourse) of for example justice, or the abstract idea of human dignity or the abstract idea of Africanisation. The moment there is order it is hegemonic in nature (Mouffe 2013:xi). One could say that any determination or naming of the Call is an attempt at colonising the Call. Different Names are given, different consistencies are created in response to the insistence, different orders are created and these orders, consistencies, Names, will be in conflict with each other. The battle between the Names is a battle between worlds, metaphysical systems, and therefore the battle is always a religious and/or political (ideological) battle where the human construction of the worlds is forgotten and the other is seen as the enemy that is out to destroy my reality. Or as Theodor Däubler says, *Der Feind ist unsere eigene Frage als Gestalt* (Mouffe 2013:v).

For example, the grammatisation of #FeesMustFall is opposed by university managements calling for rationality against "raw" emotion which is then also placed into a greater abstraction (discourse) of an economic and epistemic system that is presented as given and therefore as absolute: one cannot argue against the demands of the market, as the market dictates.

Thinking in that sense is colonial, as the Other (Call) is always reduced to the Same (Name) within the totality of some or other abstract idea (a part incarnating the whole). Thinking is an *ergreifen* of the other into a *Begriff*. Thinking is always onto-logical, where the other (*onto*-logy) is reduced to a thing (element) of my world, defined by my logos: onto*logy* (see Badiou 2009:39). The moment you question that, you question my world which can only lead to antagonism.

The insistence becomes for example black pain (a thing) within the world – a world determined by a certain understanding (abstract idea/*logos*) of justice. Or the insistence becomes a thing (irrational emotions, criminal element) within a certain understanding of the economic and epistemic "reality" of the world (*logos*), which is presented as given, unchangeable.

In that sense thinking is colonial, as it always assimilates the other (*onto*) into the world of the same, under the dominant logic of the same (*logos*). Thinking is onto-logy. This is exactly what happened with colonialism when the other was "discovered" – the indigenous people of the colonial lands, who were reduced to being the other of the European, namely determined as the Black Other, but always determined by the White Same. The black other became a thing (*onto*) within the *logic* of the European world (ontology). Thought as determining is colonial, as it colonises the insistence by submitting it to its thought, its logos.

It is important to realise that what one is always dealing with are abstractions and the students themselves are in the process of abstracting (*making* sense via psychic, collective and technical individuation as externalisation) – so this is all about abstracting, making sense, becoming human through making sense and externalising that sense: becoming human, to ex-*text* through externalisation (ex-*text*-ualisation). One could argue that what I am saying is also only a particular abstraction of what it means to be human and not *the* abstraction, but that does not change that abstraction is necessary, but insufficient.

One could choose a different word for abstraction and say that it is about externalising the insistence into a narrative (emplotting into a narrative) through the dual process of *mimesis* and *muthos* (Ricoeur 1984:31–33). By combining Ricoeur, Stiegler and Laruelle (2015) one could argue that the insistence (the Real), the Call on the level of subsistence, is emplotted, abstracted, externalised, cloned (*mimesis*) via a certain *muthos* (philosophical/ideological decision), which in turn is then internalised in the psychic individuation in conversation with the secondary and tertiary retentions (externalisations) of a particular collective.

It is for this reason that I cannot put my name on any statement, not because I necessarily disagree with the contents, or the opinions, but it is not my way of *responding* to the insistence (*the Call*), which has been externalised, cloned, under the name #FeesMustFall. My way or stance I would like to see as far as possible as a stance of non-responding by engaging all these different responses and responses still to come (texts), and using these responses as material *not to think* (non-philosophy) that which seems to be the persistent insistence, which has Called, or which drives or pulls (*Zug*) the various externalisations (clones) such as the #FeesMustFall, but also the *responses* of managements as well as the movement calling for the university to be kept open, but I would rather to try to see thinking in the *light* (or maybe it is the darkness) of the most thought-worthy (das *Bedenklichste*). When I argue for a stance of non-responding, it is not a matter of neutrality, but an attempt *not to try to determine* (Name) that which seems to be a persistent insistence (Call) on the level of subsistence, but rather by non-responding, allowing myself *to be determined* by it, or stated differently, interpreting the various responses as being determined by it, rather than determinations of "it". That is, rather than trying think "it", to determine it, to colonise it, to try and think all responses as being according to "it", and in that sense non-colonial thinking, as in Laruelle's non-philosophy (2012; 2013a; 2013b), by creating a democracy of thought and the agonism that goes with it. Not to try and think what has been abstracted as pain or as being criminal, or as being a just protest, a form of justified violence against systemic violence, or as disruption and with these responses give a singular determination of the insistence, for example the singular determination of the insistence as black pain, which is then further individuated, legitimised, justifying its various expressions and consequences and eventually reified as a dominant discourse, with a similar discourse on the side of management and government that abstracts the insistence as criminal and placing that into a greater narrative of market economy. Non-responding, that is non-determining, is understanding all thought as determined thought, as it tries to think thought as being according to the insistence (the Call), rather than determining, colonising the insistence (Naming). All thought is according to the insistence, as that which Calls-thought-forth, or which through its persistence drives, Calls, Pulls, inspires, and thereby insists on the crafting of various determinations that are now at war (antagonistic) with each other. In other words, not a solidarity with a particular determination of the insistence, which in a sense would then be a solidarity with a particular abstraction (Name) of the insistence, a particular determination of the insistence, but maybe, if it is possible, a stance with the Pull (*Zug*) of the Call, fully conscious that it is impossible, as any form of solidarity would be solidarity with an abstraction of the insistence. In this sense, a Non-Marxist Marxist approach: To acknowledge that it is the insistence on the level of subsistence that determines thought, but without the Marxist determination of that thought. Therefore, Marxism, or dialectical materialism is seen as one possible determination of it, but not *the* determination of it. As Deleuze (1984:152) argues,

[T]he individual distinguishes itself from it, but [this psychic and social preindividual fund] does not distinguish itself, continuing rather to be wedded to that which divorces itself from it. It is the indeterminate, but the indeterminate in so far as it continues to embrace determination, as the ground does the shoe.

Non-responding is not apathy nor non-commitment, but if anything, it would be a radical solidarity with the students rather than a solidarity with my or any other collective determination of the students, or a particular collective's determination of justice. By non-responding I mean *not trying to determine* that which seems to be a persistent insistence on the level of subsistence, but rather non-responding by allowing myself *to be determined* by it. Rather than seeking to think "it" and thereby determine "it", to try and think from "it", according to "it", which is impossible, but thereby understanding all thought as being determined by it, and the differences in thought are then explained via different processes of individuation.

To think all thought as being determined from that which Calls-thought-forth, which through its persistence drives, inspires and insists on the crafting of various determinations via the process of individuation or singularisation. Not a solidarity, not an individuation into a collective of concerned academics or concerned theologians, as such a solidarity is a collective individuation into a group, that has been collected around a particular abstraction (Name) of the insistence, but an attempt to think all these different determinations according to the Call (Pull) of the insistence, or the Call of the Student-in-Flesh (the Call of *was uns denken heisst*), fully conscious that it is impossible to think the Student-in-Flesh, as the Real is foreclosed to thought, although it determines thought in the last instance, as it Calls thought-forth. Naming the Call, the insistence, for example "black pain", is not biological or genetic, but political, as Stiegler argues: individuation is always political (Stiegler 2015a:47). The Call is always already grammatised, as the Body-without-Organs is always already stratified (Deleuze & Guattari 2011:134). A political body is a grammatised body, stratified body, and once stratified, once it is ordered, it is hegemonic in nature and therefore there is war against idioms and spirits,[54] other voices, the other equivalences who are then systematically excluded (systemic violence), marginalized and ostracized: voices are silenced who do not fit the dominant grammatisation. Therefore, the determinations of the pain of the black body is as colonial as the management that criminalises the black body. It is in this context that the question of decolonial thought becomes important. What would decolonial thinking be?

Of course, the subsistence of the different individuations is very different and this difference needs to be heard as there is a clear economic and power imbalance. There is a clear imbalance of power, but that is exactly what I am arguing: the *difference* needs to be heard, not individuated or singularized and eventually grammatised into an abstraction, but *differences need to be heard*. This hearing, must never be stopped or colonized into a singular individuation and/or grammatisation, not even the singular grammatisation of a *celebration of plurality or diversity*.

To try and move beyond these wars, or antagonisms, I have chosen to rather refer to Flesh, in reference to Henry's interpretation of Flesh or Life, and thereby opted not to follow Laruelle (2015) who speaks of in-person, for example, Victim-in-person, fully conscious that I might thereby already give the insistence (the Call) a particular determination by individuating or singularising it as Flesh. In that sense one can argue that any individuation, as abstraction, is counter revolu-

---

[54] Grammatisation is a war waged on spirits [*esprits*] via the technical development (individuation) of systems of tertiary retentions (Stiegler 2014:56).

tionary, at least counter the Marxist revolution, as the Flesh, the material conditions of subsistence, the insistence is not allowed to speak, but only the already idealised material conditions, particular clones, particular individuations or signalisations thereof, are allowed to speak, and in that sense it is still the ones with the means to power who control the labour of individuation, keeping the remainder as the proletariat, depriving them of that labour. As Mouffe argues, it is hegemonic in nature (Mouffe 2013:ix), or stated differently, depriving them of becoming human (noetic souls). It is in this context that I interpret Fanon's (2014) call for the humanisation of all and not just a particular bourgeoisie.

This war is not only a war between the different individuations, for example concerned academics against management, but it is also a war against Flesh, against the Real. As Laruelle argues,

Philosophy is vengeance against the Real because it is vengeance against itself, against what it believes to be the Real and then precisely because it believes itself to be this Real that it wants to repress, so that the Real is not repressible or forgettable, just foreclosed. Philosophy is inseparable from this relationship of self-destruction that moves right into nihilism (Laruelle 2015:33).

This war is the war of the so-called intellectuals, who need their own abstractions to individuate themselves, using the students as their material to justify their abstractions and their battles with other's abstractions. Or as Fanon argues, 'They use the term slavery of their brothers to shame the slave drivers or to provide their oppressors' financial competitors with an ideology of insipid humanitarianism' (Fanon 2004:28). Fanon again cautions intellectuals when he argues, 'The current behaviour of the intellectuals, who on the eve of independence had rallied around the party, is proof that such a rally at the time served no other purpose than to have their share of the independence cake. The party becomes a tool for individual advancement' (Fanon 2004:116). One can argue that not only the party, but the student-in-pain serves as a tool for the collective individuation of the concerned academic, which could also serve her or his individual advancement in the future of academia in South Africa or his or her rating as an academic. The same could be said about this book, but that is exactly my argument, meaning making is individuation into a collective.

Later, Fanon also challenges the heads of state, 'These heads of government are the true traitors of Africa, for they sell their continent to the worst of its enemies: Stupidity' (Fanon 2004:126). The same could be said of the intellectuals who sell the nation to stupidity for not thinking, not thinking *das Bedenklichste*, the most thought-worthy, but being more concerned about their individuation via their noble abstractions which then battle against each other in the halls of academia.

It is an intellectual battle of abstractions (see Laruelle 2015:vii-viii), trying to prove which abstractions are better, or more progressive, more critical, more liberal, forever with the fear of not being progressive enough, or not being politically correct enough, not being critical enough. The students themselves are much less exclusive and therefore much more revolutionary. From the meetings I attended they wanted a radical democracy where different pains could be expressed and not confined or reduced to a singular determination of pain; democracy that allows the various Names of the insistences (Calls) to speak, as each Name individuates differently, without being represented by advocates who control or police the grammatisation, but calling for a radical democracy, or even a democracy of things, or a parliament of things as Latour (1993:142f) argues, where all Names can speak. The campuses are militarized and the students' abstractions are policed by academic abstractions, and thus a moment, a possible event, is destroyed by the power battles between abstractions.

It is the so-called intellectuals who then politicise this pain into black pain so that they, the academics, can individuate, which has more to do with their individual and collective individuation than with the Flesh of the students. This again reminds one of Fanon (Fanon 2004:116) and his critique of colonised intellectuals, and of Laruelle (2015), who speaks of dominant intellectuals, dominating intellectuals who are fighting for their own subsistence survival in the academic jungle.

Therefore, I cannot sign any statement, as then I would be in solidarity with an abstraction of the Student-in-Flesh. I would be in solidarity with a determination and in that sense and that sense alone, complicit in a colonialisation of the student body or the protesting student body.

By signing I would individuate myself as either a concerned academic, progressive academic or concerned theologian. One cannot avoid individuation. To ex-ist, to write, to ex-*text*-ualise, as I am in this book, is to individuate into a collective. Yet, I believe it is a different collective, a non-collective in a certain sense that is collected around a practice of non-philosophy or a practice, as I suggest, of non-colonial thinking as a trans-metaphysical praxis. I do not want to individuate myself within one of these warring collectives, but not because I think there is a better collective. There is no better collective into which I would rather individuate, but I would rather see myself as seeking new weapons, as Deleuze argues (see Stiegler 2015a:5), in response to the control societies (the colonial societies) that seek to control not only individuation but control the desire, who want to determine the Call, by determining the insistence. Fanon does not call for such control, but calls for innovation (2004:239) rather than this control that binds into the terrestrial language of death. In theological terms, I do not want to individuate into the law of one or other grammatisation, which can only bring death, but by grace seek to become collectively human, by creating space for ever more collectives and a radical democracy of collectives, who would then interact agonistically with each other rather than antagonistically.

By signing or endorsing I would be in solidarity with a consistence, whilst my interest lies with the insistence: the Call. I am saying this not as a judgement of abstraction, as all we ever have are abstractions, and we need them, that is all we will ever have to engage with. Therefore, I am thankful for those who do craft statements. It is just not where I can be, but I say that without any value judgement, nor am I calling anyone to follow me, I am not propagating a movement, I do not want anybody to sign up or endorse what I am proposing. No, on the contrary, there is a movement already, and that movement in its various expressions is the only material that one has, and I do not want to add to or subtract from that material, nor do I want to write my own material or rewrite the material differently. I do not want to write nor underwrite any material. My interest is with that which drives the movement, which Calls the movement (thought)-forth, which determines the movement rather than that which the movement has determined.

By changing the direction from determining it, colonising it, to understanding thought as being determined by it, but without thereby trying to determine it in return, but accepting the various determinations as necessary but insufficient, they are all equally called forth.

I do not want to determine what decolonial thought is, I want to practice non-colonial thinking rather than making colonial statements about what decolonisation is or is not, and the only way to do that is to think thinking, that is to use thinking (philosophy) as material to think about thought – the most thought-worthy: *was uns denken heisst*.

It is with this desire to practice non-colonial thinking, a practice that cannot but make use of all the colonial thinking and statements, without accusing the colonial statements of being wrong, or evil or bad, as that would not be non-colonial, but anti-colonial and anti-colonial is no different from colonial, as all there is, are colonial statements, namely determinations of the Call, Names given to the Call. So to offer one more Name, determination, is not transformation, it is just more of the same. The challenge is to realise that all thought is determining. If all thought is determining, that transforms thought as it makes all thought a fiction, an abstraction, an externalisation, ex-*text*-ualisation, something grammatised, externalised, a technics. All thought is a form of *poiēsis*. It is this realisation that opens the door for something different – not a different determination, but a different praxis, which takes all determinations into account as equal fictions (Names given to the Call). Such a praxis I call trans-metaphysical.

As Fanon argues, something different is expected of us, 'Humanity expects other things from us than this grotesque and generally obscene emulation' (Fanon 2004:239) of colonial thought. Indeed, something different is expected of us, not an emulation of modern and colonial thought that is just turned around, but a new thought.

If we want to transform Africa into a new Europe, America into a new Europe, then let us entrust the destinies of our countries to the Europeans. They will do a better job than the best of us. But if we want humanity to take one step forward, if we want to take it to another level than the one where Europe has placed it, then we must innovate, we must be pioneers (Fanon 2004:239).

Fanon ends his book, *The Wretched of the earth* with this call:

For Europe, for ourselves and for humanity, comrades, we must make a new start, develop a new way of thinking, and endeavour to create a new man (Fanon 2004:239).

This takes one back to Nancy's quote earlier in this chapter, the thought that humanity needs to return to the workshop (Nancy 2013:5). I would like to read this in its dual sense, as both how one thinks of humanity and how humanity thinks. I think something of this was explored in this chapter. Therefore, I use all these materials, the various statements from the concerned or progressive academics or theologians, the students, the deans of the theology faculties, not to judge, but to return human thinking to the workshop. The practice of non-colonial thinking is to make use of these colonial and anti-colonial statements, not by judging them, as one could judge only from a colonial point of view, as only those who believe that they can conclusively determine the Call can judge another's thought. Any statement I would craft would be no different and therefore there is no point in judging. But I need to use these materials to explore a praxis that *is* non-colonial and transmodern (see Dussel 2012 & 2013), as such a praxis I believe could facilitate new spaces, create a new humanity, new weapons, with which to open a door to a democracy of things, a parliament of things to come.

Deconstruction and diversity (relativism) the meta-narrative of Global Capitalism

I am fully aware of the danger of calling all the externalisations or clones equal – a democracy of thought. The concerned academics will probably call such a position a sell-out to the status quo, or playing into the hands of the market. As Luc Boltanski and Eve Chiapello argue that such deconstructive critique, or artistic critique, plays into the hands of capitalism (see Latour 2004:231). Yes, indeed relativity, as the result of difference, is what the financial market needs, as it needs continuous differentiation, as these differentiations become the new frontiers for the expansion of the market. Deconstruction and diversity or difference can be interpreted as the new meta-narrative of global capitalism and its need for constant innovation, constantly creating difference, It needs the Other where the other (difference) becomes a market possibility. Differences, the other, are new markets to be exploited or they are seen as a threat to national security and therefore they offer an excellent excuse for more investment in the arms industry, so as to protect the self against the newly created other-as-enemy – be it the terrorist or whatever name is given to the other, the other is seen as the enemy that drives militarization.

By arguing that all thoughts are equal, equally determined by the Call, it does not exclude the fact that certain thoughts (Names) dominate and silence other voices. It is therefore no longer about truth, but about domination and silencing of voices, not because the silenced voices have the truth, but because injustice is interpreted as not giving space or voice to certain voices and therefore no democracy. Now democracy and justice will never be achieved and therefore it is something that always calls one towards more democracy and more justice.

There is, on the level of subsistence, a dominant narrative that to a large degree determines the conditions of subsistence. Deconstructing the various grammatisations might play into the hands of this dominant narrative, because these deconstructions on the level of consistence changes nothing to the conditions of subsistence, and thus offers a good deviation from the conditions of subsistence that need to be addressed.

Yet, demonising it does not really challenge it either, but also plays into its hands, as the cold war is a classic example of. Nothing drives capitalism more than a clear image of the enemy, as the arms race illustrates as well as the new wars, for example the war on terrorism which is what capitalism needs at this moment, when there are no more countries to colonize.

Recognising the democracy of thought, or the equality of all thought, and thereby losing the critical position (alternative determination) from which to judge and condemn the status quo, could be understood as playing into the hands of the status quo or the market. And yet, these so-called critical edges, might develop into lines of flight (Deleuze & Guattari 2011:116) in the rhizome, but they are very quickly assimilated back into the rhizome via the apparatus of capture and the war machines, and thus do not really offer an alternative either. On the contrary, they provide the market with new market opportunities. Thus, something else needs to be found that challenges the rhizome without being re-appropriated by it. A more radical challenge than the battle of abstractions, or the war of grammatisations, is to not seek to determine but to be determined and to think according to the Real rather than engage in the various wars against the Real (Laruelle 2015:33). That would be a true revolution, transformation – not a new thought, but a new thinking as it recognises the rhizome for what it is. Not to stratify the Body without Organs, but to think according to the Body without Organs (Deleuze & Guattari 2009:11), and the various clones are seen for what they are: stratifications, externalisations, and grammatisations on that Body without Organs. I will explore these ideas as an alternative to the war against the Real and the war of abstractions in the next chapter.

3. Thinking as war against the Real as well as war amongst equally determined thoughts, but only via the creation of evil so as to *present* one's truth as salvation.

Such an incarnation of humanity, aggregating its absolute being beyond relation and community, depicts the destiny willed by modern thought. We shall never escape the "unappeasable combat" as long as we remain unable to protect community from this destiny (Nancy 1991:5).

The war of thinking and thus the praxis of non-thought

The previous chapter ended with Laruelle's description of thought (philosophy) as a war against the Real. In a context of such a war against the Real, the temptation is to find another thought, maybe even a peaceful or a peace-loving thought to counter these warring thoughts. The temptation is to find a solution, to find salvation, to find peace in times of war, to find healing in times of pain and wounds, to find answers for all these questions. But what if this temptation is the very "problem" or "mistake" of thought? What if that which is called forth (thought) is always called forth by the desire to be *the* solution, *the* salvation, *the* answer to that which calls it forth? What if thought's problem is that it believes itself to be the remedy, the salvation, the healing, in short it believes itself to be the *pharmakon*? Thought is indeed the medicine (*pharmakon*) and the only medicine that one has and therefore it is absolutely necessary, but what is not thought in thinking is that this medicine is poison as much as it is medicine (see Derrida 1981:99). In other words, it is a characteristic of thought to be *the* response, and as response to be *the* answer: the *pharmakon*, but forgetting that it is *only the response* from which that which called the response forth withdraws and therefore the response is never that which called it forth (see Heidegger 1961:5–6).

Yet, together with thought's desire to be *the* answer, is that although thought is absolutely necessary (one cannot not respond and answer), it is and will always remain insufficient, as that which called the response (answer) forth withdraws from the response (answer). This insufficiency is there because of a gap, a lack, in Lacan's sense (see Stiegler 2015b:98), or stated differently thought remains insufficient because it is determined by différance (Derrida 1982), and because of this différance, that which called thought forth will continue calling, because it is never fully answered in any response. As that which called thought forth withdraws from thought, the thought (response or answer) never *is* or captures that which called it forth. In a sense one can argue that that which called-thought-forth (the Call) dies or rather is murdered in the answer or the response. As thought, language is a *pharmakon* (both gift and *Gift*) (see Derrida 1981:99) and therefore thought is the archive, the tomb, the pyramid of thought, it *believes* itself to capture and preserve the Real (that which called it forth – the Call), but the Real is not *in* that response, it is not captured or embalmed in the tomb, as in the tomb is only a trace or a ghost of the Call which has withdrawn from the response. If the Call was ever fully answered there probably would not be any history as everything would be fixed: finally determined.

This insufficiency of thought (language) brings about a haunting restlessness, as the Call insists to be answered, continually, insistently, persistently calls into the responsibility of responding, answering the Call. New thoughts are continually called forth and they are called forth because of the insufficiency of thought. It is in this pull (the *Zug* of the Call) that thought, and with thought, humanity stands. This *Zug*, Call, is responded to with the belief and by the belief that one is answering and responding adequately, accurately and absolutely. The "Here I am" is filled with the *belief* that one is giving a true and faithful response to the Call. The "Here I am" as the faithful response of a faithful subject (Badiou 2009:47) convinced of its faithfulness to the Call, but which is rather a faithfulness to its belief – faithfulness to its belief (decision) concerning the Call. Was Abraham faithful to the Call or was he faithful to his interpretation of who called him, and his interpretation of the promise? The *Akedah* could be interpreted that the Call once again calls Abraham to sacrifice the Thing in Bataille's (see James 1997) sense – to sacrifice the materialisation of the Call, the Thing that has been made in response to the Call, his son Isaac, so as to remain faithful to the Call and the Call alone.

Could the *Akedah* be such a radical Call away from faithfulness to the Call, to a faithfulness in a belief about the Call?

The response is an effective response because it is filled with the belief that now, at last, it offers the final and correct response in answer to the Call, by taking full responsibility for the Call and believing to offer the perfect remedy: *pharmakon* to finally fix and determine the Call. Every epoch calls for new thought and somebody will rise to the occasion and offer new thoughts and with the new thoughts new paradigms will emerge, often dramatically changing the worlds that are carried out by these new thoughts.

For example, Schleiermacher was frustrated with the contemporary thoughts, especially the thoughts that tried to take up the *respons*ibility to think religion. In his time, there were two dominant responses that took up the responsibility to name and to respond to the Call and were classified (typified) under the strata of religion. Both these options to think religion, namely theoretical thought and practical thought, were unsatisfactory for Schleiermacher. He wanted to suggest that only a completely different kind of thinking can truly *do justice* to the Call to think *das Universum*.[1] He wanted to think religion in completely different terms than theoretical and practical thought, and like with all new thoughts, he had the belief that only his thought (the thought of the faithful subject) could truly do justice to the Call, which was for him the Call of *das Universum*. A third kind of thinking was necessary, besides metaphysics and ethics, or as Schleiermacher refers to metaphysics as *Transzendentalphilosophie* and *Moral* (Schleiermacher 2001:44). Besides these two, metaphysics and ethics (*Moral*), Schleiermacher wanted to present religion as a third way of thinking, responding to *das Universum*, (the Call) which was different from both theoretical and practical thought.

This frustration with thinking has haunted thought, at least Western thought, from the very beginning, and this frustration with or insufficiency of thought has driven the history of thought, it has inspired the paradigm shifts, revolutions and reformations, each time convinced that it is responding more faithfully to the Call than all the previous responses. This frustration is repeated with every epoch as mentioned in the previous chapter. I referred to the frustration that Root, Kearney and Rollins also expressed, with both orthodoxy (metaphysics) as well as the turn towards ethics in liberal theology. Each thinker starts his or her project by expressing their frustration with the previous thoughts and thought-systems and why they are believed to be insufficient. Heidegger (1961) once argued that when reading others' thoughts, one reads them so as to read the un-thought of their work. It is exactly this, to read the un-thought in another's work and thereby identify the insufficiency in their thought. But does identifying the insufficiency (that which they did not think) truly help, or is it part of the game? Identify the un-thought in somebody's thought and you can firstly deconstruct their thought, and secondly build your thought on the basis of the previously un-thought. By knowing that there will be un-thought in any work, this creates the possibility of creating a gap for one's own work, but will it really make a difference? In this book, I argue that such a praxis would be perfectly fine, as long as one is not convinced that thinking

---

[1] Eure Transzendentalphilosophie? sie klassifiziert das Universum und teil es ab in solche Wesen und solche, sie geht den Gründen dessen, was da ist, nach und deduziert die Notwendigkeit des Wirklichen, sie entspinnt aus sich selbst die Realität der Welt und ihre Gesetze. In dieses Gebiet darf sich also die Religion nicht versteigen, sie darf nicht die Tendenz haben, Wesen zu setzen und Naturen zu bestimmen, sich in ein Unendliches von Gründen und Deduktionen zu verlieren, letzte Ursachen aufzusuchen und ewige Wahrheit auszusprechen (Schleiermacher 2001:44).

the un-thought of somebody else's thought, is thinking the truth, or believing that it is a more faithful response to the Call, as it is just thinking differently and that all the different thoughts are equally responses to a Call. The Call is captured by none of the responses, and yet determines them all, in the sense that it calls them all forth, and therefore one can say it determines them in the last instance.

Therefore, I will not try and identify the un-thought in the previous thoughts, but rather offer a praxis of non-thinking, which is not to think the un-thought, nor is it a praxis of anti-thinking, which would be stupidity, and thought has always been at war against stupidity. No, what is offered is a non-thinking, which in a sense is to embrace stupidity, but not the stupidity of not-thinking, but the stupidity of thinking (see Stiegler 2015b). Non-thinking, or non-philosophy or non-theology is to recognise the stupidity of all thinking, or the vanity of all thinking, as each thought or thought-system *believes* itself to be *the* response to the Call. Non-thinking is to think the pharmacological condition of all thought: that thought is always both gift and *Gift* (poison) and that thought therefore is a tomb that houses only a trace haunted by différance, a ghost of that which it speaks about. If thought believes itself to capture the Real or to perfectly respond to the Call, then it is stupid as it forgets that it is only a haunted tomb, with only a ghost of the Call. As Derrida writes, "cinders there are" [*il y a là cendre*] (Derrida 2014:3). There are cinders, ashes, ghosts, because how does one respond to the silent Call? How does one respond, or as Derrida asks it: 'But how can this fatally silent call that speaks before its own voice be made audible?' (Derrida2014:4).

Non-thinking (non-philosophy) is not an attempt to think the Call, or to determine the Call, but is to understand all responses as being equally determined by the Call in the last instance. Non-Philosophy is not the opposite of thought, which could be maybe a form of nihilism, but it is a democracy of all thought and therefore the proposal of a trans-fictional praxis. It is a democracy of thought, not in the nihilistic sense where all thoughts are seen as equally meaningless, nor is it a kind of pluralism where all thoughts are seen as relative, but together they create the bigger picture in the sense that only together does one have a more holistic sense of the Whole or the Real. A democracy of thought where thought is seen as a response to a Call, but where the Call withdraws from the responses, but equally haunts all the responses: there are only cinders there. To try and determine how much of the Call is captured or how little of the Call is captured would once again be just one more response. To argue that all the responses together give a full picture of the Call, would also only be a possible response, and not *the* response. There is no "*the* response", but there are responses and many responses still to come joining the responses of the past and the present, as the cinders pile up.

This book is a response, but it is not a response in the sense of seeking to determine the Call, but like all responses it is determined by the Call and instead of offering a determination of the Call, it offers a haunted description of a

Call-Response praxis in which humanity finds itself in, or into which humanity is drawn by the Call (*Zug*).

The inescapable responsibility to respond, that is to think

Schleiermacher, like many before him and many after him, was called into the responsibility to think. Badiou (2009:51–53) would call such individuals, who are called into responsibility by what he calls the Truth, and that I refer to as the Other-of-past-and-present-thought or the un-thought of past and present thought and thought-systems, faithful-subjects. In the different epochs of the history of thought there have always been these individuals (faithful-subjects) who were called into responsibility by the Call and by their response changed their world. Their world was changed because their response to the Call, their determination of the call, changed the logos and by changing the logos they changed the onto-logos, the ontology of that world (see Badiou 2009:102). As this book does not seek to determine the Call, the Call can be named (determined) different things as it has in the past and the present, for example as the Real or *das Universum* or even as the Multiple, and it always appears as Truth, at least the truth of that particular epoch or the new truth of the new world (the new ontology). But these truths are dependent on faithful subjects who respond by taking up the respon-sibility for this truth (new logos), which will change the clearing (*Lichtung*) and all that appears (ontology) in the *Lichtung,* and thus the world is experienced as changed. Paradigmatic of a faithful-subject in the Western tradition is probably Abraham who was called in his cultural-political-economic and religious world and he faithfully responds, and through his response ushers in a new faith, a new people and the promise of a new land. Is the promise of a new world (new peo-ple and new land) not always *the* possibility of responding faithfully to a Call? It was in his response to the Call that he became the father of a new faith (new religion). The faithful-subject's faithfulness, by faithfully responding to the Call, promises a new world, a new people and a new land. This is the story of Abraham and the promise he received after faithfully responding to the Call. The biblical stories help one to think these responses, or do we (in the Western world – those influenced by the Biblical texts) think this way, because these stories (consciously or unconsciously) are part of the secondary and tertiary retentions with which one makes sense of the world? These texts, the Biblical stories as well as the Greek myths and many other texts, form the tertiary retentions with which meaning is made in the West and those communities influenced by the West.

In the story of Abraham, the Call was determined as the call of the living God of history, but the Call could be determined as many things as well: the Real, *das Universum*, Badiou's Multiple, but it appears as Truth, or it could just be the un-thought other of past and present thoughts – the remnant, or marginalised, or excluded of past and present thoughts that call-out to be thought. Or it could be the pharmacological condition of thought itself, it's insufficiency, which calls thoughts forth, or as Žižek argues, 'the way the subject's own activity is *inscribed into reality*' (Žižek 2009:244 emphasis is mine, see also Meylahn 2016), the way the subject's thinking is in*scrib*ed into, or in*scrib*es reality. In other words, the other or Other or Real or Truth or un-thought, that which is believed to Call, is a consequence of the pharmacological condition of thought, of writing, of the speaking of language. In this sense it could be the Call of différance, the Call or the fate of cinders – the *pharmacological* condition of thinking. What Calls? What Calls thinking forth? All of the above and maybe the reason that there is a Call is to be found in the grammar of thinking, in différance, the pharmacological condition of thinking, the fate of thinking that all there is are cinders. The Call could thus be the haunted call of thinking itself, which ascribes the Call to something, namely that which called thinking forth, but withdrew from thought.

Whatever the reason, history is marked, traced, by the Call.

A Call could be heard as the call of the un-thought or the Other or the ghost of a particular ontology, as that which is excluded or not present in a particular ontology.

In the above paragraphs the faithful response to the Call of the un-thought was discussed, but not everybody who hears the Call responds faithfully.

Badiou identifies three possible responses to the Call, which he determines as Truth, or which appears as Truth, namely responding by recognising the truth (faithful subject), a denial of truth (reactive subject) or an occultation of truth (obscure subject) (Badiou 2009:47). Truth is what Called Badiou in his frustration with contemporary thought. For Badiou, contemporary thought is held by the conviction that there are only language and bodies (Badiou 2009:1) which he describes as democratic materialism. This conviction is insufficient for him, as there is more, there is that which is un-thought by democratic materialism, the other of democratic materialism, the remnant of democratic materialism. This un-thought other is for Badiou Truth.

'There are only bodies and languages, except that there are truths' (Badiou 2009:4). And because there are not only bodies and languages but also Truths, the body-language dialectic of democratic materialism is broken open to give way to Badiou's thought, namely: a materialist dialectic (Badiou 2009:4–5).

In other words, people respond differently to the Call. That which insists in the Call, one could say is the un-thought (other) of previous and contemporary thoughts and thought-systems. To this un-thought, the other, people respond differently, as the un-thought has the tendency to disrupt the previous and contemporary thoughts and thought-systems and thereby bring about paradigm shifts or revolutions. As Badiou argues, true change only happens when the epistemology (the way of thinking) changes, otherwise it would make more sense to speak of modification (Badiou 2009:259). Epistemological change is disruptive and disturbs the status quo, which explains why certain groups and specifically power-groups who benefit from the current ontology, have a lot of interest in either denial of the Call or occultation of the Call.

Badiou argues that for change to happen an exception is required, 'an exception to the laws of ontology as well as to the regulation of logical consequences' (Badiou 2009: 360). An exception to the laws of ontology, in other words something that is other, an exception to the current ontology, this other (the un-thought) insists and disrupts and calls to *respons*ibility. In Levinas' (1981:13) sense it is the Other who calls into responsibility, which is prior to the responsibility to Being. Levinas' ethics, as first philosophy, is to be called into responsibility by the Other, by for example Badiou's Truth which breaks open the Same of democratic materialism and thus ushers in a materialist dialectic.

Schleiermacher, often referred to as the father of modern Western theology, could be seen as such a faithful-subject who responded to what Badiou would call a Truth, but which I will call the Call, and perhaps the Call of the un-thought (other) of his contemporary thought and thought-systems.

In Schleiermacher's response he determines this Call as religion, as the response of the faithful-subject is believed to be a faithful response to that which Calls. Schleiermacher argued that for the un-thought to be thought it needed a different kind of thinking, as metaphysics and ethics excluded, left un-thought, that which called Schleiermacher into responsibility. One could argue that a similar Call called to Rollins and he responded with his mystical turn and maybe also Root who responded with his Christo-praxis, as both experienced the current options of thinking as being insufficient. In other words, the current theologies were insufficient to think that which for them was the Truth in Badiou's terms, and in my terms to think the insisting un-thought of the current metaphysics and ethics that is responding to the Call.

It does not really matter if the faithful-subject is a biologist or a physicist or a mathematician – ever since the call of Abraham there is something religious about responding to the Call. One could say that responding is the task of faith, to *believe* oneself responding faithfully to the Other (the Call) and thus to be faithful to the Truth, to God, or however one determines (Names) the Call. To be a knight of faith is the calling of the faithful-subject. What I am saying is that Badiou's faithful-subject who responds to the un-thought, who responds to the Other (the exception to the current laws of ontology), believes him- or herself to be faithful and therefore her or his response will inevitably be linked to narratives of faithful-subjects, captured for example in the sacred books of religion, as these narratives provide the metaphors with which to think a faithful-response. These sacred narratives are narratives of knights of faith – faithful subjects.

Is that not what Schleiermacher identified, that religion is something other than what was captured by his contemporary thought-systems (metaphysics and *Moral*)? For Schleiermacher, neither metaphysics nor ethics or *Moral*[2] can think religion or the Call, and therefore Religion needs its own kind of thinking. Both theoretical knowledge as well as the turn towards *phronesis* or practical knowledge will not do to think the Call, or think what Schleiermacher named Religion.[3]

A Call is that which calls thought-systems forth. But the faithful subject responds and all one ever have access to are the various responses of faithful subjects, who believe themselves to be faithful to the Call. Such faithful responses are powerful, as they changed worlds, as with each faithful response there was a paradigm shift, or a revolution, or a reformation, and history bears testimony to this and yet nothing ever really changed. Nothing changes, as there is an eternal return, a repetition, as each response is *only* a response to a Call, and all the different responses are equally only responses, which makes them equal but not the same.[4] Deleuze unpacks this repetition in his book, *Difference and Repetition* (1994), when he argues that repetition is 'above all a condition of historical action' (Deleuze 1994:91). Of-course there is change and numerous differences, as there have been tremendous paradigm shifts as well as revolutions, but have these very diverse paradigm shifts and revolutions really brought about change? Marx once argued that repetition is comic 'when instead of leading to metamorphosis and the production of something new, it forms a kind of involution, the opposite of authentic creation' (Deleuze 1994:91). In reference to Nietzsche, Deleuze argues that the eternal return is not a faith, but the truth of faith (Deleuze 1994:95). I will interpret this statement as that the eternal return is not a new religion or a new truth that calls a faithful-subject into responsibility, but it is the truth of all the faithful-subjects who have been called into responsibility by a Call, and who *believed* themselves to be responding faithfully. *Repetition is the truth of faith*, that is, repetition is the truth of the belief that one is responding faithfully to the

---

[2]   Und was tut Eure Moral? Sie entwickelt aus der Natur des Menschen und seines Verhältnisses gegen das Universum ein System von Pflichten, sie gebietet und untersagt Handlungen mit unumschränkter Gewalt. Auch das darf also die Religion nicht wagen, sie darf das Universum nicht brauchen, um Pflichten abzuleiten, sie darf keinen Kodex von Gesetzen enthalten (Schleiermacher 2001:44).

[3]   Die Theoretiker in der Religion, die aufs Wissen über die Natur des Universums und eines höchsten Wesens, dessen Werk es ist, ausgehen, sind Metaphysiker, aber artig genug, auch etwas Moral nicht zu verschmähen. Die Praktiker, denen der Wille Gottes Hauptsache ist, sind Moralisten, aber ein wenig im Stil der Metaphysik. Die Idee des Guten nehmt Ihr und tragt sie in die Metaphysik als Naturgesetz eines unbeschränkten und unbedürftigen Wesen, und die Idee eines Urwesens nehmt Ihr aus der Metaphysik und tragt sie in die Moral, damit dieses grosle Werk nicht anonym bleibe, sondern vor einem so herrlichen Kodex das Bild des Gesetzgebers könne gestochen werden (Schleiermacher 2001:44–45).

[4]   When we say that the eternal return is not the return of the Same, or of the similar or the equal, we mean that it does not presuppose any identity (Deleuze 1994:241).

Call, and that one's response is the Truth of the Call. Stated differently, repetition is the truth of the stupidity of thinking, with thinking's belief that it is the only true remedy (*pharmakon*), response to the Call, and thereby forgetting that the *pharmakon* is also poison; thinking's belief that it is the gift to humanity, forgetting that this gift is also a *Gift*. And the stupidest response would be the belief that one can escape this *truth of faith*, as this faith, this belief is necessary for humanity to be (exist), as to be is to appear, be out there, and such disclosure only happens through appropriation and thus in and through the *Ereignis* of language: ex-*text*.

Whatever the response is, it is no different from all other responses: it is a response, a *pharmakon*, a name, and therefore a tomb, an archive of the Call, with only a ghost of the Call remaining, as that which called withdraws from the Name, response, *pharmakon*. Or as Saint Paul (2 Cor. 3:6) would say, the letter of the law can only bring about death, in contrast to the Spirit which is life. Can one capture the spirit in a letter, a name, a law, or is the letter always only a tomb of the spirit, from which the spirit withdraws? Can one capture a Call in the letter of the response? No, the response is a *pharmakon*. And the *pharmakon* is always gift and *Gift* (poison) (see Derrida 1981:99). It is a gift as it *makes* the Call present in a Name [from which the Call withdraws], and a wonderful gift it is as the Name in turn carries out a new world, a new ontology, in the light of the new Logos (Name), and thereby creates the *Lichtung* and the *Lebensraum* (world) of *Dasein* in *Mitsein*. What a beautiful and tremendous gift. But it is also death as the Logos attempts to capture and bind the Call, but the Call (that which called thinking or the Logos forth) withdraws so that only a ghost is left which haunts the name, or stated differently, the name turns into or turns out to be cinders (see Derrida 2014): the name is an empty sign that points only to itself.

Schleiermacher's religion, Root's Christo-praxis, Rollins' mysticism, or Kearney's *Anatheism* – each tried to think the un-thought of their traditions, but could they escape that which they criticised? No, their responses could not escape what they criticised but only repeated the response in their faithful attempt to respond faithfully: the truth of faith is repetition. In other words, their thought, their response, could not escape being a tomb of the very Spirit that haunted them, a tomb of the Call that called them in the first place. Repetition is the truth of faith, the faith in thinking, the belief that one is responding faithfully, the belief of the faithful-subject. Badiou (2009) would argue that it is not just repetition, but that there is movement – the movement of a materialist dialectic in contrast to dialectical materialism. I would remain with repetition being the truth of this belief, even and especially the belief placed in materialist dialectic. Any thought that seeks to determine the Call, that seeks to faithfully respond to the Call, is a repetition of all previous responses and responses still to come.

For example, Schleiermacher's religion – does it escape the enclosure of metaphysics or the infinite demand of ethics? Even if the ethics is as radically open to the other as in the ethics of Levinas (see Levinas 1969:304), it remains a response which is just another metaphysics or first philosophy.[5] Kearney's hospitality in his *Anatheism* (2010) does not escape being a tomb for the Call, even if it is a hospitable tomb.

Will a new kind of thought solve the problem? Or is thought, as that which is called forth by the most thought-worthy, not always a war against the Real? Or a war against that which called it forth? In that sense, any new thought or thought-system will not really solve the problem as any new metaphysics or new ethics, even radical ethics of the Other, or postmetaphysics, still only responds to that which calls it forth, and thus is never new but only one more response, one more repetition, a turn of the wheel.

Any new thought, a new metaphysics or a new ethics, is never truly new but only repeats the cycle, which is a cycle of a war against the Real that ends in dead ends, which is death. It is the death of terrestrial writing, as Derrida argues, cinders there are, there are cinders there (Derrida 2014:13).

Transzendentalphilosophie or metaphysics or philosophy or theology or ethics wages this war against the Call; wages a war against the Body without Organs, stratifying and etching into and onto this body the various strata of differentiation and classification, but never reaching the Body without Organs.

You never reach the Body without Organs, you can't reach it, you are forever attaining it, it is a limit. People ask, So what is this BwO? – But you're already on it, scurrying like a vermin, groping like a blind person, or running like a lunatic: desert traveller and nomad of the steppes. On it we sleep, live our waking lives, fight – fight and are fought – seek our place, experience untold happiness and fabulous defeats; on it we penetrate and are penetrated; on it we love (Deleuze & Guattari 2011:150).

In the previous chapters, I have already introduced the thoughts of Laruelle and his non-philosophy, I believe that what is necessary is not a new thought nor a new way of thinking, as any new thought or new way of thinking will always be a response (repetition) to that which calls-thought-forth. Laruelle's non-philosophy might help, not in responding to the Call, but thinking this truth of responding, without offering any faith in believing its response to be the true and faithful response to the Call, as it is not a response to the Call. The Call is not its matter that it responds to, but thinking is its matter or material (science of thought, a science of philosophy), as it tries to think thinking, responding to Heidegger's call to think thinking, to think this truth: repetition.

To think non-philosophically is not to try and determine that which Calls. It is therefore not a response to a Call, and therefore it is without the faith in

5   … metaphysics, transcendence, the welcoming of the Other by the same, of the Other by me,
      is concretely produced as the calling into question of the same by the Other, that is, as the ethics
      that accomplishes the critical essence of knowledge (Levinas 1969:43).

the principle of sufficient philosophy, or the principle of sufficient psychology or sufficient theology. In a certain sense it is without faith, that is, without the belief in its faithfulness to the Call. In its faithlessness, in its atheism (non-belief) in the responses, it is perhaps faithful to the Call, faithful to the withdrawal of the Call, which is the *Zug* which calls, the *Zug* in which humanity stands as metaphysical beings.

The thinkers that have accompanied this journey, as examples Root, Rollins, Kearney and in this chapter Schleiermacher, tried to faithfully respond to the Call in the realisation that the traditions in which they stand were insufficient in responding to the Call. The traditions can be divided into two broad traditions, one that focusses on practical knowledge and the other on theoretical knowledge, or they can be divided into orthodoxy and orthopraxis.

In other words, the frustration is with both orthodoxy and orthopraxis, both theory and practice as the two ways in which the Call (*das Universum*) was determined by thought in the past. Schleiermacher argued that these two paths of thinking the Religious are unsatisfactory (insufficient), and he tried to develop a third way, to think that which affects us, to think that which Calls us, and thus the repetition continues. One cannot move beyond this repetition, as any response to the Call wages a war against the Real, trying to determine the Call, trying to capture the Call *um das Universum in ein Begriff zu begreifen*.

Theology would in this sense be a war against God or a sin against God, in that it names and seeks to determine God, which is what Rollins tried to avoid, but he tried to faithfully avoid it as a faithful-subject and thus repeated the truth of such faith, which is repetition. To move beyond repetition, if one would want to do that, one would need to avoid the faith in thinking as the truth of that faith will always be repetition. To avoid faith in thinking would be folly, and folly – the holy folly of the salos (holy fools) (see Meylahn 2013: 321ff) for example – might be an interesting option for individuals, but certainly not a political option for a community or a collective, as such a denial of the faith in thinking (existence as ex-*text*-ualisation) would make the political[6] (collective *Lebensraum,* collective ex-*text*-ualisation) impossible.

---

[6] When I refer to the political I am using this term as does Nancy (1991: x) and Mouffe where "the political" (*le politique*) is interpreted as the site where what it means to be in common is open to definition and "politics" (*la politique*) is the play of forces and interests engaged in a conflict over the representation and governance of social existence (Nancy 1991:x). Mouffe follows a similar argument, when she argues, 'The political refers to this dimension of antagonism which can take many forms and can emerge in diverse social relations. It is a dimension that can never be eradicated. 'Politics', on the other hand, refers to the ensemble of practices, discourses and institutions that seeks to establish a certain order and to organize human coexistence in conditions which are always potentially conflicting, since they are affected by the dimension of the 'political' (Mouffe 2013:2–3).

The inescapable responsibility to think and what is not thought when thinking

One is called to think, one is called to respond to the Call. Often that which calls is the un-thought (other) of previous and current thoughts and thought-systems, the exceptions or exclusions of current ontologies, which through their persistent insistence puzzle and/or disrupt and thereby Call for new thoughts, by calling for a new, different or alternative ontology. In a sense one could say that it is a call for justice. The un-thought, the other, is not included in the past and present ontologies and therefore insists and calls, calls for justice, that is, calls to be included in a new ontology that will include the un-thought, include the other and therefore will be more just than the previous ontology. Yet, as that which calls-thought-forth withdraws from thought, there will always be a new un-thought, a new other, a new excluded, a new other that is unthought. Maybe in a sense of the poor will always be amongst you (John 12:8). Therefore, it cannot be the un-thought, the excluded, the other, the poor of thought-systems that guide the thinking of thinking, as they will only drive the repetition, but the generic victim of thinking needs to be thought, which is the Call itself. It is the Call that is the victim of thinking, as thinking wages a war against it. This idea will be further explored in the next chapter, where Christ, the incarnate, offers a story with which to interpret the generic victim of thought-systems as: political-systems, or religious-systems, or ideological-systems.

Thus, one is called to think by the un-thought, but there is something that remains un-thought in this response to the un-thought, and what is not thought is thinking itself (see Heidegger 1961). In *Was heisst Denken* there are two thought paths Heidegger explores: that which calls thought-forth, but also to think what thinking itself is, as he argues *Das Bedenklichste in unserer bedenklichen Zeit ist, daß wir noch nicht denken* (Heidegger 1961:3). The most thought-worthy of this time is that one is not thinking. If one is not thinking, what is one doing? One is responding, in the belief that one is thinking the Call. All these different thoughts and thought-systems are responses, but is one thinking? Repetition is the truth of faith, the faith in thinking, but has this truth of faith in thinking been thought? Indeed, it has. Nietzsche thought it, Deleuze thought it, and so this truth of faith in thinking has been thought.

They tried to think the most thought-worthy, namely not only that which calls-thought-forth, but what thinking itself is: *was heisst Denken*? Thinking is responding, but there is an inherent stupidity in thinking and that is that it forgets that it is responding when it believes that it is thinking. This stupidity is the faith in thinking, the truth of which is repetition.

To illustrate this, I turn once more to Schleiermacher. Schleiermacher was frustrated with the two thought-paths, metaphysics and ethics, and therefore wanted to think about the possibility of another type of thought with which to re-spond to that which affects one (*was ein angeht*), that which calls not only thought but the self through thinking forth.

In other words, he realised that metaphysics and ethics, or theoretical thinking and practical thinking, are not really thinking, at least they are not thinking the most thought-worthy.

He tries to explain this by arguing that practical thought works with an idea of the ethical or the good and this good is carried into metaphysics as it is seen as a natural law or the way things are, or the way things should be according to "law" of nature.[7] Between metaphysics and ethics there is no real difference as they merge into each other. One can follow Schleiermacher's thoughts if one takes a contemporary example into consideration. For example, the idea of uni-versal human rights, an ethical argument, but as these rights are *believed* to be essential and natural to humanity and therefore universal, it becomes a metaphys-ical argument. It does not matter if one starts from praxis or from theory. Thought believes that it has captured something essential, it *believes* that it has responded faithfully (by implication truthfully), and therefore believes itself to be the true presentation (representation) of what is, and in that sense one can clearly see how human constructions are reified, whereby the human authorship is forgotten. In the previous chapter this was believed to be the role of religion as part of the so-cial construction of realities, when social constructed realities are legitimised and reified to such an extent that the human authorship is forgotten, based on the belief that one is responding faithfully. That final reification of the social construction – is that not already present in the very initial response to the Call? Is that *faith* in thinking not always already present in thinking: the faith that believes that thought responds faithfully to the Call? The faith that thought is a true reflection of what *is*. The faith that the I think *is* the I am. The faith that "my" flesh *is* my body. This faith is the very condition of being, of *Dasein*, of existence (ex-*text*-ence).

Back to the idea of universal human rights, which is a rather recent and local (Western) social construction (see Meylahn 2016b) and yet it is *believed* to be essential to humanity and therefore universal. In the name of the ethics of human rights (the belief that one is struggling for justice in the name of human rights), is a struggle that believes itself to be thinking (faithfully representing the "rights" or essence of individuals or groups), whilst "in truth" it is responding, and the response becomes solidified, reified, so much so that if forgets (does not think) that it is a response, but rather *believes* that its thought is the way things truly are, or the way things should be and therefore a fight for human rights becomes a

---

[7]   Die Idee des Guten nehmt Ihr und tragt sie in die Metaphysik als Naturgesetz eines unbeschränk-ten und unbedürftigen Wesens, und die Idee eines Urwesens nehmt Ihr aus der Metaphysik und tragt sie in die Moral, damit dieses Große Werk nicht anonym bleibe, sondern vor einem so her-rlichen Kodex das Bild des Gesetzgebers könne gestochen werden (Schleiermacher 2001:45).

fight for Truth. Thought believes that it has captured the essence, the truth of the
Real, faithfully responding to the Call, and it needs to believe this in order for it
to be the thought (the Logos) that carries out a *Lebensraum*, a world in which to
exist (ex-*text*) in. The fight for justice, in the sense of fighting for the un-thought,
or for those excluded from paradigms of thoughts, from ontologies, is based on
the belief of responding faithfully or more faithfully than the previous systems of
thought.

Yet, as with all thought there remains the un-thought, even if one believes
oneself to be thinking the un-thought, as there is the un-thought of the un-thought.

To use the example of human rights as Western rights, Graham argues concerning any universal view of humanity, 'Any common discourse of a homogeneous universal human nature is attacked as effectively muting and silencing the
experiences of those whom the Enlightenment subject as male, white, rational renders 'Other': not only women, but people of colour, dominated by neo-colonialism
and racism' (Graham 1996:25). In other words, whoever responds to the Call in
the belief that their response captures the true essence of humanity, responds from
within their embodiment (primary, secondary and tertiary retentions and protentions) and thus that embodiment becomes the truth, or the norm, whilst "essential
human nature" withdraws from that thought.

This quote from Graham highlights another aspect of thought that has not
yet been touched on, namely the question: who thinks and thereby determines
the Call, determines the Real, determines the Truth? To be human is to respond
(noetic soul), to exist is to respond (ex-*text*-ence). All thoughts are equal, as they
are equally responses, but not all are equal in the sense of the weight or the authority they hold over the collective *Lebensraum*. In other words, although all thoughts
are equal, there is an inequality of thoughts with regards to which thoughts have
the power to determine and thereby to carry out the shared world. I will come back
to the role of power and inequality in the next sections, but will continue to focus
in this section on what is not thought, which of-course has to do with power and
the embodiment of who is thinking. There are different responses to the Call, as
Badiou, as mentioned above, pointed out. The who and the how of the response
has a lot to do with power, which in turn has to do with embodiment. Who has
the power to determine how to respond, and who determines what the correct response is? There are different responses, Badiou argues: one can respond either as
faithful-subject or as a reactive subject or obscure subject (Badiou 2009:47). One
needs power to respond as faithful subject and likewise the responses of reactive
and obscure subjects is also related to power. The faithful subject often finds her-
or himself in the role of the prophet, the one who ushers in paradigm shifts, revolutions or reformations. This role of responding as faithful subject would not be
possible without some form of power, the power of education for example. The

reactive and obscure subjects in turn protect current power constellations, in other words, protect the current legitimisations and institutions of the dominant truth.

Power is linked to thinking (responding) in all three of Badiou's possible responses. Power determines what is thought, and thereby it determines what is not thought, as it determines when and how the un-thought can be thought. It was Foucault who helped one recognise the role of power in thinking and that the thinking space, the *Lebensraum* for existence (ex-*text*-ualisation) is not neutral and equal, but is riddled with power imbalances and unequal thoughts, unequal responses, where some responses are systematically silenced, resisted or obscured.

It is in such a context of unequal thoughts, unequal responses that the Call is often experienced as a call for justice, or even a call for Truth, but even such a call for justice is a call of power: relative power.

There is a double un-thought: firstly, the remnant, the un-thought, the other of what is thought, that which is not thought, or which is repressed or obscured. The un-thought in this understanding is what drives history and paradigm shifts, as each generation of thinkers (responders), faithful-subjects, believes themselves to hear the Call of the previously un-thought and they believe themselves to be faithfully responding to the previously un-thought. The un-thought in this sense is believed to be thought eventually, or there is the hope in the belief that it will be thought eventually. The truth of this belief is repetition and the eternal return, the eternal response.

There is another un-thought, not as remnant or excess, but it is *not thought* as it escapes the belief of thinking completely, and that is that thought *is a response* to a Call whilst the Call withdraws from the response. What is forgotten in that it is never thought, is that thinking *is* a response to that which called it forth, whilst that which called it forth withdraws from the response, leaving not a remnant or an excess un-responded to (un-thought), but by withdrawing from thought, leaving thought empty. Thought is an empty tomb with only the ghosts, traces of that which called, echoing in it or haunting it. The first un-thought could become the occasion to think the not-thought. Stated differently, the particular un-thought (remnant or excess of thought) could become the occasion to think the generic un-thought or the not thought of thinking.

This forgetfulness of that which is not-thought is the most thought-worthy (*Bedenklichste*), yet it is this most thought-worthy that calls thinking forth. For example, Schleiermacher's thought was called forth by the previously un-thought, namely the un-thought of metaphysics and ethics and he *responds* by thinking the previously un-thought in terms of religion. But this still leaves one with what is not thought in his response and that is that his response is a response from which the Called withdrew.

If one takes Schleiermacher as an example and return to what I shortly discussed in the previous chapter with the ideas of Religion$_1$ and Religion$_2$, one could interpret Schleiermacher saying that Religion$_1$ is the Call and it calls Religion$_2$ forth as either metaphysics (*Transzendentalphilosophie*) or Ethics (*Moral*). Yet, Religion$_2$ was unsatisfactory for Schleiermacher as it left what he felt religion "truly" is, un-thought.

This meant that for Schleiermacher there must be something more. He believed to be thinking that which is more, by determining it as the binding principle that allows for this mixture of metaphysics and ethics (see Schleiermacher 2001:45). For him it is an *anziehende Kraft*, which I refer to as Call, which he determines as Religion, which for him is the highest, because philosophy, metaphysics and ethics, are subordinate to Religion (see Schleiermacher 2001:45), as they are called-forth by this Call – *anziehende Kraft*.

Schleiermacher argues that there is a parallelism between metaphysics and ethics or theoretical knowledge and practical knowledge, and to acknowledge this and to seek to show this is for him religion (Schleiermacher 2001:46). Both these two thought systems are called forth by that which is the most thought-worthy, both are called-forth by the Call. In response to this Call the highest philosophy is developed and the greatest metaphysics and the profoundest ethics, but even with all these thoughts, one would still be on the path towards the Call, towards religion in Schleiermacher's[8] sense. It would be the task of what he names Religion, the Call, to liberate from Religion$_2$ (see Schleiermacher 2001:47).

The un-thought, or the insufficiency of the current thought, is the occasion for the Call to be heard. Critical thought always deconstructs past and present thought-systems in the Name of the Call (in the Name of the un-thought of previous thought-systems), but it repeats the "mistake" by responding faithfully to that Call and thereby determining the Call, not thinking that the Call withdraws from the response, leaving the response empty.

One cannot escape thought, therefore non-thought or non-philosophy is not a denial of philosophy or of thought, as thought is essential in the process of individuation of an individual within a collective. There is no *Dasein* without thought, there is no world without thought, and therefore non-philosophy does not deny thought, nor does it deny the importance of thought. It highlights the un-thought, that which is forgotten in that it is not thought, which is not a fault

---

[8]   Aber ich denke, Ihr sucht, von diesen Bedürfnissen getrieben, schon seit einiger Zeit nach einer höchsten Philosophie, in der sich diese beiden Gattungen vereinigen, und seid immer auf dem Sprunge sie zu finden, und so nahe läge dieser die Religion! Und die Philosophie müßte wirklich zu ihr flüchten, wie die Gegner derselben so gern behaupten? Gebt wohl Achtung, was Ihr da sagt. Mit allem dem bekommt Ihr entweder eine Religion, die weit über der Philosophie steht, so wie diese sich gegenwärtig befindet, oder Ihr müßt so ehrlich sein, den beiden Teilen derselben weiterzugeben, was ihnen gehört, und zu bekennen, daß, was die Religion betrifft, Ihr noch nichts von ihr wißt. Ich will Euch zu dem ersten nicht anhalten, denn ich will keinen Platz besetzen, den ich nicht behaupten könnte, aber zu dem letzten werdet Ihr Euch wohl verstehen (Schleiermacher 2001:46).

of thinking, but the way of thinking. There is always the un-thought, which calls
new thought forth, but then there is the not-thought of what thinking is, namely
that thinking does not think itself, but always is an attempt to think (determine)
the other (the previously un-thought). This stupidity (forgetfulness, or that which
is not thought) needs to be thought, but for that to happen thought needs to be
thought, as that which believes to be able to determine that which called it forth.

Thinking as a war against stupidity, forgetting the stupidity of war and the role of this war in individuation of individuals within a *polis*

Ever since the Enlightenment, thinking (reason) has been seen as a war against
stupidity in the name of forming a *mündige* (mature or majority) public which
was the necessary basis of sovereign politics (see Stiegler 2015b:2). The task to
form, to educate a *mündige* (mature or majority) public was given to education
(schools and universities). Schools and universities were given the task to form
mündige subjects, which was the necessary basis for a sovereign republic, where
people govern themselves through reason. For Kant, *Mündigkeit*, human reason, is
formed only through humans emerging (being liberated) from *Unmündigkeit*, that
is, to emerge from 'the inability to use one's own understanding without the guid-
ance of another' (Stiegler 2015b:3). To become a noetic soul one needs to struggle against 'unreason [*déraison*] that manifests itself in many forms – between
stupidity [*bêtise*] and madness [*folie*]' (Stiegler 2015b:17). In the context of the
above, the calling of reason is to think the un-thought of the previous generation
and thereby to conquer the "stupidity" of the previous generation. The movement
from *Unmündigkeit* to *Mündigkeit* for Kant is a conquest, a conquest in the name
of the *Aufklärung* against stupidity (see Stiegler 2015b:3). In this struggle against
stupidity of previous generations through education, independent thinking individuals who respond faithfully to the previously un-thought are individuated into
a community, an enlightened collective, namely to become for example citizens
of the modern secular Enlightened city. It is a war against stupidity (un-thought)
of the previous generations, but what is forgotten, in that it is not-thought, is the
stupidity of this belief, the truth of this faith, which is that stupidity is repeated.
That stupidity is repeated, is not thought, but as Stiegler argues, there is also a
return of stupidity at the end of Western Enlightenment. This return of stupidity
might become an occasion to think the stupidity of repetition.

There is a return of stupidity in the sense that there is a return to *Unmündigkeit*
(minority) through the conservative revolution in the West, which inverted the Enlightenment goals and which includes rationalization or reification as Adorno and
Horkheimer (see Stiegler 2015b:44) refer to it, and with it the 'extension of stupidity, which is also to say one of submission, infantilization and regression to
minority' (Stiegler 2015b:23). Or as Adorno and Horkheimer argue, that human-

ity, instead of entering the truly human state of being a noetic soul are sinking into a new kind of barbarism (Adorno & Horkheimer 2002:xiv). This barbarism, the infantilization and regression to a minority, is the result of rationalization (reification), which is the characteristic of capitalist becoming according to Weber, and thus knowledge becomes stupidity (Stiegler 2015b:17). Knowledge becomes stupidity, or has it always been stupid? There are different interpretations and descriptions of stupidity. There is the stupidity of not-thinking, not-thinking for oneself, which was believed to be the state of humanity prior to the *Aufklärung* and which seems to be the state that humanity in the West is returning to, and then there is the stupidity of not thinking thinking. I will return in a moment to the stupidity of thinking as such, the faith of thinking. The not-thinking for oneself, to return to being a minority, is interpreted as being the result of rationalization, where the noetic powers necessary for individuation, have passed into the hands of the market. The market controls the cultural artefacts, the secondary and tertiary retentions and protentions, and thereby determines what people are to think. This is what Polanyi refers to as the 'self-regulating market' or what Gramsci described as cultural hegemony that de-forms reason (see Stiegler 2015b:17). This reminds me of Heidegger, who argued that with machination and the focus on lived-experience, the truth of the modern Being is revealed (see Meylahn 2013:43ff). Machination, based on the idea that the world can be objectively explored and discovered and thereby manipulated, is echoed in lived experience, as the modern lived experience is the experience of an objective world (see Livingston 2003:331). In such a state the role of thinking is completely forgotten, as thought is believed to be a transparent medium. This lived experience of the forgetting of the role of thought is very close to the non-thinking of thought. Thus, this epoch becomes an ideal occasion to think what is not-thought in thinking. Likewise, with the return of stupidity, it might be a good occasion to think the stupidity of thinking.

From the above paragraphs, three forms of stupidity or non-thinking can be identified. Firstly, the previously un-thought that calls thought forth, together with subjects not-thinking-for themselves, in other words that which called the Enlightenment as war against stupidity forth; secondly, the un-thought as a result of commercialisation, what Stiegler calls symbolic misery (Stiegler 2014:10); and thirdly, the stupidity (non-thinking) of thinking itself, as it believes (has faith) that thought could be the cure, the *pharmakon*, for stupidity. Similar to Laclau's (2014:17–18) ideological dialectic as incarnation and deformation, reason forms and deforms itself (Stiegler 2015b:17). It is the 'pharmakon of writing that produces a state of *bêtise* as much as of stupidity' (Stiegler 2015b:31), as stupidity is tied to the externalization (ex-*text*-ualisation) of thinking humanity.

Ronell Avital (2002:5) argues that 'stupidity does not allow itself to be opposed to knowledge in any simple way, nor is it the other of thought'. Knowledge cannot be separated from stupidity, as these two are not opposites, but stupidity is part of the war against stupidity, it is the characteristic of ex-*text*-ualisation, as it is the condition of the *pharmakon*. Stupidity is the transcendental structure of thinking (Stiegler 2015b:49). It is a pharmacological situation as stupidity is the law of the *pharmakon* and the *pharmakon* is the law of knowledge (Stiegler 2015b:33). Thus, if there is a war that needs to be won against stupidity it is not in the name of reason or in the name of knowledge, but by thinking thinking (*was heisst Denken*), in other words, thinking the pharmacological situation, or as Stiegler argues, to practice positive pharmacology, or what I call *poiēsis.* Not to be a knight of faith, as a knight of faith (faithful subject) only repeats, but to be a poet of faith, as Deleuze (1994:95) argues in reference to Kierkegaard. A poet of faith, faithfully responding as poet and not as knight, by being fully aware of one's poetry, in other words, not believing poetry to be anything more than poetry, that is literature.

The pharmacological situation, or ex-*text*-ualisation, which is the law of knowledge and thus the law of stupidity is linked to individuation. As argued in the previous chapters, individuation is externalization (ex-*text*-ualisation). In other words, individuation is the pharmacological situation. Or as Deleuze (1994:152) argues:

Stupidity is neither the ground nor the individual, but rather this relation in which individuation brings to ground to the surface without being able to give it form (this ground rises by means of the I, penetrating deeply into the possibility of thought and constituting the unrecognized in every recognition). All determinations become bad and cruel when they are grasped only by a thought which invents and contemplates them, flayed and separated from their living form, adrift upon this barren ground. Everything becomes violence on this passive ground. Everything becomes attack on this digestive ground. Here the Sabbath of stupidity and malevolence takes place. Perhaps this is the origin of that melancholy which weighs upon the most beautiful human faces: the presentiment of a hideousness peculiar to the human face, of a rising tide of stupidity, an evil deformity or a thought governed by madness.

Thought as war against the Other in the name of the Other, but absolutely necessary for *Dasein* in a particular *Mitsein*

Psychic individuation and social individuation are intertwined as the one can never happen without the other (see Stiegler 2015b:54). The individual responds to the Call with the 'Here I am' in which the I is individuated *in* the response, but the response is always a response from out of a specific embodiment, namely the primary, secondary and tertiary retentions and protentions of the specific context in which the I find herself or himself.

Stiegler (2015b:105–120), giving a poststructuralist reading of Hegel's *Phenomenology of Spirit*, explores the link between psychic individuation and social individuation and how the 'Here I am' is socially embodied so much so that the enunciation, 'Here I am', is a reading[9] – one could say a reading of his or her embodiment. That the enunciation is a reading has to do with the secondary and tertiary retentions and protentions that the me, who becomes an I, and as I, is embodied in.

That this reading is a pro-duction, that is, a kind of writing, and not just a reception is due to the fact that any true reading (passing to the act of reading) is a selection from among the *primary* retentions (what I retain in what I read) operating according to those criteria that *secondary* retentions constitute for the reader, that is, according to memories that are themselves woven together as *this* reader, and not as another (Stiegler 2015b:113).

Thus the 'Here I am' in response to God or 'Here I am' in response to Physical Reality or 'Here I am' in response to the Absolute Spirit, depends on the secondary and tertiary retentions and protentions of the me that responds in becoming an I. This individuation of the individual psyche together with the social is what was called understanding (Stiegler 2015b:54): the creation of meaning and the making of sense. Stiegler speaks of a transindividual situation as the creation of meaning.[10]

To hear the Call is to experience dissatisfaction as a modality of incompleteness, to experience a lack, just as Schleiermacher experienced dissatisfaction with the two forms of thinking religion (metaphysics and ethics). Any thinker who has presented his or her "new thought" individuates into that new thought as an individual (faithful-subject), together with the new school of thought that is founded (social individuation) on these new ideas. Thereby thought is transformed, and with thought the social-political and even the economy can be transformed as a "new" world is carried out. The "new" thought shines a "new" light (*Lichtung*), a clearing in which a "new" world appears.

The process of individuation into a collective happens via the identification of the other, either the other as the previously un-thought, or the other as the enemy in the sense of those who do not recognise this "truth", in Badiou's sense the obscure or resistant subjects. It is in hearing the call of the other (the previously un-thought) that one individuates oneself into a collective ("church" of the faithful-subjects) against those who are obscure or resistant subjects concerning this "truth" or this Call. Keeping in mind that the hearing of the Call is a reading

---

[9] The substance is still enclosed here in the predicative form of proposition, such that it lies outside of this subject of the enunciation who is the reader of the statement, who does not know (not yet) that he or she becomes the subject of the enunciation by reading – that is to pass in actually to the act of reading is to become the author of that which is read (Stiegler 2015b:113).

[10] … the transindividual presupposes artefacts technical objects, which are also object-images that must be understood as hypomnesic supports, *hypomnemta, pharmaka* and everything that Derrida analysed as *supplementarity* in that history of the supplement… (Stiegler 2015b:54–55).

(production or naming) of the Call, which is dependent on the primary, secondary and tertiary retentions into which one is embodied.

One can say that the process of individuation, as it is always a process of individuation into a particular collective, is a political process. This was discussed in the previous chapter in conversation with the thoughts of Laclau, but also as Charl Schmitt argues that such an individuation into a collective (*polis*) is only possible via the clear identification of the enemy, as the figure of the enemy is the condition of the political as such (see Derrida 2005:67).

... for Schmitt, it is indeed nothing more and nothing less that the political as such which would no longer exist without the figure of the enemy and without the determined possibility of an actual war. Losing the enemy would simply be the loss of the political itself (Derrida 2005:84).

An enemy (an identifiable other) is necessary to establish the identity of a group or an institution or a *polis*. Mouffe (2013:5) argues that one needs to understand that 'every identity is relational and that the affirmation of a difference is a precondition for the existence of any identity – i.e. the perception of something 'other' which constitutes its 'exterior'. We can understand why politics, which always deals with collective identities, is about the constitution of a 'we' which requires as its very condition of possibility the demarcation of a 'they'".

Stiegler continues this thought by arguing that the entry into the political sphere (the *polis*) coincides with an exit from war – *polemos* (Stiegler 2015b:86), in other words, that those who live together have overcome their differences perhaps by identifying a common difference (other-enemy).

Both are necessary: a clearly defined other (enemy) as well as an exit from *polemos*, and maybe the one is the condition of the other. The individuals need to ignore their individual differences to become a collective, but to become a collective a common good (*theos*) needs to be found or a common enemy needs to be identified. It is through the common good or enemy that the individual differences become relative enough to form a community.

Some would argue that one is living in a "civilised" world and openly declaring civil war is something of the past (although there has been a lot of talk of war lately). In the "civilised" liberal West open displays of power and military aggression is frowned upon, and therefore more subtle forms of power and coercion needed to be found, or more powerful images to demonise the enemy as terrorist for example.

In later sections I will discuss the discreet or not so discreet use of power to control society and establish political identities. The polis, the political,[11] that

---

[11] I use the term political as Mouffe (2013:2–3) does in comparison to politics. 'The political refers to this dimension of antagonism which can take many forms and can emerge in diverse social relations. It is a dimension that can never be eradicated. 'Politics', on the other hand, refers to

needs war to be established needs to find a different form of power and war that is not so blatantly obvious, and thus sooth the liberal conscience. The war has never stopped in liberal democracies. Only the weapons have changed, as war becomes logical disputation and the weapons become those of the law (Stiegler 2015b:86), the laws of the market, for example.

The university in South Africa today has become a contested space and there is a war fighting for this space, as it is a battle for the *soul [essential truth] of the university*. All these different statements that are calling for endorsements, petitions calling for signatures, in a sense they are are a call for decisionism and as Derrida says, 'decisionism, as we know, is the theory of the enemy' (Derrida 2005:67). The battle lines have been drawn, and every academic of the university must decide on which side they stand in this fight for the soul of the university. Every member of staff and every student must decide, are you with us or against us – one cannot get more modern than that.

The space for individuation, for responding, is a space riddled with power dynamics

It is a war, and wars are about power. The question thus is, Who has the power to grammatise this space, whoever wins will have the power to determine the space into a singular determination, even if that singular determination includes the plural, multiple and diverse, and therefore it is a battle for the presumed *singular* soul of the university. Who has and who will in future colonise the university? But colonized the university will remain, unless thinking moves beyond such antagonisms and the division into friend and enemy, or good and evil, towards a truly non-colonial thought. As the battle lines are currently drawn, the movement is not about decolonisation, but is rather a matter of re-colonisation and who the coloniser will be.

Who has the power to colonise spaces, who has the power to determine the Call, determine the Real, determine what the Good is, who God is, who has the power to say what Religion is?

Michel Foucault (1965; 1973; 1979; 1980), a French intellectual who regarded himself as an "historian of systems of thought," tried to think thought. He thought thinking in relation to the role of power in thinking. He traced the role of power in these cultural, political and historical practices of thinking, or the praxis of *Dasein* (ex-*text*-ualisation) in a world where the things of the world are objectified and so also the other humans of that world are objectified, and thereby all is subjugated under the dominant logos, which carries out that particular world. If the world is

---

the ensemble of practices, discourses and institutions that seeks to establish a certain order and to organize human coexistence in conditions which are always potentially conflicting, since they are affected by the dimension of the 'political".

carried out by a particular logos depending on who has the power to determine the logos, they will be in a position to determine the ontological place of each thing and each person within the ontology of that world. In Laclau's (2014:18f) sense, who has the power to identify which equivalence will incarnate the whole? Whoever has the power will also determine what remains un-thought and to what extent the Call to think the un-thought is resisted or obscured.

For Foucault, language is an instrument of power, and people have power in a society in direct proportion to their ability to participate in the various discourses that shape that society, the dominant discourses that determine the Call and by determining the Call, determine the world that is carried out by that *determined-Call*. In other words, there is an inseparable link between knowledge and power: 'the discourses of a society determine what knowledge is held to be true, right, or proper in that society, so those who control the discourse control knowledge' (Freedman & Combs 1996:38). Who or what decides which knowledge is true, right and proper? Or how is this decided? Who decides which equivalence (floating signifier) incarnates the whole, who decides which fiction will be chosen as *the* determination of the Real? In a previous chapter this was all seen to be part of the social construction of reality and the central role that religion plays in legitimising and reifying the believed whole. The question could be asked, who are the priests, who have the power to decide – to decide on the meaning of the signifiers circling around the Call, and thereby creating the institutions that legitimise and reify the Truth-that-determines-the-Call, determines and fixes the meaning, the interpretation and understanding, so as to create such comprehensive systems that the human authorship is forgotten?

A powerful logos is the metanarrative, the metaphysics that carries out a world, legitimizes it, and eventually reifies it into a world of which the human authorship has been forgotten. Graham argues that any metanarrative is an abuse of difference, and with her I will argue that any Logos, any metaphysics is an abuse of difference, and specifically an abuse of différance, by 'absorbing and smothering variety and pluralism into a global universal homogeneity' (Graham 1996:21).

In the choice of a particular floating signifier, or a particular equivalence, particular fiction to incarnate the truth is always at the exclusion of all the other possible equivalences and all the other fictions, which will need to be silenced in this incarnation.

In Laclau's sense incarnation will always be linked to power – the power of the priests, those who have the power to determine, to give a name to the Call. The incarnation of Christ in the previous chapter is different as it was not linked to power, but was associated with those equivalences, fictions, other floating signifiers who were not chosen, but rather excluded from the incarnation and deformation dialectic of ideology. In other words, Christ's incarnation was not into power, but into powerlessness as it says in Philippians 2:5–8.

Graham in her war against stupidity proposes that one needs to expose these dominant views of reality, these dominant metaphysical systems, as she says that 'Ideas and theories are tested and verified not in relation to their degree of congruence to some external and transcendent reality, but in relation to their effectiveness in enabling us to manage and manipulate the world' (Graham 1996:22). She does not want to propose a truer view of the Real or a truer interpretation of the Call, but expose the dominance of certain views that silence other views. The critique is no longer as with the materialists, who wanted to challenge ideology with the Real, the material. For example, the critical scholars of the Frankfurt School are no different from what they challenged as their thoughts remained a philosophy of mastery, as Stiegler (2015b:78) argues. They too wanted to master the Real, master the Call and give it a singular determination. So, what would be the basis of critique, especially taking Laclau's (2014:11) argument into consideration that any claim to be extra-discursive is the ideological illusion par excellence? The prophetic voice, traditionally in the name of the poor (excluded or silenced fictions or other equivalences), challenges the power of the priests. Ideology is traditionally challenged by what is believed to be materialism, that which ideology excludes, yet, as discussed in the previous chapter, to believe oneself to be speaking from the excluded and as *the* excluded is just the choice of a different equivalence, a different fiction, indeed a previously excluded fiction but a fiction all the same. The moment one speaks, by choosing a new or different equivalence, that speech is equally incarnated and deformed as an ideology, with the end result that prophets tend to become priests. Even the voice of the previously voiceless who need to be given voice, when they do speak, they speak ideology. A prophet who speaks in the name of the excluded, poor, marginalised becomes priest the moment that she or he believes that the particular poor, excluded, marginalised are the new or true incarnation of the whole.

Most incarnations do not recognize their own deformation, but rather believe themselves to be the incarnation of the Truth. They believe to have captured the Real, have responded correctly and completely to the Call. It is this illusion, this belief that there is an extra-discursive point of view, that there is a non-ideological point of view, in other words, that there is an objective *Begriff* (comprehension) of reality, that needs to be challenged – not with a new thought, but with an embrace of the pharmacological condition. Heidegger (1984 §40) argued that in the epoch of machination and lived experience something of the truth of being is revealed. If one continues in this line of thought one could argue that this age, which Gramsci calls cultural hegemony or Polanyi's self-regulating market, which is the logical consequence of objectifying scientific or technical reason (see Stiegler 2015b:17), reveals something of the truth of thinking or the return to a minority, and this stupidity reveals something of the stupidity of thinking as scientific reason believed itself to be free from ideology and therefore have direct and objective access to the Real, which then later developed into rationalisation of everything. Anything, any theory or movement that believes to be the voice of the Real is captured by the illusion of its own hidden ideology. Graham follows Foucault to expose this ideological illusion of the scientific paradigm, and argues that the scientific that presented itself as "illusion free" was and is very much captive of its own illusion, captive of its own stupidity, but that does not deny that it is highly effective, as it gave itself the absolute power to objectify, classify and dominate the whole world (Graham 1996:21). A classic example is how psychology, believed to be a scientific discipline, gave itself the power to classify people and on the basis of those classifications institutionalize people.

The dominant ideology believes itself to be presenting and/or representing the real-world, and with the real-world also what it means to be human. Such a dominant view always mutes other voices, and mutes differences as already discussed above.

The majority for Stiegler experience the positive and constitutive effects of power, but what about the power that one is subjected to through the normalizing "truths" (the legitimation and reification role of religion that presents the world as a given) that shape lives, realities and relationships? Who decides which "truths" are legitimate, who establishes the norms, and who controls the institutions (including the media) that legitimate certain norms, "truths", as all these are constructed or produced as an operation of power?[12] Therefore, it is important to be conscious of one's own dominant Logos, one needs to be aware of the world in which one is embedded (embodied), as this world is not perceived or experienced as a social-construct (with powerful priests in powerful institutions holding it and keeping it all together), but is viewed as the way things truly are, and more importantly it is viewed as the way things should be. On the basis of this *"should be"* one judges others and classifies others as being uncivilized, or underdeveloped, or undeveloped, or as *the* other.

One has forgotten the ideological illusion that one is caught in, one has forgotten one's embodiment as one's own dominant world appears *as if* it is given this way, believed *to be* this way, either because of the laws of nature, or because it is believed to be this way as this is how God created it, and/or as God, or the laws of nature, wanted it, or designed it to be. This world or this civilization has forgotten that it is constructed, this forgetfulness is the perfect ideological illusion, or stupidity as Stiegler (2015b) refers to it. This is the *belief* of thinking,

---

[12] There can be no possible exercise of power without a certain economy of discourses of truth which operates through and on the basis of this association. We are subjected to the production of truth through power and we cannot exercise power except though the production of truth (Foucault1980:93).

and even if one has a lot to criticise about one's world, for example the Western world, one cannot help but believe (think) that *this* world, in its ideal form, is the best or the only real solution to the globe's problems. In other words, for most Western middle class communities there is the general belief that this civilization, "Western" civilization with its democracy and human rights, has what it takes to guarantee justice and altruism in the global world, and therefore should be the norm for the globe. As norm for the globe it has the right and the duty to police the globe, and therefore is justified to wage war on "terrorism" – where terrorism is seen as that which is against this norm, in other words, that which is believed by the norm to be rogue. Graham argues that such a belief is no guarantee for justice, but on the contrary, 'it may merely provide humanity with greater instruments of oppression' (Graham 1996:24). Greater instruments in the name of a good, and in the past in the name of a God, as Schleiermacher argued that good (morality and ethics) becomes the highest being and thus in the name of God, holy wars are fought, or wars of truth are fought, or wars in the name of justice. In the context of the above one could say that all wars are holy wars, all conflicts are religious conflicts.

In an enlightened "Western" society it would be a shock to argue that the West is fighting a holy or religious war, as they believe their wars to be in the name of truth, universal humanity and human rights and democracy, in other words, in the name of all that which is "true", essential to nature or to humanity – the ideological illusion par excellence.

The power that is used needs to be seen not as repressive or oppressive, although for large portions of the earth that is exactly how power is experienced, but for middle to upper class westerners it needs to be interpreted as something "positive", but positive in the way that Foucault understood positive. When Foucault argues that power is something positive he is not arguing that power is something desirable or beneficial (White & Epston 1990:72). Power is positive in the sense that it is constitutive, that it shapes individual and collective lives.[13] In Western and middle class society power is not predominately experienced as repressive or oppressive, but as the constitutive power that shapes individual lives in accordance with certain normalising truths. The media and the cultural industry provide dominant or invasive tertiary and secondary retentions through which the primary retentions and protentions are shaped, in which and through which individuals individuate themselves, that is view and read-write (ex-*text*-ualise) themselves, read-write their experiences, actions and their gestures.

---

[13]   We must cease once and for all to describe the effects of power in negative terms; it "excludes," it "represses," it "censors," it "abstracts," it "masks," it "conceals." In fact power produces; it produces reality; it produces domains of objects and rituals of truth. The individual and the knowledge that may be gained from him belong to this production (Foucault 1979:194).

This is vitally important when attempting de-colonial thinking, not to accept the "norms" and "truths" that were imposed upon the other by the Western norm, or Western universal humanity.

This power is difficult to identify as it is not direct power, but in an Enlightened Western world the use or rather the misuse of power or force cannot be as direct as it was in previous times, in other words, public torture, or public executions would not be acceptable use of force or power. Thus new mechanisms of social control needed to be found – power as social control, which according to Foucault is the ever-present gaze (White & Epston 1990:24). Or the even more refined use of power and control which is the belief that one's freedom and essence lies in consumption (this belief is necessary for profits), whilst keeping people under the illusion (see Stiegler 2015b:12) that they are free because they have choice in what they consume, as in Lacan's discourse of the capitalist (see Meylahn 2010c).

For Foucault, it is not just ideology, as discussed in the previous chapter in the construction of a political, but his concern is with the effects and the social control by the various dominant ideologies (White & Epston 1990:25). His focus was also on the techniques of power that are required for the construction, development and protection of knowledge (the institutions of knowledge, for example universities, and what is accepted as "true" knowledge):

It is both much more and much less than ideology. It is the production of effective in-struments for the formation and accumulation of knowledge – methods of observation, techniques of registration, procedures for investigation and research, apparatuses of con-trol. All this means that power, when it is exercised through these subtle mechanisms, cannot but evolve, organise and put into circulation a knowledge, or rather apparatuses of knowledge which are not ideological constructs (Foucault 1980:102).

According to Foucault, in recent history Western society has increasingly relied on the practices of objectification of persons and their bodies to improve and extend social control (White & Epston 1990:66). The modern history of the objectifica-tion of persons and their bodies coincides with the proliferation of what can be referred to as the "dividing practices" (Foucault 1965), dividing and classifying everything. The Body without Organs is stratified as everything is classified and differentiated. Depending on who is stratifying, who is classifying, who is divid-ing things and persons, that person or group will have the power to classify cer-tain things, certain individuals or groups of people (cultural groups, racial groups, religious groups or groups according to mental and physical ability) as being not-normal or deviant from a norm, and thereby exclude them or marginalize them by for example medicating them or institutionalising them.

The praxis of *Dasein* has to do with the individuation (ex-*text*-ualisation) of an individual into a collective via ideology or religion. In the last few paragraphs the role of power in this ex-*text*-ualising space has been discussed. Because of the differences in power, certain people or groups have more power than others and therefore can determine the space, can determine the ontology by determining the logos of that ontology. This power either belongs to people or groups or through continuous rationalisation reification this power has been given to the market, the self-regulating market or cultural hegemony. The space is determined as the market and by the market and therefore it also has the power to determine the personal and social identity of people. Foucault unpacked this power, a power that for him was essential to the operation of the modern state – the modern state that needs to govern people as well as bodies of people, and the best way to govern is to control the individuation, or actually the dis-individuations, via control of the tertiary and secondary retentions. In this way, people can be subjugated and individuals are forged into "docile bodies" (White & Epston 1990:67) which are easily controlled.

Foucault introduces a few metaphors to understand the use of power in the modern state, to control bodies and thereby control the individuation of people into political collectives, evaluating people and fixing them into predetermined groups, for example: the Panopticon and the gaze that work as forms of normalizing judgement. The question became, How to create docile bodies, because docile bodies are easily controlled, yet Stiegler (2015a:26) argues that a generalized proletariat is not easily controlled, but becomes unpredictable, or predictably unpredictable and therefore dangerous.

The creation of docile bodies and the danger of a generalized proletariat

The Panopticon was an architectural form developed by Jeremy Bentham in the 18th century. Bentham proposed this architectural form as an "ideal" model for the organization or arrangement of (White & Epston 1990:67) persons in space that would effectively "forge" them into "docile bodies", as docile bodies could be more easily transformed, manipulated and used or controlled (White & Epston 1990:68). The belief in an all-seeing eye was an ideal way to ensure that people are obedient to the dominant norm, just as children were often told by their parents that God sees everything. The idea of an all-seeing God was to ensure that the children did nothing wrong, because God is watching. God was not only watching, but would also punish any wrongdoing.

In short, to substitute for a power that is manifested through the brilliance of those who exercise it, a power that insidiously objectifies those on whom it is applied; to form a body of knowledge about these individuals, rather than to deploy the ostentatious signs of sovereignty (Foucault 1979:220).

The Gaze

In the model of the Panopticon every space was observable from the observation tower (the all-seeing eye), which was perfectly situated in the center of the courtyard. In the tower were believed to be the guards, from which they had an uninterrupted view of all the activities taking place in the individual spaces (White & Epston 1990:68). The people in the different spaces were made to believe that they were the objects of perpetual observation. These spaces were: '... small theatres, in which each actor is alone, perfectly individualized and constantly visible' (Foucault 1979:200). Important for the Panopticon to work, was that the people in the different spaces never actually saw any guards, as it was important that the eye as such is never seen. As the other was never directly visible (only the tower was visible), the invisibility of the other created the *belief* that the guards were constantly watching them, and so the prisoners became the subjects of the guardian's gaze 24/7. This incited the prisoners to act as if they were constantly being observed (White & Epston 1990:69).

Evaluation and the Fixing of Lives

This constant feeling of being observed, constantly being exposed to the gaze of the guards, became a normalizing gaze (White & Epston 1990:69). Every person in these different spaces under the gaze believed themselves to be constantly evaluated according to the rules and the norms of that specific institution that carried out these spaces. This normalizing gaze subjected each person to a 'whole micro-penalty of time, of activity, of behaviour, of speech, of the body of sexuality' (Foucault 1979:178). Just as the gaze controlled people, so also the idea of fixing people in files, written documents, placed them in boxes and categories (see White & Epston 1990:69). Individuals are captured and fixed in files that contain all sorts of written documents, from reports to behaviour cards. This fixing of life already begins at birth with the first medical files, and the filing continues through school into adult life with all the reports and performance evaluations. As I write this sentence, I realise that in writing this sentence I am normalising my life. Just because my life is documented in this way, it is certainly not true for most lives on this planet. The numerical majority of the earth's population are undocumented, and for that very reason excluded from the benefits of citizenship, medical aid schemes and international travel. I mention this to indicate how easily one takes one's own world as the norm, as a universal expression of what *is*.

Although large parts of the earth's population are undocumented, that does not reduce the importance of files and statistics in the dominant Western world. Files and statistics provided the technics to the dominant Western world to fix people according to universal norms and the construction of unitary and global knowledge about persons (White & Epston 1990:70). Individual's physical and mental health was measured according to such norms and recorded in medical and psychiatric files. The normalizing gaze and files fundamentally contributed to the reduction of Life to writing.

Where religions once demanded the sacrifice of bodies, knowledge [*Western knowledge*] now calls for the experimentation on ourselves, calls us to the sacrifice of the subject of knowledge (Foucault 1984:96).

The Panopticon provides a model for a particularly modern system of power that relies on the technique of "normalizing judgment." (White & Epston 1990:70). White and Epston (1990:70) argue, as discussed above, that such a reduction of humanity to written documents silences many other possible interpretations of what is human or what it means to be human. This whole system provides for a system of social control 'in which persons' performances are judged according to certain standards or specifications' (White & Epston 1990:70). In this context, meticulous examination replaces moral judgment (White & Epston 1990:71). People are judged according to performance that is measurable via written documents, stored in files. One just needs to think of performance management that so many people in Western institutions are subjected to, where performance is reduced to certain measurable outcomes. Lecturers' abilities are judged by student evaluations that are based on predetermined norms and criteria. In these institutions, it is not an offense to do "wrong", but it is an offense not to perform according to an external norm of what is interpreted as being performance (see White & Epston 1990:71).

Self-subjugation

It is amazing how this system works, it does not only reduce the human to an objective measurable entity, but it co-opts the individual into her or his own objectification[14] (*Verdinglichung*), which is translated as reification (see Stiegler 2015b:45–45). Again, this is the role of religion, the highest good that determines everything, includes everything into its ontology and in so-doing co-opts individuals into their own objectification. This modern system of power is one that not only renders persons and their bodies as objects, but also recruits persons into

---

[14] Under these conditions, people would become ever-vigilant with regard to their own behaviour, as they evaluate all their actions and gestures against norms specified by the particular organization they are part of, or collective they are part of (White & Epston 1990:71). Once they have identified any "anomalies" or "aberrations" in their own conduct, actions or gestures, 'they would be induced to relate to their own bodies as objects, that is, to engage in disciplinary and corrective operations to forge their own bodies as docile. Thus, they become their own guardians. They policed their own gestures. And they became the objects of their own scrutiny' (White & Epston 1990:71).

an active role in their own subjugation, into actively participating in operations that shape their lives according to the norms or specifications of the organizations (White & Epston 1990:71). Is there an escape from these 'chains' as Nietzsche refers to them? No, there is not, 'If man can suffer (from having that which he is not), then it is 'only from *new chains* that he suffers: "Free will" really means nothing more than *not* feeling his new chains' (Stiegler 2015b:54). And therefore it does not help to be critical of ideology, critical of religion, critical of all that which is believed to hold humanity captive, as captive humanity will be. Deleuze in his interpretation of Nietzsche argues not for liberation from chains, but for a reinterpretation of repetition and the eternal return. For Deleuze, Nietzsche liberated the will from everything that chains it by making repetition the very object of willing (Deleuze 1994:6). Chains are *pharmaka*, just as repetition is *pharmaka* (Stiegler 2015b:67). Repetition is that which chains, and yet even as it chains, it is also repetition that heals and saves; there is no outside repetition, only a different view of repetition. Repetition can be viewed as the determination of the Real or it can be viewed as being determined by the Real in the last instance. Repetition 'presents itself as the pharmacological object par excellence' (Stiegler 2015b:67).

Yet the chains of capitalism are different in the sense that they create their own truth as in Lacan's discourse of the capitalist (see Meylahn 2010c).

It is difficult to escape the chains of capitalism as 'consumerist capitalism has taken control of the transindividuation process through a hegemonic monopolization of the retentional supports and systems that condition all psychic and collective individuation … This is what Deleuze described as the 'realization' of the universal by the market, and by marketing which creates 'the market' and imposes its rule, the range of which itself extends across the planet (Stiegler 2015b:63).

Can one escape the chains of capitalism?

… liberate us both from the state and from the type of individualization which is linked to the state. We have to promote new forms of subjectivity through refusal of this kind of individuality which has been imposed on us for several centuries (Foucault1982:216).

It is impossible, there is only the possibility of a preferred subjugation. The war on the Real continues and/or the war on madness (stupidity) (see Stiegler 2015b) continues only to produce more stupidity, but there is no escaping ideology, religion or stupidity, or repetition. Yet, this epoch of late-capitalism does reveal a certain truth about thinking and that truth needs to be thought. I will come back to this shortly.

The church's priestly complicity with the normalising gaze, as well as its prophetic alternative, which is never an alternative, but more of the same

The role of the church, as stated in the first chapter, seems to always want to present the world with some or other form of salvation. As Wilson (1997:1) writes about his book: 'This book is also written under the conviction that the changes taking place in Western culture present a wonderful opportunity for faithful witness to the gospel, as the church in the West re-examines its own life and witness and discovers once again the power of the gospel of Jesus Christ to redeem humanity.' The church wants to present the *pharmakon* as medicine as salvation of the world.

It was clear that the normative in the church or in Christianity, more specifically in practical or public theology, can no longer just be the direct application of the law (ten commandments), but power and normativity needed to be transformed to become more palatable in the modern world, just as was discussed above – the normative needed to become more discrete. Things have changed and they have changed dramatically for the church and her role in society. For example, according to MacIntyre, the moral tradition prior to the Enlightenment depended upon a threefold structure: (1) humanity as we are; (2) humanity as we should be and (3) how we can get from where we are to where we should be (MacIntyre 1984:54). Instead of the moral law as to how humanity should be, Gerkin (1991:69) suggests a shift towards common sense, sound judgement and the development of an aesthetic taste. Therefore, instead of telling people what is morally right or wrong and punishing them for immoral behaviour, rather invite them to interpret their lived experience differently, for example on the basis of common sense, sound judgement and aesthetic taste. Yet, beneath common sense, sound judgement and aesthetic taste, lie the secondary and tertiary retentions and protentions of the community. The believed central purpose of ministry, in Gerkin's model, is to assist individuals as well as communities to interpret their experience via their primary retentions and protentions, which are shaped and formed by the secondary and tertiary retentions and protentions of the *faith* community. Dominant in the faith community is the role of the Scriptures, as tertiary retentions and protentions. Therefore, to share in the common sense of a faith community means that the individual's mythic story fits into the basic or foundational stories of that specific faith community (Gerkin 1991:59). The individual with his or her primary retentions is individuated into the community through the secondary and tertiary retentions and protentions of the faith community. In this sense individuals in the faith community interpret their reality in the light of the Scriptures. New members, or the youth are individuated into the stories of the community and taught to interpret their experiences in the light of these artefacts (narratives). The priest's work is thus to make sure that these stories are known, and are told over and over again at important moments in the community's life as well as the individual's life. It could be argued that in certain Western communities it is difficult to distinguish between what is perceived to be a good and civilised life from a secular, Christian or Buddhist or Jewish interpretation of a good and faithful life. In other words, the common sense values, sound judgement as to what is good and right and even aesthetic taste seems to be more or less the same irrespective of which religion one belongs to, or even if one professes to be agnostic or atheist. In such a situation, the church's role, or the role of any faith community, would be to raise "good" citizens. Good citizens are citizens with "good" common sense, sound judgement and aesthetic taste, and it does not matter which religious sacred texts one uses to do this, as long as they are individuated into being good citizens. The priest would then have the typical role of protecting and proclaiming the common good of that particular community and initiating new members into this good.

Besides the role of the priest helping people individuate within and with the narratives of the community, there is for Gerkin also the role of the prophet.

From a prophetic perspective, there is a difference between the values of the *polis* and the values of the faith community, or maybe there should be a difference between the values (the good) of the faith community and the good of the *polis*.

In many contexts that distinction has become rather vague. Therefore, besides the priest there is also the need for the prophets, who identify what is wrong, lacking, un-thought in the *polis*, and then present the church as saving or healing alternative.

The prophetic voice, contrary to the voice of the priests who keep the status quo in place, is to disrupt the status quo by questioning the status quo. Questioning of the status quo can take on different forms. It can identify the lack, the un-thought in the sense of offering the status-quo correctives to improve the common good of the polis. The role of the church would then be to be the moral conscience of the *polis*. Or the prophetic role could be more radical as it does not want to improve the common good (make it more inclusive for example), but radically or fundamentally challenge the common good. In this radical sense, the prophetic voice is not, like the priests, to enclose into the system, or even to offer improvements to the system, but to disenclose the system. Opening the system for an other and thus a different system. The prophet is always shaped by the traditions that she or he is seeking to break free from and to assert a new freedom of God (Gerkin 1991:71), to seek a new freedom of a new good, a new Logos. The task of prophetic ministry is to nurture, nourish and evoke a consciousness and perception of reality that is different or an alternative to the dominant culture (Gerkin 1991:71). The prophet identifies what is wrong, or lacking, or un-thought in the dominant culture and proposes a different (alternative) *pharmakon*.

A new or a different or an alternative metaphysic has been proposed numerous times by different prophets or faithful-subjects throughout history, thus bringing about revolutions or reformations. They do this, as stated above, by responding to the un-thought of the system, responding to the other of the system, but what they do not think is that all an alternative or different metaphysics is, is a repetition.

The truth of the faithful response of the prophet is repetition.

The prophetic voice is a response, and as response it is necessary, but it is as insufficient as all other responses – past, present and responses still to come. It is necessary, as it is believed to be a faithful response to the Call (call of God, call of the un-thought, call of the Real, call of the Flesh), but the Call (God, the un-thought, Flesh, the Real) withdraws from this response, just as it withdrew from all other responses.

The priestly and the prophetic responses, or the responses of faithful-subjects, reactive-subjects or obscure-subjects are part and parcel of the same. They form the truth of repetition. In Deleuze and Guattari's (2011) terms they are part of the rhizome, where lines of flight are formed only to be captured again.

A trans-fictional praxis is not prophetic in this sense, but something different – not a different or alternative metaphysics, but seeking to exist (ex-*text*) in the context of multiple metaphysical systems, traversing each other. A trans-fictional praxis does not seek to be prophetic, nor priestly, but acknowledges priestly and prophetic responses as responses to the Call, but determined by the Call in the last instance.

The prophets proclaim an alternative *pharmakon* as the antidote for that which is wrong (lacking) in the status quo protected and upheld by the priests. As Nietzsche argued, all this does is to replace one set of chains for another; a free will or a free God is only an illusion.

This prophetic ministry that Gerkin is developing is based on the metaphysic (or aesthetic) vision contained in the primal story of the Christian community (Gerkin 1991:69). The role of the practical theologian in this context is that of an interpretive guide, who guides the community to interpret their reality differently according to an alternative Logos, an alternative world (metaphysics). Yet, what would be the reason to swop worlds, or to swop metaphysical systems? What would be the motivation to swop to a different *pharmakon*? Why should the alternative be better? On the basis of what norms are congregations enticed to interpret differently? The normative element comes from relating the particular to the whole, the particular to what is believed to be the universal, through fostering a mutually critical dialogue between the particularity of the community's situation and the wisdom contained in the grounding Christian tradition (Gerkin 1991:70). This might have some similarity to what MacIntyre refers to as the living tradition, which for him 'is an historical extended, socially embodied argument, and an argument precisely in part about the goods which constitute that tradition' (Mac-Intyre 1984:222). The call to newness and alternatives is based on God's promises and the eschatological expectation (Gerkin 1991:71). What Gerkin suggests is to identify certain *themata* from the contemporary experience of life and bring these into dialogue with the themes in Scripture and tradition (Gerkin 1991:93). A new authority which is not moralistic or conforming is found and it is the authority of sound judgement, and aesthetic vision (Gerkin 1991:93). Gerkin focuses on the following themes:

- Presence (Gerkin 1991:91–116), where he first unpacks the contemporary long-ing for presence and then brings this into conversation with God's presence and Christ's presence or incarnation.
- Community (Gerkin 1991:117–143), as again the longing for "true" community and fellowship is a strong desire in contemporary Western culture, where life has become so isolated and focussed on the individual. This longing is then brought into conversation with the biblical narratives of community.
- Vocation (Gerkin 1991:144ff), the idea of a calling, a purpose in life, is another theme that captures the longing of many in the Western culture and again the Bible can offer an antidote, a *pharmakon* for this condition.

Does theology really offer an alternative, or only an alternative *pharmakon*, by first identifying the lack or the un-thought in the present and past thought, and then bringing this lack into conversation with similar themes in the Bible and thus offering a Biblical interpretation? Or perhaps rather a particular interpretation of the Bible, as *the* Biblical interpretation, as any interpretation of the Bible, only appears (is disclosed or revealed) to the extent that it is appropriated within a cer-tain worldview, a metaphysical system. What Gerkin offers is to interpret the lack in the lived experience in conversation with a particular interpretation of a Bibli-cal view, as *the* Biblical view. Root offered to interpret the lack, or the impossible, with the help of theological ideas of *creatio ex nihilo* and a Theology of the Cross.

Beyond war, beyond antagonism towards Trans-fictional agonism

If one speaks about battle for the soul, from within Western tertiary retentions, one cannot but also bring in God and the Satan who are believed to battle each other for the human soul.

It is clear from the language of the various statements surrounding the #FeesMustFall movement that a decision has been made as to who the good or the just are, and who the bad or evil ones are. Once that decision has been made there will be victimisation and vilification on both sides.

War always ends in dehumanisation on both sides, because evil will always be interpreted as absolute evil and there is absolute evil on both sides. Two absolute evils and the whole university becomes hell, or as Fanon argued, 'The theory of the "absolute evil of the colonist" is in response to the theory of the "absolute evil of the native" (Fanon 2004:50).

Thus, management criminalises the students, who are seen to be unruly and emotional (non-rational) and therefore not completely living up to the norm of what it means to be human, that is to be rational. In a certain sense, they are seen to be less than completely human, which is a way of saying they are beasts? On the other side, some in the movement see management as no longer human, but a beast with unjust practices. For example, the slogan "murdering the black child", makes of management murderers and they are seen as beasts.

If one grammatises this event for the sake of this book, by reducing it to these two opposing positions with management (government) on the one side and the students from the #FeesMustFall movement on the other, then on both sides there is a clear good (God) and a clear evil (Satan). Words of justice and lawlessness are thrown around to clearly indicate who the enemy is, calling all those who read the statements to decide, and thereby become part of their collective; to individuate according to this particular grammatisation – grammatisation which seems to always be a grammatisation of a certain good (and the implied evil that goes with it).

There is need to individuate, individually, collectively and technically and this always happens in the name of the good and by implication through the materialisation of an evil (clearly identified enemy) and thus the need for Satan, the enemy, to create a collective (*polis*). The need to individuate, to be or become a noetic soul, is understood as this battle against the beast, (devil) or the battle of reason against unreason or stupidity.[15] Yet, in forming itself it deforms itself[16] as with Laclau's dialectic of ideology. It seems that one would need to create the devil to present Jesus as the saviour. One needs to create the devil so that one's abstraction, remedy, can be presented as the only salvation or truth, which of course is a rallying call, an altar call – come forward and sign so that you are on the right (godly-righteous) side.

The academics with their truth claims, pronounced with such conviction the justness of their cause, yet their abstract truth is no different to the abstract truth of their enemies. Fanon speaks of colonised intellectuals, and Laruelle (2015:36) refers to dominant intellectuals that are fighting for the soul of the university. Or as I call them, myself included, determining intellectuals, who want to determine the

---

[15] To pass into the act of reason, which Aristotle called *noēsis*, is precisely and above all to struggle against that unreason [*déraison*] that manifests itself in many forms – between stupidity [*bêtise*] and madness [*folie*] and prospering on the terrain of ignorance, fantasy and, nowadays, the industrial exploitation of the drives, that is, as the planetary-wide extension and universalization of what Gilles Deleuze described as *baseness* (Stiegler 2015b:16–17).

[16] If reason forms itself (in passing through a *Bildung*), this is also and above all because it deforms itself (Stiegler 2015b:17).

insistence, determine the soul of the university. In the end, it is not about transformation. It is just about the turn of the wheel of history between slave and master and who has the right to determine. This is not decolonial or postmodern or transmodern, but completely modern with no transformation. It is for this reason that I suggest a non-colonial thought in tradition of Laruelle's (2012; 2013a; 2013b) non-philosophy.

I am not proposing an alternative, as any alternative would just be another turn of the wheel and therefore not an alternative at all. One cannot escape making sense of one's world by determining the world, and yet in this book I seek a praxis of how to engage these different worlds, a practice that I determined in the end of the previous section as non-colonial or as a trans-fictional praxis.

Why must one always create a devil to justify our saving or redeeming abstraction: our saving Jesus? Can one not move beyond Schmitt and his argument that a city cannot be built without an enemy? Or must grammatisation always be a war of spirits (Stiegler 2014:53&55; 2015a:116), a colonisation of the other, the typical modern purification by division into distinct ontological zones (Latour 1993:10–11)? Is grammatisation always a form of colonialism? Is grammatisation always a stratification of the Body without Organs? Does grammatisation always have to be modern, that is via division (stratification) and purification?

A division, and consequently a purification, is only possible on the basis of a decision of what the good is. Is individuation as noetic soul, always a participation in *Theos*, the good, as Aristotle argues (see Stiegler 2015a:24) – in other words, no individuation without decisionism?

Is individuation (psychic, collective and technical) only possible via the decision of what is Good (God) and what is Evil and the consequent purification: war on spirits?

The good in which the noetic soul participates is the sovereign, which needs to be clearly distinct from the beast, but in the sovereign's purifying war against the beast, does it not itself become the beast and so the wheel of history only turns, but nothing changes, only repetition?

In the end, all that is left are two beasts, as the sovereign becomes the beast, or the sovereign is the beast (see Derrida 2009:18). This logic seems to always end with two absolute evils as Fanon argued, and the consequent dehumanisation of all.

Is the *poiēsis*[17] of a we, the individuation of a we through technics, exteriorisation that is then interiorised, only possible via this war on spirits, war of grammatisation?

---

[17] I use the word, *poiēsis* as a creative act, the noetic acting out, as Stiegler describes it: 'This logical and semiotic horizon, which I have also just called symbolic, is, however, originally a *technical horizon*: noetic acting out is technical, a *tekhnē*, which is to say, an art' (Stiegler 2015a:31).

In such a confining space where all is dehumanised, is violence the only option? It becomes a situation where violence becomes the only *poiēsis* for the individuation of the proletariat, for example Fanon argues, 'The colonized man liberates himself in and through violence' (Fanon 2004:44). Or again violence seems to be the only possibility for acting out when a population has been reduced to a generalised proletariat within contemporary symbolic misery, as Stiegler argues (2014:61), reflecting on the various violent mass shootings in the USA.

Is there not something of a radical evil (Arendt 2006:xiv) in all this, in contrast to absolute evil? Evil can be understood as being radical, in contrast to absolute. Radical evil is interpreted where evil destroys not only its victims, but also the means by which survivors might seek to respond (that is radical evil understood in the sense of dis-individuation). Stiegler argues that dis-individuation occurs when 'retentional funds from which the individual is constituted, to which it is linked, which it inherits, and which support its own retentions, have been amortized in the sense that they have become dead, as well as mortifying' (Stiegler 2015b:115).

Radical evil is interpreted as general proletarianisation of humans through robbing them of the possibility of the labour to externalise, to write, to create, *poiēsis*, to be human, to be noetic souls. That is if being human is understood primarily as 'individuation which is constitutive of ex-istence, and which is thus distinguished from the subsistence that is the fate of sensitivity and nutritivity' (Stiegler 2015a:32). Stiegler continues and argues:

The noetic circuit of sense, as an exterior projection, is also the technically engrammed and transmitted accumulation of what noetic souls have sensed by giving to be sensed, which is to say, by ex-pressing from the originary possibility of exteriorization that is the noetic life as technical life – this is the mobility belonging to a life that places itself outside itself by projecting itself in its *technai*, and which, in this way, ex-ists (Stiegler 2015a:32).

Radical evil would be the silencing of voices, preventing them from individuating, amongst other reasons, because of the commodification of tertiary retentions, which Stiegler (2014:10) describes as symbolic misery. Radical evil is then to control or police ex-istence (ex-*text*-ence), controlling and limiting individuation by determining the grammatisation into which one could individuate. Radical evil is when I only have two choices: for or against, as that limits my psychic, collective and technical individuation.

If these are the only options, what hope is there but war or antagonism?

If the management dehumanises the movement and the only way the movement can individuate itself is with the counter dehumanisation of management, by declaring the management as the enemy of the black child, what hope is there? In this war of grammatisations, this war of abstractions, this war of clones, the sovereign and the beast continuously exchange places in these two opposing narratives.

Why does one need Satan so?

One needs evil or the good because one is a worker, a labourer, as one is a poet, creating (writing) oneself through ex-*text*-ualisation via various primary, secondary and tertiary retentions. The human labour is one's poetry, one's *poiēsis*, one's technics and technology that becomes the organology that carries out one's world. Exteriorizing (ex-*text*-ualising) oneself into a *Dasein* of a particular world, populated with things (ontology), these things, this ontology, carries out a world and thus one's individuation (psychic and collective and technical) is the creation of one's world, and is therefore, one could argue, truly created in the image of a creator God who is – according to Genesis – the creator of the world, and humans as images of the Creator God are likewise creators of worlds. It is one's *poiēsis* that makes one an image of God, humans according to the tertiary retentions of the Jewish-Christian influenced worlds. However, it is exactly this *poiēsis*, this labour, this work, these technics that makes one an image of God, that likewise brings humanity into close proximity to the temptation of Satan in the Garden of Eden, namely, to eat of the fruit of knowledge. It seems as if the creation of humans in the image of God and temptation of Satan cannot be separated, at least not in Western philosophy or metaphysics. To be an image of God is to participate in God through externalisation and thus as noetic souls participating in God, but this participation is equally a participation in the eating of the fruit of knowledge of good and evil. This participation in God, through deciding what is good, is equally a participation in Satan's temptation if one wants to remain in the Jewish-Christian tertiary retention of the Genesis story. It seems unavoidable that participating in God is to fall into this temptation. According to Aristotle the noetic soul participates in *Theos* (Stiegler 2015a:24), in the movement from potential to act, through the *decision* of what is good and by implication evil. The human participates in God, participates in *Theos*, the good, by being able to judge (decide) what is good for her own psychic soul as well as the collective soul, and this is humanity's noetic labour, *poiēsis*. This labour, this *poiēsis*, is to participate in *Theos* (good) through a decision, which includes the creation of evil, and so the battle between the sovereign and the beast begins, where sovereign and beast become indistinguishable. Or the slave becomes master, or the colonised becomes coloniser and thus the wheel of history only repeats, but nothing transforms.

Therefore, what is needed, according to Enrique Dussel, is transmodern thinking rather than just modern (colonising) thinking. Although I have great appreciation for his transmodern paradigm and the various forms of de-colonial thinking, especially because of the geo-political and historical necessity thereof, decolonial thought (although necessary) needs to remember that it is as insufficient as are all other thoughts and thought-systems. If it forgets that it is insufficient it remains to a large extent caught in the basic modern assumption that truth can be discovered. Many decolonial theories were and are strongly influenced by critical theories, often offering singular interpretations of Western modernity and often proposing singular explanations of various decolonial thoughts (see Meylahn 2017e), or abstracting the victims of colonial thought in the fashion of true leftist and politically correct intellectuals, and thereby creating a new abstracted system, and consequently not challenging "Western modernity" but just turning the table around between master and slave, and therefore not escaping the master-slave dialectic.

This chapter is based on an interpretation of what it means to be human, namely a noetic soul, but that is particularly from within the Western tertiary retentions (Greek, Jewish-Christian), and therefore it seems that one would need to abandon this Western world and seek salvation in other worlds – African or Far Eastern, or amongst the First Nations of the Americas.

Colonialism and Globalisation have closed this door of seeking salvation amongst the Others as the Other is always the Other of the Western Same.

It seems impossible to escape the Western Same, as the Face of Christ, as Deleuze and Guattari (2011:167–191) name the abstract machine of the West, has truly become global and inescapable. All thinking is Christian, or at least all Western thinking is Christian as Nancy (2008:142) argues, and this includes basically the whole globe, at least all thinking that has been influenced by Western paradigms of primary, secondary and tertiary education (see Gaztambide-Fernández 2014:202). In such a context, any alternative to Western thought, which is *crafted as alternative*, will not be an alternative, but part of the same. It will be the Other of the West and therefore remain the West's Other.

What is the point of seeking dialogue, for example in discursive ethics, when only those can partake in the dialogue that are present to each other or are present to view, and therefore available for dialogue? It then becomes a question: in which logos, or in whose logos will the dia*logos* take place? Any dia*log*ue is firstly limited to that particular ontology, as only those visible or present (the *onta*), those or that which is within the view or *Lichtung* of a particular logos, are able to participate in the dialogue to develop a discursive ethics. In other words, dialogue has to do with ontology – only those who are present (part of a specific ontology) can partake in the dialogue of that ontology. Dialogue is always a dialogue within a particular ontology, where only those partake in the conversation who are present to a particular view, who come into view through a particular light, or who come to presence in a particular light (logos), and therefore a particular onto-logy, the logic of a particular world.

The dialogue is limited firstly to those who are visible in the logos of the ontology in which the dialogue takes place, and secondly, they can only speak in the language (logos) of that ontology for them to be visible and to be heard.

Things are disclosed as they are appropriated in and as the event of language – whose language or which language offers the space for dialogue or discursive ethics, as the language will determine who is disclosed enough to participate, and it will determine which voices are heard.

Dussel (2013:128) therefore counters discursive ethics with his argument for a material ethics. Certain things or people or groups first need to become visible (be disclosed), move out of the shadows, before they can partake in the dialogue. Two things need to be critically thought concerning discursive ethics: firstly, who participates and secondly, in which language (logos) does this discussion take place. It is not just a question of participation, but the logos (epistemology) of the possible dialogue needs to be up for discussion, in other words there is not just one logos for the dialogue but different possible logoi. If disclosure always happens in relation to appropriation, it cannot only be a question of what is disclosed (who becomes visible), but *in what* do they become visible, into whose world do they become visible? In what or into what are they appropriated? Within the logic of any world and even in the dia*logoi* (trans-logoi) between differing worlds, there will always be those with more power (masters) and those with less power (slaves) or even those without any power (the excluded, invisible, those in the shadows). One could change the power imbalance and thereby rearrange the furniture in a particular ontology, the masters and the slaves could exchange places for example, but the ontology as such does not change. One could also expand the horizon by continuously including previously invisible things (people or groups) within the ontology and thereby have an ever expanding horizon that transcends itself so as to include the "Other", but it remains the Same. It is only a graciously expanded ontology of the Same, or it has become a hospitable ontology, but it is still the same ontology that has become hospitable. Or will it allow the guest to become host (see Derrida 2008b) and thereby change the logos of the onto*logy*? But even if the logos does change and thereby the ontology is changed, it is still an ontology of a master logos, a different master, but a master all the same. History will not have changed, but only repeated itself.

Nietzsche argued that the slaves in a particular ontology can present their values in such a way as to instil guilt in the masters, and thereby turn the wheel of history. Nietzsche argued that this slave mentality that instils guilt in the powerful is part and parcel of the Christian ethic.[18] This combination of ressentiment

---

[18] In *The Genealogy of Morality*, Nietzsche contrasts the masters' self-centered world view, in which "goodness" is synonymous with excellence – that is, with a health, a beauty, a wealth, and a strength that they confidently think they embody – with the equally master-centred "slave" outlook. Coveting their oppressors' power but unable to access their privileges, the "slaves" sti-

and guilt still seems to drive the altar call to sign or endorse the statements, but that only turns the wheel or rearranges the furniture, but it does not challenge the ontology. Victimology that challenges the values of the master by opposing the master's values with the opposite values of the slave will not bring about change, but only a turn in the wheel, as the values of the slave once in the position of power (master) are transformed into the values of the master, as these opposite values are each other, just as the sovereign is the beast and the beast is the sovereign. This turning of the wheel does not change the ontology. The dialogue still only happens between those who are present, and they are present because of a particular light (logos), but what about those who are invisible, those in the shadows, those that are neither masters nor slaves?

Yet, even if one would make the invisible, the excluded, those in the shadows, one's *starting point*, by seeking to make them visible, one would make them visible in that particular ontology where they were previously invisible, as the Other of that ontology, or as the previously invisible ones. They would become visible in a foreign language, as they articulate themselves, become visible, only in the logos of the dominant ontology, and only once present can contribute to the dialogue, or challenge the dialogue. On the other hand, one always articulates oneself in the language of the other (Derrida 1998:59), in the language of the secondary and tertiary retentions that one did not create, but found, and into which one individuates oneself, into which one was thrown. In that sense, one always speaks the language of the other. Yet, in another (often forgotten) sense, language *is* the other, as language is the response and never the Call. The Call which called language (response) forth, withdraws from that which it called forth.

In other words, all becoming present, all articulation is an articulation – becoming present in a foreign light, the light of the world into which one becomes present, but which is not that which called it forth.

It seems that the only option left is not to seek an alternative, or to speak from the slave or to speak from the excluded, those in the shadows, as that does not challenge the ontology. It might broaden the ontology (expand the horizon), but not change it, as to focus on the Other and thereby *believe* oneself to be creating an alternative or a disenclosure of the enclosure of Western thought, will not be an alternative but will still be Christian, as Nancy (2008:10) argues. The disenclosure

---

fle their envious hostility, which Nietzsche calls precisely ressentiment, and create a morality based on compassion, renouncement, and meekness, which reverses the masters' values and, once insidiously instilled in the latter, loads them with guilt and causes them to relinquish power, thus eventually allowing the rise of the weak. This moral schema seems to me analogous to the coloniser/colonised relationship in which, to the former's confident Eurocentrism, the latter opposes a moralising discourse of victimisation and/or self-negation. In such a relation, however, "the rise of the weak" is not the end of the story; as will be developed in the final section of this essay, the discursive strategies of the subaltern are appropriated by the dominator not to atone for, but to act as a cover for his/her domination (Chouiten 2011:3 of 28).

is as much part of Christianity as the enclosure. Or in Deleuze and Guattari's (2011) thoughts, any lines of flight will be re-assimilated into the rhizome and will not truly create an alternative or an escape. Thus, alternative (anti-colonial) thought is not truly an alternative, but becomes part of the rhizome, becomes part of the face of Christ, it expands the horizon, making its reach more effective.

Something radically new needs to be found, or as Fanon argues, something truly innovative, but not an alternative to Christ. As has already been shown, such an alternative is no alternative, but more of the same. Prophetic ministry in the end is no different from priestly ministry. The two faces of Christ or the two names of Christ – Christ the servant or Christ the king – continually become each other.

I suggest that one has to *think through Christ, think through* the face of Christ, *think through* the abstract machine that produces both enclosure and disenclosure, that produces the Same and the Other, master and slave, excluded and included, shadow and present, i.e. that produces all these binaries. I believe that Laruelle might offer a path to think through the abstract machine of the West, the Face of Christ, with his Christo-fiction (Laruelle 2015c). In other words, what is necessary is not a thinking *against* Christ or *with* Christ or *in* Christ or *for* Christ, but *through* Christ. If Christ is the abstract machine creating culture, creating externalisations, creating technics (all the different Western forms of individuation), it cannot be a matter of *thinking* Christ, in other words offering one more and maybe with the belief of offering *the* final Christology, as the ultimate saviour of the Real, or the saviour of God or saviour of humanity or the earth, but of thinking *through* Christ as the abstract machine of the West; thinking through Christ, as the abstract machine of the dominant ontologies: the logics of the Western worlds and thus global worlds. Thinking through Christ creates a trans-fictional space, as all the metaphysical worlds created by the abstract machine are seen as equal. The prophetic as well as the priestly are equally called forth. They are equally necessary *and* equally insufficient, and therefore they are seen as different fictions. Yet, although all the fictions are equal in the sense that they are equally called forth from that which called them and yet withdraws, they are not equal with regards to the internal power relations. In other words, the worlds that these fictions create (carry out) are very different. None of the worlds is more real, they are equally fictive worlds, but they are different fictions.

Thinking through Christ not towards anything, and therefore not as any final or conclusive thought of the Real, the Same or the Other, but thinking through Christ as the abstract machine of the West.

To think through Christ towards nothing, therefore not as a response to a Call but a thinking through or a thorough thought, therefore thinking what thinking is, that does not open onto anything, but onto thought itself, to think the *Bedenklichste*, that which is most *thought-worthy*, namely thought itself. This is arguably thinking only Western thought, but in the above paragraphs it was clear that trying to think an alternative to Western thought will only ever be the other of West-ern thought, in other words, the Western other. But perhaps by thinking through Western thought it is decolonised, it is de-Westernised, as it is a non-philosophy of Western thought. It is the non-determining, non-responding thinking through thought.

Thought is thought and thus all thoughts become equal, as in equally in need of being thought, and what becomes clear is not a final determination of what thought thinks, but thought itself. Nothing is revealed but thought itself, and it is revealed as equally *necessary and insufficient* and therefore making the battle between binaries non-sense, and the binary between hybrids and binaries would be interpreted or revealed as just one more attempt, *necessary but insufficient*, at thinking (determining) the Real. No thought can determine the Real, but all thoughts are equally determined by the Real as *necessary but insufficient*, whilst the Real (the Call) remains foreclosed to thought. This can be acknowledged by understanding the fictional character of all thought and how thought is produced. One metaphor for understanding the production of thought is the abstract machine, specifically the production of Western thought, the abstract machine of the West, namely the face of Christ. The idea is not to seek an alternative abstract machine or to challenge the ontology of the West with an alternative ontology. All that will happen is that a new binary will be created between Same and Other, and the singular ontology (horizon) will be expanded as the rhizome grows.

The Christo-fiction helps as it offers a metaphor, a fiction with which to inter-pret the fictional character of all thought. In a sense it is a metaphor of metaphor, or a fiction of fiction. Thus, a Christo-fiction helps in thinking thought, thinking how thought is produced. It helps to think the most thought-worthy, the *Beden-klichste*. It offers a metaphor, a fiction, to think how individuals are individuated through thought (ex-*text*-ualisation), how ideas are singularised within collectives and through the technics of the collective, via the primary, secondary and tertiary retentions. The Christo-fiction offers a fiction of thought, a fiction of Western thought. The Christo-fiction offers a way to understand the face of Christ as the abstract machine of the West and by implication the face of the globe. Any al-ternative will only be an alternative produced by the face of Christ and therefore one has to think through Christ rather than *against*, *with* or *in* Christ. By thinking through the machine, one can not necessarily escape, as any escape will still be within the rhizome, within the Face, but one could create something different – weapons that think through control societies, weapons that think through colonial thought and thus offer a possibility of non-colonial thinking and a trans-fictional praxis. No longer a dialectic, nor Dussel's analectic,[19] but rather fictional: thinking

---

[19]   Analectics, which comes from the Greek root *ano* (beyond), takes as its point of departure the unmitigated transcendence of the other. The other is never the mere shadow – a faulty, incomplete image or realization of the same, the I, the one. The other is beyond the horizon

the pharmacological condition. Thinking *through* thought, not towards anything, but thinking thought.

What does thinking through Christ mean? It means understanding the Christo-fiction as a fiction with which to understand fictions, that is, understand abstractions, externalisations, technics, the necessary but insufficient thoughts with which humanity individuates through creating meaning (understanding). The face of Christ is a metaphor of the abstract machine of the West and Christo-fiction is a metaphor of the metaphor, a story (fiction) to interpret the production of Western (global) fictions. What does thinking through Christ mean? It means to think through the Christo-fiction with its Christic kernel of incarnation, crucifixion and resurrection (ascension). Thinking through the Christic kernel helps to interpret through a fiction how disenclosure and enclosure continually interact with each other, creating the rhizome, but not challenging it.

Andrew Root's *Christo-praxis* (2014:138), responding to a frustration with contemporary practical theology's reliance on Aristotle's interpretation of human actuality and potentiality, points one in the right direction towards a praxis of Christ: Christo-praxis. Root's Christo-praxis does not follow Aristotle's path of human action which has the potential to 'create a possibility for itself from itself' (2014:138), but Root interprets the Christo-praxis in the light of *theologia crucis* and *ex nihilo*.[20] Christo-praxis would be a praxis out of nothing, (*ex nihilo*), that is the experience of the impossible (death or law), and then out of nothing (*ex nihilo*) the experience of the possible impossible (resurrection, grace, faith, Christ alone). If one would think this thought further, the Christian individuation (discipleship) would not be a participation in the good (*Theos*), but an inclusion by gift or grace and faith alone through creation *ex nihilo*, and through total reliance (*Sola Christus*) on *theologia crucis*, in other words, this could be one way of avoiding the creation of both God and Satan, as a move beyond decisionism.

---

of what is already experienced and comprehended. The method of the self-mirroring (and self-projection of the same) is dialectics, and it is this method that has ruled all of Western philosophy at least since the pre-Socratics (Parmenides and Heraclitus). But dialectics is war, the war of the same and the I to affirm itself in and through the other, and to wrest from the other what makes the other inassimilable alterity the horizon of comprehension and existence of the I is a totality. Dialectics is the production of the totality. The other is an exteriority that is irreducible to the totality of the self-same. As long as we subscribe to an ontological approach, the otherness of the other will remain inscrutable alterity. To open ourselves to the other requires that we destroy ontology and in its place institute ao metaphysical approach, one that sets out from the fundamental principle that the truth of the world is always beyond what is never exhausted by the given. To put it formulaically, ontology is to dialectics as metaphysic is to analectics. The former is mobilized by exclusion and war, the later by expectant openness and solidarity (Dussel 2003:5).

[20] ... it is possibility through nothingness that embeds my Christopraxis perspective in the theologia crucis (Root 2014:147).

Is it possible to move beyond decisionism? Can a noetic soul individuate without participation in *Theos*? Does Root's Christo-praxis move one beyond decisionism? Or does his Christo-praxis become the new decision, the new alternative, a new truth, a new *pharmakon* that individuates a new collective and a certain orthodox grammatisation of that collective's individuation, which is exactly what happened after the Reformation with Lutheran orthodoxy, and therefore a repetition of the identification of good and evil? Even with his Christo-praxis there might not be the moral good or the moral evil, but there are faithful-subjects who understand their reliance on grace, faith and Christ alone through Scripture alone, and reactive subjects who reject this "good news" or obscure subjects, who obscure this truth. Root's Christo-praxis is presented as a possible new good or new norm for practical theology. Root uses Christo-praxis, the justification through Christ, as a hermeneutic to interpret experiences of God.[21] To use Christo-praxis as a hermeneutic rather than a revelation of truth, is what I will return to in later paragraphs, but not as a hermeneutic to interpreting experiences of God in the independent objective reality, but as a hermeneutic for interpreting fictions, or as Henry argues, the phenomenology of phenomenology (Henry 2003:25). The Christ-*poiēsis* that will be developed in the following chapters is thinking through the Christ-event, where the Event is not interpreted as a response, nor is it an attempt to respond to the Christ-event by responding through the creation of a theology or Christology. Christ-*poiēsis* is to think through Christ.

As soon as Christ's liberating praxis becomes a new truth, there is decisionism. The moment that one interprets Christ as a presentation of a truth (as the true or faithful response), or as a presentation of good, presentation of Reality, the Reality of impossible possible, presentation of the truth of *theologia crucis* and *ex nihilo*, one is again in the role of the advocate presenting a truth about something, truth of life, truth of reality, truth of God, etcetera.

Laruelle's Christo-fiction does not offer a new truth, nor does it offer the correct, for example historically or dogmatically correct interpretation of Christ. It does not present Christ as the new truth, nor as the correct hermeneutic for interpreting experiences of God in the independent objective reality, as such an interpretation would at best be a new necessary but insufficient determination of God, Reality, Life, Salvation, but Laruelle offers a fiction to help understand the fictional character of all thought. If Christ would be the interpretation of God in the independent objective reality, then Christ would be the name, the response to the Call, Christ would be the determination. And in that sense Christ would be sin, the creation of an image of God, the name of God. Christ emptied himself of God

---

[21]   I use justification not as the retrieval of doctrinal history but as a hermeneutic, a lens, that gives
       vision to the action of God in and through the concrete experience of human beings as they
       encounter the event of God's action of ministry (Root 2014:120).

according to Philippians 2 and did not seek equality with God, thus did not seek to be *the* determination of God.

In other words, Christ is not a truth about something, but the story of Christ (Christo-fiction) is fiction about fictions and in that sense reveals something about the truth of fictions, the truth of thought. 'I am the truth' (John 14:6) Jesus says – not the truth about something, but He *is* the truth as he is the way. He is the way of truth, as his story (Christ event) is the way of thinking. Not the truth as *adequatio* or as representation, but the truth as revelation: *aletheia*. But what is revealed? The Real is not revealed, but the truth of thinking is revealed.

This Christo-fiction might inspire not truth, or individuation, but if anything a praxis – a messianic praxis that never ends. Another critique against Root's Christo-praxis is that because it only focusses on the crucifixion without also taking the incarnation into account, his praxis becomes apolitical and does not truly challenge the political and/or ethical systems, but reduces faith to personal (evangelical) experiences of God.

The incarnation can be interpreted as the becoming flesh of truth, as a revelation of truth, and thereby enclosing a world around that truth. Or it could be interpreted as the disenclosure of a dominant truth – through Christ's preferential option for the poor and marginalized, he challenged the enclosure. The Crucifixion will then either be interpreted as the world's rejection of the truth or as the death of the dominant gods, the death of the dominant sovereign and therefore the creation of the possibility of new life. The danger is exactly with the resurrection, the new life, liberated life, which is too quickly individually, collectively and technically individuated into a new community: a church. This new individuation is then a re-enclosure of the disenclosure and thus the rhizome grows and history repeats itself.

Can one remain in the crucifixion? This question alone already makes it impossible as the thought of remaining presupposes something in which to remain, in other words some form of individuation or some form of singularisation has already taken place for the decision to want to remain. Thus, a singular interpretation of the crucifixion is given in which one seeks to remain. Many of the early monks or desert fathers tried to live in Christ, remain in Christ alone. That is a form of radical discipleship, and yet it proved impossible, as even an inoperative community (see Nancy 1991) would still be a community. It is for this reason that one might turn to the Holy Fools, the *salos* (see Meylahn 2013:331ff) who refused any form of following (discipleship) and thereby any form of collective or technical individuation. They might still be the best example of a non-philosophical life, but without community.

The messianic praxis, inspired by the Christo-fiction, is a continuous incarnation amongst the poor, marginal, shadows or excluded, even the poor and marginal and shadows of those individuated as poor and marginal, in the true sense of the idea: Christ alone (*Sola Christus*), by faith alone and grace alone, without law, tradition, grammatisation or individuation.

In my interpretation of the reformation, the reformers tried via various confessional statements to remain true to Christ in an attempt to create a living body of Christ rather than an institution, i.e. a collective individuation around dogmatic grammatisations, but did not succeed. They had hoped that with confessional statements they could capture something of the need for continuous reformation, but with the capture they entrapped themselves in the old temptation of Satan to know what is good and what is evil.

Henry (2015) tries with his incarnational philosophy to remain open to Life (God as Life and as the Living God of history) as that which determines thought in the last instance, but with his philosophy he determined the Call as Life – Life as that which insists and through its insistence drives the history of grammatisations, and therefore one could determine this insistence as Life or as God, but through that determination one would create one more necessary but insufficient thought (philosophy or theology, for example a theology of Life or the Insistence of God). Henry's determination of that insistence as Life, was the law, the grammatisation which killed Life.

Making sense of the insistence happens in community (collective individuation) and thus the determination and community (collective individuation) go together as was discussed in the previous chapters. What is sought is a thinking through this process not to offer an alternative, but to offer nothing, but without that nothing (*ex nihilo*) becoming the new determination or the new collective non-community.

Christo-fiction does not take one to the truth, does not take one to any new understanding of the Real, Life, God or the Call, or Humanity, but gives one a fiction of thought, a metaphor to interpret thinking of the noetic soul. It does not open the way towards true Life, it is the way of life, it is the truth of life (insistence), as Jesus once claimed that he is the way, the truth and the life. It does not open onto anything, and nothing new or revolutionary is revealed, it does not claim to be the final thought, the final all-encompassing philosophy, it only opens thought, not to its truth, which would only be the belief of thought, and the truth of that belief is repetition, but to its fiction and all the future fictions still to come – the various fictions, all equally necessary but insufficient, and thus the possibility of trans-fictional democracy of thoughts and of thoughts still to come.

With the immanent ecological and political crisis, do we not need more wars in the name of healing?

I am not denying the disastrous effects of global capitalism. Many public theologians have written extensively on the immanent ecological and economic-political crisis that the globe is facing. There is certainly a need for action and saving. In a previous study, I also discussed the economic-political crisis and proposed how the church can become an alternative community, and thus offer hope. In that study I proposed that hope is found in communities of the cross (see Meylahn 2010a; 2010b), communities of the cross I would today interpret as trans-fictional communities of Christo-*poiēsis*. Such communities would not be seen as remedy, not as *pharmakon*, but taking the pharmacological seriously, and recognising that late-capitalism has revealed something of the pharmacological truth to the world, and using that truth to think thought and develop a trans-fictional praxis rather than offer a new theory.

From Stupidity to *poiēsis*

Stiegler (2015b) argues for a toxic pharmacology, which I believe is a tautology, as the *pharmakon* being a remedy is also poison according to Derrida (1981:99) and thus to argue that the *pharmakon* is toxic, is repeating what the *pharmakon* is. The turn to *poiēsis* is to turn to literature, which is to embrace the *pharmakon* as both gift and *Gift*. That is what I propose: to embrace the *pharmakon*, whilst suspending any principle of sufficient philosophy (Laruelle 1999: 287). In other words, to suspend the *belief* in philosophy, the belief in thinking, but to think thinking, and thus to think the *pharmakon,* or to think the stupidity of thinking. To embrace the *pharmakon* as gift and *Gift* and thereby embrace the truth of the faith of thinking: repetition, and then not to develop a positive pharmacology as Stiegler (2015b) suggests, but a *poiēsis,* or rather (being inspired by Kierkegaard) not a knight of faith, but a poet of the faith, as Deleuze argues, 'in short a humourist' (Deleuze 1994:95). What is it that makes the *pharmakon* toxic? It is that the *pharmakon* is not recognised for what it is, but it is believed to be the true reflection or presentation of things, thanks to the reifying work of religion, ideology and the belief of thought. Deleuze called for new weapons – not to fight a war against stupidity, but to forge new weapons (see Stiegler 2015b:74). Do we need new weapons? Will new weapons not just be different *pharmaka*? Will any new weapon not just be a repetition? The new weapons are not new truths, but to re-think differently the *pharmaka of thought*, in other words, to think thinking, as Laruelle would argue: to develop a science of philosophy, rather than develop a new philosophy. Stiegler argues, 'to rethink and rearm thought is to rethink the *pharmakon* itself as arm, as weapon – and, of course, as a double-edged sword' (Stiegler 2015b:74).

Therefore, a non-philosophy is necessary to challenge that belief in philosophy or the belief and trust in thought (forgetting its stupidity), whilst accepting the necessity of a *pharmakon*, but likewise recognising its insufficiency.

4. Can Christ save from these Sovereigns that are Beasts?

> *Wars. So many wars. Wars outside and wars inside. Cultural wars, science wars, and wars against terrorism. Wars against poverty and wars against the poor. Wars against ignorance and wars out of ignorance. My question is simple: Should we be at war, too, we, the scholars, the intellectuals? Is it really our duty to add fresh ruins to fields of ruins? Is it really the task of the humanities to add deconstruction to destruction? More iconoclasm to iconoclasm? What has become of the critical spirit? Has it run out of steam (Latour 2004:225)?*

The previous chapter interpreted thinking as war against the Real, with the result that there are too many wars. It seems as if these wars against the Real are unavoidable and that the dream of peace is utopian. This chapter will not be one more attempt at seeking global peace, nor arguing for a just war, but exploring possible ways, a praxis, to work *with* and or amongst the different warring factions against the Real, and therefore a trans-fictional praxis.

There is the war in the name of critical knowledge, as well as a war in the name of Enlightenment as a war against what is perceived to be the darkness of stupidity. There is the war in the name of the good against evil. There is the war in the name of what is believed to be right against what is wrong. There is the war in the name of justice against injustice.

For most people, such wars would be perceived to be justified, as they are fought in the name of knowledge against stupidity, justice against injustice, the good against evil and what is believed to be right against all that is wrong.

So many wars as Latour in the above quote says. But is war necessary?

Yes, war against the Real is necessary as it is inevitable that knowledge, the response, seeks to grasp the Call, seeks to colonise the Call, as it determines and names the Call. This naming as such is already a war against the Real, but with all the different names there is also a war amongst the different names given to the Call. Such war or such antagonism is unavoidable, as the colonisation of the Call (the Real) is always a hegemonic process and therefore about power,[1] where other voices, other names are silenced.

---

[1]   War or antagonism is unavoidable as Chantal Mouffe argues, 'It is because of the existence

But can all these wars be grouped together as if there is no difference between them? There is always difference, but what makes all these wars equal, is the idea that thinking is a war against the Real, which brings a certain *equivalence* of all these different yet similar wars to the fore. And it is because of the equivalence that politics, according to Mouffe and Laclau, is always about antagonism and hegemony (Mouffe 2013:1). It is because they are equal in the sense of equally called forth, and equal responses, that there is a battle between the responses, the battle for hegemony.

The Call withdraws from thought, or the Call withdraws from the response and thus all one is left with, is the response, the name. Yet, it is the response, the speaking of language, that carries out the world in which one is (exists – ex-*texts*). One ex-*texts* differently depending on the text (narrative or metaphysical systems) that carries out the world in which one is, and therefore it is of vital importance who or what determines the language that carries out the world, as the language will determine one's hierarchical place in the world. Therefore, there is not only a war against the Call, but there is a war amongst the names seeking to determine the Call, as different names will carry out different worlds. The worlds that are carried out are indeed very different, and some might be argued to be better than others, but not better because they are more Real, or more truthful, but better according to a different norm, but such a different norm would only be another name. And who decides, who has the power, the hegemony, to declare certain norms universal, with which to judge the different worlds?

It is only because of hegemonic power that a certain group can choose a certain equivalence and make it representative of the whole (universal) and thereby silence and even exclude other possibilities, or declare certain worlds rogue or terrorist.

Criticism or critical thought can no longer be in the name of Truth or the Real, but one can challenge the power, hegemony, with the consequent exclusion or silencing of certain voices, or the exclusion of certain names, responses to the Call.

Can war in the name of justice, and a "just war on terrorism," be equated with each other? War against stupidity cannot be equated with imperialistic wars. Surely certain wars are more just or can be better (easier) justified than others? I am not only speaking of physical wars with weapons, but also the war of words that are debated and fought. Can certain wars be justified? They are justified all the time. The question is rather, justified by what or by whom? Who sets the norm, who determines the name? Is a universal norm not necessary, because without it,

---

of a form of negativity that cannot be overcome dialectically that full objectivity can never be reached and that antagonism is an ever present possibility. Society is permeated by contingency and any order is of a hegemonic nature, i.e. it is always the expression of power relations' (Mouffe 2013:xi).

would that not open the door for the total relativity and in the end stupidity wins the day? Or is it stupidity that is winning anyway, and always wins, as long as there are winners and losers, good and evil, right and wrong?

What happens to the critical spirit if there is no war? Does the critical spirit need war? If there is no Real against which to wage war, where would the critical spirit's steam come from to fight all these wars? Wars are easily fought in the conviction that one knows the truth, that one is fighting for the Real material conditions, that one is fighting for the emancipation of the Real human, as long as one knows who or what the Real human is, or what the Real material conditions are, or one knows the Truth. The steam for these wars, as well as the justification of these wars, is this *belief*. The belief in the Truth, in the Good, or the belief that one's knowledge, one's reason, is the only correct, right knowledge and reason, and therefore the war is a just war or a war in the name of justice, because of the belief that one knows – knows the Truth, the Real or the Good, or God.

The Beast of war is the flipside of the Sovereign (see Derrida 2009:32). Derrida quotes La Fontaine from his fable, *The World and the Lamb*, where La Fontaine argues the reason of the strongest is always the best (Derrida 2009:7). The Reason of the strongest, as Mouffe and Laclau argue, is about hegemony, the strongest reason wins the day, and therefore it is the reason of the strongest that wins. The sovereign is the one who as the power to decide. The power to decide which equivalence represents the whole.

Wars, or struggles, are often believed to be sovereign struggles, as they are believed to be fought in the name of truth, or in the name of a justice, or in the name of a messiah who can save the world, as the Messiah is believed to be the Truth of the world.

Or stated differently, can the Messiah save from the beast or is the beast necessary to present the Messiah as the saviour?[2] If that is true, then one could argue that without a beast a Saviour or Messiah would not be necessary! This would make the beast a precondition for a Messiah as Saviour. Such a precondition would make the Beast the cause or the reason for the Saviour's existence. What would be the role of the church in this Beast-Saviour relationship? If the Beast and the Saviour need each other and become each other, that would make of the church as bride of the Saviour, by implication the bride of the Beast, as the church would be dependent on the Beast, the bad, the evil, the lack, the problem so as to present her Saviour as the saving answer. The church would need to be the bride of the beast so that it can offer her Saviour as the answer. Thus, if the church is believed to be a saving instrument, or as necessary for salvation, there would need to be

---

[2]   See Laruelle (2015b:77–78) who argues, 'Its inversion, which is to say the hierarchical primacy of Evil (or of not-Good) over Good, is only tolerable by a mutation of transcendent Evil as it is imagined by religions and philosophies. But as has been said, this not-Good is necessary to the Good, which itself is not "sufficient" to completely exhaust the ethical real.'

something in the world that one needs to be saved from in order for the church to have a reason for her existence, and therefore her existence, as salvation for the world, would be dependent on the existence of the Beast (evil, devil, etcetera), to which the church and her Saviour are the answer.

It would seem that the church needs sin to exist. Or stated differently, without sin there would be no need for a church (as a saving instrument). This is also true for the Saviour: without sin there would be no need for the Saviour. Therefore, the existence of a Saviour is dependent on the existence of sin (evil). Beast and Saviour, Beast and Sovereign, do not only co-exist, but they also turn into each other, which might explain the numerous atrocities of the church, or the old saying that says that the road to hell is paved with good intentions. It sometimes feels as if more beastly and ghastly things have been done in the name of good than in the name of evil.

Such criticism of the church and or of religion is not new, but it is an old criticism that has found new impetus with thinkers like Richard Dawkins (2008) and his *The God Delusion*.

Radical atheism, anti-religion, is to think that one can *solve* the problem (save the world) of sin and salvation by proclaiming God dead, or proclaiming evil dead, or sin dead, but that would translate into not to have thought at all, similar to those thinkers who believe that they are free of ideology.

Laruelle argues that the radical challenge is not to think that God is dead as in the various radical theological traditions, as atheism is just an inverse of theism, nor is it to remain undecided between atheism and theism in a form of anatheism, but the real challenge is to think God as a malicious god.[3] To think God, irrespective of which God, is the God that is being thought, but to think God as a malicious God. The challenge is to think the God of any thought as a malicious God. In other words, the God that appears in thought, that exists (ex-text) in thought is a malicious God. Why? Name it God, or name it Reason, or name it the Philosophical decision together with the principle of sufficient philosophy, or name it Truth – whatever one names it, it is malicious. It is malicious because it is the illusion of thought. Something Calls and this something that Calls is believed to pre-exist thought and it does pre-exist thought as it Calls thought forth. The thought that is called forth responds to the Call by determining that which pre-exists thought

---

[3]   The true atheism is not as simple as philosophy imagines it to be. It occurs in two stages: the banal refusal to believe in a God is self-contradictory and satisfies those who think little, but the refusal to believe in a good God is true rebellion. There is always a God lying in ambush, preparing his return in whatever negation is made of his existence, even a materialist one, but it is important that it be a malicious God, a thesis that only an "ultra"-religious heresy can face. The atheism of indifference is weak and lays down its arms along with its speech to philosophy; the second is a strong heresy, the "non-" theological radicalisation of a malicious God, his extension to every divinity that would appear as One or Multiple, as Sole and Great or even as natural and pagan (Laruelle 2015b:21).

and calls thought forth. It has determined that which pre-exists thought and with thought pre-exists the world, God for example. It has also been called other things: matter, and it has been called form (idea), and thus one has materialism and idealism. Religion decides what to call it, or philosophy decides what to call it, but whatever or whoever names it, it is believed to pre-exist thought and call thought forth, but only in thought is *it* (the name decided upon) made to pre-exist thought. That decision, that name, is malicious, because for it to exist and to determine the world that the name carries out, its creation in human thought must be forgotten.

Therefore, the challenge is thus not to think a different name, but to think the malicious nature of that Name, the name that is believed to be above and before any other names.

The whole idea of God, or religion or philosophies' decision to name, and to believe that their name is the good or the right name is the problem, or perhaps already wanting to identify the problem, is the problem.

The language of the Beast and the Saviour no longer makes sense. If such language no longer makes sense, does that not automatically mean that all is acceptable? That there are no longer any atrocities? That there is no evil or no wrong in the world? No, of-course there are evils, wrongs and too many atrocities, just like there are truths, the good, and too many Saviours. I am not arguing, as some secularists might, for a world without Gods and Beasts in the belief that such a world would usher in world peace. Not atheism nor theism or anatheism will save the world [that is if one believes that the world needs saving], but maybe to think the malicious god/s, might create an interesting space for a different praxis.

There is not much sense in trying to kill God, as one would need to kill God over and over again. Kill the God of theism and the God of atheism rises, kill the God of atheism and anatheism rises. What I am arguing is that there will necessarily always be a name given to that which is believed to pre-exist thought and calls thought forth to receive thought. It is the *Zug* of thinking in which humanity stands as *the* metaphysical being.

To declare God dead, or to kill God, will only be repeated as God (the Name given to that which calls thought forth) will always resurrect; God is immortal, and therefore neither God nor atheism can save the world, only a recognition of a malicious god. Only once one realises the need for god, the necessity of a god, and that there is no escaping god, even if the god that one is speaking of is an atheist god or a materialist god or an immanent god, can one perhaps begin thinking differently – not about god, but about thinking.

The malicious god that Laruelle is referring to is the god *of* thinking. Malicious in the sense that she/he/it is believed to pre-exist thought so as to call thought forth and then receive thought. Malicious as whatever it is that is believed to pre-exist thought, so as to call thought forth, and then to receive thought remains a trick (illusion) of thought. It *is* a creation of thought and yet Called forth by

something Other than thought. To believe in a malicious god is to perhaps begin
thinking the most thought-worthy.

What I am arguing, is that these Beasts with their corresponding Saviours, or
these Saviours and their Beasts, are created within contexts, as political-religious
acts of sense-making and meaning creation and therefore are necessary. No sense
or meaning without Gods and their corresponding Beasts.

I would even argue that Gods and Beasts are integral and necessary to the
processes of collective sense-making and meaning creation. Sovereigns (God,
saviours and messiahs) are as necessary as Beasts (Satan and Devils) in the creation of worlds, so much so that one can say without God and the Beast there
will be no world. In that sense God [Beast] truly is the creator of the world, often a world created in answer to a lack, a problem, an experience of evil and/or
darkness, in response to meaningless chaos.

In other words, God and by implication Beast are necessary, but insufficient,
which includes the belief of atheist and belief in all the different philosophical
decisions and the principle of sufficient philosophy. These philosophical decisions
can be interpreted as humanist or materialist, or immanent versions of religious
gods. Whatever is believed to pre-exist thought, and thus believed to call thought
and with thought individuals and worlds forth, can be given the name God, as a
generic name for all the different possible names. But it is a malicious God.

In returning to the world in which I am embodied, and many of those reading this book, one is embodied in a Western influenced world with various post-
colonial contexts seeking to respond with decolonial thoughts. In these worlds,
there is also a God creating the decolonial worlds after having identified the other,
the evil, the beast, whatever it is from which the post-colonial world needs saving
or liberation. In this context of beasts and gods, what is the role of Christianity?

Yet, before one can even attempt to respond to such a theological or Christological question, one needs to acknowledge the cultural-social-political and economic role of Christianity in colonization, modernity and postmodernity. One
needs to acknowledge the role that Christianity has played in the thinking of the
West. One cannot speak of decolonisation without thinking the role of Christianity in colonisation, as Fanon argues that for many Christianity is a white man's
church.[4] Yet on the other hand, the role of Christianity needs to be thought more
fundamentally than just from a mission perspective with the old cliché, that land
and its mineral wealth was exchanged for the Bible. If Christianity has played
such a dominant role in the birth of modernisation, colonisation and capitalism,
it would seem impossible to seek salvation from these in Christianity. Yet, Christianity has been part of both modernity as well as postmodernity, capitalism as

---

[4]   The Church in the colonies is a white man's Church, a foreigner's Church. It does not call the
      colonized to the ways of God, but to the ways of the white man, to the ways of the master, the
      ways of the oppressor (Fanon 2004:7).

well as socialism and communism, colonialism as well as often playing a leading role in the liberation, playing an important role in the various wars of independence from colonialism. Christianity seems to always be on both sides of all these binaries, binaries that have characterised the story of the West, and consequently the story of the globe. The global village is carried out, it ex-*texts*, in the light of this Western narrative.

Christ is part of the grammatisation in each of these dominant narratives that have shaped the West, and consequently has also shaped and formed the narrative of the global village. To understand this role of Christianity, or rather the role of the Christian texts, I turn to Deleuze and Guattari (2011:167–191) who argue that the face of Christ is the abstract machine of the West.

If one accepts their argument, how can turning to Christ be of any help? If Christ is so implicated in the rhizome, even to be seen as the creator (abstract machine) thereof, how can one turn to Christ in search of salvation from the rhizome? This question has been asked numerous times in the history of the West and it has been answered, but it has always been answered unconsciously and/or consciously in-Christ. In other words, there is no escaping Christ and therefore it is time to maybe change the question: should one not think *through* Christ rather than trying to think against or outside of Christ?

The question: how can Christ be of help? In the past, and in most critical intellectual's minds, the immediate answer that comes to mind is that Christ and/or religion cannot be of any help at all, as Christianity (religion) is part of the problem, or even *is* the problem. Critical intellectuals have often argued that minds (consciousness) need to be liberated from religion (gods and beasts), as religion was perceived as false-consciousness and even bad consciousness. The "just" war of critical scholarship has in the West, in the tradition of the Enlightenment, been a war on religion and specifically on Christianity. Yet, in response to secular critical thought, critical liberal theology returned the favour, and waged its battle by defending critical theology's right to remain a faculty at a public university serving the public good of the citizens. Critical liberal theology incorporated the weapons of critical secular scholarship into their Christian thought, so much so that Ernst Bloch could write in his book, *Atheismus in Christum: 'Nur ein Atheist kann ein guter Christ sein, nur ein Christ kann ein guter Atheist sein'* (Bloch 1968). In response to this kind of critical thinking, theologies without God developed, or the school of radical theology or God-is-dead-theology emerged with theologians like: Thomas J Altizer, Mark C Taylor, John D. Caputo, Paul Van Buren, John Robinson, to name a few of its proponents.

Is atheism the answer? Is a *God is dead theology* the answer? Laruelle responds, 'Atheism is, in all respects, a hasty mediocre, and thoughtless solution, passive and naïve, as is materialism itself' (Laruelle 2015c:2). This does not mean that Laruelle returns to a theism or anatheism and neither will I in this book, but

rather turn to a malicious God, or the inescapable trick of the belief of thinking –
the inescapable malicious trick of the belief of thinking, namely the belief that
thought is sufficient, for example, sufficient to capture (think) the Real, the Call.
Instead of pondering the existence or non-existence of God or the existence or
non-existence of anything, rather ponder the *Zug* of thinking in which humanity
finds itself, and in which humanity is the metaphysical, as discussed in a previous
chapter in reference to Heidegger.

For a moment back to radical theology, which seems to have become the intellectual postmodern theology of the West, and that is exactly it: it is very much a
Western theology, whilst in post-colonial countries liberation was sought from the
white patriarchal Christian God and not God as such. In the liberation theological
tradition, God was to be found amongst the poor, marginalised and ostracised or
God was re-discovered (re-invented) in a feminist reading or womanist reading of
the Biblical God, in response to white patriarchy. So often theology (the prophetic
side of theology) sought liberation from the priestly side of state-religion or state-
theology. Theologies born in post-colonial contexts also sought liberation from
critical liberal Western theology, which in a sense was also a form of state theology – the state theology of liberal Western states.

There is a very long tradition of prophetic or reformation theology's battle for
liberation from the dominant priestly or state or empire theologies, which sought
to dominate and control theologies. This tradition of critique against priestly theology is already found in the Bible, with the prophetic tradition vs the priestly tradition. In the early church, there was the example of the monastic movement – the
desert fathers who moved out of the cities, controlled by their bishops and priests,
into the desert, in protest (see Meylahn 2013:331–337) and seeking a prophetic
alternative to the priestly theology of the cities. The Reformation can be interpreted as a prophetic protest against the priestly (papal) corruption of the church.
The various liberation theologies are prophetic voices that arose in protest against
colonialism and capitalism, or eco-theologies speaking out against (protesting)
capitalism and globalisation. Many of the critical (liberation) traditions inside and
outside of Christianity took inspiration from the Christian texts and/or, where appropriated, by liberation theologians. The result is that Christ is found on both
sides of the war, as either the priestly Christ of the church and state (Christ the
Lord and Prince) or Christ of the poor and marginalised. Even the Christ of God
is dead theology is a priestly Christ of the liberal intellectual secular city.

In the previous chapters I tried to understand and describe the praxis of being
human and that part of this praxis of being human is ex-*text*-tualisation. The *me*
that is called becomes the *I am* of *here I am* through ex-*text*-ualising in response
to a Call. This ex-*text*-ualising is never done in isolation, but in social-cultural
(textual) contexts of the primary, secondary and tertiary retentions and protentions of the *I*'s embodiment. Meaning is made, sense is created in this con*text*ual

embodiment. Embodiment, which is con*text*ualisation, is the collective sense-making (past and present) of the con*text*. It does not really matter if one calls it common sense, or aesthetics, this sense-making is always a political-religious praxis, as it is the sense-making in-common of a community or of a specific context. In this sense, it is a political praxis: being-in-common as making-sense-and-creating-meaning-in-common. Such a political praxis needs to be clearly differentiated from politics, just as Nancy sought to understand *the political* as something very different from *politics*.[5] Making-sense and creating-meaning-in-common is a political-ideological-religious act where a particular equivalence is chosen to represent the whole, and thereby *incarnates* the whole, but is deformed in that incarnation as it can never represent the whole. A particular name is given to that which is believed to pre-exist thought, call thought forth, and receive thought again, but whatever is believed to pre-exist thought only exists in-thought (there is nothing outside of text), but this is forgotten. Therefore, whatever is believed (made) to pre-exist thought is in-thought and thus is deformed – it is no longer that which pre-exists, but it is that which ex-*texts*.

In the previous chapters political, ideological and/or religion were used interchangeably, without thereby denying the important differences between them, but the focus was on the collective (being-in-common) creation of meaning and sense-making as binding (*religare*) the in-common.

Thus, no sense-making or meaning-creation is free from ideology, free from religion, free from politics and therefore free from illusion. I am not saying that all religions, politics and ideologies are illusions, but what I am saying is that they are fictions. To be able to judge that they are illusions I would need to believe myself to be free from illusion, which is impossible. Only somebody who is free from illusion can judge others to be caught in illusions, but this belief that one is free of an illusion, is the illusion par excellence, or stated differently *is* the illusion of ideology par excellence. All the different freedom struggles, believing themselves to be the struggle to liberate the people from illusion or false-consciousness, were indeed only replacing one set of chains for another, as they *believed themselves to be free*. They were only free because they could not recognise their new chains (new illusions) in which they were ensnared. So many liberation struggles have been fought in the name of this belief (freedom, liberation) that once liberated from false-consciousness there is a 'real' world behind the appearances of ideol-

---

[5]   Jason Smith in his introduction to, *Hegel: The Restlessness of the Negative*, writes, 'kind of proto-political sociality that would not yet be political in any identifiable sense, an *ontology* of being-in-and-as-common whose claims could not simply be articulated in inherited political idiom?' (Nancy 2002:x). As well as Christopher Fynsk in his Forward to Nancy's *The Inoperative Community*, '… what Nancy calls in the preface to this volume "the political (*le politique*: the site where what it means to *be* in common is open to definition) and "politics" (*la politique*: the play of forces and interests engaged in a conflict over the representation and governance of social existence)' (Nancy 1991:x).

ogy or behind the appearances of false-consciousness; the belief that on the other side of illusion, false-consciousness, "free" subjects are to be found. For example, the belief that there is a real Africa behind the appearances, namely the way colonialism deformed Africa as the European's black other. I unpacked this belief of finding true Africa in the pre-colonial past in a previous project (Meylahn 2017e). So often liberation or post-colonial thinking believes that there is a pre-existing essence to be found once the dominant (colonial or patriarchal) thought constructions are removed. What such thoughts do not realise is that such belief is the truth of all thought, and the truth of that belief is repetition.

Or the belief that the "truth" of what it means to be a woman can be found once the cage imposed on women by patriarchy is destroyed. Such beliefs are not new, but have driven history in the West for centuries. It was this belief that truth is to be found once human constructions are lifted that inspired the search for the historical Jesus. Or that inspires historical critical exegesis. The idea that one can get closer to the truth by deconstructing the constructions of power and ideology. In a certain sense, such belief is justified. It is justified in the sense that the cracks in and of thought-systems reveal the truth of those thought-systems, but not the truth of the Real, or that which called thought forth. The cracks reveal the truth of thought-systems, namely that they are deformations. However the cracks are not the truth, but they are the sites or the occasions for the truth of thought-systems to be revealed. Feminism is the occasion for the revelation of the deformation of patriarchy, not the revelation of the truth of humanity or women. Black consciousness is the site or the occasion for the revelation of the deformation of white supremacy, but not the truth of humanity. The mistake would be to make more of the occasion than a revelation of the truth of the thought-systems, by making it into its own thought-system, based on the belief that one knows what pre-exists deformation. That is, to believe that feminism or black consciousness knows what pre-exists white patriarchal thought.

This belief has certain similarities and might even still be part of the very tradition that ushered in the Enlightenment and later positivism. It is a tradition that believes that the true nature (the Real that pre-exists thought) could be found (discovered) once the veil of myth, tradition, religion and ideology has been lifted. Battles in the name of freedom or in the name of liberation are in the end nothing more than counter-hegemonic practices 'that attempt to disarticulate it in an effort to install another form of hegemony' (Mouffe 2013:2), but hegemony will remain as part of the being-in-common as a political praxis. It is this political praxis that Mouffe (2013:2) calls *the political* that can never be eradicated, as it is part of being-in-common. Therefore, one will need to accept that there will always be "illusions" or rather deformations as particular equivalences are chosen to represent the whole, and that one will never be free of such deformations (ideology/religion). Therefore, the necessity to believe in a malicious God.

There is always a cage in search of a bird as Kafka said in his *Third Notebook* on the 6th of November 1917, 'I am a cage in search of a bird'. The moment there is a bird, (the moment something exists, it ex-*texts*), and therefore *it* (the identifiable something) will always be a caged bird, as *there is* no such existence as an uncaged (un-texted) bird – the text is always there once there is ex-*text*-ence. Critique and criticism seemed to only function with the steam of this belief, the belief of having access to the Real behind or before (prior) the various appearances of ideology and/or false-consciousness (see Latour 2004). If this belief in the Real behind the veil is no longer believed, what happens to critique? What happens to critical thought? Or is one forced into passivity by the equivalence of all "illusions"? Is critique still possible or has it run out of steam?

Does one still want critique or should one attempt to move beyond good and evil, beyond the idea of Saviours (Messiahs) and Beasts? What is the point of Beasts and Sovereigns as they turn into each other anyway (see Derrida 2009:32)?

What would happen to Christianity or religion and even politics if it was no longer about saving souls or people from the bad, the evil or the Beast?

From the previous chapters one realises that to create the opposite, in the sense of anti-narratives, does not help, as the opposite Other soon turns into the Same. Christ is part of the enclosure (State theology, Empire theology) and part of the disenclosure (Liberation Theology, Prophetic Theology, Black Theology, African Theology, Feminist Theology, Womanist Theology). Christ is both in the enclosure of metaphysics as well as the disenclosure of metaphysics, as Nancy argues, 'Christianity is at the heart of the dis-enclosure just as it is at the centre of the enclosure [*clôture*]' (Nancy 2008:10).

It can therefore not just be about a hermeneutics of liberation, or a prophetic hermeneutics, but a more radical hermeneutics is necessary, so radical that it is no longer hermeneutics, understood as Hermes the mediator or interpreter between thought (language) and the Real, but where humans are seen as creators of meaning: noetic souls as poetic souls. Hermeneutics is no longer just about reading texts, but realising that reading is writing texts.

It is no longer about caged birds and free birds, but about different cages, and creating a preferred cage.

Or as Latour (2010) argues, it is about composition,[6] not just deconstructing all the fictions, but collectively composing an inclusive fiction of a possible common world. Yet, the question will always remain: Who composes? Who decides what and who is included in the common world? Is the common truly common, in the sense of being radically inclusive? Such questions of who or what is included in the common, is also the question that the European Union is asking itself: who is

---

6   While critics still believe that there is too much belief and too many things standing in the way of reality, compositionists believe that there are enough ruins and that everything has to be reassembled piece by piece (Latour 2010:475–476).

part of the European Union? And who makes that call, who decides? The answer will always be: the reason of the strongest is best. Collectives are determined by collective meaning and sense, which in turn is determined by hegemony. Critique of such collectives is determined by counter practices seeking to determine an alternative hegemony.

What is the point of having the hammer of deconstruction and debunking, all the illusions, if there is nothing behind these illusions, no real world, no real Africa, no real woman, no real or essential human is revealed?[7] The question is, what meaning can be *created* of being an African or a woman, whilst recognising the wounds of the past and present with its violence against the black and female body? There is a long history of "dehumanisation" of certain groups and people. Not dehumanisation because one knows what it means to be human, but dehumanisation in the sense of depriving individuals the opportunity to co-write their bodies.

Laruelle argues that these actual historic victims are the occasions for the generic intellectual[8] in contrast to the media intellectual[9] to think the victim-in-person. The generic intellectual understands that the victim is a victim as a subject in a world.[10] The victim is a victim as body, as being embodied (ex-*text*-ualised) in a world where the body is *classified* (stratified) as black body, female, a body with a certain sexual orientation and a certain gender, or as a disabled body, etcetera. But the victim-in-person is not that body, but the "Flesh" that is classified and stratified and therefore makes all flesh a victim, just as it makes all bodies criminals.[11] All flesh is a victim, but there are bodies that are victims and there are

---

[7]   With a hammer (or a sledge hammer) in hand you can do a lot of things: break down walls, destroy idols, ridicule prejudices, but you cannot repair, take care, assemble, reassemble, stich together. It is more impossible to compose with critique than it is to cook with a seesaw (Latour 2010:475).

[8]   ... we will distinguish "generic" (or "under condition," or even "non-standard") "intellectuals," who use philosophy out of necessity, but as a simple under-determined means, without finality as to the real of victims, ultimately dedicated to the prior-to-the-first defense of victims (Laruelle 2015b:51).

[9]   In this sense, "intellectuals" are the symptom of that which philosophy becomes when it takes victims to heart and takes care to attend to them and raise them to the status of principal object, between image and phantasm (Laruelle 2015b:50). We will call a media intellectual, engaged or embedded, he who uses media in order *to be invested in the media* (Laruelle 2015b:50).

[10] Their duality is unilateral: the subject has Man for its condition, rather than presupposing him, whereas Man presupposes the subject and its relations to the world only occasionally. In this hypothesis, it is understood that it is the subject who is victim, not Man-in-person, even though it is the subject's necessary but non-sufficient condition and a priori material form. Here is in fact the principle of what will be "resurrection:" Man-in-person or the glorious lived experience is the negative condition of death, of the subject, but it itself does not die when the subject dies (Laruelle 2015b:93).

[11] We are spontaneous criminals and persecutors condemned to be able to actually become so because we are in-the-last-instance victims, and this for the very same reason: our humanity

bodies that are persecutors in particular worlds carried out by particular fictions (politics, religion, ideology). The media intellectuals jump onto the bandwagon of some or other liberation politics, that (mis-)uses the *bodies* of victims in defence of their politics. The generic intellectuals have compassion with the victim as victim-in-person and therefore do not jump onto particular political band-wagons, but take a *stance* with the insurrection of the victim-in-person as a resurrection. The bodies of victims are an occasion to reveal the truth of the thought-systems that made them the bodies of victims. This occasion can be used, and thus the bodies of victims are used to present a new or alternative embodiment, via a victimology. In other words, the *bodies* of victims are used to carry out a new political-religious-ideological collective. Or the *bodies* of victims can be the occasion to think from the flesh of the victims, the victim-in-person, or from the generic victim, believing, knowing there is a malicious God, who deforms flesh into bodies. A stance with the victim-in-person knowing that bodies that exist are victims and persecutors in the particular thought-world.

This is a stance that does not seek to use the bodies of victims, the determined bodies of the victims, to determine a world, but interprets all the bodies as determined bodies, and thereby the insurrection of the Flesh, the insurrection (Call) of that which calls different determinations of bodies forth on the basis of what is believed to pre-exist thought.

There is a resurrection of the Flesh, the resurrection of the Call, after the crucifixion of subjects (bodies). The glorious Flesh can rise, the Call can call again, only after the crucifixion of the body, crucifixion of the subject. History crucifies the bodies of actual victims, and the call for specific justice is the call of the actual historic victims, yet it is in-response to that call that the victim also becomes persecutor, and thus it is only the Call of the victim-in-person that insurrects as the resurrection of the Call.

This hammer of the media intellectual debunking illusions with his or her sledge hammer, believing itself to be breaking down walls, crushing false-consciousness – is it not still inspired by the same belief as the first hammers of modernity, that believed that once the veil of myth and tradition is broken the secular world will reveal itself? These hammers fighting the battle for justice are in truth just fighting for an alternative hegemony.

Is it not still the same modern hammer that hammers away at this world, believing itself to be in search of the Real that can be found once all the layers of social construction have been broken away?

Its limitations are greater still, for the hammer of critique can only prevail if, behind the slowly dismantled wall of appearances is finally revealed the netherworld of reality. But when there is nothing real to be seen behind the destroyed wall, critique suddenly looks

(Laruelle 2015b:93).

like another call to nihilism. What is the point of poking holes in delusions, if nothing more true is revealed beneath (Latour 2010:475)?

The hammer of war against the Real only functions as long as there is the belief that the Real and thought are separated and mediated by language.

One is no longer just a reader and interpreter of texts, but author of texts (see Stiegler, 2015b:113). It is about *poiēsis* and later I will argue why the *poiēsis* could be a Christ-*poiēsis* in a global village where the West has played such a dominant role. In exploring a trans-fictional praxis as Christ-*poiēsis* I will enter into conversation with Latour's composition as well as Mouffe's agonism.

Without hammer?

What if the hammer is no longer used to break down the walls and veils to reveal the Real, but it has been transformed into a pen that writes fictions, various differ-ent fictions carrying out different worlds, with the result that there is a democracy of fictions? In each fiction, the Man-in-person[12] becomes a body that is a some-body – a subject. In these fictions, some bodies will always be victims and others will be persecutors. Each of these philosophies is a war on the Real, and therefore a crime against Man-in-person. But what if these wars were interpreted as fic-tions, as necessary but insufficient fictions: Philo-fictions? Would such an attitude make a difference to these wars? If the wars are no longer in the name of Truth, Real, Justice, God or the Good, but the question is rather, which fiction creates a better (more inclusive) common world, would that not change the wars? It would change the wars, as the wars would be without hammers, although they would still be persecutors with regards to Man-in-person.

On the other hand, does a democracy of fictions not open the door for all sorts of new problems? If thinking is no longer a war against the Real in the name of Truth, Justice, God or the Good, then everything is possible, including the denial of climate change. Such denial would be on equal footing with the climate scientists, various conspiracy theories are then equal to "scientific" theories. There is no way to differentiate between fake news and "real" news, or in a certain sense all news is fake – as they are fictions. Latour (2004) takes up this criticism when he argues:

Do you see why I am worried? I myself have spent some time in the past trying to show "the lack of scientific certainty" inherent in the construction of facts. I too made it a "pri-

---

12   I follow Laruelle's form of writing Man-in-person and thereby not intending to exclude woman-in-person, but specifically follow Laruelle to thereby link it to his thought. The differentiation between male and female is part of the embodiment, as gender is a construction and therefore it is impossible to bring sexual difference into Man-in-person as Man-in-person is prior-to-the-priority of sexual differentiation.

mary issue." But I did not exactly aim at fooling the public by obscuring the certainty of a closed argument—or did I? After all, I have been accused of just that sin. Still, I'd like to believe that, on the contrary, I intended to emancipate the public from prematurely naturalized objectified facts. Was I foolishly mistaken? Have things changed so fast? In which case the danger would no longer be coming from an excessive confidence in ideological arguments posturing as matters of fact—as we have learned to combat so efficiently in the past—but from an excessive distrust of good matters of fact disguised as bad ideological biases! While we spent years trying to detect the real prejudices hidden behind the appearance of objective statements, do we now have to reveal the real objective and incontrovertible facts hidden behind the illusion of prejudices (Latour 2004:227)?

Has too much been challenged and now one is left with nothing, a nihilism that makes everything possible leaving critical thought with no basis for critique? What about a critique of critique? 'Or should we rather bring the sword of criticism to criticism itself and do a bit of soul-searching here: what were we really after when we were so intent on showing the social construction of scientific facts?' (Latour 2004:227) What if this road leads to criticism of those things one cherishes?[13]

Latour's response to such criticism is that this road was never to take one away from reality into the fictional, but to bring one closer to reality.[14] It was all about hearing the Call. To hear the Call, to think that which calls thought forth, and it was never to enter into the "free play" of fictions. This differentiation needs to be kept in mind. Yes, radical critique, namely critique of critique, might have made what traditional critical thought would call "uncritical" thought possible, or might even have made what traditional critique would call "stupidity" possible. There is indeed a rise in stupidity, together with what Stiegler (2014, 2015a) names symbolic misery. That accusation stands, as radical critique in the sense of critique of critique has made uncritical thought possible and thereby the inability to decide between conspiracy theories and so-called facts or fake news and so-called facts, but only if it heeds a nihilist Call and thereby determines the Call as nihilist. If one determines the Call as being nihilist, then nothing has changed as one is still as modern as the modern thought such thinking criticises. To determine the Call is modern, even if the Call is determined as nihilist. One can only not differentiate between fake news and real news if there is nothing, only pure construction.

---

[13] There is no sure ground even for criticism. Isn't this what criticism intended to say: that there is no sure ground anywhere? But what does it mean when this lack of sure ground is taken away from us by the worst possible fellows as an argument against the things we cherish (Latour 2004:227)?

[14] My argument is that a certain form of critical spirit has sent us down the wrong path, encouraging us to fight the wrong enemies and, worst of all, to be considered as friends by the wrong sort of allies because of a little mistake in the definition of its main target. The question was never to get away from facts but closer to them, not fighting empiricism but, on the contrary, renewing empiricism (Latour 2004:231).

But there isn't nothing, only nothing outside of text, but these texts with their différance are still responses to a Call (which is not nothing, just as it is not not-nothing, it is undecidable as it is foreclosed to thought), but it determines thought in the last instance, as that which calls thought forth. It (thought) remains in response to the Call (which is foreclosed to thought), but still determines thought in the last instance, and therefore it is not a free fall, and everything goes. The hammer that has been exchanged for a pen remains an embodied pen that writes and reads, or reads as it writes in response, and is determined in the last instance by that which calls it into responsibility. The pen that writes fictions is not irresponsible but totally and completely *respons*ible, as it is nothing but a response. It is absolutely responsible, and this twice over:

1. It responds to a Call, *was uns Denken heisst*, and therefore it is *respons*ible thinking.
2. It is guided by a fiction of the creation of fictions, namely to think thought, or as Laruelle might argue to develop a science of philosophy, a science of thought.

The subject of the pen (author) is a response to Man-in-person and has a responsibility to Man-in-person, and it is specifically the Victim-in-person that is the ethical modality of Man-in-person (see Laruelle 2015b:8). Ethics is no longer determined by what is good or by what is just, but the ethical modality of Man-in-person is the Victim-in-person, and the actual victim is the occasion for this ethical modality. The actual historic victim is the occasion for an ethical modality, that is, an ethical stance, but not an ethical theory of what is believed to be good or right, or just, or what is believed to be Real.

It is not a free for all, irresponsible, pen scribbling fiction, but a responsible pen, which is a doubly responsible pen responding to a Call, and responding by thinking the responding, whilst responding. Responsible in responding and in being responsible for the response.

What has this double responsibility got to do with Christ and the Christ-*poiēsis* of this book?

Why focus on Christ?

One might also ask why focus on Christ, if Christianity is so implicated? The question can also be asked: why not focus on Christ, if Christ is so implicated? In a sense it is like believing that if one is free of illusion that is the greatest illusion, likewise to believe that one can think in the Western influenced world without Christ, is to think Christ. Therefore, instead of trying to avoid thinking Christ, to actively think *through* Christ, similar to the only way to avoid illusion is to think through illusion: that is, know that all thought is an illusion (fiction).

It is because Christ is so implicated that one should think through Christ. If one truly wants to think non-colonial and/or transmodern and therefore a trans-fictional praxis, one has to think through Christ, which means through the abstract machine of the West, otherwise one would just create possible lines of light (liberation) from the rhizome, which will be re-captured by the apparatus of capture (Deleuze & Guattari 2011:424ff) and integrated into the ever-expanding rhizome, just as the prophet inevitably turns into the priest.

As argued above, Christianity is implicated in modernity and colonialism, but just as much as Christ is implicated in the disenclosure of metaphysics, in the various liberation movements (Black theology, African theology, Feminist and Womanist theologies) and thereby in the various independence struggles.

Disenclosure becomes enclosure and enclosure becomes disenclosure, any of these binaries become each other, turn into each other, because there is no real change, only repetition. It is therefore not an attempt to move beyond metaphysics, as any beyond, or anti, or post or Other is only a re-creation of that which one has left, that is a creation of an alternative metaphysics, but which is still metaphysical. This is what one needs to move beyond: acknowledging that any movement beyond, in the sense of an alternative, is not a beyond, but only a turning of the tables, shifting the furniture in a particular ontology, or increase the size of the particular ontology.

The dominant world is carried out by the abstract machine of the West, which has been described as the Face of Christ, and for that reason Christ has to be thought-through, if one wants to be responsible and respond to the dominant responses. But more importantly the story of Christ offers a story (fiction) of not only the abstract machine, but also of thinking. And therefore Christ-*poiēsis* offers the space to fulfil the double responsibility. This will be unpacked in more detail, later in the chapter.

Christ-*poiēsis* as more radical hermeneutics

Therefore, more radical hermeneutics is needed than a disenclosing hermeneutics, more radical hermeneutics than a sledge hammer of critical hermeneutics, more radical hermeneutics is needed than a liberation hermeneutics, or a black hermeneutics, African hermeneutics or feminist hermeneutics, or a decolonial hermeneutics, hermeneutics that does not carry (or mediate) meaning, but creates meaning. Hermeneutics that writes when it reads, and reads when it writes, that is a *poiētics*.

There is nothing to be revealed after critique, only one more illusion of ideology, one more metaphysics, and this continues *ad infinitum*. In that sense, there is no transcendent that can be reached. One remains in the text: there is no outside text (see Derrida 1997:158). The Call, the moment it is recognised, it is read, it is written as a determined Caller *in* the response (text), the Man-in-person is alwa··· a victim-in-person *in* the response, irrespective if s/he is embodied as victim or .

persecutor in a particular world. But, there is not nothing outside text! On the contrary, there is probably too much outside of text, namely all that which Calls the text forth, *was uns denken heisst*, but that which calls thought forth is not captured in thought, yet it can only be thought in thought (it only appears – is disclosed as it is appropriated), it only exists to be read when it is written, that is if it ex-*texts*. I am a cage in search of a free bird only ever to find caged birds in the cage that I am. Man-in-person is always outside the text, but the moment one believes to be able to read Man-in-person, it ex-*texts*, it is written.

Once one makes "peace" that one only ever "finds" caged birds, and stops hunting for the free bird by breaking all the cages, one can move from dis-articulation towards re-articulation, but re-articulating differently. Or as Mouffe[15] argues, not only a dis-articulation is necessary, but a re-articulation. The re-articulation is not just more of the same, it is not repetition, because it is re-articulation without the faith in thinking. It is without the faith in thinking, as the truth of the faith in thinking is repetition. A re-articulation without the faith or the belief of knowledge is literature (fiction). Literature as a re-articulation without repeating the *faith* or the *belief* of *knowledge* of the articulation that it dis-articulated in the first place. A re-articulation that recognises the importance and the necessity of faith for the creation of meaning and sense-making, but simultaneously recognising the insufficiency of that faith, belief and knowledge. Literature in the sense of recognising the necessity of faith, whilst recognising its insufficiency or its fictional nature.

More radical hermeneutics is necessary, which is so radical that it is no longer hermeneutics, but a creation, a composition, a *poiēsis*, in the attempt to forge new weapons. To forge Deleuze's new weapons, for what? To fight a new war? No, not a war, but to forge new tools, by transforming the swords and the spears of critique into ploughshares and pruning hooks of cultivation. 'They will beat their swords into ploughshares and their spears into pruning hooks. Nation will not take up sword against nation, nor will they train for war anymore' (Is. 2:4). What kind of peace is possible with fictions? What kind of peace is possible with all the different necessary but insufficient philo-fictions or faith-fictions? Wars are fought because of the necessity of truths, the necessity of the Good, the Just the Right, and/or the God, but maybe peace is possible in the recognition of the insufficiency of these necessary philo-fictions or religious-fictions? Wars against the Real will remain, as they are necessary, but if their insufficiency is recognised, maybe one can move from antagonism towards agonism.[16]

---

15 This is a complex process that cannot merely consist in separating the different elements whose discursive articulation constitutes the structure of the current t hegemony. The second moment, the moment of re-articulation, is crucial. Otherwise, we will be faced with a chaotic situation of pure dissemination, leaving the door open for attempts at re-articulation (Mouffe 2013:73).

16 My argument, however, is that the authoritarian solution is not a necessary logical consequence

The dreams of Peace

What kind of peace is this that is forged from the previous tools of war? Is it the cosmopolitan peace-dream (in the sense of David Held's (2010), Daniele Archibugi's (1995) or Ulrich Beck's (2006) cosmopolitanism) of a united Western rational world, where reason, preferably Western or even Habermasian secular reason, wins the day over "primitive" emotional arguments? Habermas rightly saw the need for rational disputation with the other (Habermas 1998), but it is exactly that: rational and therefore the emotional side is silenced and side-lined.

I agree with Chantal Mouffe and her criticism of cosmopolitanism when she argues that her 'main objection to the cosmopolitan approach is that whatever its formulation, it postulates the availability of a world beyond hegemony and beyond sovereignty, therefore negating the dimension of the political. Moreover, it is usually predicated on the universalization of the Western model and therefore does not make room for a plurality of alternatives' (Mouffe 2013:20). In other words, it denies the need to make sense and create meaning as a political-religious act. Then there are those cosmopolitans who take the political and specifically the power imbalance in the world seriously, and seek to build a cosmopolitanism, taking these imbalances of power into consideration.[17] All these different cosmopolitan movements follow a universalist approach, and therefore still the hammer that believes that once all the differences (economic, social, cultural and political) have been debunked there remains a universal humanity beneath all the layers of construction. Mouffe (2013:22) argues not for a universalist approach, but a pluri-verse approach. One needs to accept that any identity 'is constructed as difference, and that any social objectivity is constituted through acts of power' (Mouffe 2013:4). Identity and social objectivity is only possible through exclusion, as it is exclusion that governs the constitution of objectivity and identity. It is for this reason that Laru-

---

of such an ontological postulate, and that by distinguishing between 'antagonism' and 'agonism', it is possible to visualize a form of democracy that does not deny radical negativity (Mouffe 2013:xii).

[17] Next to the traditional Kant-inspired universalist cosmopolitanism of those who, like Martha Nussbaum, assert that our primary allegiance should be to the 'worldwide community of human beings', we find a growing number of 'new cosmopolitans' who reject such a perspective and want to bring cosmopolitans down to earth by recognizing the realities of power and acknowledging the need for politically viable solidarities (Mouffe 2013:20).

This new cosmopolitanism exists in a variety of forms, among them the 'discrepant cosmopolitanism' of James Clifford, the 'vernacular cosmopolitanism' of Homi Bhabha and Dipesh Chakrabarty, the 'multi-situated cosmopolitanism' of Bruce Robbins, the 'decolonial cosmopolitanism' of Walter Mignolo and the 'critical cosmopolitanism' of Paul Rabinow. All these theorists try to reconcile cosmopolitanism, seen as an abstract standard of planetary justice, with a need for belonging and acting at levels smaller that the species as a whole (Mouffe 2013:20–21).

elle (2015b:113) turns to the victims, those or that which is excluded, as the site of exclusion reveals the fictional nature of worlds. Laruelle argues, '... Man-in-person as the "savior" that comes-under-to-victims' (2015b:113). Laruelle refers to Man-in-person, Deleuze and Guattari refers to the Body without Organs, Henry refers to Flesh or Life, and in this book, I have tried to interpret all these different names, as different names (determinations) of that which calls thought forth, and referred to that which calls thought forth as the Call. The Call, Man-in-person, Flesh (Life), Body without Organs "is" the Victim-in-person, or the generic victim, as it is the Call that is sought to be determined (captured – *in einen Begriff ergriffen*) in the response. It is the Call that is "persecuted" by the very thinking that it called forth. It is the Call that is hunted by thought, which it called forth in the first place, but from which it withdraws. The Call, as the victim-in-person or generic victim, is hunted, persecuted by thought and therefore every called-forth-thought has its victim, as thought never *does justice* to that which withdraws from thought. Therefore, justice is always still to come. The subjects that are carried out by thought, in which they are subjects, are as much victims of their thought as they are persecutors of all the objects that they determine in their embodied worlds. Yet, to understand something of the generic victim, that is the victim of thought, the actual historic embodied victims are the occasion. In this sense Laruelle can argue that the victims are the *ultimata* or the *eschata* from which we are able less to judge the world than to transform it, which has only a generic sense' (Laruelle 2015b:113). I will return to the victim-in-person and the historic embodied victims as the occasion for an ethical modality later in the chapter.

The question is, if peace is possible? Cosmopolitanism has been shown to offer peace at a price, and the price was to sacrifice difference. A trans-fictional praxis does not want to sacrifice difference, nor celebrate difference, but acknowledge differences.

Mouffe recognises the danger of a unified world, and therefore argues for the necessity for a multi-polar world, in my argument multi-fictional worlds, as different worlds are carried out by different metaphysical systems, different narratives carry out different ontologies and therefore a trans-fictional praxis, with various *logoi* and thus multi-polar. But this is only the first step, to acknowledge and recognise the pluri-verse nature of multiple worlds of a trans-fictional praxis. The second is an *ethical modality* of such a trans-fictional praxis, so that the pluri-verse worlds do not fall victim to total relativity. The ethical modality of trans-fictional praxis is a Christo-*poiēsis*, based on Laruelle's victim-in-person, when he argues, 'We assemble this research under the generic name of Victim-in-person, an ethical modality of Man-in-person' (Laruelle 2015b:8).

Besides cosmopolitanism there is also the belief of peace under communism.

Can peace be found in "true" communism, where the community is free from illusion and thus liberated, where it can rule itself in its material truth, as many on the left argue that only a revival of communism can *save* the world (see Mouffe 2013:83)? Again, Mouffe argues that these revivals of communism deny the political nature of humanity in the creation of meaning and sense-making. The only way that communism and cosmopolitanism can work is if a new mega-truth is believed in and all believe in it – a universal truth or foundational truth whose necessity is recognised, but whose insufficiency is denied. Another *way* is necessary, not another truth that trumps the previous truths, but a way needs to be found to live in a pluri-verse world, which is multi-polar and thus a trans-fictional praxis, but without resigning to relativity.

These cosmopolitan and communist dreams of rational individuals in equal speech communities, unaffected by their emotions, have not really moved beyond the hammer. Now it is the emotions that are hammered into non-existence. Communism, as Sartre argued, is the 'unsurpassable horizon of our time' (Nancy 1991:1) and so many believe that the only solution is to return to the common of communism. As the word communism stands

as an emblem of the desire to discover or rediscover a place of community at once beyond social divisions and beyond subordination to techno-political dominion, and thereby beyond such wasting away of liberty, of speech, or of simple happiness as comes about whenever these become subjugated to the exclusive order of privatization; and finally, more simply and even more decisively, a place from which to surmount the unravelling that occurs with the death of each one of us – that death that, when no longer anything more than the death of the individual, carries an unbearable burden and collapses into insignificance (Nancy 1991:1).

Yet, the materialism of communism believes that the "true" material conditions can rule themselves once they are liberated from ideology; that the Real, if given a chance, will carry out a perfect world, and the evil that needs to be overcome is ideology and false consciousness. All these different ideas of a possible harmonious utopia have not transformed the hammer into ploughshares and pruning hooks, as there is still too much hammer. Still a hammer trying to find, not necessarily a secular realm, but still a realm filled with too much *belief* in reason or true liberated consciousness.

Latour (2010:485) argues for the *composing* of a common world, rather than finding a common world. Yet, who writes the score, who determines this composition, who is the composer, or who are the main authors, the dominant authors, and how many voices are excluded from this composition? For Latour (1993:142) it is important to give a voice to as many as possible, even the non-human, and therefore he argues for a parliament of things, where as many as possible things are included. But what about the irreconcilable differences between these different voices, what mega-narrative silences these conflicting voices or arbitrates between these conflicting voices? It will still be about hegemony, and which narrative or which ring binds them all. Something that Tolkien maybe recognised in *The Lord of the Rings*, that power always seeks that one ring to bind them all. This could also be turned around, that whatever binds all the different pluri-verse narratives into a common world, is power. One has not moved beyond the malicious God, but it is important to recognise the necessity for such a God for meaning creation and sense making.

Mouffe (2013:6–7) argues, 'The crucial issue then is how to establish this us/them distinction, which is constitutive of politics, in a way that is compatible with the recognition of pluralism.' She argues for a politics that is compatible with pluralism, but who decides on this politics? What ring binds them all? There still will be *the* hegemony – *the* politics – the in-common of the various competing and agonistic hegemonies, under one power, or united (bound) in one narrative.

What reason, which rationality, which *logos* guides the space of this parliament, and who decides on who or what is allowed to speak and who not? What metaphysics creates the parliament of things? What logos carries out a politics of pluralism? Or is it the things that carry out the parliament, just as things carry out the world and the world grants the things their place (see Heidegger 1971:200–202)? This is for Heidegger the speaking of language, but it still is a question of which Word is spoken, because in different Words different things will be disclosed to carry out that world.

If it is the things that carry out the place (world, parliament), then new voices or new things will carry out a different world or parliament, but who makes sure, what authority legitimises which voices may speak, who decides who has a voice and who not? What light allows certain things to appear and others to remain hidden? It thus becomes a question of who is allowed to speak, who is invited, which Other is recognised as guest and who as enemy, which is currently the question that many spaces are asking. Which other, foreigner or migrant, is invited to enter and who is seen as enemy, or as terrorist who is believed to come and destroy the home? Derrida unpacked this dynamic entanglement between hospitality and hostility (Derrida 2008b) by coining the word, *hostipitality*.

As Latour argues,

Once you begin to trace an absolute distinction between what is deaf and dumb and who is allowed to speak, you can easily imagine that this is not an ideal way to establish some sort of democracy... ... But no doubt that it is a fabulously useful ploy, invented in the seventeenth century, to establish a political epistemology and to decide who will be allowed to talk about what, and which types of beings will remain silent (Latour 2010:476).

Who decides? Again I turn to Laruelle (2015b:8) and his victim-in-person, who guides this question and offers not an answer but an ethical modality, which is not an ethics based on some or other philosophy or religion, but an ethical *stance*. To turn to victims is not new, most liberation movements, most revolutions, prophets turn to victims, as they seek to counter the status quo by offering their counter hegemony of which the prophets are the priests. Hegemony will remain, either as the hegemony of the priests or that of the prophets who have become priests of a different hegemony.

Laruelle therefore does not turn to the embodied victims of historic worlds, because such a turn to embodied victims ends up in a victimology, a hegemony in the name of the victims, where the prophets turn into priests, but he follows a stance with or in accordance with the victim-in-person, namely the generic victim.

Is it possible to remain prophet without becoming priest? Is it possible to stand with embodied victims without developing a victimology?

For example, the idea of minorities, victims acting together in a *multitude* is the idea that was put forward by Paolo Virno (2004), 'The democracy of the Multitude expresses itself in an ensemble of acting minorities that never aspire to transform themselves into a majority and develop a power that refuses to become government. It is 'acting in concert', and while tending to dismantle the supreme power, it is not inclined to become state in its turn' (Mouffe 2013:70). There is a sense of a messianic praxis in the multitude, that disrupts, but without ever creating or articulating a government or world. This idea could also link up with Nancy's (1991) myth-interrupted of the inoperative community. A constant challenge to the systems, constantly challenging, disrupting the politics of the day, a constant challenge to the metaphysics of the day by interrupting the dominant myths, but without necessarily creating a new myth.

Myths are created the moment a specific victim is identified and a victimology is articulated.

The task of identification is often the task of the intellectual, who uses the victim for a specific ideology or politics to challenge the state, but who *uses* the victim, by embodying the victim in his or her abstraction (victimology), with the *belief* that they are fighting for justice and a new world. This is where prophets turn into priests, and to avoid this one needs an inoperative community or myths continuously interrupted. Myths continuously exposed as literature, and the occasion for this are the embodied victims, but without the victims becoming a new myth. Mouffe's (2013:70ff) problem with such a continuous interruption of myth is that the status quo in a certain sense is accepted as given. I would argue that what is accepted as given is not the status quo, but the interchanging of priests and prophets and the only way to interrupt these two sign regimes is to think through them and not in them or as one of them, and thereby to interrupt their myth and all myths with literature.

If it is no longer just about reading (be it the dominant myths or anything else), but about authoring a text, even authoring a new myth, this would be opposing reading to writing, or reading to authoring. Maybe thinking *it* as a hybrid is more useful as Latour seems to propose, but a hybrid is still thinking *it*, just giving it a different name. I suggest a calling-responding, not as a hybrid or a continuum, but a mutual *erklingen* between the insistence *in* and *with* the primary, secondary and tertiary retentions-protentions. The one *erklingt* in the other, so much so that one is never sure what called and what or who responds and where calling and responding is impossible to differentiate; they are One – a determination or an *erklingen* in the last instance by a Call believed to be heard by the respondent, a Call read into the text as it is written in the response to a Call. One could maybe think of it as a vibration in the rhizome, like a spider's web – if you touch it on one corner, the whole web begins to vibrate. What is therefore necessary is a rhizomatic reading-authoring, which does not determine, but which is determined, or rather an awareness thereof, where the rhizome is not a determination of … , but is determined according to the Call [in the last instance]. This awareness does not bring one any closer to the truth, to *Das Ding*, therefore, what is called for is a praxis, a way, not a truth, not determining, but of being determined, by acknowledging that all responses are determined in the last instance by a Call.

Not a truth in the sense of representation or *adequatio*, but a truth as a way, as Jesus spoke of himself: as a way, a truth and a life (John 14:6). A way, as a praxis of truth, and a fiction to guide it. A fiction to mentor this praxis, not a theory-laden praxis, but maybe a fiction-laden praxis, as a continuous messianic praxis where one is continuously "saved" from any determining Messiah, where myths are continuously interrupted by literature.

I believe that Root, in his book, *Christo-praxis*, tried to move into this direction, in the sense that he sought to save the Real,[18] or at least not to fight a war against the Real. He wanted to bring the Real back into conversation and not leave *everything* to social construction.

Yet, I also believe that Root's Christo-praxis remains a war against the Real, as his praxis still determines the insistence (that which Calls), by determining it through the metaphors or with a hermeneutic of *theologia crucis* and *ex nihilo*.

Is it possible to avoid this naming (determining) of the Call, and by determining it, making or taking a decision? Is this not exactly what I am also doing, by naming it a "Call" or deciding to call it a Call? I am not determining it as Call, I am not saying that it, whatever it is, *is* a Call, but I am generically referring to that which calls thinking forth as the Call. I am referring to that which is believed

---

18 Justification is the reinstating of the real. It is judgement against epistemological hubris and a return to the priority of ontology. It is the assertion that human beings are not creators of reality, but rather reality as sin and death impinges on us, confusing and so easily making opaque our epistemological conceptions of reality (Root 2014:197).

to pre-exist thought, but which calls thought forth only to receive thought as the most thought-worthy, as it is that (whatever that may be) that calls thought forth, but withdraws from thought. It withdraws from thought through no characteristic or essence in itself, but because of the essence of thought as *pharmakon*. Thought, language, thinking is haunted by différance. It is because of différance that that which called thinking forth withdraws from thought, leaving only a trace, a ghost of itself in thought.

This book has focussed on the Call, as that which calls thinking forth, and yet withdraws from thinking and thus placing humanity into the *Zug* of the call, placing humanity in the withdrawal, as the being that points into the withdrawal naming and responding to the call and therefore a metaphysical being. As there are different responses a trans-fictional praxis is proposed. This Call can for example be named God, and God would probably be a very good name for it, but the Call would not be God. The idea of a Call (that which calls thought forth, but withdraws from thought) has numerous similarities with certain (non-religious, anti-idolatry) interpretations of the Biblical God: God who creates, calls forth thought and with thought humanity and all that ex-*texts* but who is not the creation, sounds a lot like the Call. But one needs to remember that the Call is nothing but the *Zug* (the Call-pull) in which humanity finds itself as being a sign that indicates in the direction of the Call. Thus one cannot say that the Call is God. God is one possible name for the Call, as every Other is wholly Other. God, who must not be named, is probably a good name to give to the Call and its withdrawal from thought (from names). Maybe it could be useful not to read-write the story of God as a story telling one about God, thereby determining God, but rather as a story that reveals something of the way of God, and in that sense also something of the way of the Call, which would be the way of thinking (the way of being human).

Is this Biblical God of faith an interpretation of the Call or is the Call an in-terpretation of the Biblical God? The two resonate in each other: that the Call is thought when thinking through Western thought systems, will resonate in numer-ous of the secondary and tertiary retentions and protentions of Western thoughts, which includes the Biblical texts. Therefore, the Call and God will haunt each other, or resonate in each other, which explains the return to religion, or a return to messianic religions in post-structural thoughts. As I indicated in a previous chapter, my intentions is not to save God. I do not want to give a Biblical-God interpretation of postmodernism, nor give a postmodernist interpretation of the Biblical God, but accept that the one resonates in the other, as tertiary retentions tend to do in making sense, and creating meaning.

Christo-poiēsis I interpret as an awareness of the poetic character of all thought and a fiction to read-write which accompanies it, helping to remain in literature, rather than becoming a myth with the belief that one can determine the Real or determine the Call. A Christ-*poiēsis* acknowledges all thought as fictional (necessary but insufficient), yet determined in the last instance by the Real (the Call). It does not present itself as the answer, nor does it argue that the other answers are wrong, as it acknowledges that all there are, are answers (responses) and that these responses are all equal. Although, as Latour (2010) argues, there are better compositions and there are bad compositions that might be in need of decomposition. Criticism has run out of steam (Latour 2004), as it can no longer judge or critique absolutely, but only relatively or contextually by arguing for better or worse compositions, or as Freedman and Combs (1996) would say, argue for preferred realities.

What is this poetic praxis that is guided by a writing-reading of a fiction and where one is never sure if one is reading or writing? The fiction, which to read-write through, is the Face of Christ as the abstract machine of the West, and as such, the abstract machine of the global village. In trying to think through the Face of Christ I will reflect on the story of Christ as represented in the gospels. The Christ event, as the incarnation, crucifixion and resurrection, will be the way to think through the Face of Christ.

Trans-fictional praxis as Christ-*poiēsis*, as a praxis of criss-crossing of various narratives, various metaphysical systems past, present and future needs something to guide it, as it is no longer guided by the Real or by Truth or by what is believed to be right or good. Trans-fictional praxis does not have a myth as Nancy (1991:52ff) would say and therefore does not have a logos with which to bind (*re-ligare*) into a community. All it perhaps has is an interrupted myth, or a crucified myth and an insurrection-resurrection that goes with it. An interrupted myth is a myth that knows that it is a fiction, and therefore its faith, its belief is interrupted. Nancy (1991:52) argues, 'The tradition is suspended at the very moment it fulfils itself. It is interrupted at the precise and familiar point where we know that it is all a myth'. A few pages on he argues, 'Myth is interrupted by literature precisely to the extent that literature does not come to an end' (Nancy 1991:64). The myth is interrupted by *poiēsis* – writing, textualisation: literature.

This interruption as literature (*poiēsis*) needs a story to guide it, but which story, and who decides which story is to be taken? Well, the preferred fiction would be the fiction of the creation of the various fictions, of how a Call is incarnated in the various responses as *the* incarnation of the Call. Thus, incarnation needs to be part of the story that guides a praxis of continuous interruption of myths by literature (fiction) – this interruption is the interruption by literature, and as literature which never comes to an end. The *poiēsis* is continuous. Secondly, the failure of these incarnations, or as Laclau would argue, the deformation of the incarnations can be understood by taking into consideration the role of power and the powers that be in the various constructions of meaning, through the establishment of dominant narratives (hegemony), but also the failure or the insufficiency of these myths or *logoi*, which are interrupted by their deformation, or stated differently by their fictional nature: literature. Myths are interrupted – not by a truth, but by their mythical nature, that is, myths carrying out worlds are interrupted by their insufficiency: that they are myths. This second movement of deformation or interruption of myth can be interpreted with the help of the crucifixion, as the crucifixion is in the name of the ruling powers, the hegemony who crucify Christ. In Laclau's thoughts the incarnation is necessary, but it is a deformation, it is revealed as myth, that is: as insufficient, it is crucified.

Last moment of the Christ event is the resurrection. The resurrection can be interpreted as the creation of new stories and new communities. As Nancy (1991:125) argues, resurrection is not 'the end of the process, nor is it the final appropriation of the Living Concept'. According to Nancy, 'Resurrection is the manifestation of the god inasmuch as he comes in his own withdrawal, leaves his mark in his own obliteration, is revealed in his own invisibility (it is not a "resurrection," it is not a return)' (Nancy 1991:125). If resurrection is interpreted only as a return, there would be nothing unique or interesting about it, as all gods resurrect, as they are immortal. Resurrection as return is not specific to Christianity – all gods (Osiris, Dionysus, Christ) resurrect, it is part of their immortal nature, to resurrect (Nancy 1991:125), and as Nietzsche claims they are more radiant, more powerful, more glorious once they resurrect (Nancy 1991:125). Yet, maybe the resurrection of a crucified Christ is different?

This is not a dialectic: the gods are immortal. "Death" and "resurrection" do not apply to them. What does apply to them is what they have in common with the heavens, without the heavens being their mediation: the sovereign interplay of darkness and radiance, of radiance withdrawn into darkness and of darkness as manifest as radiance (Nancy 1991:126).

It is the resurrection of the crucified one, the darkness, God-forsakenness that is manifest as radiance, as some interpret the Gospel of John, where the crucifixion is the enthronement. Thus, the resurrection could be interpreted as freedom, the freedom to compose, free of myth as the myth/Logos has been crucified. The illusion has been exposed! It has been exposed to be what, an illusion? Is the revelation of illusion the resurrected truth? Is the truth of the Christ-narrative the truth of the belief of thinking, namely repetition? That all is illusion and that in truth there is nothing, God-forsakenness? Is the Christ-event a revelation of this darkness manifest as radiance? The resurrection would then be the stamp of approval of that nothingness of the crucifixion. Is the resurrection the freedom of the child, once it has transformed from being a Camel and a Lion (Nietzsche 2000)? Such an interpretation of the Christ-event would make the Christ-event a revelation of a very specific truth, namely the truth of Nietzschean nihilism, and the Call would once again be determined as nothing.

The Christ-*poiēsis* that I am trying to develop, the Christ-event (the story of Christ) does not reveal any truth, it is not a determination of the Call, but reveals only itself. The story of Christ can always be interpreted as the revelation of the Truth, even the revelation of a non-truth, but what is forgotten in such a reading of the story is that the story that is read is also the story that is written by the reader. Whatever truth the reader believes to find in the story, is the truth she or he wrote into the story.

A Christ-*poiēsis* is not a hermeneutic, it does not seek to interpret the story or reveal the truth of the story, as it recognises that any reading is a writing of the story, but reads-writes this story as a story of reading-writing.

The story is about nothing but itself. Like the Call it is foreclosed within itself, but it calls out to be read and interpreted (given a meaning), but in any interpretation it can be made to reveal all sorts of truths, and the history of theology or the history of the various Christologies is a witness to this. Christ or the Bible has been made to mean all sorts of things in the history of theology and biblical studies.

What if the story is read-*written*, in other words, it is read conscious that by reading it is written, therefore a Christo-*fiction*, but read-written as a fiction devoid of any belief about some or other truth, which is then read into the story, but as a fiction about thinking (textualisation)? The Bible or the Christ narrative is not the truth that is written into or onto the text, and then believed to be discovered in the text as the truth of the text. The truth of reading-writing this text is not something outside this text, it is not outside or transcendent to the text, as the text is not about something, but the text is the text and what it is believed to be about is written onto and into the text, and then read from the text. What if the text is written-read as not being about something outside of the text, but about the text itself, the text alone – a text about that which happens to and in texts, a text about textualisation, a text about incarnation, a text about embodiment in texts?

Any truth, as well as such a truth, would be a truth written into and onto the text and then read from the text. Unless it is not such a truth that is believed to be outside the text of which the text is but the mediator, the text does not reveal a truth, but the text is the truth of itself and this specific text tells the story of that truth. In this sense, a self-revelation, the text is *written* and then read to reveal the story of texts. Henry argued that the Christ event is the phenomenology of phenomenology, in other words, the text still pointed to something beyond itself, and thus that truth was written into the text, only to be read from the text again. But what if the truth is not written into the text to be read from the text, but the text is written to be read as text (literature)? And what happens to texts when they become literature?

It is read-written as the story of thinking, which is also a story about the Call, that calls thinking forth, but without determining that Call.

The truth that the story of the Christ-event reveals is the story of Christ alone (*sola Christus*), as one has no other access to Christ, but through the texts (*sola*

Scriptura). What Christ means is something that is written into the story that is read, and then it is no longer Christ alone, but Christ and the truth written into the story of Christ and *believed* to be found in the text.

Christ is not the incarnation of some or other determination of the Call, but the Christ-event is read-written as the fiction of fiction, or the thinking of thinking.

Why is a reading-writing of the text important? It is important as the reading-writing of the text as Christ-*poiēsis* takes the reading-writing of texts into consideration and does not seek to move beyond that to some Real or Truth beyond the text, to which the text is believed to point.

A few paragraphs above I reflected on a Nietzschean interpretation of the Christ-event, or as Nancy interprets the Christ event, but would argue that these interpretations of the incarnation and crucifixion are written into the text, as the texts are still read as if they reveal this truth: the truth of the crucifixion, the truth of the incarnation.

Laruelle responds to such a nihilist interpretation, and argues against this play or interplay of darkness and radiance, as he interprets Christ's resurrection as insurrection. 'The victim carries with it resurrection, or rather the prior-to-the-first-insurrection, against the dialectic of being and nothingness, which has no real or lived sense' (Laruelle 2015b:44). If the Christ-event is written-read as the fiction of thinking, then Christ, the crucified, rises and rises as the glorious flesh of the risen, and not the rising of some or other truth. The resurrection is then not the victory of some or other truth written into the story, but the resurrection is the resurrection of the text, or the Call, in other words, the resurrection of that which called thinking forth, or which called interpretation forth, after the interpretation or after the response is crucified.

This glorious risen flesh is the flesh of the victim-in-person, it is the flesh of Man-in-person, but as Man-in-person in its ethical modality as victim-in-person does not arise, but only ever appears as subject in the world, the resurrection of victim-in-person is an insurrection: an interruption of the myth.

Christ-*poiēsis* as a reading-writing of the story of Christ with its three moments – incarnation, crucifixion and resurrection – is read-written as the story of thought and therefore an ideal story to guide the thinking of thinking. Or as Laruelle (2015b:125–127) argues, that it calls for imitation of Christ[19] rather than an interpretation of Christ.

Such a reading-writing of the Christ-story provides one with the metaphors with which to think the ideological dialectic as Laclau calls it (2014:18). It is a story that can guide the interruption of myth, it is a story that can guide thinking, and specifically the history of thinking. Laruelle argues that 'Christ is not just a

---

[19]   This is the de-philosophication of Logos, the de-Christianization of the Word, the de-Judaization of the Torah, something else entirely than deconstruction or de-mythization; it is their human or weak oraxiomatization, our imitation of Christ (Laruelle 2015b:127).

religious model to be imitated in his existence or in his sufferings, the founder of
a new religion that ceaselessly returns to interpret and solicit him, but (he is) the
author of a logia that must be read as the protocols and axioms of a new science
of humans – and humans, moreover, insofar as they are committed, as beings of
belief, and rites, to the world' (Laruelle 2015c:33).

Such a Christ-*poiētics* can guide a trans-fictional praxis, by offering it an ethical modality, without determining a good or a right orthopraxis, or determining
the Call in some or other form of orthodoxy, understood as right belief.

A trans-fictional praxis is guided by the things that are visible, that exist (ex-
text), and because they exist they carry out the parliament of things. But what
about all that which is excluded because it is not visible, or because it is silenced?
What motivates the inclusion of previously excluded things, those that do not have
ex-*text*-ence, that do not yet have a voice, as they are not recognised?

In this reading-writing, Christ's incarnation is not the incarnation of a particular equivalence guided by power, but Christ's incarnation is guided by powerlessness (see Phil. 2:7). Christ is incarnated into and amongst those who are nothing
so as to shame those who are (1 Cor. 1: 27–28). The classical interpretation (writing) of this is to interpret Christ's incarnation into the ideological dialectic of
the prophets, that is, into a victimology, which challenges the status quo. In this
reading-writing (interpretation), the story of Christ is used to develop a specific
Christology: a liberation Christology.

What if one reads-writes this differently, where prophets do not become
priests, as it is not about determining, as it is not about belief of what is true
or Real?

As long as there is such belief, the interpretation of the Christ-event or the
interpretation of his ministry will guide the reader to seek out the repressed, invisible, excluded, the shadows in the web as the truth and thus develop a victimology,
as an alternative hegemony. But any alternative hegemony is just another addition
to the web, with the result that such an alternative becomes only a momentary
escape, a line of flight, which is eventually re-captured again through the war machines (Deleuze & Guattari 2011:351–423) or apparatus of capture (Deleuze &
Guattari 2011:424–473). One has not thought through the Christ-event, but one is
still thinking in Christ and in thinking Christ expanding the rhizome.

But the web, the rhizome can be brought to constant vibration, as the myths
are insistently interrupted, not by truth, nor by the Real, but by their being myths,
their insufficiency.

Their insufficiency, their literary nature, is not exposed by an alternative determination of truth or the Real, but by their insufficiency, by their literature. Myths
are not interrupted by some truth that appears or the Real that appears, but by
being myths. By being myths, the myths are interrupted, when their faith (belief) is interrupted, their faith, namely that they believe they know what pre-exists

thought and calls thought forth. This faith is interrupted once it is revealed that what pre-exists thought has been created (made), that is, it is literature.

Myths are interrupted when their insufficiency is exposed, their literature is revealed, and the occasion for such revelation is not Truth or the Real, but the victims of the myths.

Myths are interrupted when focusing not on the lines of flight, but on the repressed, the generic repressed, or Victim-in-person (Laruelle 2015b), thus bringing about constant lines of flight, without those lines of flight becoming the Other which is then re-appropriated as a new market opportunity.

Badiou (2009:369) argued that the event is the ontological figure of the instant, it appears only to disappear. The event of truth disappears the moment it appears, the disenclosure is recaptured (enclosed) the moment it appears and can be recognised, named, and responded to. Derrida speaks of invention with the following words:

... if I can invent what I invent, if I have the ability to invent what I invent, that means that the invention follows a potentiality, an ability that is in me, and thus it brings nothing new. It does not constitute an event. I have the ability to make this happen and consequently the event, what happens at that point, disrupts nothing; it's not an absolute surprise (Derrida 2007:232).

One cannot have a politics of disruption or a politics of insurrection, as such would only be possible with its own myth or logos, its own hegemony.

Christ-*poiēsis* and non-colonial thought

The repressed of every individuation or grammatisation opens this individuation grammatisation to its fictional (abstract or externalized – ex-*text*-ualised) character and thereby invites all those in need of collective individuation and psychic individuation to the labour of individuation (*poiēsis*), to find new weapons against the various forms of control society with its dis-individuation. An invitation to a radical *poiēsis* of all noetic souls, or to create a space for a parliament of all things (Latour 1993:145): where all things are invited to individuate to become noetic souls in a collective individuation where the various secondary and tertiary retentions are employed *together with the repressed,* and thus a trans-fictional approach; where different expressions of the modern (not just a singular expression), including the repressed expressions of the modern are part of the individuation. A collective individuation, where voices are not silenced, although grammatisation is always a war against spirits (Stiegler 2014:55), thus the realization that the individuation has no end, the conversation has no end: the myths are continuously interrupted by exposing their mythic nature.

One cannot get beyond myth, but one can be aware of the violence of myths and grammatisation and therefore always seek an openness or an interruption of the myths, by allowing the repressed to challenge the war on spirits: the dominant grammatisation. As Fanon argued, the land belongs to *all* who work it (Fanon 2004:133), the nation belongs to those who work: those who individuate, individually, collectively, via the primary, secondary and tertiary retentions without a grammatisation police seeking to control, but within a democracy of things. The challenge is to develop as many as possible noetic souls, to develop a national consciousness and or national literature in Fanon's language.

It is only from this point onward that one can speak of national *literature. Literary creation* addresses and clarifies typically nationalist themes. This is combat *literature* in the true sense of the word in the sense that it calls upon a whole people to join the struggle for the *existence* of the nation. Combat literature, because it informs the national consciousness, gives it shape and contours, and opens up new, unlimited horizons (Fanon 2004:173 my emphasis).

To develop a national literature in a very literal sense of the word literature, thus not to develop a national myth, but interrupt national myths with national literatures. Fanon argues that this can only happen once the colonized intellectual changes his/her perspective[20] and no longer has the coloniser in mind.

What one learns from decolonial thought is that all knowledge is situated knowledge and that the geo- and body-politics always needs to be taken into consideration.[21] The body, the subject is always Man-in-person appearing as a stratified body in a specific world. *Dasein* in a world is to exist, but to exist is to ex-*text*. This text (body) that one is, is not written only by oneself, but by the con*text* (secondary and tertiary retentions and protentions). The bodies carry out a world, but

---

[20] Whereas the colonized intellectual started out by producing work exclusively with the oppressor in mind – either in order to charm him or to denounce him by using ethnic or subjectivist categories – he gradually switches over to addressing himself to his people (Fanon 2004:173).

[21] By setting the scenario in terms of geo- and body-politics I am starting and departing from already familiar notions of 'situated knowledges'. Sure, all knowledges are situated and every knowledge is constructed. But that is just the beginning. The question is: who, when, why is constructing knowledges? ... The shift I am indicating is the anchor (constructed of course, located of course, not just anchored by nature or by God) of the argument that follows. It is the beginning of any epistemic de-colonial de-linking with all its historical, political and ethical consequences. Why? Because geo-historical and bio-graphic loci of enunciation have been located by and through the making and transformation of the colonial matrix of power: a racial system of social classification and invented Occidentalism (e.g. Indias Occidentales), that created the conditions for Orientalisms; distinguished the South of Europe from its center (Hegel) and, on that long history, remapped the world as first, second and third during the Cold War. Places of non-thought (of myth, non-western religions, folklore, underdevelopment involved regions and people) today have been waking up from the long process of westernization. The anthropos inhabiting non-European places discovered that s/he had been invented, as anthropos, by a locus of enunciations self-defined as humanitas (Mignolo 2009:2–3).

the world grants bodies their place, and bodies have different places in the world, as they are differentiated, stratified into strata – hierarchical strata (layers) which has social-economic and political consequences. Decolonial politics and liberation movements focus on the colonised world, focus on the colonised subjects, the colonised bodies of that particular world who have been identified as victims.

The generic intellectual heeds the Call of the victim-in-person as the ethical modality of Man-in-person, recognising the colonial wound in each subject, recognising the *etching* (writing) into and onto the Body without Organs as the Body with Organs appears (see Deleuze & Guattari 2011:149–166). The colonial wound of thinking is the cut into the Body without Organs, from which the subject is cut, differentiated so as to appear in the light of a particular world carried out by a particular logos.

Mignolo argues that the de-colonial option is the singular connector of a diversity of de-colonials, which have one thing in common: the colonial wound (Mignolo 20069:3). This colonial wound is however more generic than Mignolo argues – it is the wound of every single and determined body that appears in a world. It is the wound of the victim-in-person. It is indeed the wound that makes the subject and differentiates subjects and thereby the possibility to classify subjects, as Mignolo argues: the wound which is the 'fact that regions and people around the world have been classified as underdeveloped economically and mentally' (Mignolo 2009:3). The wound of thinking, and not just the wound of colonial thinking, but all thinking as colonial. Non-colonial thought takes this idea into consideration, that all thought is colonial, and therefore non, in the sense of non-philosophy. As thinking determines, thinking differentiates, it cuts, it etches, it writes by carving a subject from the Man-in-person. To think differently is not to think Man-in-person, but to always think the human as it appears, and it is not to liberate Man-in-person from false consciousness or colonised consciousness, but it is purely to shift the subject from one determined world to another determined world.

To call the victims to rise up in revolt so as to create a new world is not a liberation, but a swopping of cages, and indeed there are better cages and therefore these revolts are justified, but not in the name of freedom or truth, but only in the name of better or preferred cages.

A generic intellectual does not think the victim *for* her or his cause (philosophy), but seeks to *not*-think (non-philosophy and non-colonial thought), but rather has compassion with the victim-in-person – compassion as a communal pathos, as being communally affected by that which calls thought forth; compassion as communally wounded, communally affected by the power of that which calls thought forth, and communally colonised by thought, which nobody escapes. But likewise thought affected by the com-passion, the communal-pathos of the Call (man-in-person) that calls thought forth. It is not a call against thought where thought is seen as the enemy, the new evil, but to recognise that thought is determined in the last instance by com-pathos and which then in turn determines the pathos as Flesh, Life, God, Real, etcetera.

Thus, non-colonial thinking is to expose the colonial nature of all thinking and then not to think otherwise, but creating space for as much as possible thought, allowing all in the land to work, to labour, to write, to create, *poiēsis*. A parliament of the whole land, where all things are included, and that is truly a national literature, or a national individuation, without nationalist determinations, where all souls participate, therefore countering a generalised proletarianisation. This can only happen if the war on souls is stopped with exclusive and violent grammatisations. Radical evil is not countered with declarations of absolute evil, but it is countered by creating spaces where individuals can individuate, become noetic souls, or as Fanon argues: 'We must elevate the people, expand their minds, equip them, differentiate them and humanize them' (Fanon 2004:137).

It is as Césair said: "To invent the souls of men." To politicize the masses is not and cannot be to make a political speech. It means driving home to the masses that everything depends on them, that if we stagnate the fault is theirs, and that if we progress, they too are responsible, that there is no demiurge, no illustrious man taking responsibility for everything, but that the demiurge is the people and the magic lies in their hands and their hands alone. In order to achieve such things, in order to actually embody them, we must, as we have already mentioned, decentralize to the utmost. The flow of ideas from the upper echelons to the rank and file and vice versa must be an unwavering principle, ... (Fanon 2004:138).

My suggestion is, that as with postmodern, decolonial thought it does not help to create the opposite, but to think the colonial or the modern through, to radically think it, to think what it means to think (*was heisst Denken*). Maybe the same could be said of Christ: not to turn from him, but to radically turn to him and think through him and in him alone.

Christ is of no help if Christ is grammatised together with the Good, if Christ is seen as the redemption from evil, that was first created with the decision for the good, which in turn was created with the individuation into the good. Christ becomes part of this battle between good and evil, but maybe there is a Christ beyond good and evil? It is the good that is evil, or at least the decision for the good that is evil. As Laruelle argues, it is not radical to think that God is dead, but the radical thought that is necessary is to think God evil, or to state it more correctly, that any idea of God is evil (see Laruelle 2015b:21). This might not be that different from Luther (see Althaus 1983:33f) who argues that anyone who seeks God outside the cross will not find God, but the devil. In other words, anyone who seeks God outside of the death of God, finds not God but the devil, but this needs to be radicalised, that anyone who seeks God outside the death of God as well as the death of the death-of-God, does not find God, but the devil.

Andrew Root (2014), in his Christo-praxis, rediscovers something of Luther's *theologia crucis* and the tradition of *ex nihilo*, where Christ is interpreted via theology of the cross and *ex nihilo* as the movement from death (impossible) to life (possible). In a sense, Christ becomes a line of flight from the powers of death and the laws of the possible to new possibilities. Possibilities that under the law were impossible, which is then Christologically interpreted as resurrection or as salvation through grace alone.

Root's Christo-praxis focusses on *theologia crucis* and *ex nihilo*, yet as soon as Christ is grammatised into a *theologia crucis*, or as soon as believers are individuated into a *theologia crucis* as the new good, or the new salvation it becomes *theologia gloriae* and one is back to square one. One would have to find a way to remain in the *theologia crucis* without it becoming a good (the *Theos* for the noetic soul).

The moment you create these binaries, or opposites with the one being good and the other evil, they turn into each other: the sovereign becomes beast and the beast sovereign, *crucis* becomes *gloriae* and *gloriae* becomes *crucis*.

Is there a way beyond this? It seems as if *theologia crucis* was an attempt at a way beyond, as it was a liberation from the good, the possible, a liberation of the *theos*, as the *theos* is crucified and therefore one is liberated from the Gods, the *Logos*, the Law, crucifixion as the insurrection of Man-in-person. Crucifixion as the insurrection of Christ as the Son-of-Man.

One is maybe also liberated from the need to judge, but the problem comes with the desire to individuate collectively as a church, or as followers of Christ. The problem is, once this liberation becomes a good that seeks followers, it is in that moment that a singular equivalence incarnates *the* Good and thereby is deformed. Then that good automatically becomes a *Theos* that individuates individuals and collectives into communities, churches, congregations, denominations, and the wheel of history repeats itself.

I am aware that I am reading the Bible, both the creation story as well as the Christ-narrative with a specific hermeneutical lens, with an anti-religious (iconoclastic) lens. A reading that contrasts the living faith of the fathers of faith to the idols and ideologies of the surrounding nations and cultures. A reading that is in a sense iconoclastic, destroying idols, destroying the good and thereby an attempt to liberate from this repetitive wheel of history. Latour argues (2001) that there is no iconoclasm, but only iconoclashes and I agree, that one only ever displaces the gods, as one cannot escape them, gods once killed tend to resurrect, even if they resurrect as dead gods, as in atheism.

So although such an iconoclastic approach might be in close proximity to the liberation theological hermeneutic, it is not, because the moment liberation theological hermeneutic is used to individuate individuals or collectives, this prophetic liberation theology becomes priestly, where the priests in Deleuze & Guattari's (2011:114) sense circle around a new "liberating" signifier, that becomes the dominant grammatisation, controlling it, purifying it, waging a war on all the spirits that disagree and silencing others.

Yet, these two traditions of either the enclosure (grammatisation that is guarded and projected by the priests) or the disenclosure (that is professed by the prophets), belong together and together create the face of Christ, the abstract machine of the West.

Therefore, something else is needed, as even a non-religious, living-God hermeneutic does not escape being a religious hermeneutic, as soon as individuals and collectives individuate around it, it becomes *the* Good. The disenclosure becomes an enclosure, the prophet becomes the priest, which is what inevitably happens with any opposition, any binaries: the opposites become each other. There is therefore a need to find a completely new way of reading, rather than a new reading which is not a reading, new thinking which is not thinking, in other words: a non-philosophy, a non-theology, a non-Christology. But how? How to think without decisionism, without individuation, which seems impossible? How to be in-common with the myth interrupted? Maybe a way beyond good and evil is to individuate with a conscious fiction that has no pretence to determine *Das Ding*, nor the Good, but if anything is and remains a fiction, a *poiēsis*, a fiction of individuation, a fiction of the noetic souls, without any aspiration of seeking to determine it; if anything, recognizing the determination of all thoughts by *Das Ding in the last instance.*

From the above it is clear that no new thought is called for, as any new thought would only be a re-colonisation, but what is called for is thinking the calling forth of thought. Thoughts are determined in the last instance by a Call, but thought will always be an attempt at determination – *Das Ding* via a process of individuation, singularisation through a decision and knowledge of the Good (*Theos*). An awareness of onto-*logy*, that is, the dependence of things on the logos that gives them a place (individuation or singularisation) within a certain world.

After the death of God and the death of the death of God one is left with death, cinders

"There are cinders there," "Cinders there are" (Derrida 2014:13)

One is left with cinders, ashes, if anything, only traces. Traces of what? Cinders of what? What is totally burnt, what is completely sacrificed: a holocaust? Is it the texts that turn to ash as they are revealed as myth or fiction? Is it the subject, the author who disappears in the con*text* (*Mitsein*)? Is it Man-in-person sacrificed in the subject (*Dasein* in a world)?

What is sacrificed and who is sacrificed, and what is sacrificed by whom? What is left after all these sacrifices and to whom is it sacrificed? Knowledge is sacrificed, belief is sacrificed, what is left? Faith? Abraham the father of faith, called to sacrifice that which called him onto this journey of faith: the promise of land and offspring. Then the one who called him, calls him to sacrifice the incarnation of the promise, the materialisation of the promise, the embodiment of the promise: Isaac. There are cinders! Faith in what? The promise is taken (sacrificed), the embodiment, the incarnation, the materialisation of the promise (the call) is taken: cinders there are! One is called to sacrifice even the hope of the promise, as Abraham was called to sacrifice his son, the incarnation of the promise (see Meylahn 2017d); sacrifice or the recognition of the stupidity, recognition of the *pharmakon* and that all there is are cinders, the ashes after the sacrifice.

In writing this way, he burns one more time, he burns what he still adores although he has already burned it, he is intent on it (Derrida 2014:25).

Indeed, Kierkegaard's knight of faith, Abraham, who has faith with nothing in his hand, with nothing to show, with no-showing, no appearance, no revelation, no manifestation, except maybe the showing of Nothing: the revelation of Nothing.

Cinders are nothing, but nothing is still something. Again, one is haunted by this nihilism that so easily becomes the new God and therefore the need for less than nothing.

Laruelle argues not for a belief in the sufficiency of God, but faith is the non-sufficiency of Christ (Laruelle 2015c:xi). Thus, on the one side there is the beliefs in the sufficiency of theology, philosophy, knowledge (collectively the sufficiency of thinking) which all turn to cinders and on 'the other side (the side from which our struggle is prosecuted) a necessary but nonsufficient faith' (Laruelle 2015c: xii). A necessary but nonsufficient faith so as to give account for the cinders, the literature, the writing, the *pharmakon*. Yet, one must give account of these ashes. As Derrida says: 'I had to explain myself to it, respond to it – or for it' (Derrida 2014:4). No longer called to be knights of faith, but poets of faith (Deleuze 1994:95). Poets who create meaning and sense, who create literature with necessary but insufficient faith, and thus give account for the cinders.

An attempt at a Christ-*poiēsis*

Can Christ save, can Christ save one from Christ and can Christ save one from the desire to be saved? How can sacrificing Christ, the crucifixion, be this saving that does not need to be saved?

How does one think through Christ? How does one think and thus ex-*text*-ualise through Christ? Ex-*text*-ualise through Christ, I interpret as a Christ-*poiēsis*, fully conscious of the pharmacological condition of all texts, and thus all thoughts as ex-*text*-ualisations. To think through Christ will be no different, also an ex-*text*-ualisation, but a Christ-*poiēsis*, in other words, an ex-*text*-ualisation, that is firstly through Christ and secondly a conscious *poiēsis*, without the faith of thought, the truth of which is repetition.

The Christo-fiction as the narrative to guide thinking through Christ, as a fiction to help think the pharmacological condition of thought. Or as Laruelle reflects on a Christo-fiction, when he says: 'then it is urgent that we revise our categories which are still those of our beliefs; that we take the leap of thought that is called fidelity, and forge fiction capable of upholding this fidelity' (Laruelle 2015c:x).

A Christ-*poiēsis* is not against theology. It is a non-theology and a non-Christology in the sense that what Christ-*poiēsis* offers is something different to the Principle of Sufficient Theology or the Principle of Sufficient Christology.[22] Christ-*poiēsis* is to invent a Christ that is our contemporary (see Laruelle 2015c:18). A Christ-*poiēsis* creates a space for a trans-fictional-praxis of following Christ in the sense of *imitatio-Christi* – a space for necessary but insufficient faith rather than belief. In other words, no belief in any principle of sufficiency, no belief in any sufficient dogma, but faith[23] alone through grace alone, that is, without faith in any human work or construction, even without faith in *poiēsis*, rather a fidelity to *poiēsis*. A fidelity to literature in the sense of a fidelity to thinking, without the faith of thinking, which is literature. That means a fidelity to the insufficiency of *poiēsis*. Dogmas like philosophies, that are exposed as being necessary but insufficient, is contrasted with a necessary but a consciously insufficient faith (see Laruelle 2015c:xi), as it is not *my* faith, but Christ-event alone, as the fiction of the fiction of thought, and therefore *sola Christus*. This insufficient faith is what traditionally theologically creates the dependence on Christ alone through grace alone. No knowledge of Christ, not even faithfulness to Christ, is believed to save one, as faith as work is always insufficient, and therefore Christ alone. In life and in death the Christian's only hope is Christ, the Christian's only hope is not knowledge or faith in Christ, but *Christ* alone, without knowledge, without belief, but by grace and insufficient faith alone.

Christ-*poiēsis* is no Christology, as Christologies, as idealist Christologies, are always 'mere interpretations of Scriptures using the means of philosophy, or the dogmatisms of the Church' (Laruelle 2015c:30).

---

[22]   Our problem is the *Principle of Sufficient Theology* (PST) that has taken hold of them. Believing themselves sufficient to think Christ-in-Person (the Christ of the faithful rather than that of believers), they lack a second dimension – let us a theologically and christologically nonstandard dimension (Laruelle 2015c:x).

[23]   Perhaps a new kerygma is announced here: belief is the sufficiency of God, but faith is the nonsufficiency of Christ and thus of humans who abase or bring down the sufficiency of God (Laruelle 2015c:xi-xii).

Laruelle argues that in his Christo-fiction it will be instead 'a matter (after a great deal of explanation) of philosophizing "in" that science which *is* the Christ-event' (Laruelle 2015c:30).

To think (philosophise) not Christ or the Christ event, as that would be to develop an idealist Christology, but to think thinking, to think philosophy (a science of philosophy), thus to think humanity and the being of the human as a noetic soul in-Christ. To think this thinking, to think the *Bedenklichste* in-Christ. To think thinking through Christ, through the Christ-event, which is made up of these three movements: incarnation, crucifixion and resurrection.

And by identifying in Christ and in him alone the subject bearing a *generic science* – that is to say, a subjective science, a science of religions. Such is our primary thesis. To philosophize in Christ does not affect the grandeur of Reason if it really is a question of a science-in-Christ. This would be to place philosophy, and therefore theology, as complexes of knowledge and belief, under condition of a new theoretical but practical *stance*, to determine them and transform them by way of a science whose blinding yet invisible, clear yet silent principle would be contributed by Christ. Christ is not just a religious model to be imitated in his existence or in his sufferings, the founder of a new religion that ceaselessly returns to interpret and solicit him, but the author of a logia that must be read as the protocols and axioms of a new science of humans – and humans, moreover, insofar as they are committed, as beings of belief, and rites, to the world. An important nuance here: it is not the Christian religion, still less "Christian science," that is the science of other religions; it is Christ who announces the protocols of a science for all religions, Christianity included. Christianity is here no more than what we could call a "formal" or else "primary" religion, to be placed under condition, a christic condition (Laruelle 2015c:33).

To think thinking *in* and *through* Christ and thereby not think Christ, as the purpose is not to develop a Christology or a theology of Christ, but to think das *Bedenklichste*.

To philosophize "in" Christ? The solution already depends on what we understand by this "in": through, according to, because of, for? We are evidently involved in a theory of immanence that Christian philosophers controlled through the subjective interiority of faith, others through that of the transcendental ego, and yet others through the interiority of the mystical body of the Church or that of scriptural texts. Whence idealist christologies, which are mere interpretations of Scriptures using the means of philosophy, or the dogmatisms of the Church. For us it will instead be a matter (after a great deal of explanation) of philosophizing "in" that science which *is* the Christ-event (Laruelle 2015c:35).

A Christ-*poiēsis* needs to take on both sign regimes of the abstract machine of the West (Face of Christ) into consideration to be able to become a scientific *stance of Christ* that takes as its object all religions as well as all philosophies, all thought-systems, all metaphysical systems and therefore it can guide the trans-fictional praxis.

The two sign systems:

1. 'paganism as *illustrated* by philosophy in its Greek origins or by the *Logos*' (Laruelle 2015c:35) or what Nancy would call the enclosure, and
2. monotheism as *illustrated* by Judaism and the Torah (Laruelle 2015c:35) or prophetic theology of the various liberation movements, or as Nancy would say, disenclosure.

In Christianity, these two systems are at times combined in various forms into a synthesis and other times the focus is more on the one (priestly theology) or on the other (prophetic theology), thus creating the ever expanding abstract machine of the West, as prophetic theology (lines of flight-disenclosure) is re-captured into priestly theology (enclosure).

Laruelle in his Christo-fiction or science of Christ wants to develop 'laws that, without being those of representation, even religious representation, are capable of explaining the latter as that which falls to humans' (Laruelle 2015c:36). The latter that he is speaking of is thinking Christ as contributing a type of intelligence that is faith or messianity itself (Laruelle 2015c:35). Here, Laruelle is not that far removed from Nancy's (1991) myth interrupted – the prophetic intelligence that falls to humans, but without this developing into a religion or a humanism with its own myth. I would rather opt for a *poiēsis*, a fiction to imitate rather than a law to determine. This is possible according to Laruelle, if one has faith in Christ as *in faith according to Christ*, that is, faith in imitating Christ rather than believing in Christ. 'We do not have faith in faith, nor faith "in" Christ but, really, faith "in" (according to) Christ, or "informed" by him' (Laruelle 2015c:37). The question is "how can we invent a generic practice of Christ and of messianity" (Laruelle 2015c:44), or how can we invent a generic practice of myth-interrupted? How to invent a praxis, how to compose a Christ-praxis and therefore Christ-*poiēsis,* so as to not think Christ (Christology), but to think in-Christ and through Christ?

It is to think in and through the Christ-event, as a fiction of thinking. As already stated the Christ-event is made up of these three moments: incarnation, crucifixion and resurrection, as it is these three moments that all four gospels agree upon and Christologies seek to interpret. I will not attempt to interpret these three moments, as that would be to develop theology or Christology, but use these moments of the Christ-event to think thinking and thereby think in-Christ or through-Christ, by allowing thought to imitate Christ or Christ to imitate thought. The messianic kernel does not seek to determine the Real (the Call), or explain the Real, it is not a truth in a representational or adequate sense, but a narrative that mimics (*mimesis*) the narrative of thinking, without necessarily determining thought, what thought thinks of, but the focus is that thought thinks.

A trans-fictional praxis as Christ-*poēsis* gives account (take or be given responsibility) for the cinders as well as offering an ethical modality in the trans-fictional space, without that modality becoming an orthopraxis.

I will shortly unpack a possible Christ-*poiēsis* by following the three moments of the Christ-event.

Incarnation

As mentioned in a previous chapter, Laclau already spoke of incarnation as part of the thinking and more specifically thinking ideology, as incarnation is part and parcel of the dialectic of ideology. A specific equivalence is chosen (a decision is made) to represent the perceived whole and thereby the whole is incarnated in the particular equivalence. The Word (Logos) becomes flesh, as the word made its dwelling amongst us. This equivalence which represents the whole, represents the good and thus is interpreted as God (*theos*) that binds – not only binds into community, but it also is that which calls the noetic soul into being, as individuals in community individuate into this *theos*, this good, the representation of the whole.

In the various theologies and Christologies, Christ is *interpreted* as the incarnation of God, or the incarnation of Truth, or the incarnation of true humanity, or the incarnation of Flesh (Henry), the incarnation of materialism. Whatever truth one believes, Christ is interpreted as the incarnation thereof and thus there are different Christologies and different theologies – but likewise also different thoughts and different thought-systems, different metaphysical systems, all based on this dual action of incarnating the Logos or Truth or Whole and interpreting the incarnation as a true representation of the Logos, Truth or Whole.

The Call calls forth a response and in the response the Call is identified and in the identification the respondent becomes a subject (a human). The Call is incarnated in the response, it is materialised in the response, and through this materialisation the respondent becomes a subject of the Here I am in a world.

Christ's incarnation becomes a fiction to help think thinking, to help think human subjectivity, to help think the political, the religious, and the ideological. But one has not thought Christ as such, as there are a plurality of Christs past, present and still to come. Yet, all these Christs are different incarnated truths or *logoi* or interpretations of what is believed to be the Whole, are based on Christ, one could say are called forth by Christ, but Christ remains foreclosed to all these Christologies, metaphysical systems, theologies, thought-systems. He, or his story of the incarnation, calls these theologies or Christologies forth, but he is not determined by them, but determines them in the last instance. Laruelle (2015c) uses science and mathematics to think in-Christ, specifically quantum theory. This does not mean that he thinks Christ from a quantum theoretical perspective. He does not develop a quantum-physical Christ, but uses the metaphors of quantum physics, namely: superposition and idempotence to think the incarnation and how so many different theologies and Christologies and metaphysical systems and ideologies can be called forth without changing or determining that which called them forth.

Christ, who is foreclosed to thought, and yet determines all thought in the last instance, Laruelle thinks with the help of the imaginary.[24]

Christ is believed to pre-exist creation (John 1), that is pre-exist pre-ex-*text*-ualisation. Christ is believed to pre-exist thought, yet he becomes incarnate in thought. This is the basic story of thinking. That which is believed to pre-exist thinking calls thought forth, and awaits to receive thought and thus is believed to be incarnate in thought.

Incarnation can be understood with the idea of cloning. Christ-in-person is cloned in the various Christs of the different theologies and Christologies (see Laruelle 2015c:24). One could also argue that Christ-in-text is cloned in the various interpretations of the text. But he is not this clone. Postmetaphysical theologies clone Christ as the deconstructor of philosophies, for example Caputo (2007), with his *What would Jesus deconstruct* or any of the other post-metaphysical theologies. But Christ *is* not the deconstructor,[25] he can be cloned as such within a post-metaphysical theology, but Christ-in-person is not *the* deconstructor. In such a theology Christ would be the deconstructor, but Christ-in-person would remain undetermined by Christ-the-deconstructor, or Christ-the-hospitable-host, or Christ-the-stranger. Christ-in-person, who is not the historical Jesus, would underdetermine any determination. The call of Christ-in-person would not stop with any of the determinations of Christ in any theology or Christology or Anatheism, and thus Christ-in-person underdetermines all determinations of Christ.

There is an interesting twist in the story of Christ's incarnation. As already mentioned earlier in this chapter, Christ's incarnation is not into power, but into powerlessness. Christ's incarnation is not the incarnation of power or hegemony, but the incarnation into weakness. It is exactly this incarnation amongst the weak (those who are not who bring to shame those who are), that brings a non-philosophical, non-colonial and non-ethical ethical modality to the Christ-fiction.

---

[24] Alongside the real but historical Jesus Christ, Christ the religious object of theology, there is another Christ that we could call "imaginary" or paradoxically, "scientific" because of its proximity to the algebraic or complex imaginary number – a messiah factor, more precisely, charged with making the cognizance of Christ pass from the state of a body of theological knowledge to its generic (that is to say, scientific and more particularly quantum) state – truth (Laruelle 2015c:48). It is obviously not a question of a theology of quantum physics, still less a Far Eastern one. At most one could say that the complex imaginary number or, geometrically speaking, the quarter-turn find a functional equivalent in the messianic function, and that, inversely, the force of Christ's insurrection in history and philosophy can be intuitively figured by the algebraic impossible (Laruelle 2015c:84).

[25] He is not even the deconstructor of philosophies, since he calls into question the ultimate presuppositions of deconstruction (Laruelle 2015c:30).

Not an ethics based on a philosophical decision of what is good and by implication evil, but rather an ethical stance than a worked out ethical theory. An ethical stance that underdetermines any determined ethics. The incarnation amongst the victims, as the victim-in-person. In the double sense of being victim-in-person, Christ becomes the victim of hegemony, he becomes the victim of the dominant ideology, as well as the dominant religion, as he is crucified by the incarnated powers of whatever political-religious world of his ministry, but likewise the various clones of Christ make him a victim of these clones, he is a victim-in-person of our various theologies. He is the victim-in-person of the various Christologies.

The Christo-fiction with Christ's incarnation amongst the least of the brothers and sisters (Matt. 25), offers an ethics without an ethical system based on some or other philosophical or religious decision, as it offers a stance without the stance becoming a determination of what is right, correct and/or good, because the right hand does not even know what the left hand is doing (Matt. 6:3), nor did those who entered the kingdom (the righteous), know when and where they served the Christ (Matt. 25:37). An ethical stance beyond the knowledge of good and evil, as the victim-in-person is the victim of such knowledge.

Incarnation and ministry amongst the least of the brothers and sisters.

Laruelle argues for a non-philosophy, which turns to Man-in-person and not the subject of some or other metaphysical system, either the Greek metaphysics of Being or the Judaic metaphysics of the Other (Laruelle 2015b:6). An ethics beyond the ethics of Priests and their enclosure, but also an ethics beyond the ethics of Prophets and their disenclosure. Not an ethics based on intellectual (philosophical) exercises of the philosophizing intellectual and their victimology (Laruelle 2015b:5), but a different ethics that is not based on any of the metaphysical systems but that can function as an ethical modality of a trans-fictional praxis without judgement, and therefore beyond good and evil. Such a praxis is based on the ethical modality of man-in-person, and the ethical modality (beyond knowledge of good and evil) of man-in-person is the victim-in-person (Laruelle 2015b:8). The man-in-person is the victim-in-person the moment s/he exists (ex-texts) as man or woman, in a world where the subject is called into ex-*text*-ence: that ex-*text*-ence is the existence of a body (somebody, but often also as a somebody classified as a no-body by the dominant narrative), of which the man-in-person is a victim. A victim of stratification, where the texts of ex-*text*-ence have been etched into the flesh (man-in-person) to transform the flesh into a body. Therefore victim-in-person is the ethical modality of man-in-person. Victim-in-person is the Call of the free bird that only ever exists in the cages of the I am.

It is in Man-in-person that for Laruelle salvation is found (Laruelle 2015b:7). Or as he asks: Who still deserves to arise? And then responds: '*Only victims, that is, humans in-prior-priority, deserve to arise and are likely able to do so*'

(Laruelle 2015b:11). In other words, if one wants to speak of freedom, liberation and salvation, it could only be the salvation of Man-in-person. Salvation would be a free bird, but birds only exist in cages. It is because birds only exist (ex-text) in cages (text) that salvation would be a free bird. Therefore, salvation is to be found in the destruction (deconstruction) of cages (texts), or at least that is the common belief, or the common conclusion that seems to necessarily follow.

The victim-in-person could be argued is another name for the Call, or rather the cry, which one could argue is the Cry for Justice, or the Cry for democracy still to come. Laruelle argues concerning the victim (victim-in-person), 'The victim forces us to discover at the core of its generic passivity an inversion of classical phenomenological intentionality, such that it is now the world that transcends or transgresses toward man, and not man toward the world, to which he is instead indifferent or foreclosed' (Laruelle 2015b:24). Man-in-person is foreclosed to the world, indifferent to the world and yet it is man-in-person that calls the world forth in which Man-in-person exists (ex-*texts*) as man or woman.

If the victim-in-person is the ethical modality of man-in-person, then the way of an ethical modality is to associate with the generic victim (Laruelle 2015b). The ethical modality for a trans-metaphysical praxis is to stand with the free bird when only caged birds exist. Yet, how to stand with something that does not exist, but only is believed to Call ex-*text*-ence forth and yet withdraws from any ex-text-ence? How to stand with that, which becomes a victim of the very thing it calls forth? Specifically, if one knows that the moment one stands with some*thing* that one believes exists, one is the persecutor, as one's belief (thought) is the cage of the encaged bird.

This was discussed in the previous chapters with regards to the student movements. One believes to take a stand with the students, yet by taking such a stand, such a conscious stand, one has marked the student-in-person, one has marked the flesh of the student-in-person into a defined body. The stance that Laruelle proposes is with the generic repressed, the generic victim and not the specific victim or specific repressed (see Laruelle 2015b:23). The generic repressed or the generic victim of grammatisation is not the specific repressed of a particular grammatisation.

How different is such a stance from the typical stance of liberation? Not that different and yet completely different. Liberation is the liberation of the Life, liberate the Real from social construction, liberate Truth from false-consciousness, liberate the Flesh (Life) from the confines of the imposed body. The ethical modality and its stance with the generic repressed is not a stance with Life (Flesh), as Life (Flesh) would again be a determination of that which is believed to pre-exist thought (social construction) and in that sense the ethical modality of the victim-in-person is an impossible stance, as there is no *place* or *time* to stand. It is a placeless and timeless stance, as it is without metaphysics, without narrative that gives time and place for things to exist. Such a stance would be a stance without a *Zeit-Spiel-Raum,* without a myth and thus an impossible stance, because there would be nowhere to stand.

A time-less and place-less stance that does not seek to determine what pre-exists thought (social construction), but which views all determinations as called forth, by whatever is believed to pre-exist thought; that views all thoughts as determined in the last instance, and therefore as necessary (called forth), but insufficient (where the Call withdraws). The ethical modality of the victim-in-person leads into a trans-fictional praxis, because from this stance all determinations of what is believed to pre-exist thought are seen as necessarily called forth, but insufficient. From this stance all determinations (philosophies, religion, metaphysical systems, ideologies) are viewed as fictions. Thus the stance of the victim-in-person as the ethical modality is a trans-fictional praxis.

The stance, or a trans-fictional praxis, is not where one seeks to first determine and then stand with whatever one has determined, in the belief that it pre-exists social construction, as such a stand would still be in the conviction of belief. The truth of such a faith (belief) would be repetition. A trans-fictional praxis as an ethical stance is to view the different constructions as necessary, but insufficient and thus beyond belief, but with a fidelity to thinking, but without being faithful to what thought believes itself to think.

In every liberation, emancipation of a repressed, there is a new repressed. The media intellectuals with the victims they identify have no real interest in the victim-in-person, as their interest lies with their abstract victimology and their collective individuation around their abstract concepts. Laruelle (2015b:23) writes, 'One does not want to defend a victimary interpretation of history and add it onto philosophy, to contrast a "victimodicy" to theodicy, but rather to think the victim's minimum possible real, that is to say, to think *according to the victim.*'

To think according to the victim is to think according to Christ or to think in-Christ. Christ who is cloned in the different theological and Christological systems is the victim-in-person, and as such is the ethical modality of Man-in-person. The Christ event is a way to interpret and understand the generic victim. The Call is the generic victim of thought-systems, political-systems, religious systems. As the Call withdraws from knowledge, from the response, from thinking, as it is separated from thought and thought-systems, this separation can be interpreted as sin. The story of the Fall of humanity can help in interpreting this withdrawal in which humanity stands. Humanity is separated from that which called it forth through humanity's *believed* faithful response to the Call, on the basis of its *believed* correct knowledge of what called it forth.

The generic victim could be interpreted as the victim of sin, the victim of separation, and the Call would then be the generic victim of thought, thought-systems, including political, religious and ideological thought-systems. Christ-event becomes the story, the story of this generic victim. The Christ-event becomes the story of Man-in-person, or the story of the Son-of-man, as the story of thinking.

It is interesting how the Call can be interpreted with the story of God, or the story of God, who should not be named, becomes a story of the Call. There is a mutual *Erklingen* when trying to think through the thinking of the West. It is to be expected as the Biblical texts form a dominant part of the tertiary retentions and protentions of Western thought. Therefore, if one wants to think through thought, then these texts will play a role in that thinking, which again only strengthens the argument that for non-colonial thought one has to think through Christ.

The story continues as the incarnation is an incarnation into a ministry. This ministry has been interpreted, in specifically the liberation and contextual theological traditions (prophetic traditions), as a ministry with a specific bias or preferential option for the poor.

Such a prophetic interpretation of Christ focuses on certain texts in the Gospels. For example, that according to the Gospels Christ's incarnation was in a stable, on the margins of society, in Bethlehem. The birth in a stable is important as it is on the border between human and non-human life, literally on the margin that Christ is incarnated in the worlds. His body, his embodiment, is an embodiment on the margin. The world had no room for him, thus in a sense he was homeless when he came into the world and soon thereafter, having to live as refugee in Egypt, before he could return to his ministry in Palestine. Christ is interpreted as being incarnated into homelessness and as a refugee, thus for example making homelessness and refugees sites of truth in such prophetic traditions.

As mentioned earlier Christ-in-person is incarnated not into the power of the dominant hegemony, but as a victim of those powerful hegemonies, be it the hegemony of the Roman political Empire or that of the Pharisaic religious system.

In Laclau's ideological dialectic, incarnation is cloning via a decision of the powerful, those who determine the clone, incarnation is a hegemonic choice of an equivalence to represent the whole. The story, as depicted in the Gospels, tells the story of Christ's birth in a stable and it tells the story of his family having to flee to Egypt to live as refugees. This is the story, and this story can be *made to mean* that the truth of the world is to be found amongst refugees and the homeless, in other words, this story can *be made to mean* the incarnation of a certain truth, the truth of the prophets.

If one stays with the story, as far as that is possible, without making it mean anything, Christ's incarnation is an incarnation into a world. A world like all worlds that is carried out by power, namely those who have the power to decide and control the Logos: the priests. In the story of the gospels, the priests are the Scribes and the Pharisees as well as the Roman authorities (Pilate). What one can know from the story is that his ministry brought him into trouble with these authorities, as there is a clear confrontation between them and Christ. What does that mean? What this means, will again depend on what meaning is *given* to this story. Whatever meaning is given to the story is the meaning that is *believed* to pre-exist the interpretation, and the interpretation is believed to discover this meaning as the truth of the text. What is forgotten in such exegesis is that one does not read texts, but one writes text as much as read texts.

The "naked" story never appears, as what appears as a text to be read, is already written by the reader.

Heidegger wanted to create an awareness of what is called thinking, *Was Heist Denken* (Heidegger 1961:3–4), not to understand thinking, but to become aware of that which calls thought forth, namely that which determines thought. That which calls one to think is the most thought-worthy (*Bedenklichste*), but it is the impossible to think, and the confusion is to confuse what is thought with thinking, to confuse an interpretation of the text with the text. For example, Marx and Henry tried to come as close as possible to that which calls thought forth. Henry, with his idea of Life or Flesh, has moved perhaps as close as it is possible to the most thought-worthy, but they are still caught in their thought and have not thought through to *Das Ding*. Henry thought it as Life or as Flesh, in Marxist tradition they have thought it as the material conditions, but by thinking it, they have individuated it and grammatised it as such.

It is impossible to reach that which calls forth thought, because one is caught in thought. To think thinking as such, to become aware of thinking and specifically to become aware of Western thinking, the thought which has been shaped and determined by Greek and Jewish-Christian thought, to think this thinking through, not with the idea of reaching the final thought or *Das Ding*, but by creating a fiction of thinking that is aware of the fictional character of all thought. The Christ-narrative not only is implicated in all these thoughts, but maybe it can help with this fiction of thinking through thought, to think the *Bedenklichste*, thereby not to think, but to think through, not to arrive at *Das Ding*, but to be aware of how *DAS DING* always appears in thought. As Christ-in-person is cloned in the various theologies and Christologies, so Christ always appears in-thought, but Christ-himself (Christ-in-person) is never thought. Therefore, one could argue that one is saved by Christ alone (*sola Christus*), that one is saved by Christ-in-person, but the Christ that we think saved us, is never Christ-in-person, but always the Christ of a specific theology or Christology. The Christ of belief is never Christ-in-person. The Christ-event tells the story of thinking, and specifically the belief in thinking. So it is not about interpreting Christ in the priestly tradition of protecting the status quo in the form of state theology, nor is it about interpreting Christ as the prophetic messiah, who proclaims the truth of the under-side against the status quo. Either way it would be an interpretation that is read into the story of Christ.

Christ the incarnate, as Henry (2003; 2012; 2015) understands the incarnation, is incarnation into and incarnation of the Flesh, thus an immanence, Life. For

Henry, the Christ-event reveals the truth of Life, it reveals the phenomenology of phenomenology. Laruelle's Christo-fiction does not reveal Life, does not reveal Truth as in Henry, but tells the story of thinking. The truth that is revealed is not the truth of the Real, the truth of the Call, but the truth of a way, the truth of a praxis. And this truth of a way, this truth of a praxis, not in the sense of an orthopraxis, as it is not the right way, but the way of thinking itself and the Christ-event is the fiction of the fiction of thinking.

After a deviation, I return to the first moment of the Christ-event, the incarnation.

For me the incarnation cannot be separated from Christ's ministry, as it was an incarnation into a ministry, therefore the incarnation is not a theo-ontological-determination, but a way of life: a practice, a ministry. His incarnational ministry can be interpreted as a preferential option for the marginalised, those deemed unacceptable to the law, to the norm, one could say a preferential option for the repressed of the dominant norms or the dominant law. The danger is to translate this preferential option for the poor into a theology of resentment that instils guilt in the master, as Nietzsche criticized Pauline Christianity. Such an *interpretation* of his ministry (practice) will clone Christ into the prophetic (disenclosing) ideology or religion or orthopraxis.

Yet, Christ's ministry in the gospels is not about instilling guilt in the masters, it is more radical than that, as instilling guilt in the masters only turns the wheel. Christ's ministry can be interpreted as questioning the wheel as such.

Christ's messianic practice of associating with the repressed did not make the repressed the new norm, he did not develop a victimology or as Laruelle calls it a victimodicy (Laruelle 2015b:23).

Nor did it present the values of the marginalized as the new norm. It was not about the slave becoming the new master as Nietzsche argued. Christ's association was not a victimology by instilling guilt in the master's conscience, but an occasion to reveal something about the law. An occasion to reveal something about thinking, the truth of thinking.

The law, thinking, response is revealed, in Badiou's terms, as terrestrial writing which is death. Christ challenged the law, but not in the name of a new law, but challenged the law by challenging the letter (construction) of the law, the grammatisation of the law with the spirit of the law, the very spirit(s) against which grammatisation wages its war in the first place. Those outside the law, those deemed unfit or unclean, did not become the new law, but they were the occasion to expose, in the language of Paul, the death of the letter. Christ's association with the least of the brothers and sisters (victims), by becoming the ultimate victim,[26] was

---

[26] The idea of the ultimate victim is a play on Benjamin's concept of the ultimate criminal, as the one who challenges not one law or two, but who challenges the legitimization of the law (see Meylahn 2014b). An ultimate victim is not a victim of a particular grammatisation, but is the

to expose the death of terrestrial writing, the cinders that are.

It is this perspective that was too disruptive for the powers that be that they had to judge him as an ultimate criminal (see Meylahn 2014b). A criminal that does not contravene a law, but challenges the basis of the law, challenges the carrying out of the respective worlds, thereby challenging the order of the world – the logic of the worlds, disrupting the myth. He challenged these worlds carried out by their laws (logos), not by presenting a different logos, nor by presenting an anti-logos, or a logos from below, but by exposing the logos, the law for what it is: the terrestrial writing of death.

Thus, the Christ-fiction (the messianic fiction) guides thinking, it is a way and a truth and a life, but without determining truth or life or an orthopraxis where the right hand would know what the left is doing. It exposes thinking as terrestrial writing, it exposes the law or the logos as a malicious god, from which the "living spirit" or the Call withdraws.

The Christ-event in this interpretation, as fiction about fictions, does not become a metaphysical principle, or a *theologia gloriae*, as Christ is not thought, determined or cloned into any theology, neither priestly theology nor prophetic theology, but his practice is imitated in accordance with the victim, rather than determining the victim, thereby under-determining both the priestly as well as the prophetic theologies (enclosure and disenclosure), by not determining at all, but being determined, being called insistently: a messianism without determined Messiah, a messianism always still to come in the form of a messianic praxis.

If Christ-fiction helps in thinking thinking, then it will also help with non-thinking, as a non-philosophy and non-theology, that is, with non-colonial thought.

The challenge of non-colonial thinking is not anti-colonial thinking, as anti-colonial thinking would be colonial, but to truly understand that thought is determined rather than determining. That thought is always responding, by naming, by abstracting the call, and in the response individuating oneself individually as well as collectively in exteriorising (ex-*text*-ualising) oneself through technics (writing). Of course, this awareness creates a democracy of all thought. All thoughts are equally fictional, which would play into the hand of the dominant narrative of the status quo of late capitalism, but as discussed previously, demonising the dominant narrative also plays into the hands of the capitalism by offering capitalism a clear enemy.

Narratives can be deconstructed by that which they repress, the voices that are silenced, marginalised, but this is a continuous process, as those voices should not be colonised in a victimology or a prophetic theology, which becomes priestly

victim of grammatisation as such. Christ is the victim of cloning, ideology, thinking, theology as such. He is the victim-in-person.

theology. It is a *never ending call* (an insistent and persistent call of the victim-in-person) for democracy and justice *always* still to come. Or the specific victim becomes the occasion not to expose thinking for being wrong, unjust or evil, but the specific historic victim becomes the occasion to expose thinking as mythical in the name of the victim-in-person.

Two possible interpretations amongst many other interpretations: the one oscillates between the priest and the prophet and the other exposes the priest and the prophet and the various variations thereof as fictional (myth interrupted by myth or literature).

The Face of Christ has been interpreted as a combination of the priestly and the prophetic, and thus functions as the abstract machine of the West.

The prophetic is interpreted in the various forms of disenclosure. For example, there are historic victims, and the prophet rises to the occasion, develops a victimology and thus challenges the status quo, but in the process, becomes a priest.

Another example, the un-thought of any thought-systems calls for faithful-subjects, the Truth calls for faithful-subjects, the faithful-subject responds faithfully, first as prophet against the reactive and obscure subjects and later as priest, and the result is the repetition of history, but this time as materialist dialectic (Badiou 2009). Materialist dialectic is a challenge to both democratic materialism as well as dialectical materialism, but the rhizome still grows, as lines of flight are re-captured and thus it expands – the Face of Christ colonises new lands.

A continuous call for a new humanity, new creation, new weapons with which to fight the powers of capture, in the name of the prophet or in the name of faithful-subjects, expands the rhizome. It is such a call from the insistence that seeks always new responses, which makes the rhizome expand, grow, colonise. Virno's multitude of minorities, multiple prophets refusing to become priests, might make the rhizome constantly tremble, vibrate, constantly disrupting the myth, but without faithful-subjects believing a new myth. Such vibration might bring it to life, with constant individuation in the rhizome and thereby undermining (under-determining) the apparatus of capture (control societies) as well as the war machines, with their killing and dis-individuation, by offering a celebration of noetic souls, including the nutritive and sensitive souls in a parliament of things. This could be a practice of non-colonial thinking that does not seek to determine, but sees all thought as determined, and therefore the call for non-centralised individuation of all things, a democracy for all things, but without the myth of a new life, a new humanity, or a new creation.

Crucifixion

The Christ-event does not end with the incarnation and a ministry amongst the victims as victim-in-person, but it continues to the crucifixion. A Victimology can be incorporated into the rhizome, can be incorporated and even made profitable, both economically and politically, as the groups who have individuated around an abstract victim (determined victim) score both political and economic points. History bears witness to this, how prophets become priests. Yet, what is to be done with the ultimate criminal, the ultimate victim as victim-in-person, not the victim of a specific discourse on race, class or gender, but the victim of thinking as such; the victim-in-person, who exposes the myth of the myths, who exposes terrestrial writing as death? The victim-in-person is the victim of thinking, the victim of cloning (incarnation-deformation). Such a victim cannot be captured by the system, by the apparatus of capture or its war machines, as it is a victim of both, and therefore under-determining their determinations. Therefore, the victim-in-person becomes ultimate criminal as it challenges not the legitimisation of a law, but challenges thinking, as determination, as colonialism. Christ challenged the law, the letter of the law with the spirit of the law, according to Paul (2 Cor. 3: 4–6) and according to most interpretations of the Sermon on the Mount (Matt. 5– 7). Christ challenged cloning (colonialism of thinking or determining of thinking) with the spirit (Call) of thinking, that which calls thinking forth. Did Christ do all this? Or does the Christ-event help us think this? It is a Christo-fiction that helps us think thinking, in a sense exposing the insufficiency of thought, revealing thought as fictions, namely as attempts at grasping, but left with only cinders: fictions, literature, writing, *pharmakon*. Such a challenge is too radical, too ultimate, and therefore the priests and the prophets, as well as the Christian synthesis of the two, had to crucify him, and will crucify him again and again.

In a previous study, I argued the death of God was not in the crucifixion, but in the incarnation, in the sense that the transcendent dies in becoming immanent, and that the crucifixion was the death of the death of God which did not translate into the life of God (Meylahn 2013:310ff). The crucifixion was interpreted as the death of the way of life, as the death of any form of orthopraxis, as the messiah, the way, is crucified.

Laclau, in his ideological dialectic discussed in the previous chapters, argues that ideology is made up of incarnation and deformation. Deformation could also be interpreted as crucifixion or the death of the incarnation, as a *pharmakon* (writing – thinking) is both gift (incarnation) and Gift (death – crucifixion). The Cross is cinders, it is a holocaust, everything is sacrificed, nothing is left. The cross *is* nihilism, the abyss of total forsakenness. Such an is-statement would seek to determine the cross, would seek to incarnate the cross in a singular meaning and thus would need to be crucified.

So many ways to clone, to determine the cross, as Luther said in the Heidelberg Disputation of 1518 (Thesis 19 and 20), that only he or she is a true theologian who has a *theologia crucis* (see Meylahn 2013:319). So indeed, it is in the cross that things are *decided*, but it is exactly the decision that is the problem. True theology begins with *theologia crucis*, but is any interpretation of true theology not also in need of crucifixion? Does *theologia crucis*, once understood as true theology, not become *theologia gloriae* and therefore needs to be crucified? The cross, like Christ, is cloned in various theologies of the cross, and just as various gods are crucified, so various theologies of the cross need to be crucified. All is crucified – there are cinders, there are cinders there.

The cross, just like the incarnation amongst the least of the brothers and sisters (the crib and the cross belong together), is under-determining, leaving only cinders. Is this the final victory of the abyss, of nihilism as the last truth, the truth of cinders? No, as Derrida says, of these cinders we must give account. But without finality, as whatever determination is given, it is crucified, as it is deformed.

Thus, like Abraham, who was called to sacrifice the incarnation of the promise, the embodiment of the promise, all is left are cinders, the holocaust. From such a holocaust only a glorious Call can resurrect as insurrection. If there are cinders there, and cinders there are, it is the Call that rises not from the ashes like a phoenix, or like all immortal gods, but because of the ashes the Call rises and not from the ashes. The holocaust does not have the last say, nihilism does not have the final word, but the Call, as the Call calls thought forth. The difference being that as the Call calls thought forth, the called forth thought knows that it is literature.

Resurrection as insurrection

In the cross from the cinders, it is not the phoenix that rises, it is not a return of the gods, it is not the resurrection of the gods, who are immortal anyway and always rise, as such resurrection would only be the eternal return, but it is the glorious flesh of the victim-in-person who rises with a glorious body clearly marked by the wounds. Revelation chapters 4 to 5 tells the story of the glorious body of the risen Christ, as a wounded body, the body of the slaughtered lamb and not the Lion of victory.

The risen glorious-wounded body is not some final victory of some or other God or truth or determination, but the insurrection of the Call that calls to account when there are cinders there. All there are, are cinders, but still Called to account, to account for these cinders, still Called to respond, as the Call has not been crucified, not been burnt or sacrificed. It is the resurrection of the glorious flesh of the victim-in-person, the Lamb that was slain, that rises as an insurrection, as a Call to account for the cinders, a Call to account for the hope that is in us (1 Peter 3:15). The hope for the future, the call of the future, not beyond cinders, but the hope in cinders, in-Christ and him crucified. The hope for *poiēsis* still to come, the kingdom to come, the world to come – worlds carried out by *poiēsis,* composing new worlds, re-articulating new worlds, but remembering that these new worlds are cinders to come.

This event (incarnation-crucifixion and insurrection-resurrection of the glorious Call of the Victim-in-person) helps to think thinking, at least thinking in the West, helps one to think through the Abstract machine of the West, the Face of Christ, revealing both sign regimes (priestly and prophetic) as myths, as terrestrial writing, as death, namely cinders.

The Call is cloned (a Caller is determined, cloned) in-the-response (a Caller is incarnated) and deformed (crucified), but the Call is not silenced, but insurrects or under-determines all determinations, and thus the Call is resurrected. John Schad (1993) wrote an article, "Hostage of the Word": *Poststructuralism's Gospel Intertext*, in which he argues that the heresy of the Johannine Prologue is that God and speech share the same impossible beginning and therefore are always already identical, or coextensive (1993:1). I have argued that thinking and Christ are identical and coextensive, the one is the fiction of the other.

Can one still speak of a theology? Is this a theology? No, it is not, and if it is anything, it is an *imitatio Christi*. What does this mean for theology and specifically practical theology?

Is it a praxis? It is an imitation, to imitate thought, which is itself an imitation and thus the imitation of imitation, a fiction of fiction, exposing the myth of myth – doing this not in the name of truth, but doing this is the truth, the truth of the way of thinking. The truth of the faith of thinking is repetition, the truth of the way of thinking is resurrection as insurrection, but without the faith of thinking.

Should one want more than that? Anything more will once again by determined by a sufficiency and not an insufficient faith.

In the final chapter of the book, I will turn to unpack these ideas within the context of practice within community and between communities: trans-fictional praxis as Christ-*poiēsis*.

5. In-conclusion: a trans-fictional Christ-*poiēsis* as praxis for imagining non-colonial worlds emerging from the shadows of global villages

Non-colonial worlds are colonial worlds of which the fictional character is thought.

Books, as do texts, have beginnings and endings, introductions and conclusions, but because of the content of this book it cannot really offer a conclusion, but needs to remain inconclusive, open to the Call. Yet, in this last chapter of the book, as a conclusion and therefore in-conclusion, I would like to offer a few ideas as to how a trans-fictional Christ-*poiēsis* can be a praxis for imagining non-colonial worlds emerging from the shadows or the cracks of global villages. There can never be a non-colonial world, just as there cannot be non-philosophy, but a recognition that all worlds are colonial, and that recognition allows for a non-colonial stance towards the worlds emerging from the shadows. A stance that recognises the fictional character of these worlds, and thereby disrupts the inherent colonialism of these worlds.

The idea of *de*colonialism, or *de*colonial thought, would probably fit perfectly with the stance of this book, as it links up with the thought of *de*construction, or rather auto-deconstruction. Decolonial thought, understood as that which auto-deconstructs, auto-disrupts and disturbs the various colonial narratives or the dominant narratives because of the insistence of the Call, the insistence of the Flesh, or Life, or the persistent insistence of the Victims of the various colonial discourses. Yet, I will rather refer to non-colonial thought and non-colonial worlds, as de-colonial thought can too easily be understood as a stance that understands itself as speaking for or in the Name of the Call, or Name of the Flesh or Name of Life, or Name of the Victim, which is then not decolonial but colonial, as it identifies and determines the Flesh, the Life, the Victim or the Call. In these chapters I have referred to victim-in-person rather than victim and will in this chapter refer to the [Call] in square brackets, but even such styles of writing remain writing. Even when writing something under erasure it remains legible and therefore is identified and determined. That which Calls is less than erasure, less than square brackets, in a sense even less than foreclosure, as all these are already thoughts and thus legible determinations and identifications. Non-philosophy takes cognisance of this and therefore all determinations and identifications turn to ash, cinders, and yet these cinders are all that one has. Non-colonial thinking thus is not in the name of, but if anything in the name of thinking and therefore disrupting thinking not in the name of anything, but in the name of thought as cinders. Non-colonial worlds are colonial worlds of which the fictional character is thought.

In this chapter the focus will not be on an application of the ideas developed or reflected upon in this book, but rather exploring how these ideas can interact with specific contexts of practice. The contexts of practice are part and parcel of my embodiment. The student protests have accompanied much of this book, and therefore I will not return specifically to their protests, but explore how these ideas, or this *imitatio* of thinking through the Christ event, and therefore thinking through Christ, can be of help in community work, individual or group counselling or sojourning, as well as reading and interpreting, for example, the Bible, but with the conscious focus of imagining non-colonial worlds emerging from the cracks and/or shadows of global villages.

Trans-fictional Christ-*poiēsis* as praxis for imaging non-colonial worlds

Trans-fictional Christ-*poiēsis* as praxis for imagining non-colonial worlds, can be interpreted as an *imitatio Christi*. Yet, this *imitatio Christi* could in turn be interpreted as an *imitatio* of the thinking of thinking, as an imitation of the movement the Call calls forth, and as a faithfulness to the Call rather than a faithfulness to the responses. The Call calls forth thinking, which includes theology, philosophy and science and it is in responding to the Call that the subject is called into *respons*ibility and through responding the subject as subject comes into ex-*text*-ence. The subjects called into responsibility are called in or from a specific community, as they respond and ex-text as embodied subjects, as contextual subjects. If they are faithful-subjects responding to a new Truth, their responses call a new community of disciples into ex-*text*-ence.

In this book, it has been argued that the Call can be determined as being numerous different things, depending on the embodiment of the one responding. It has been determined as Life (Henry) for example, and then the praxis could be an imitation of Life, as a theology of Life (2003 and 2012) or a philosophy of incarnation (Henry 2015). If the Call is determined as God, as in the God who Called Abraham, then this praxis could be interpreted as a divine praxis, or praxis of faith. If the Call is determined as the material Real then this praxis would be a form of Marxism or non-Marxism (see Laruelle 2015d). The response *determines* the Call, which is a determination of that which affects thinking (that which calls thinking forth). The Call calls thinking forth and through the response thinking subjects are individuated and communities are bound together. This is the *work* of thinking, or the labour of thinking as the labour of *Dasein*: determination of the Call, and in the determination of the Call a subject is individuated or called-forth and a community is bound together by the specific determination of the Call. This is the *work* or *labour* of thinking, the labour of responding: ex-*text*-ualisation or ex-*text*-ence as *Dasein* in a specific world. This book, in following Laruelle, has not tried to offer one more response by determining the Call, but has responded by attempting to think this thinking of thinking, whilst recognising the work of thinking through a science of philosophy. It has tried to think the *Bedenklichste,* that which gives to think, that which is most thought-worthy, that which calls the work of thinking forth. It did not attempt to offer one more work of thought, by offering a particular determination of the Call and thereby individuating a particular subject(s) who are collectively bound together into their specific community of belief or knowledge (the determination of the Call), which carries out a particular world, but to think this working of thinking.

As long as thinking believes it can determine the Call, the truth of this belief will be repetition. Between the different believed determinations there will be antagonism and holy wars, be they religious, philosophical, scientific or political-ideological determinations.

Thus, maybe responding by referring (determining) that which calls-thinking-forth as "Call" is already too much of a determination, as determining it as "Call" is only possible *in* that which the Call has called forth, namely thought or a response to the Call. Calling (determining) "it" a Call is already a response and therefore one should maybe write [Call] in square brackets and thereby under-determine the Call by the [Call].

In the rest of this chapter I will therefore write the [Call] in square brackets to acknowledge that the [Call] is not a determination of that which calls thinking forth, but is only in reference to that which calls thinking forth, and that it is always determined in the response, but remains foreclosed whilst determining the response in the last instance as that which called it forth.

In this last chapter of the book, I would like to explore the praxis of such a stance, from the [Call] in the midst of the various differing responses and therefore a trans-fictional praxis. I refer to it as a stance as it is not a thinking as such, as it is not a determination of the Real or the [Call], but it is a stance, in the sense of taking a stand with or in accordance with the [Call], unilaterally looking at the various determinations of the past, present and those still to come.

It is a last chapter, but it is and will always remain an inconclusive chapter as the story continues, and no conclusion is offered, no finality is offered, only a stance that realises the necessity of all the past determinations and the necessity of future determinations, and it does not offer a non-determinative thinking, as non-determinative thinking or nihilist thinking is still determined thinking.

Trans-fictional praxis as Christ-*poiēsis* is not a work of thinking, but a stance regarding thinking, and as stance a way of life. Not the truth that is thought, but the truth of thinking and therefore as Christ said about himself (John 14:6), I am the way the truth and the life. A Christ-*poiēsis* that seeks to imitate Christ is a way and a truth of thinking, without that truth determining anything, but a truth about thinking itself. Yet, likewise, the imitation of Christ is an *imitatio* Christi and not a determination of Christ. Therefore, Christ is not "used" as *the* hermeneutical key with which to unlock, interpret and determine any truth, but in imitating Him one stands in a stance of a praxis, which is a way and a truth and thus a life. It is a way that is the truth about life, which always appears as *Dasein*, as *Mitsein*.

Christ is not a hermeneutical key with which to determine Reality and determine the truth about the Real, about the [Call], but it is a way of engaging with *Dasein* as *Mitsein*, but from the stance of that which called *Dasein* as *Mitsein* forth. *Imitatio Christi* and participation in Christ does not reveal *the* Christ. It is not an attempt at offering a Christology where Christ is determined, but through imitation and participation a truth about the worlds in which one exists is revealed, a truth about human works, the labour of being, the labour of thinking is revealed, the truth about *Dasein* is revealed, but not in the sense that it is the truth of *Dasein* where *Dasein* is determined in a particular way, but a truth about the various determinations of *Dasein*. The moment Christ, as hermeneutical key, becomes a way towards a particular determination, then it is no longer Christ alone (*Sola Christus*), but Christ and the determination of Christ. That determination of Christ is then what is *believed* to save and therefore no longer saved by Christ alone, neither by Grace alone (as it is that determination of Christ that saves, that *labour* (work) of *Dasein* that saves), neither saved by faith alone, but by the knowledge of that truth. Christ is not a way to a Truth, but Christ is the truth, the truth of a way, a stance in life. To stand with Christ does not reveal a particular world, for example a Christian world. There is no Christian world, but the worlds are revealed in their truth, in their fictional nature, through Christ.

This needs to be stressed. It is a stance, a way, a truth, that fully appreciates the necessity of determinations of the [Call], all the Truths about the Call, but also recognises the insufficiency thereof. However, the insufficiency does not cancel the necessity thereof. Philosophies, religions, sciences and ideologies are necessary, as we cannot do without them, because we cannot *be* without them, neither as individuals nor as communities.

There is no *Dasein in Christ*. *Dasein* is always to be, to ex-text in a particular world, but there is a Christ-*poietic* stance in that world, to participate and imitate Christ.

It is a Christ-*poiēsis* as one sees the world through Christ, but not in the sense that a Christian world is revealed. A Christian world will only be revealed (carried out) if Christ is interpreted as *the* interpretation or *the* determination of the [Call] and then one has Christ and this determining Truth and no longer *sola Christus*, *sola gratia* or *sola fide*, but one is saved by one's labour, by the labour of thinking, the labour of *Dasein*. Christ is not determined as some cure that is then presented as the answer to a determined and identified problem, but a Christ-*poiēsis* is a stance of imitating Christ and participating in Christ through which one is liberated from the various determinations of the [Call], determinations of the Lack to which the determined Jesus would be the answer. It is this liberation from the work of determining the [Call] and the belief in this work, which can be interpreted as liberation from sin, where sin is understood as seeking to determine the good; and furthermore such liberation opens the space for an ethical-stance that is beyond the knowledge of good and evil, just as the "saved" in Matthew 25 did not *know* the "good" they had done by serving the least of the brothers and sisters.

As discussed in the first chapter, this is not an attempt to save Christ or to offer an apologetics of the four pillars of the protestant faith. With what arrogance would one seek to do that? I am not attempting to offer a post-structuralist interpretation of Christ or these pillars, as I am not offering an interpretation of them, a determination of them, but a stance of thinking through Christ: not a determination of Christ which causes a burning sensation in the heart of a mutual *erklingen*, but a stance, a participation, an *imitatio* Christi which is the Truth of the way of Life.

It is not a Truth that can be known, because to be known it has to be determined, but a truth that is the way – the way of life.

Christ-*poiēsis* does not carry out a world, does not create a world, but through Christ the worlds are revealed in their truth: their fictional (crucified) truth. Therefore Christ-*poiēsis* is not a world creation, but a stance in the different worlds, a stance for a trans-fictional praxis or as was discussed in the previous chapters an ethical modality in a trans-fictional praxis.

There is no existence without text (externalisation), no ex-*text*-ence without philosophy, religion, science or ideology. Yet, these are all philo-fictions, they are fictions as they are insufficient and do not conclusively capture the Real or the [Call]. One therefore finds oneself in a transversal space between philo-fictions, but as each of these various fictions seek to determine the [Call], individuate subjects and bind a community together, they are different metaphysical systems that carry out their respective worlds. Therefore, a trans-fictional praxis would be totally impotent in the face of such equally determined worlds in the last instance. All the different worlds are equal, as they are all equally philo-fictions (metaphysical systems), in the sense of being equally determined in the last instance by the

Real [Call], as each of them has been called forth by that which they *believe* called them forth: called them into being.

Such relativity would leave one totally impotent to act in a trans-fictional space. Or as Latour (2004) argued: the steam for criticism, the steam of critical discernment is gone. The steam is gone, because steam for criticism is based on the ability to judge. Judgment is in turn based on the *belief* to have finally, correctly and conclusively determined the Real or to have responded correctly to the [Call] that called the response forth. If one accepts that there are no conclusive determinations of the Real or correct responses to the [Call], then it seems that the only option left is to resign to total relativity. However, because one has not given up on that which calls thinking forth, the [Call] remains the determination in the last instance of all thinking as it is that which calls thinking forth. The [Call] insistently calls, as it haunts all the determinations. No response finally or conclusively determines the [Call] as that which called the response forth, and yet every single response is determined in the last instance by that which called it forth: the [Call].

The stance is not a stance amongst powerless (insufficient) philo-fictions, but the stance is a stance with the [Call], driven by a passion to think the *Bedenklich-ste*, that which is most thought-worthy, as it is that which calls thought forth. The stance is not a stance in total relativity which would translate into an impotent democracy of thought, but a stance with or in accordance with the [Call]. And it is a passionate continuous *respons*ibility in response to the insistence of the [Call] that calls thinking forth. It is the affectivity of the [Call], the pathos, that is the steam – not of critique, but of a praxis that seeks to remain *faithful, but faithful* in the sense of remaining responsible to the [Call]. This responsibility to the [Call] seeks to remain responsible to the [Call] in that it does not view any of the responses as the final correct and conclusive response. In other words, it is a faithfulness to the call without a faithfulness to the belief of the responses, but a view of all the responses as being only determined in the last instance by the [Call] and none of them *the* Determination of the [Call]. In the biblical language, each determination is viewed as an idol, and therefore a *faith* that seeks to be faithful to the [Call] against the *belief* of the various responses. But a trans-fictional praxis is not iconoclastic, as it is a name (determination) and therefore, of what would it be a destructor of determinations? It would rather be what Latour (2001) argues for: iconoclashes. It is an agonism between the various philo-fictions.

In this inconclusive chapter, as the story will always continue, I would like to reflect on the consequences of such a passionate (*pathos* called faithfulness to the [Call] rather than following the belief of any of the responses) praxis for sojourning with individuals in communities as well as between communities in ecumenical or intercultural contexts. How does one journey with individuals without knowledge, but with the faithful *pathos* of a trans-fictional stance? How does one engage in communities, in the political landscapes of injustice, without knowledge of what is just or right or good, but rather with a passionate stance (in accordance with the insistent passion of the [Call]) and with the desire to remain faithful (responsible) to the [Call]? Like Abraham, to remain faithful to the [Call] even if this faithfulness means sacrificing any incarnation of the [Call], sacrificing any determination of the Call, as he was Called to sacrifice the only tangible sign he ever had of the promise of offspring: Isaac. The question in this chapter will be: Is it possible to sojourn with individuals and communities with such a stance in a trans-fictional praxis? A trans-fictional praxis where there is no orthopraxis, nor an orthodoxy. If there is no orthopraxis or orthodoxy, can such a stance call a community together, for example a community of non-philosophers, of non-theologians, a society of trans-fictional practitioners? Could there be a community of those who take this stance, or who are taken into this stance? This question was asked by Laruelle: is it possible to organise a society of non-philosophers (Laruelle 2012b:151ff)? To sojourn with individuals and communities without knowledge (determination) or belief, but in faithfulness, in responsibility to the [Call] alone? Are communities possible, without the political act of being (externalising)-in-common? Are communities possible without communally individuating into a common-good or against a common enemy?

Non-colonial communities or movements – communities or movements in-Christ

Can communities be created without a founding or binding myth? Can communities be formed with myths-continuously-interrupted? Can there be non-colonial communities, or are communities always colonial, as they colonise the [Call], colonise the Real? In the context of the previous chapter, can there be such a thing as a community of imitators of Christ? This question in a sense *is* the question of the church: can the church be? Is it possible to be church? Can a church, as body of Christ, be? Can it exist, can it ex-*text*? Can it ex-*text* without *the Text,* in the sense of ex-*text*-ting without *the* determination of the [Call]? What if it ex-texts with literature, with writing, *poiēsis*? One finds throughout history that there have been faithful-subjects (Badiou 2009) who responded to the truth – the idea that a [Call] can call individuals – and the sacred books are filled with testimonies of such faithful individuals, heroes of faith, knights of faith, or poets of faith, for example: Abraham and Moses. But what about a community? Is it possible to create a community of knights of faith? Is it possible to create a community of poets of faith? Can a community of faithful subjects be bound (*religare*) by a Truth, in Badiou's (2009) sense? Or will that Truth, once it calls a whole community-forth, be a deformed-incarnation (Laclau 2007; 2014)? Will the truth that calls a community into being-in-common not be a wounded truth, a deformed truth that is a deformed incarnation? It will always be a deformed incarnation. The ultimate truth or good of any community will necessarily be a deformed incarnation.

If one turns to the stories of the exemplary faithful-subjects, what does one read in their attempts to "lead" a faithful-community? This turn to these stories offers nothing more than a language of faith, or a liturgy of faith, and one needs to be very mindful not to transform this language of faith into a determination of belief.

Moses was called to lead a people out of bondage towards freedom, yet for him to be able to lead them into the Promised Land, there had to be a Text. A text carved onto stone tablets before the "people of the living (liberating) God" could be formed into the liberated people of God and enter the Promised Land. The liberating Call, which called the faithful-subject Moses forth, had to be incarnated and deformed on stone tablets before it could form a community, before it could bind a community. Yet, the text that was carved onto the stone tablets clearly stated that they should not create for themselves an image: a deformed incarnation of their liberating God. Here, in the story of Moses and the *liberated* people, one finds an attempt to incarnate without deformation, by incarnating a law that forbids deformed incarnations. Was this an attempt to bind freedom into a law and thus create a community, create a political-religious identity, but through forbidding idolatry (deformed incarnations)? Yet, this very law, placed in the ark, became a deformed incarnation, it became a determination of belief, rather than a liturgy of faith.

The will of God incarnated in the written Law clearly stated that they should not deform the [Call] that liberated them into an idol. The Ten Commandments clearly forbid the creation, construction, composition of an idol, idea, theory or theology. Yet, to bind (*religare*) liberated slaves into a people (a people with a political identity), something that could bind them (*religare*) was needed. A God needed to be found into which they could individuate and become subjects of a particular community, *Dasein* of a particular *Mitsein*. For subjects to emerge, faithful subjects of a faithful and liberated community, a *Theos* ('I am the Lord your God, who brought you out of Egypt, out of the land of slavery'– Exodus 20:1) needed to be determined. The moment there is a determination, a name, an idea, there is the possibility of self-justification. With such a determination there is knowledge with which to distinguish between what is right and wrong, good and bad, and so this knowledge of what is good, right and just (the ten-commandments) was transformed into a Monument of stone. This Text (this Law) placed into the ark and later into the holy of holies became the heart of the temple, around which, in concentric circles, the priests circled, and all the people were differentiated and classified, stratified into layers of good, righteous, and clean all the way to those who were unclean and thus excluded not only from the temple, but even the temple grounds. A new god had been created from the law that forbids the creation of images, and idols.

Faithful-Subjects-of-truth, like Luther in the Reformation, also responded to a Call with *Here I am*: "Here I stand. I cannot do otherwise. God help me, Amen!" Yet, for a faithful-community of faithful subjects to be formed they needed something more, namely a bind that binds them together (*religare*). The language of faith had to be transformed into a determined and determining Text of belief. Luther responded to this need with his texts and confessional writings, which could maybe be interpreted as language of faith, as liturgies of faith, but this language of faith in the next generation, or in Berger and Luckmann's (1976) language, these habits of faith, were transformed into typifications, legitimisations and eventually reified into Texts of correct Belief and thus Lutheran orthodoxy.

The early church, seeking unity, had to formulate, create and write confessions. Confessions that till today still unite the church, bind the church into an ecumenical communion. The reformers also wrote their confessions and confessional statements as expressions of the language of faith, as liturgies of faith. Maybe they wrote them as reminders, as living memories, to inspire constant reformation against monuments, but as these new emerging communities (churches–denominations) needed monuments to become communities with identities, for example as Lutheran or Reformed, they needed to transform these confessions, these narratives of faith, languages of faith, liturgies of faith into texts of belief, idols, works, laws: the dogmas of Lutheran and Reformed orthodoxy. There are languages of faith, liturgies of faith and as such they are memories written on the flesh of the heart, but they eventually became Texts of belief written on stone and thus monuments. Assmann argues that signs become monuments so as to create political identities (see Assmann 1991:11–14). Did the sign of God's liberation from Egypt become a monument in the stone tablets, which were placed in the ark to become the holy of holies? For the churches of the Reformation, are the confessional texts not the new holy of holies? Did the signs of unity, and confessions as signs (memories) of faith as in the various confessional writings become monuments in orthodoxy (Lutheran or Reformed)?

A monument is an idol, it is something with which to justify oneself, it is a captured Truth, a determination of what is Good, it is a Text of belief which can be used to justify oneself as well as judge others. It is the knowledge that is gained when eating of the fruit of the tree of knowledge of good and evil. It is a work, a construction, an ark, a cage, an idol that captures the Truth, determines the Truth, the Good, the [Call], and therefore it is sin. The moment theology becomes a work (*technics*) it destroys the immanent working of faith. Can there be a church without theology? How to be a church of the spirit rather than a church of the letter? Is it possible? It seems it is impossible, which raises the question, is church possible? Or was the church something that emerged in a context of political necessity? Luther never wanted to create a separate church, but the Reformation was an insurrection as resurrection within the church-community, as at that stage church and community were one. The stories of the "early" church, the stories of the People of the Way, are stories of insurrectional events, insurrectional moments within religious (Jewish and/or Greek-Roman) communities as unbinding events (insurrection-resurrection). All those affected by the insurrection, all those who rose with Christ, needed to legitimize themselves, justify themselves and there- fore needed some form of institution and finally reified into the way the world *is*, or at least believed to be. Berger & Luckmann (1976) help one understand this process of social construction of the new reality, the "risen" reality in-Christ that in its realization destroys the in-Christ.

Can communities be created in *imitatio*-Christi? Can a community imitate Christ and in imitating be bound together without a myth, without a logos, without a decision as to what is the good, right, or righteous, in other words, without orthodoxy or orthopraxy? Is community possible, is the political possible without hegemony, without the incarnation and deformation of ideology?

No, it is not possible, as a community to be community needs something that binds (*religare*), it needs religion or politics (ideology) to bind it together. The var- ious ideas of the multitude as disruptive movements, tried to develop something of an inoperative community (Virno 2004). Disruptive movements without their own specific political agenda, without there being something specific that binds them, and yet something brings them together as a collective movement (multi- tude) – it is not a *theos* that binds them, but it is a collective enemy. What binds the multitude is not their determination of the good, but their collective determination of the enemy of the people, namely the state or the Empire, or capitalism. The various occupy movements were known for their diversity and that they did not have a common political or economic agenda, yet they had a common enemy. Not a good, *theos* that binds, but a collective enemy that binds the multitude together with their different particular agendas.

To be totally without *religare* would be impossible. As Laruelle argues, 'The Church is the subject of antigrace, the grasping reception of a gift that it persists in wanting to deserve. Such is the self-justification of the works that have diverted faith from its immanent work' (Laruelle 2015c:97). In other words, the church or any identifiable community or even an identifiable movement, is the subject of anti-grace. It needs self-justification, it needs a decision of the good or of the evil, whereby it can justify itself, or legitimize itself and consequently judge others as either being with us or against us, included or excluded from the community, church or movement. Community, church, movement per definition destroys what Laruelle calls the immanent work of faith, destroys the *imitatio Christi*. It destroys the immanent work of responsibility to respond to the [Call]. It is maybe for this

reason that the Salos, the Holy Fools, did not seek community and certainly rejected any form of discipleship (see Meylahn 2013:331ff).

Is this the only option: individuals as faithful subjects guided by a language
of faith, a liturgy of faith, but never faithful communities?

Has one not once again created a binary: community vs faithfulness? The binary is Community vs the [Call], Church vs In-Christ, victim vs Victim-in-person,
Subject vs Man-in-person.

New battle lines have been drawn up and maybe new weapons, or maybe these
new weapons are not so new, as it is the old weapons which are just being repeated.
The weapons remain the weapons of self-justification through knowledge, gained
from eating of the tree of knowledge with which to determine the [Call] and place
it in the ark of the Holy of Holies so as to classify and stratify all that circles or that
comes into appearance in the light of this Holy of Holies. Is it a binary? Are these
opposites? Or is it a unilateral movement of thought, as thought is called forth by
the [Call] and therefore determined by the [Call] in the last instance, without the
[Call] being determined in return?

If it is a unilateral movement of thought (as determining) called forth by that
which determines it in the last instance, then there is a community of determining
thoughts that are all equally called-forth: a democracy of thoughts (philo-fictions).
The question is no longer who is correct, who has the correct determination, whose
holy of holies is *the* holy of holies, but a recognition of the absolute necessity
of having a holy of holies in a temple somewhere, even if the temple has been
destroyed, but likewise a recognition of the insufficiency of these holy of holies to
finally and definitely capture the [Call] that called it forth in the first place, as the
[Call] remains foreclosed to thought. Even that foreclosed-to-thought cannot be
captured (determined or be determining), as it itself is but *a* possible determination
and not *the* determination determined in the last instance by that which called it
forth.

With all the faithful subjects of the past, present and future, who ushered in
various determinations, one is left in this trans-determined space of a democracy
of thoughts, a space that I have called trans-fictional with all the different holy
of holies. But without these different holies of holies being bound together in a
new meta-metaphysics or a super holy of holies, which binds them together into
a harmonious plurality, where each part is believed to only see a part and only
when all views are taken together does the whole come into view. No, that would
be meta-metaphysics and not trans-metaphysics, as the parts do not make up the
whole, they are all equally fictional or illusional, but to speak of fiction and illusion presupposes that somewhere there is the Real. Yes, there is the [Call], the
victim-in-person, the Real, Man-in-person, and determination of the Real has been
called forth by the Real and thus is determined by the Real in the last instance,
but because there are different determinations the space that is created is an an-

tagonistic space as each determination believes (and *necessarily believes*) it has determined the Real conclusively, and is therefore in competition (and necessarily in competition) with all the other determinations. It is only the recognition of the insufficiency of these determinations that transforms antagonism into agonism.

Mouffe (2013) argues not for an attempt to move beyond any hegemony or antagonism, but to embrace this political factor and work towards an agonistic approach. Agonism is good in pluralistic societies, as Mouffe argues that conflict 'cannot and should not be eradicated, since the specificity of pluralistic democracy is precisely the recognition and the legitimation of conflict (Mouffe 2013:7). She argues that what is important is that conflict does not take the form of antagonism (struggle between enemies), but the form of agonism (struggle between adversaries) (Mouffe 2013:7). A more radical democracy is needed, a parliament of things, as Latour (1993:142) argues: A parliament of things where the animals and plants, who according to Heidegger (1983:261ff) are *Weltarm,* and the stones who are *Weltlos* are also included in the democracy. Thus, a conscious bias needs to be given to the silenced voices of the various worlds, not because these voices have the truth, but because their silenced voices stand in the stance or posture of being in accordance with the [Call] rather than fighting about which determination is better. Yet, because it is not their voice that is the new truth, I prefer to speak of generic victims, or victim-in-person, because it is not their specific voice that is now *the* truth, but their voice is the *occasion* for insurrection. Trans-fictional praxis alone would be an agonistic praxis, and therefore it needs a Christo-*poiēsis, as an ethical modality* to turn towards justice and incarnation amongst the least of the brothers and sisters: the victim-in-person, with the historical victims as the occasion.

A trans-fictional praxis that recognizes the political necessity, but likewise the insufficiency of determining. A trans-fictional praxis that recognizes the gift and the *Gift* of the *pharmakon* and therefore can enter the trans-space between metaphysical worlds, between political worlds, between political ideologies. This trans-fictional praxis is *not* a new meta-narrative of let us all be friends as our political differences are only different fictions, and therefore these differences can be put aside and we can all work together towards peace and harmony. No, trans-fictional praxis is agonistic, but not antagonistic, as it is not a battle-to-the-death of the gods. But it is more than Mouffe's agonistic approach, as this agonistic trans-fictional praxis could easily end in relativism; and is it only the differences that are the motivator for agonism? What would be the steam that drives critique as Latour (2004) asked? The different metaphysical systems argue with each other, taking the power imbalances into consideration, taking the social-economic and educational differences into consideration. However, besides arguing about whose determination is best, what would drive discernment between the worlds? What would inspire discernment, where would the steam of deconstruction come from?

In the previous chapter, the steam for discernment would come from the victims of each of these metaphysical worlds. Each world is created around a holy of holies, and yes, each holy of holies has its unclean and unfit that are left to beg on the steps of the temple, and those who do not even appear in the light (radiance-radar) of the temple: the invisible ones. The victims, as argued in the previous chapter, are "the *ultimata* or the *eschata* from which we are able less to judge the world than to transform it, which has only a generic sense" (Laruelle 2015b:113). The steam for critical engagement (discernment) with the metaphysical systems is not a super determination, as if somebody has a god's eye view of the Real, but it is a stance with the victims of each of these worlds carried out by the various metaphysical systems, yet without making these victims of the worlds the new determination or the new truth, and therefore a stance with the generic victim or victim-in-person, whilst standing with the various "actual" victims, as the actual victims are the occasion for discernment as insurrection: an exposure of the fictional nature of the various philo-fictions with their principles of self-sufficiency or principle of self-justification. Each metaphysical world excludes and marginalizes the actual victims of that particular metaphysical system, and it is that particular victim that is the site of discernment of that system, as they carry the burden of that system, they carry the weight of that system, and therefore they expose the "truth" of that system, i.e. that it is a deformation (an illusion, a fiction). Yet, the danger is to transform these actual victims into a victimology or a victimodicy, and therefore the ethical modality of the stance or the steam or pathos of the stance comes not from the actual victim, but victim-in-person, and the actual victim is the occasion for the insurrection, but never a new truth.

In following Laruelle, the victim-in-person is interpreted as the generic ethical modality of Man-in-person. The steam for discernment comes from the victim-in-person (that is the generic victim) and the actual historical victim becomes the occasion for discernment.

It is the victim-in-person that disrupts and insurrects *each* metaphysical system and no system is above this insurrection as resurrection of Man-in-person or the Son of Man. It is for this reason that trans-fictional praxis needs a Christ-*poiēsis* as its ethical modality or its steam for critical engagement in the agonistic interaction.

It is through a Christ-*poiēsis*, as an *imitatio-Christi* approach, that the agonistic interaction is not just a respectful democratic conversation between differences, but is insurrectional, as it is a stance that is in accordance with the victim-in-person. It does not engage in a battle of the gods, a political debate, but insurrects the various political worlds in accordance with the victims-in-person, without thereby creating a victimology or a victimodicy.

Can such a praxis create (bind-into-community), or would such a praxis be an in-operative community (Nancy 1991) or even an anti-community or a continuously reforming community as it is an insurrectional community? The reformation interpretation of the church as continuously reforming, in the sense of *ecclesia reformata, semper reformanda secundum verbum Dei* can again serve as a guide to understanding a possible community of such praxis.

The church as the risen body of Christ is interpreted as body that is called by the insistent and insurrectional Call of Christ-in-person (Christ-in-person understood as Christ without any Christology). A church needs to consciously and continuously reform, as it knows that each new form is a deformation – a church, community, movement, continuously and consciously responding to the Call alone (Christ-in-person), through grace alone (not through any human work, thinking, philosophy or theology) and in faith alone (an insufficient, but necessary faith). In the book, *Church emerging from the cracks* (Meylahn 2012), I tried to develop such a praxis, with the five steps of a dance-movement as a continuously reforming community, reforming rather than deforming in response and in responsibility to the Call of Christ-in-person.

In the above paragraphs, the praxis was explored in conversation with being a community of those who take a particular stance with the victims-in-person by standing with the actual victims of the various worlds.

What can accompany, inspire such a praxis? The church is called into responsibility by the Word, needing to be mindful not to transform the Word into a determined Text. Can the Bible be read as a language of faith, as a liturgy of faith, without it being transformed into a determined Text of belief?

The Bible as agonistic book or a book in its multiple voices called forth (inspired) by the Call

The Bible as agonistic book or a book in its multiple voices *called forth* (inspired) by the Call and thus maybe a book in accordance with the [Call]: a language of faith rather than a Text of determined belief.

The Bible as a book, or rather as the Texts of the church, could be interpreted as an agonistic book, as it is made up of plurality of books, a whole library of books that often contradict each other, for example the priestly tradition versus the prophetic tradition. Yet, these different voices are not enemies that stand antagonistically against each other in open conflict or war, but as Mouffe argues (2013:7) with regards to her concept of agonism, as adversaries struggling with each other. In their struggle transforming the book into literature. March-Alain Ouaknin (1995), a French rabbi and philosopher, wrote a book, *The Burnt Book: Reading the Talmud*, in which he argues that the text should be 'elusive, impregnable, and should never take on the form of an idol' (Ouaknin 1995:64). The biblical text should never be read as a determining Text of clearly defined belief, but as a determined text of faithful response.

He continues and argues that the Cabalist explains that the Text, the Torah and God are one and 'in refusing to lay one's hand on the Text, one also refuses to lay one's hand on divinity (Ouaknin 1995:64). Henri Atlan calls this the atheism of writing[1] (Ouaknin 1995:64–65): the atheism of writing in contrast to the theism of the Text, the atheism of literature in contrast to the theism of Dogma. The Bible with its multi-agonistic voices always again becomes literature rather than *the* Book or *the* Text, and thus becomes cinders as Derrida would say. In that sense one could argue that it is a book that is inspired by the [Call]. The Bible is a compilation of different books written in different contexts and at different times, yet as a book it incorporates these conflicting differences. One could argue that each of the books and genres is a different response to the [Call]. I would not even dare to say same [Call], as thereby I would be determining it as being the Same. Is this a possible way to interpret the divine inspiration as inspired by the [Call], a text which would be determined by the [Call] in the last instance, without determining the [Call] in return? That the plurality of agonistic books is according to the [Call], with the different books being different clones that are adversarial toward each other, creating an agonistic library, or a library that constantly deconstructs itself as different voices and new voices keep emerging? In that sense, it would be a book (library of books) that when read together prevents monuments, but keeps each of the books as signs and memories rather than monuments, and therefore it remains literature, remains *poïesis* and not idol or Truth. It remains a language of faith, rather than a Text of belief. Ouaknin challenges the classical historical approach (1995:57–58), but likewise challenges the existential or situational approach (1995:58–59) and suggests the "caress" (1995:62–64). This idea of the caress he takes from Levinas (1969[2]). The caress is a form of interpretation that realises that no interpretation ever really bites into the text (Ouaknin 1995:62). The text, just like the [Call] and just like the Real remains foreclosed; it cannot ever be fully and conclusively determined and yet it determines in the last instance every text and likewise every interpretation of the text. The text as such can never be attained, it can only be caressed. 'It [the text] reveals itself only to withdraw immediately. The text is both "visible and invisible" at the same time; ambiguous, its meaning twinkles, it remains an enigma' (Ouaknin 1995:63).

---

[1]   The primary preoccupation of the biblical teaching is not the existence of God, theism as contrasted with atheism, but the fight against idolatry. In all theism there is the danger of idolatry. All theism is idolatry, since expression signifies it, thereby freezing it; except it, somehow, its discourse refutes itself and so becomes atheistic. In other words, the paradoxes of language and its meaning are such that they only discourse possible about God which is not idolatrous is an atheistic discourse. Or: in any discourse the only God that is not an idol is the God who is not God (Henri Atlan quoted in Ouaknin 1995:65).

[2]   The caress consists in seizing upon nothing in soliciting what unceaselessly escapes its form toward a future never future enough, in soliciting what slips away as though it were not yet (Levinas 1969:257–258).

In that sense the text, any text, is like the Real, like the [Call], which has been determined as God by some, as Flesh or Life by Henry or the Multiple by Badiou. All these different determinations are real in the last instance, but the [Call] remains foreclosed to thought.

Such a book, if it's different books are read together, can only call agonistic communities into being, ecumenical communities, intercultural communities as different communities; or individuals find resonance in different books of the Bible because of their particular primary, secondary and tertiary retentions and protentions. The Bible as a whole brings the different groups together in agonistic tension, yet united as people of the book. A book that, because of its nature, remains a book (literature) and does not become *the* Book. Each of the books calling a community into being, but together calling a plurality of communities together in agonistic and yet *ecumenical* struggle. What is said about the different books of the Bible could also be said about the different religious or sacred texts and thus offer a way of engaging in inter-religious conversations as agonistic conversations and yet ecumenical.

Could the Bible, if read in this way, create adversarial communities, thereby protecting each other from idolatry? To such an agonistic approach to reading the Bible (as library of adversarial books), a Christ-*poiēsis* approach could add an ethical modality to the reading. A Christ-*poiēsis* approach understood as an imitation of Christ, and thereby an incarnation amongst the least of the brothers and sisters, with a bias for the unheard voices, the marginalised voices, the suppressed voices in the reading of these books, which would deconstruct any singular reading as *the* reading.

Non-colonial conversations seeking preferred worlds

Is the task of journeying with individuals, irrespective if one calls it therapy, pastoral counselling or spiritual mentoring, to liberate from false consciousness? From the above and previous chapters such a task would be an illusion, as one cannot possibly liberate from false-consciousness, but only exchange one false-consciousness for another, exchange chains, and perhaps at best one can together seek preferred chains, seek a preferred false consciousness, but who decides which chains are preferred and preferred by whom? Firstly, they should be preferred by the client and not the preferred (normative) chains of some or other external expert. A preferred reality, carried out by a preferred metaphysical system, is not only the preferred reality of the client, but also the preferred reality of the collective the client is embodied in, that is, by all those in the sphere of influence of the client, with a particular interest in the preferred chains of the victims or marginal ones of the sphere of influence of the client. A Christ-*poiēsis* could guide such a practice of sojourning with individuals, families and/or communities with its special focus on the silenced voices of both the individual's story as well as the silenced voices of the individual and collective's embodiment, seeking to include as many bodies as possible, but with a specific focus on the silenced or marginalised bodies of the client's embodiment.

The aim in the past has been to liberate from false consciousness or to heal an individual from a flaw (something that is perceived to be deviant from an established norm, yet the norm is always established by "outside" experts). Who are the experts that establish the norms that have changed throughout history (see Foucault 2009), and what would healing or wholeness or normality mean in such a context? Meaning is created, sense is made, and therefore the meaning of healing and/or wholeness is something that is continuously created or re-created, and it depends very much on who has the power to determine the norm. In other words, what is normal, what is healthy and what it means to be healthy or whole is dependent on the meaning that is ascribed to these terms, and this meaning is always ascribed within a particular context. The meaning of these terms is thus dependent on the historical as well as the cultural-political and religious context of their creation, as health and the meaning of health has always been linked to power – for example the power of knowledge, as only certain individuals in a community have the necessary knowledge and skill to heal, and in that sense it is an industry that is linked to power and profit. The pharmaceuticals want to sell their medicine, and for them to sell, somebody will need to prescribe these drugs and others use them.

If the aim of therapy is not to heal, to guide individuals or communities towards some external view of wholeness or development, nor is it to transform them into somebody's conception of normality, then what would be the purpose of therapy, or rather what would be the aim of sojourning with individuals, families and/or communities?

Lacan was critical of the schools of psychoanalysts, who interpreted the aim of psychoanalysis to be to get the analysand to implicitly or explicitly identify with the analyst, that is, to take on the truth of the analyst.[3] The psychoanalysis that Lacan was critical of, understood psychoanalysis to be completed once the analysand accepted the truth of the analyst, internalised the analyst's diagnosis. In other words, the analyst (doctor, therapist, pastor, counsellor) is the expert who knows, and therapy is complete or has come to its conclusion only if the patient, the analysand, accepts the expert diagnosis of the expert. The expert is the one who knows what is *good* or *better* for the client (patient, analysand). The experts are the ones who know and one is, healed when one internalises their expert knowledge.

---

[3] Isn't it similarly clear that there is no other criterion of cure than the complete adoption by the subject of your measure? This is confirmed by the common admission by certain serious authors that the end of analysis is achieved when the subject identifies with the analyst's ego (Lacan 2006:425).

Whatever is interpreted as being good, better or correct (normal) carries out a community that is presented as "normal", "healthy" and/or "flourishing". What is believed-to-be-good is *believed* to have been "discovered" by scientists or experts in their respective fields. Latour would argue that this knowledge (good or truth) has been *composed*. What is believed to be good, healthy and flourishing has been composed by "rigorous" scientific research through teams of experts (each legitimised by their institutions) and their "findings" are published in reputable scientific journals (institutionalisation) and thus their truths are reified to be unquestionably confirmed. Therapy is "complete" or "successful" if the patient, analysand (client), accepts these truths (knowledge) of the experts and agrees with the expert that they are sick, not-normal and therefore in need of medication or therapy so as to return to a state of normality (health). In other words, therapy has reached its aim if the analysand, patient, not only accepts the external (expert) diagnosis about him- or herself, but has internalised this opinion (diagnosis). The same could be said with regards to development of communities. The development of a community is successful the moment the community accepts the external analysis that it is underdeveloped and needs the development programmes that are offered by the experts.

Without denying that such expert systems work, and the tremendous good work that has been done in helping and "healing" people in the past and which will probably continue to be highly effective in the future, what would be an alternative approach to sojourning with individuals, families and communities? What would be a different aim if not to transfer the knowledge of the expert, in the sense that the patient accepts the diagnosis of the expert? It is in this sense that psychoanalytical transferal has often been misunderstood, as the transference of a norm of what is good from the expert (who must know as she or he is the expert) to the patient, who then claims this diagnosis as a truth about her-or himself (internalised), that is, when the patient identifies with the diagnosis. Even in spiritual and/or religious matters, a member of the faith-community comes to the priest, pastor or religious leader (expert), spiritual mentor because they are believed to be experts in matters of religion, spirituality and/or morality. The "success" of the therapy, mentoring or "healing" or conversion depends on the member accepting the truth (knowledge) of the expert, and internalising that truth. In classic conversion language, somebody has converted when they accept the truth of the other as their own truth.

In narrative therapy, there is the notion of a not-knowing-position (Freedman & Combs 1996:45). The not-knowing-position is not that the therapist or mentor does not know anything, on the contrary they probably know a lot and they are indeed experts in their respective fields (therapy, spirituality, religion, etcetera), but taking the previous chapters into consideration – what are they experts in?

They are experts in the secondary and tertiary retentions and protentions of a particular expert community. If it is a psychoanalytic community, they have read numerous texts as well as the founding texts of the psychoanalytic tradition. If they are psychologists, they probably have been trained in some or other psychological tradition and therefore are well acquainted with the secondary and tertiary retentions of that tradition. The same could be said about the different specialists in the medical profession. Likewise, spiritual or religious mentors or leaders will have received some form of training in their respective fields and therefore know the secondary and tertiary retentions and protentions of their tradition. They are very knowledgeable, but knowledgeable only in various secondary and tertiary responses of the past and the present to the primary response of the patient or analysand or client through her or his primary and secondary retentions and protentions, which in turn was or is already a response to a Call – an insistence. Something that persistently insists because the primary retentions and protentions of the client struggle to contain, make sense or create meaning of this insistence (Call). It is clear from the above that the focus here is on making meaning and sense and not on bio-chemical actions and reactions nor on neurological functions. Yet, bio-chemical actions and reactions and/or neurological explanations are in themselves not beyond hermeneutics, as they are also responses and attempts at sense-making and meaning-creation, but in a different paradigm.

The focus is on sense-making and meaning creation, and that sense-making and meaning-creation always happens in a particular world (paradigm). It is a spiritual world or a bio-chemical world or a neurological world or a social-cultural world, and depending on the world the meaning or sense will be different. It is for this reason that there are differences in opinion, and differences in different scientific traditions. Michael White and David Epston (1990:6), in their book *Narrative Means to Therapeutic Ends*, draw up a table of analogies where they unpack these different worlds (positivist physical sciences, biological sciences and the social sciences) and each of these sciences with their different traditions or sub-disciplines. In each of these worlds the "symptoms" will be *written* differently and likewise the "medicine/pharmakon" that is offered will be different.

In a trans-fictional praxis (the approach developed in this book), it is not about offering one more answer or response to the insistent [Call] of such a tradition, but it is about seeking to understand thinking (sense-making and meaning-creation) and how this happens in contexts (worlds). A trans-fictional praxis is not part of a particular world of meaning, but exists in the trans-space amongst the various fictions (traditions). Therefore, the approach followed is not from the stance of an expert who seeks to determine the [Call], but the stance in accordance with the [Call] which is interpreted as unilaterally determining the various expert's determinations in the last instance. Such a stance cannot and does not offer any critique of the various expert opinions, but views all these different opinions as exactly the opinions that are all equally necessary, but insufficient.

For Jacques Lacan, the analyst does not give the analysand his or her expert diagnosis, but all that she or he can give to the analysand is nothing else than his or her desire.[4] For Lacan, the aim of psychoanalysis changed throughout his career as his ideas developed and towards the end he developed the idea of giving to the person one is sojourning with, nothing more and nothing less than one's desire. This idea of Lacan, in the context of this book, one could translate to mean that one can give to the person one is sojourning with nothing more and nothing less than the responsibility to the Call. To give the responsibility to the [Call], the *desire* to respond to that which calls one's thought forth, and that through thought individuates the subject. One of his final thoughts on the aim of psychoanalytic therapy was that the therapy is concluded when the analysand identifies with his/her sinthome.[5] Sinthome, which the client has created and which she or he has not received from any Other, as Lacan argued that new knowledge can only be created at the place of lack in the Other (see Verhaeghe & Declercq 2002). In the context of this book, new knowledge can be created only once the fictional nature of the different knowledges is exposed, by the lack of or by the victims of that knowledge. One could argue that the sojourn is completed when the client becomes a noetic soul, consciously co-constructing his or her *Dasein* in a preferred world – a preferred world that emerges from the shadows of the dominant worlds.

The sojourn does not offer one more *poiēsis* of the symptom and its proposed "cure", but thinks according to the [Call]. To think according to the [Call] is to see all these symptoms being determined by the [Call] in the last instance, rather than determinations of the [Call]. But as it does not offer an analysis or a diagnosis itself it cannot do away with the different (equal) diagnoses determining the Call in the different traditions and schools, but sees them as absolutely necessary, yet insufficient.

These different analogies do not need to be antagonistic, but indeed will be agonistic (Mouffe 2013) with each other.

---

4   What the analyst has to give [to the analysand], unlike the partner in the act of love, is something that even the most beautiful bride in the world cannot outmatch, that is to say, what he has. And what he has is nothing other than his desire, like that of the analysand, with the difference that it is an experienced desire (Lacan 1997:299–300).

5   The identification of the subject with the object *a* does not only replaces this Symbolic suppletion with a more stable, Real one, but has in addition creative effects: the jouissance of one's own drives creates the "Other gender". To be sure, this Other is a fiction, but it is a fiction that does not turn the subject into a dupe because he has created it by himself, based on his particular way of jouissance. Lacan calls this self-created fiction a *sinthome*: a particular signifier that knots the three registers of the Real, the Symbolic and the Imaginary into a particular sexual rapport (Verhaeghe & Declercq 2002:14–15).

It is a trans-fictional praxis, which allows cooperation or encourages cooperation between the psychiatrist, psychologist, medical doctor, social-worker as well as religious or spiritual leader or guide, but most importantly cooperation, as in co-construction of meaning, *with* the client and not *for* the client. The sojourning proposed here is to journey with a client in these trans-fictional spaces, where different experts offer their analysis (their knowledge as truth), but only the clients experiences are affected (called into responsibility) by the [Call], and it is the client who is struggling to make sense and meaning of the insistence of the [Call]. Whatever it (the insistence) is, it could be disturbing the "normal" (what is normal for the client) function of the client as inter-personal individual, or as biological individual, or as emotional or spiritual or psychological individual, or as individual in relationships, or as individual in a family or in a social context like a community or a work environment. The client asks for help in making sense and meaning of whatever it is that is disturbing him or her, and by making sense of it, integrating it into their narrative of a preferred life (normal functioning again according to *their* understanding of normal).

The insistent Call appears as disturbance because the primary and secondary retentions and protentions of the client cannot make sense of it, or it calls from the boundaries, the limits of the client's language. It is often that these primary and secondary retentions and protentions fail to make sense of the "disturbance", as they fail to integrate it into the clients' narrative of past-present-and-future, and therefore they turn to ask for help. The secondary and tertiary retentions and protentions that are generally available to the client are the dominant narratives, the colonial narratives that have been determining the meaning and sense within the community of the client.

For example, something disturbs the "normal" functioning of the biological body and the client goes to see a doctor. The doctor gives an explanation, the doctor gives a determination of that which disturbed [Call] and gives it a medical name (diagnosis) and suggests a possible procedure: medicine or therapy of some kind. The approach presented here is not to challenge this determination by the medical world, for on what grounds would one want to challenge it? One could only challenge it if one *believes* to have a better or alternative diagnosis, if one *believes* that one can better interpret and determine the disturbance; but in a trans-fictional praxis it is no longer about waging a war against the Real, but it is about thinking according to the Real. Such a praxis does not seek to offer a better determination (diagnosis). The client seeks conversational partners, as this medical determination is experienced as insufficient. Not incorrect, or false or wrong, but only insufficient, but in its insufficiency it remains absolutely necessary. It is insufficient, not because of a lack of expert knowledge on the side of the medical team, but it is insufficient because thinking is insufficient, whilst remaining absolutely necessary.

One could argue that a person, the client, is more than a biological individual. She or he is also an emotional, spiritual, psychological and social individual, and in that sense the medical diagnosis is indeed insufficient, as it only addresses the biological-chemical individual.

In that sense, a trans-disciplinary approach is required.

What is the difference between a trans-disciplinary approach and the trans-fictional praxis proposed here? Although there are numerous similarities between a trans-disciplinary approach and a trans-fictional praxis there are also important differences. The different disciplines in a trans-disciplinary approach are united in their *belief* in the necessity and correct determinations of their different knowledge systems. It is because of this belief that a trans-disciplinary approach can often become antagonistic, as expert fields overlap, for example when a social scientist makes biological claims, or a religious person makes medical claims, and then the different determinations clash. A trans-disciplinary approach, for example, could be interpreted to *believe* in a holistic approach, because it believes that there is something like an essence of what it means to be human, and this essence is made up of different parts: spiritual, emotional biological, social-cultural and economic-political. In other words, Flesh, Life calls to be interpreted, calls to be thought, and trans-disciplinary thinking responds by determining Human Flesh, Human Life as: spiritual, emotional, biological, social-cultural and economic-political. If this is what a trans-disciplinary approach *believes* then it makes sense to listen to the various disciplines in treating an individual, so as to address the whole human. Yet, this belief would be one more fiction as it offers a particular determination of what it means to be human.

This approach has its *belief* in what it *means* to be human. It is not what a human *is*, but what it *means* to be human. In other words, it is one possible interpretation of what it means to be human. It might be a very good interpretation and it might even be a very effective interpretation, but it remains one possible interpretation. Such an interpretation of a trans-disciplinary approach still essentially functions within a modern Western metaphysical system, with its *belief* that the essence of being human can be discovered through scientific research, forgetting that it is not discovering, but establishing (composing) this knowledge with the help of empirical data, laboratories, computer programmes that process the data, etcetera.

A trans-fictional Christ-*poiēsis* praxis is aware of the necessity of metaphysics, but also its insufficiency, yet an insufficiency that cannot be supplemented with any *supplement*. On the contrary, all there ever is, are supplements of supplements.

A trans-fictional praxis can therefore not only engage different modern Western disciplines, but can also engage in conversations with Eastern and African metaphysical systems or approaches, even those that have been declared by Western paradigms as being non-scientific. Yet, again, it can engage with these so-called non-scientific approaches not because it *believes* they have a better truth, or that they actually have discovered the true essence of humanity, but because it does not *believe* in any specific determination, but in the *working of this faith,* which is the faith of thinking, and the truth of this faith is repetition. The working of faith is the [Call] that calls a faithful-subject into being, who in turn calls disciples into following a new Truth. One could say that all these different metaphysical systems are the works-of-faith. The focus of a trans-fictional praxis is on the works of faith rather than the different products of this work, namely the different beliefs and belief systems: metaphysical systems.

It is the work of faith that allows these different metaphysical systems to appear, like Abraham who responded as faithful subject to the call. Thinking *is* the work of faith, as it is the faithful *response* to a [Call], yet the [Call] remains foreclosed to the *belief* of the response, even if the response remains faithful to the [Call].

As in the previous sections and chapters, a trans-fictional praxis finds itself in a trans-fictional space that is characterised not by antagonism, but agonism: agonism which takes the power relations into consideration between the different metaphysical systems, that specifically in the health industry, power and finance play such a dominant role. Yet, is agonism enough? How does one sojourn with an individual or a family or community in this agonistic trans-fictional space? An ethical modality is necessary to guide such a praxis and the proposal is a Christ-*poiēsis*.

Christ-*poiēsis* as the ethical modality in agonistic trans-fictional spaces toward non-colonial conversations.

There are always dominant metaphysical systems, who have the material and political means to legitimise and institutionalise themselves globally and thereby become reified as universal "facts". These dominant narratives are not only externalised in institutions but are in turn internalised in individuals and communities as they take these "external" universal truths to be their internalised truths. Indeed, there are numerous systems in place that promote this internalisation of external "truths", for example the media, which has become a very effective global player. Individuals and families live with internalised ideas of what is good, beautiful, normal, right and correct. They live with internalised ideas of what is health, happiness, development and flourishing and thereby their own *poiēsis* of beauty, through their local primary, secondary and tertiary retentions and protentions is supressed as they often internalise foreign conceptions (creations) of the meaning of beauty, health, happiness, development and flourishing.

This dialectical process of externalisation and internalisation is part and parcel of the creation of meaning and the construction of realities and therefore it is a necessary and unavoidable dialectic. This dialectic is bound to the communities it binds (*religare*), but if this process is exported through colonialism and global capitalism in the global village, the local communities' reality is displaced by this global externalised-internalised reality. It is not that the local reality is more real than the global media reality, as is the *belief* of various forms of nationalist or indigenous movements, but such local processes would allow more people to be actively involved in meaning and sense creation, rather than being docile bodies who just accept the meaning imposed on them from outside. Stiegler (2014:10) refers to the generalised proletariat as those who have been estranged from the fruits of their labour, but here labour (work) is understood as thinking, and thus estranged from the work of thinking, of externalising-internalising themselves. If it *is* human to partake in this dialectic of externalisation and internalisation, then vast populations are deprived of this humanity, as this process is supressed by the dominant fictions, or the colonialism of dominant fictions, although the process in itself is and always will be colonial, in the sense of it being a war on the Real.

These narratives are necessary for the creation of meaning and sense, as well as necessary for political reasons, to establish the in-common of a community. But, as this book has argued, it is also insufficient. Because of this insufficiency, the [Call] will persist. Its persistence will call new faithful-subjects into existence. The dominant metaphysical system might suppress and marginalise such subjects, but because of the insufficiency cannot silence the persistence of the [Call]. Individuals, as well as certain communities, might act in accordance with the [Call], but because they have internalised the dominant narrative, they do not interpret their action in the light of *their* primary response, but rather in the light of the secondary and exported tertiary retentions and protentions of others which they have imported and internalised. For example, communities, families, marriages and individuals might "actually" be coping or surviving, but because of the dominant interpretation they believe themselves to be failing, as they compare themselves to a norm that is foreign to their community. Such indigenous knowledges (responses) are suppressed by the dominant narratives and therefore are not recognised. To try and identify the suppressed narrative, Michael White following Jerome Bruner argues that one needs to differentiate between two landscapes: landscapes of action and landscapes of consciousness (see Freedman & Combs 1996:96). If one focusses on the action that is *actually* taking place in an individual, family or community, it might be very different from how these actions become conscious to the individual, family or community. The actions are often interpreted and/or become conscious in a foreign dominant narrative. For example, an individual might have been diagnosed with some or other condition, that according to the norm says that the individual will not be able to cope, and yet the individual is actually coping. It depends how coping is interpreted, as getting up in the morning and making tea in one world will not be recognised as coping, but in another it might be recognised and even celebrated as an achievement. In a world where a dominant fiction has convinced individuals of what it means to live a normal life, and that normal life is broadcasted via the media, then such daily actions will never be recognised, as according to this dominant external norm these daily achievements are irrelevant and therefore not recognised, they are not conscious.

The individual in her or his world might not be performing as the norm expects, but they are coping, they are getting up in the morning and making a cup of tea, and that might be coping in their world, and something unrecognised by dominant diagnosis makes that getting up possible. Likewise, with families that have been determined (labelled) as being dysfunctional families, there might be moments when the family functions, it might function differently to the norms of functional families established by the experts, but they function – how did a dysfunctional family manage to do that? Communities that have been declared doomed economically, socially or politically according to the dominant theories, and yet there is life in these communities, social-life, political-life and economic-life, there might even be flourishing in these communities, but not flourishing as interpreted by the development experts, but flourishing in a different local way. There is Life that might not be visible to the dominant narrative, but it is there and just because it does not fit the dominant theory, does not mean it does not exist. These responses under the radar of the dominant narratives, which White believes might be identified, focusses rather on the landscapes of action. There landscapes of action need to be recognised and explored as they might provide indigenous knowledge, local knowledge, and it is this knowledge that is interesting. In the context of the previous chapters, it is the knowledge of the victim (the unrecognised, marginalised, side-lined knowledge) that insurrects the dominant knowledge systems. This is a political activity, without it being necessary to be developed into an alternative ideology, and yet it still challenges the techniques that subjugate persons to a dominant ideology (White & Epston 1990:29). It is not about finding truth, but helping people individuated (externalise) locally rather than internalising foreign determinations and thereby becoming docile bodies: proletariat who are estranged from being noetic souls.

It is these local or indigenous responses that disrupt the dominant discourse, it is these responses that are decolonial because they disrupt the norm, but not because they are sufficient.[6] These responses are as insufficient as any other, but

---

[6]   I also believe that it is through the re-emergence of these low-ranking knowledges, these unqualified, even directly disqualified knowledges... and which involve what I would call a popular culture... that it is through the re-appearance of this knowledge, of these local popular knowledges, these disqualified knowledges, that criticism performs its work (Foucault 1980:82).

they create life-spaces for alternative meaning and sense beyond the power of the dominant narratives (see also White & Epston 1990:26).

The idea is not to create an antagonistic alternative knowledge, but as Foucault (1980) specifically argued, these knowledges are an insurrection against the 'institutions and against the effects of the knowledge and power that invests scientific discourse" (Foucault 1980:84). This insurrection is not opposed primarily to the "contents, methods or concepts of a science, but to the effects of the centralizing powers which are linked to the institution and functioning of an organized scientific discourse within a society such as ours' (Foucault 1980: 84).

'We can expose subjugating dominant discourses by asking about contextual influences on the problems' (Freedman & Combs 1996:68). Through a focus on the indigenous knowledges the docile bodies can become enlivened spirits (White & Epston 1990:31), they become noetic souls who individuate themselves through their own local *poiēsis* rather than the *poiēsis* imposed upon them from outside.

It is in this context that in narrative therapy the idea of externalizing conversations was developed (see White & Epston 1990:30). Externalization of the problem is a necessary counter to the internalization of the dominant narrative, the dominant metaphysics.

If one has internalized the "truth" of the dominant narrative and begins to believe this truth, one is a subjugated and docile body of that truth. If the problem is externalized, one can begin to see the local knowledges, or the landscapes of actions: the local responses to the [Call]. This could also be stated differently: if one knows that these imposing, imperial and colonizing truths are fictions, are understood as externalisations, understood and interpreted as ex-*text*-ualisation, then a space for alternative textualisation becomes possible.

In the process of journeying with the victim (understood very broadly), space needs to be created for deconstructive listening.[7] Deconstructive listening and not destructive listening: it is not listening with a sledge hammer, destroying the myths, the false consciousness in the name of a *belief* in some or other truth that is buried beneath the layers of construction; but deconstructive listening that is creative, as it accepts the creation of literature (fictions) and thereby invites individuals, families and communities to re-write their stories, composing their stories with their retentions and protentions that have been side-lined or silenced by the dominant fiction. White seeks to create such spaces through deconstructive listening and deconstructive questions that externalise the problem.[8]

---

[7]   We call the special kind of listening required for accepting and understanding people's stories without reifying or intensifying the powerless, painful, and pathological aspects of those stories deconstructive listening. Through this listening, we seek to open space for aspects of people's life narratives that haven't yet been storied (Freedman & Combs 1996:46).

[8]   Consequently, I have concluded that, among other things, this practice:
      Decreases unproductive conflict between persons, including those disputes over who is respon-

Through such spaces an awareness is created of the power of the dominant fiction, and once that power has been deconstructed, a space is created for unique outcomes[9] to emerge and to be recognised.

Christ-*poiēsis* as non-colonial conversation.

A Christ-*poiēsis* as a non-colonial conversation is interpreted as following Christ, *imitatio Christi*, as an imitation of the movement of thinking and thereby facilitating a space for noetic souls rather than a generalised proletariat, who have been estranged from their externalisation (thinking). In this section I will follow the three moments of the Christ-event as moments of sojourning with individu-

---

sible for the problem;

Undermines the sense of failure that has developed for many persons in response to the continuing existence of the problem despite their attempts to resolve it;

Paves the way for persons to cooperate with each other, to unite in a struggle against the problem, and to escape its influence in their lives and relationships;

Opens up new possibilities for persons to take action to retrieve their lives and relationships from the problem and its influence;

Frees persons to take a lighter, more effective, and less stressed approach to "deadly serious" problems; and

Presents options for dialogue, rather than monologue, about the problem (White & Epston 1990:39–40).

[9] Once these techniques have been identified, unique outcomes can be located through an investigation of those occasions when the person could have subjected himself or others to these techniques but refused to do so (White & Epston 1990:31). Unique outcomes are experiences that would not be predicted by the plot of the problem-saturated narrative (Freedman and Combs 1996:67). Three kinds of unique outcomes White (1990:56–61).

Historical Unique Outcomes

Unique outcomes can be identified through a historical review of the person's influence in relation to the problem . . . . There persons can be encouraged to recall "facts" or events that contradict the problem's effects in their lives and in their relationships.

A subcategory of these historical unique outcomes is comprised of those that occur between sessions, or those that can be framed within the context of the history of the therapy.

Current Unique Outcomes

Some unique outcomes present themselves in the course of the session. These are usually brought to the persons' attention by the therapist's curiosity about them and by her/his invitation to such persons to render them sensible.

Future Unique Outcomes

Unique outcomes can have a future location . . . These can be identified in a review of person's intentions or plans to escape the influence of the problem or through an investigation of their hopes of freeing their lives and relationships from certain problems.

Unique outcomes and Imagination

Imagination plays a very significant part in the practices of externalizing the problem, both for the therapist and for those persons who have sought therapy . . .

It is important that the therapist imagine what could be possibly be significant to the person seeking help and not be blinded by his/her own criteria of what would signify new developments in her/his life and relationships (White & Epston 1990:56–61).

als and/or families or communities. I will be unpacking a possible interpretation
of the Christ-event, without making any claims as to this being *the* interpretation
of the Christ-event. In other words, this section should not be understood as a
Christology. I am not seeking to determine Christ, but I am seeking to imitate
the three moments of the Christ event: incarnation, crucifixion and resurrection
as a metaphor for thinking thinking, as a way of thinking through Christ the abstract machine of the West. The Christ-event or Christo-fiction is a metaphor of
metaphor, or fiction of fiction, as a fiction to think thinking. I have used the three
moments of this fiction, the three moments that are part of the four Gospels' record
of Christ, to colour-in this fiction of fiction and thereby to think the thinking of
thinking, making no claims as to the nature of Christ or the nature of Truth, or
God or the Real, but if anything only on the nature of thinking and thus on the
nature of being a noetic soul.

Incarnation

To enter into the local con*text*; to enter and appreciate the local (individual or
family or community) fiction. Important in entering this local con*text* is to enter
it without expert knowledge, with a not-knowing position. This not-knowing position is that one truly does not know what the [Call] is, one does not enter into
this context with knowledge of the [Call] – the Real; one does not have a determination of it, nor does one have a determination that one wants to transfer to the
client or impose on the client.

   Thinking through a particular interpretation of the Christo-fiction guides this
thinking of thinking. If one takes the Carmen Christi of Philippians 2:6–7 into
consideration, where Christ is interpreted as not seeking equality with God, but
he emptied himself of the divine, this can guide the incarnation into the context,
emptying oneself of all determinations of the [Call]. The incarnation in the Carmen Christi is not interpreted as Laclau does as an incarnation of power, where
the particular is chosen to represent the whole, but the incarnation empties itself
of any possible determination of the whole or of God. This kenosis can be interpreted as an emptying of the divine, kenosis of knowledge of the Real or the [Call].
One enters the conversation without any expert knowledge of God, the Real or the
[Call], not because of a belief in nihilism or a belief in anything particular, but in
faith – faith in the working of faith, namely that the [Call] calls thinking forth and
the thought called forth *believes* itself to be a correct response to the [Call].

   In following Christ, one enters into the context – the very context that is created (carried out) by the particular determination of the [Call]. Yet, one also is
aware of the antagonistic trans-fictional space that one is entering. That there are
dominant ideologies (incarnations-deformations of the [Call]) that are competing
to determine the subjects and community called forth. Thus, following Christ, *imitatio Christi*, one enters the context carried out by the dominant determination

of the [Call] with all the other determinations antagonistically competing with this dominant determination, but the incarnation is not into the dominant or the competing determinations of the [Call] nor is it to enter into this fray as *the* Determination of the [Call], but to enter into the antagonistic context of dominant and competing determinations in the spirit of *kenosis*, without determination, empty of determination.

The first moment of the Christ-event is the incarnation as *kenosis*: entering the context with a not-knowing position, that is, without expert knowledge, nor with the desire to determine the Real, the [Call], thus not with the desire to convert the dominant determination nor the competing determinations to Christ as *the* Determination of the [Call]. With the same mind as Christ, in imitating and participating in Christ kenosis, emptying of all determinations, and a stance in accordance to the [Call] that called all these determinations forth in the last instance.

This thinking through Christ, Christ-*poiēsis*, imitates Christ by following Christ into the context: not as the determination, nor as a competing determination, but in the *kenosis*. This *poiēsis* does not create a world, but this imitation reveals the worlds as the work of *poiēsis*.

The imitation of Christ does not end with the incarnation, but the incarnation was an incarnation into a ministry, actions and parables that Christ did and told, according to the Gospels.

Incarnation and ministry

Christ's incarnation was in a stable in Bethlehem, which already indicates that his incarnation is different from the incarnation-deformation of ideology, which is always an incarnation into power – the power to determine the [Call]. The Carmen Christi once again guides the imitation of Christ, as the incarnation of Christ, which one is called to follow (to have the same mind as Christ) is not directed by power, but powerlessness and servanthood. Born not into power of a palace and the princely life of a king to be, but born on the margin between human and animal world, on the margin, as Heidegger would say, between those who create worlds, and those who are poor of world (animals). On the margin between those who create worlds, and those who are forced to be docile bodies in worlds.

Various stories of Christ's ministry, and specifically Matthew 25, tell the story of the last judgment, or maybe it can be interpreted as the *end of judgement* based on knowledge of good and evil. It is the end of judgement in the name of good and evil, as those "judged" worthy did not *know the good* that they did, and yet they did it to the least of the brothers and sisters. The end of judgement happens when good and evil are no longer determined, but when one is determined according to one's response to the victim-in-person. Jesus' solidarity with the victims is not based on a decision (ethical or political or ideological), but *is* thinking in accordance with

Man-in-person, or is the mind (life), the *stance* of the Son of Man in its ethical modality as victim-in-person.

It is not an ethical or political decision, it is not a decision for a particular good interpreted as a bias for the poor, but it is the stance of the Son of Man, as Man-in-person. It is the stance in accordance with the [Call]. It is the stance of remaining faithful to the working of faith rather than the product of faith, which is *belief* reified into Dogma as to what is good or evil.

It is the stance in accordance with the Body without Organs, (man-in-person) who is the victim-in-person of the various determinations of man or woman as subject of some or other political, philosophical, religious or ideological world. Man-in-person is the victim-in-person of *Dasein* thrown into a world, as appearing within a particular world. The victims of a particular world, the poor that will always be with you (Mk. 14:7 & Matt. 26:11), are the occasion that reveal the insufficiency or the fictional nature of these determined worlds: political worlds, religious worlds, ideological worlds. In that sense the poor, who will always be with you, are the occasion that reveal the truth, the *ultimata* or the *eschata* of these worlds (see Laruelle 2015b:113).

No wonder that those who stand, take a stance with the victims – not in a victimology stance, but in accordance with the victim – will be in conflict with the powers that be, that incarnated *an* arbitrary equivalence as *the* Truth in the first place and thereby carried out a particular ideological (political/religious) world, just as Jesus soon found himself in conflict with the authorities, whose function was to protect their world, either the Roman political-religious world or the Jewish religious-political world of the Pharisees.

In sojourning with individuals, families or communities in the stance of *imitatio Christi*, one identifies with the poor, marginal and victims of a particular world as they are the *ultimata* and *eschata* of that world, but not in one's search for truth. Not with the desire to incarnate a particular equivalence as *the* determination, but in a Carmen Christi movement of kenosis. Not in one's search for a new determination, but in compassion affected by the [Call]. The stance in accordance with the Call, rather than seeking to determine the [Call], brings one into compassion with that which the determination excludes or subjugates, the docile bodies, the generalised proletariat. In journeying with individuals and/or families or communities, the *kenotic* stance towards the various determinations that seek to control and determine the individual, family or community brings one into solidarity with that which these determinations exclude or marginalise. A solidarity which is not an ethico-political decision, but a compassion that is born of the passion (desire) of the [Call]. This compassion is a stance in accordance with the landscapes of action and thus facilitating spaces for the individual or family or community to externalise, ex-*text*-ualise and therefore to be (*Dasein*), and no longer be docile bodies. These ex-*text*-ualisations are not truer or more real, but they are their ex-*text*-ualisations and thus the docile bodies are transformed into noetic souls.

Crucifixion and resurrection

Jesus' conflict with the religious and political leaders led to his crucifixion.

The death of the gods as well as the death of the death of God. Cinders there are. Fictions there are, literature there is, *poiēsis* there is, but a *poiēsis* guided by the imitation-Christi: Christ-*poiēsis*. Such a possible Christ-*poiēsis* is insurrectional and thus a celebration of the resurrection of noetic souls.

The aim of sojourning with individuals, families or communities is to facilitate spaces for the emergence of noetic souls, individuals that externalise rather than just internalise somebody else's externalisation.

Furthermore, it can be argued in the context of this book that externalisation always takes place in a trans-fictional space, but that the trans-fictional praxis has an ethical modality, namely Christ-*poiēsis*. A space is created where individuals and/or families or communities are aware of the different metaphysical systems that seek to determine them, and instead of just internalising these determinations of the Other, a trans-fictional praxis creates space for them to respond individually or collectively to the [Call] as they determine it and thereby individuate themselves as subjects of *their* world, creating their preferred reality rather than living in somebody else's preferred reality. Maybe two examples to illustrate.

Somebody is diagnosed with a specific illness (cancer, depression, or anything else). The medical and or psychiatric world determines the individual as ill and to a certain extent they become docile bodies of the medical world's determination and are treated in accordance with the prescribed *pharmakon*. The aim of sojourning with them in a trans-fictional Christ-*poiēsis* praxis is not to challenge the diagnosis or to offer them a better or alternative diagnosis. Christ-*poiēsis* as thinking through Christ is kenotic, it does not seek to determine the [Call], but sees all worlds as being determined by the [Call] in the last instance. Therefore, it does not offer an alternative determination, it does not enter the antagonistic trans-fictional space with another fiction, but the trans-fictional space is revealed in its truth, its fictional truth, and this already transforms the antagonistic space into a possible agonistic space.

The aim is a stance of *imitatio-Christi* where one stands with the individual, becomes flesh with the individual (incarnation) in their determined world, determined by the various determinations of the [Call]. To enter into the worlds of the individual kenotically, and therefore to view the various determinations that seek to determine the individual as a subject [object] of a particular world, by seeking to transform the individual into a docile determined body, an object of expert knowledge. Yet, this expert determination has cracks in it, as it can never fully capture the Life or the Flesh or the [Call] of the individual, family or community. Guided by the incarnation and the ministry of Christ the focus is on these cracks, on the unheard stories, on all that which escapes the dominant determination. Creating a space for these unheard stories to be externalised, to become audible and visible, the dominant narrative is questioned and crucified (deconstructed) by that which haunts it: the [Call]. Through this crucifixion of the dominant narrative the docile body can resurrect by seeking to respond to the "sick" body with "Here *I* am", as a subject rather than object of determinations. A subject that responds with its own primary and secondary protentions and retentions (its own knowledge), as well as the secondary and tertiary protentions and retentions of her or his community, as well as the retentions and protentions of all the expert communities that are circling around the individual, determining it with their expert knowledge.

The subject of Here I am, the noetic soul, the resurrected body is not judged by any expert system, but judged alone by that which it excludes, namely the victims of that newly resurrected body. It is judged only by the Flesh of the newly determined body.

A trans-fictional praxis as Christ-*poiēsis* seeks to move beyond determinations of the [Call], beyond determining what is good and right and correct and thereby be in a powerful position to judge others as well as justify oneself, but seeks faithfulness to the [Call] by entering the trans-fictional space in accordance with the [Call], which reveals all the different determinations as fiction: fiction that do not determine the [Call], but are determined by the [Call] in the last instance.

In this trans-fictional space that is carried out by a Christ-*poiēsis*, a trans-fictional praxis as Christ-*poiēsis* imitates Christ, thinks through Christ, as the Abstract machine of the West, by taking a stance with the victims-in-person, not because of a political-ethical decision of a particular interpretation of what might be politically correct or good, but in faithfulness to the stance of the [Call]. Such a praxis might create spaces for non-colonial worlds to emerge from the shadows of global villages.

To end this book, this text, by giving the word back to Fanon, 'For Europe, for ourselves and for humanity, comrades, we must make a new start, develop a new way of thinking, and endeavour to create a new man' (Fanon 2004:239).

Bibliography

Adorno, Theodor & Horkheimer, Max, 2002, *Dialectic of Enlightenment*, Standford University Press, Stanford.

Althaus, Paul, 1983, *Die Theologie Martin Luthers,* 6. Auflage' Gütersloher Verlagshaus Gerd Mohn, Gütersloh

Archibugi, Daniele, 1995, Cosmopolitan Democracy: An Agenda for a New World Order, Polity Press. Cambridge.

Arendt, Hannah, 2006, *On Revolution*, Introduction by Jonathan Schell, Penguin Books, London.

Assmann, Aleida, 1991, Kultur als Lebenswelt und Monument, in: dies.; D. Harth (Hg.), *Kultur als Lebenswelt und Monument*, Frankfurt/M., 11–25,

Avital, Ronell, 2002, *Stupidity*, University of Illinois Press, Urbana.

Badiou, Alain, 2009, *Logics of Worlds: Being and Event,* 2, translated by Alberto Toscano, Continuum, London.

Bataille, Georges, 1986, *Erotism, death & sensuality*, translated Mary Dalwood, City Lights Books, San Francisco.

Beck, Ulrich, 2006, *The Cosmopolitan Vision*, Polity Press, Cambridge.

Bennington, Geoffrey, 1993, 'Derridabase', in Geoffrey Bennington, & Jacques Derrida, *Jacques Derrida*, translated, Geoffrey Bennington, University of Chicago, Chicago

Berger, Peter, 1967, *The Sacred Canopy: Elements of a Sociological Theory of Religion.*, Doubleday, Garden City, NY.

Berger, Peter & Luckmann Thomas, 1976. *The social construction of reality*, Penguin Books, New York.

Bloch, Ernst, 1968, *Atheismus in Christentum*, Suhrkamp, Frankfurt am Main.

Biko, Steve, 2004, *I write what I like: a selection of his writings*, Picador Africa, Johannesburg.

Bons-Storm, Riet, 1989, *"Hoe gaat het met jou?" Pastoraat als komen tot verstaan*, Kok, Kampen.

Browning, D 1991. *A Fundamental Practical Theology: Descriptive and Strategic Proposals,* Fortress Press, Minneapolis.

Caputo, John, D. 1993, *Demythologizing Heidegger,* Indiana University Press, Indianapolis.

Caputo, John, D, 2006, The Weakness of God: A Theology of the Event, Indiana University Press, Indianapolis.

Caputo, John, D., 2007, *What Would Jesus Deconstruct?: The Good News of Postmodernism for the Church*, Baker Academic, Grand Rapids

Caputo, John, D., 2013, *Insistence of God: A theology of perhaps*, Indiana University Press, Bloomington, Indiana.

Chouiten, Lynda, 2011, "The Other Battle: Postcolonialism and Ressentiment" in *Journal of Postcolonial Theory and Theology*, Volume 2, Issue 3, Sopher Press

Dawkins, Richard, 2008, *The God Delusion*, A Mariner Book Houghton Mifflin Company, New York.

Deleuze, Gilles 1994, *Difference & Repetition*, translated Paul Patton, Columbia University Press, New York.

Deleuze, Gilles and Guattari Felix 2009, *Anti-Oedipus: Capitalism and Schizophrenia*, translated by Robert Hurley, Mark Seem and Helen R. Lane, Penguin Books, London.

Deleuze, Gilles and Guattari, Felix, 2011, *Thousand Plateaus: capitalism and schizophrenia*, translated by Brian Massumi, University of Minnesota Press, Minneapolis.

Derrida, Jacques, 1981, *Dissemination*, translated Barbara Johnson, University of Chicago Press, Chicago.

Derrida, Jacques, 1982, *Margins of philosophy*, translated Alan Bass, Harvester, Brighton.

Derrida, Jacques, 1994, *Specters of Marx: The state of the debt, the work of mourning and the new international*, translated by Peggy Kamuf, Routledge Classics, New York.

Derrida, Jacques, 1995, 'Sauf le nom', in J. Derrida & T. Dutoit (ed.), *On the name,* transl. D. Wood, J. J. Leavey & I. McLeod, pp. 35–88, Stanford University Press, Stanford.

Derrida, Jacques, 1997, *Of grammatology*, transl. G.C. Spivak, John Hopkins Press, Baltimore

Derrida, Jacques & Caputo, John, D., 1997, *Deconstruction in a nutshell: a conversation with Jacques Derrida*, edited with commentary John, D. Caputo, Fordham University Press, New York.

Derrida, Jacques, 1998, *Monolingualism of the Other, or the prosthesis of origin*, translated Patrick Mensah, Stanford University Press, Stanford.

Derrida, Jacques, 2005. *The Politics of Friendship*, translated by George Collins, London, Verso.

Derrida, Jacques, 2007, 'A Certain Impossible Possibility of Saying the Event', translated Gila Walker, in W. J. T. Mitchell and Arnold I. Davidson (eds), *The Late Derrida*, University of Chicago Press, Chicago.

Derrida, Jacques, 2008, *The animal that therefore I am*, edited by Marie-Louise Mallet, translated David Wills, Fordham University Press, New York.

Derrida, Jacques, 2008b, 'Hospitality' in *Acts of Religion*, London, Routledge, p. 356–420

Derrida, Jacques, 2009, *The Beast & the Sovereign, Volume 1*, transl. G. Bennington, University of Chicago Press, Chicago.

Derrida, Jacques, 2014, *Cinders*, translated Ned Lukacher, University of Minnesota Press, Minneapolis.

Dussel, Enrique., 1985, *Philosophy of Liberation*, translated Aquilina Martinez and Christine Morkovsky, Wipf & Stock Publishers, Eugene, Oregon.

Dussel, Enrique, 2003, *Beyond Philosophy: Ethics, History, Marxism, and Liberation Theology*, edited by Eduardo Mendieta, Rowman & Littlefield Publishers, Inc., New York.

Dussel, Enrique, 2012, "Transmodernity and Interculturality: An Interpretation from the Perspective of Philosophy of Liberation, in Transmodernity: *Journal of Peripheral Cultural Production of the Luso-Hispanic World*, 1 (13), p27–59.

Dussel, Enrique, D., 2013, *Ethics of Liberation: In the Age of Globalisation and Exclusion*, translated by Eduardo Mendieta, Camilo Pérez Bustillo, Yolanda Angulo, and Nelson Maldonado-Torres, Duke University Press, London.

Failing, Wolf-Eckart & Heimbrock, Hans-Günther, 1998, *Gelebte Religion Wahrnehmen. Lebenswelt – Alltagskultur- Religionspraxis*, Kohlhammer, Stuttgart.

Fanon, Frantz, 1967, *Black Skin/White Masks*, Grove Press, New York.

Fanon, Frantz, 2004, *The Wretched of the Earth*, A new translation from the French by Richard Philcox, Grove Press, New York.

Foucault, Michel, 1965, *Madness and civilization: a History of insanity in the age of reason*, Random House, New York.

Foucault, Michel, 1973, *The birth of the clinic: an archeology of medical perception*, Tavistock, London.

Foucault, Michel, 1979, *Discipline and punish: the birth of the prison*, Peregrine Books, Middlesex.

Foucault, Michel. 1980, *Power/Knowledge: Selected interviews and other writings*, Pantheon Books, New York.

Foucault, Michel 1982, The subject of power, In H. Dreyfus & P. Rabinow, (Eds), *Michael Foucault: Beyond structuralism and hermeneutics*, Chicago University Press, Chicago.

Foucault, Michel, 1984, Nietzsche, genealogy, history, in P. Rabinow (Ed), *The Foucault reader*, Pantheon, New York.

Foucault, Michel, 2009, *History of Madness*, edited by Jean Khalfa and translated by Jonathan Murphy and Jean Khalfa, Routledge, London.

Freedman, Jull & Combs Gene, 1996, *Narrative Therapy: The social construction of preferred realities*, W.W. Norton, New York.

Ganzevoort, Ruard, 2009, *Forks in the Road when tracing the sacred: practical theology as hermeneutics of lived religion*, Presidential address to the ninth conference of the IAPT in Chicago 2009, accessed from www.ruardganzevoort.nl on 20 May 2013.

Ganzevoort, Ruard, 2013, *Spelen met heilig vuur. Waarom de theologie haar claim op de waarheid moet opgeven*, Ten Have, Utrecht.

Gaztambide-Ferández, Rubén 2014, 'Decolonial options and artistic/aestheSic entanglements: An interview with Walter Mignolo, in *Decolonization: Indigeneity, Education & Society*, Vol. 3.No.1, pp. 196–212.

Geertz, Clifford, 1993, Religion as a cultural system. In *The interpretation of cultures: selected essays, Geertz, Clifford*, Fontana Press, Oxford, pp. 87–125.

Gerkin, Charles, V., 1991, *Prophetic Pastoral Practice: A Christian Vision of Life Together*, Abingdon Press, Nashville.

Gerkin, Charles, V., 1997, *An Introduction to Pastoral Care*, Abingdon Pres, Nashville.

Gräb, Wilhelm, 2000., *Lebensgeschichten – Lebensentwürfe – Sinndeutungen. Eine Praktische Theologie gelebter Religion*, 2. Aufl. Gütersloher Verlagshaus, Gütersloh.

Gräb, Wilhelm, 2002, *Sinn fürs Unendliche: Religion in der Mediengesellschaft*, Kaiser, Gütersloh.

Gräb, Wilhelm, 2005, Practical Theology as Theology of Religion: Schleiermacher's understanding of Practical Theology as a discipline, *International Journal of Practical Theology, 9*, pp181–196

Gräb, Wilhelm., 2012, Practical Theology as a religious and cultural hermeneutics of Christian practice: an enthusiastic support of Bonnie J. Miller-McLemore's corrections of the five misunderstandings of Practical Theology based on Schleiermacher's concept of theology, *International Journal of Practical Theology, 16(1)*, pp. 79–92.

Graham, Elaine L, 1996, *Transforming Practice: Pastoral Theology in an Age of Uncertainty*, Mowbray, New York.

Grözinger, A. & Pfleiderer, G., 2002 (Eds.) *Gelebte Religion als Programmbegriff Systematischer und Praktischer Theologie*. TVZ, Zürich.

Habermas, Jürgen, 1998, *The Inclusion of the Other: Studies in Political Theory*, MIT Press, Cambridge, MA.

Held, David, 2010, Cosmopolitanism: Ideals and realities, Polity Press, Cambridge.

Heidegger, Martin, 1961, *Was heisst Denken?* Zweite, unveränderte Auflage, Max Niemeyer Verlag, Tübingen.

Heidegger, Martin, 1965, *Unterwegs zur Sprache*, Dritte, unveränderte Auflage Frühjahr 1965, Verlag Günther Neske, Pfullingen.

Heidegger, Martin, 1971, *Poetry, language, thought,* transl. A. Hofstadter, Harper & Row, New York.

Heidegger, Martin, 1983, *Die Grundbegriffe der Metaphysik: Welt – Endlichkeit – Einsamkeit,* Freiburger Vorlesung Wintersemester *1999/30,* Herausgegeben von Friedrich-Wilhelm von HerrmannVittorio Klostermann, Frankfurt am Main.

Heidegger, Martin, 1984, 'Grundfragen der Philosophie: Ausgewählte "Probleme" der Logik', in *Gesamtausgabe, B. 45,* Klostermann, Frankfurt.

Heidegger, Martin, 1989, *Gesamtausgabe,* vol. 65: *Beiträge (Vom Ereignis),* Klostermann, Frankfurt am Main.

Heidegger, Martin, 1998, *Pathmarks,* edited William McNeill, Cambridge University Press, Cambridge.

Heo, Chanwook, 2015, *Stufenweg zum Heil*, Lit Verlag, Münster

Henry, Michel, 2003, *I am the Truth: Toward a Philosophy of Christianity*, translated Susan Emanuel, Stanford University Press, Stanford

Henry, Michel, 2012, *Words of Christ*, translated Christina M. Gschwandtner, William B. Eerdmans Publishing Company, Grand Rapids, Michigan.

Henry, Michel, 2015, *Incarnation: A Philosophy of Flesh*, translated Karl Hefty, Northwestern University Press, Evanston, Illinois.

Hofstadter, Alfred, 1971, 'Introduction', in M. Heidegger, *Poetry, language, thought,* pp. ix-xxii, Harper & Row, New York.

James, Craig, 1997, Georges Bataille (1897–1962): Introduction, in Ward, Graham edited, *The Postmodern God: A theological reader*, Oxford, Blackwell Publishers, pp. 3–15.

Kearney, Richard, 2010, *Anatheism: Returning to God after God*, Columbia University Press, New York.

Küster, Volker, 2005, "Interkulturelle Theologie"' in: Schreiner, Peter; Sieg, Ursula; Elsenbast, Volker (Hg.): *Handbuch Interreligiöses Lernen*, Gütersloher Verlagshaus, Gütersloh, pp. 179–191.

Lacan, Jacques, 2006, Ecrits: The First Complete Edition in English, translated by Bruce Fink, W.W. Norton, New York.

Lacan, Jacques, 1997, The Seminar of Jacques Lacan: Book VII The Ethics of Psychoanalysis 1959–1960, edited by Jacque-Alain Miller and translated by Denis Porter, W.W. Norton, New York.

Laclau, Ernesto, 2007, *On Populist Reason*, Verso, London.

Laclau, Ernesto, 2014, *The Rhetorical Foundations of Society*, Verso, London.

Laruelle, François, 1999, A Summary of Non-Philosophy, translated by Ray Brassier, in *Pli: The Warwick Journal of Philosophy* (8), University of Warwick, Warwick, p. 138–148

Laruelle, François, 2010, *Future Christ: A lesson in heresy*, translated by Anthony Paul Smith, Continuum, New York.

Laruelle, François, 2012, *From Decision to Heresy: Experiments in non-Standard Thought*, Edited Robin Mackay, Sequence Press, New York.

Laruelle, François, 2012b, *Struggle and Utopia at the end times of Philosophy*, translated by Drew S. Burk and Anthony Paul Smith, Univocal, Minneapolis.

Laruelle, François, 2013a, *Philosophy and Non-Philosophy*, translated Taylor Adkins, Univocal Publishing, Minneapolis

Laruelle, François, 2013b, *Principles of Non-Philosophy*, translated Nicola Rubczak and Anthony Paul Smith, Bloomsbury, Kindle version, London.

Laruelle, François, 2015a, *Intellectuals and Power: the Insurrection of the Victim* François Laruelle in conversation with Philippe Petit, translated by Anthony Paul Smith, Polity Press, Cambridge, UK.

Laruelle, François, 2015b, *General Theory of Victims*, translated Jessie Hock and Alex Dubilet, Polity Press, Cambridge.

Laruelle, François, 2015c, *Christo-Fiction: The Ruins of Athens and Jerusalem*, translated Robin Machay, New York, Columbia University Press

Laruelle, François, 2015d, *Introduction to Non-Marxism*, translated Anthony Paul Smith, Univocal Publishing, Minneapolis.

Latour, Bruno, 1993, *We have never been modern*, translated by Catherine Porter, Harvard University Press, Cambridge, Massachusetts.

Latour, Bruno, 2001, What is Iconoclash? Or Is there a world beyond the image wars? In *Iconoclash, Beyond the Image-Wars in Science, Religion and Art*, edited by Peter Weibel and Bruno Latour, ZKM and MIT Press, pp. 14–37.

Latour, Bruno, 2004, Why has critique run out of steam? From matter of fact to matters of concern, *Critical Inquiry* 30:2, University of Chicago, Chicago, 225–248

Latour, Bruno, 2010, 'An attempt at a "Compositionist Manifesto", *New Literary History 41:3*, p. 471–490.

Levinas, Emmanuel, 1969, *Totality and infinity: An essay on exteriority*, translated Alphonso Lingis, Duquesne University Press, Pittsburgh.

Levinas, Emmanuel, 1981, *Otherwise than being: Or beyond essence*, transl. Alphonso Lingis, Martinus Nijhoff, The Hague.

Livingston, Paul, 2003, 'Thinking and Being: Heidegger and Wittgenstein on machination and lived-experience', *Inquiry* (46), 324–345.

MacIntyre, Alasdair, 1984, *After Virtue: A study in moral theory*, University of Notre Dame Press, Notre Dame.

Meylahn, Johann-Albrecht, 2010a, *The Church in the Postmodern Global Village: Towards Pastoral Redemptive Communities Volume One*. Lambert Academic Publishing, Saarbrücken Germany

Meylahn, Johann-Albrecht, 2010b, *The Church in the Postmodern Global Village: Towards Pastoral Redemptive Communities Volume Two*. Lambert Academic Publishing, Saarbrücken Germany

Meylahn, Johann-Albrecht, 2010c, Holistic Redemptive Pastoral Ministry in the Fragmented Transit Hall of Existence, *HTS Teologiese Studies/ Theological Studies* 66 (1), Art. #426, 9 pages. DOI: 10.4102/hts.v66i1.426

Meylahn, Johann-Albrecht., 2012, *Church emerging from the cracks: a church in, but not of the world*, SunMedia Press, Bloemfontein.

Meylahn, Johann-Albrecht, 2013, The Limits and Possibilities of Postmetaphysical God-talk: A conversation between Heidegger, Levinas and Derrida, *Studies in Philosophical Theology 52*, Peeters, Leuven.

Meylahn, Johann-Albrecht, 2014a, 'Imagining the beauty and hope of a colourful phoenix rising from the ashes of Marikana and service delivery protests: A postfoundational practical theological calling', *HTS Teologiese Studies/ Theological Studies* 70(1), Art. #2616, 6 pages. http://dx.doi.org/10.4102/hts.v70i1.2616

Meylahn, Johann-Albrecht., 2014b, Imitatio Christi and the Holy Folly of Divine Violence: The church as ultimate Criminal, *Acta Theologica 2014: 34(2)*

Meylahn, Johann-Albrecht, 2014c, 'No title, no name, nothing, maybe waste', *HTS Teologiese Studies/Theological Studies* 70(2), Art. #2647, 9 pages. http://dx.doi.org/10.4102/hts.v70i2.2647

Meylahn, Johann-Albrecht, 2016, 'Non-philosophical Christ-poetics beyond the mystical turn in conversation with continental philosophy of religion', *HTS Teologiese Studies/Theological Studies* 72(3), a3542. http://dx.doi.org/10.4102/hts.v72i3.3542

Meylahn, Johann-Albrecht, 2016b, An ethos of deconstruction in multi-cultural and multi-religious contexts, *Religion & Theology Volume 23 (3–4)*, p. 368–385.

Meylahn, Johann-Albrecht, 2017a, 'Fictional metaphysics of fiction: Metaphysics and imagination in the humanities', *HTS Teologiese Studies/Theological Studies* 73(3), 4699. https://doi.org/10.4102/hts.v73i3.4699

Meylahn, Johann-Albrecht, 2017b, 'The universal imperial power of the Christian Text and yet the vulnerability of its message', *HTS Teologiese Studies/ Theological Studies* 73(4), a3857. https://doi.org/10.4102/hts.v73i4.3857

Meylahn, Johann-Albrecht, 2017c, Response to Richard Kearney's *Anatheism*: Anatheism and Holy folly, paper presented at the conference *The Philosophy of Richard Kearney* at the University of Pretoria 13 May 2017. To be published in 2018.

Meylahn, Johann-Albrecht, 2017d, 'Theologia and the Ideologica of Language: The calling of a theology and religion faculty in a time of populism', *HTS Teologiese Studies/ Theological Studies* 73(4), a4717. https://doi.org/10.4102/hts.v73i4.4717

Meylahn, Johann-Albrecht, 2017e, 'Practicing Ubuntu beyond, against or with Christian texts' in *Practicing Ubuntu: Practical Theological Perspectives on Injustice, Personhood and Human Dignity*, Edited Jaco Dreyer, Yolanda Dreyer, Edward Foley, Malan Nel, Lit Verlag, Zürich, pp. 123–134.

Mignolo, Walter, D., 2009, Epistemic Disobedience, Independent Thought and De-Colonial Freedom, *Theory, Culture & Society*, SAGE, Los Angeles, London, New Delhi, and Singapore, Vol. 26(7–8): 1–23 DOI: 10.1177/0263276409349275

Mignolo, Walter, D., 2011, Cosmopolitan Localism: A Decolonial Shifting of the Kantian's Legacies, *Localities Vol. 1*, pp. 11–45

Mouffe, Chantal, 2013, *Agonistics: Thinking the world politically*, Verso, London.

Nancy, Jean-Luc 1991, *The Inoperative Community*, Edited by Peter Connor, University of Minnesota Press, London.

Nancy, Jean-Luc, 2002, *Hegel: The Restlessness of the Negative*, translated by Jason Smith and Steven Miller, University of Minnesota Press, Minneapolis.

Nancy, Jean-Luc, 2008, *Dis-Enclosure: The deconstruction of Christianity*, trans. Bettina Bergo, Gabriel Malenfant, and Michael B. Smith, Fordham University Press, New York

Nancy, Jean-Luc, 2013, *Adoration: The deconstruction of Christianity II*, trans. John McKeane, Fordham University Press, New York

Nietzsche, Friedrich Wilhelm, 2000, *Also sprach Zarathustra*, e-book, Projekt Gutenberg, viewed from http://www.gutenberg.org/cache/epub/7205/pg7205.html

Ó Maoilearca, John, 2015, *All Thoughts are Equal: Laruelle and Nonhuman Philosophy*, University of Minnesota Press, Minneapolis.

Osmer, Richard, 2008, *Practical theology: An introduction*, William B. Eerdmans Publishing, Grand Rapids.

Ouaknin, Marc-Alain, 1995, *The burnt book: reading the Talmud*, translated by Llewellyn Brown, Princeton University Press, Princeton.

Ricoeur, Paul, 1984, *Time and Narrative,* vol. 1, transl. K. McLaughlin & D. Pellauer, University of Chicago Press, Chicago.

Rollins, Peter, 2006, *How (not) to speak of God*, Brewster, Paraclete Press, Massachusetts.

Root, Andrew, 2014, *Christopraxis: A Practical Theology of the Cross*, Fortress Press, Minneapolis

Rumscheidt, Barbara, 1998, *No Room for Grace. Pastoral Theology and Dehumanization in the Global Economy*, William B. Eerdmans Publishing Company, Cambridge, UK.

Schad, John, 1993, '"Hostage of the Word": Poststructuralism's Gospel intertext', in *Religion & Literatures* 25(3), 1–16.

Schleiermacher, Friedrich, 2001, *Über die Religion: Reden an die Gebildeten unter ihren Verächtern*, 1799, Herausgegeben von Günter Meckenstock, Walter De Gruyter, Berlin.

Spivak, Gayatri Chakravorty, 2010, Can the subaltern speak?, in *Can the subaltern speak?: Reflections on the history of an idea*, edited Rosalind Morris, Columbia University Press, New York, p. 66–111.

Stiegler, Bernard 2014, *Symbolic Misery: Volume 1: The Hyperindustrial Epoch*, translated by Barnaby Norman, Polity Press, Cambridge.

Stiegler, Bernard., 2015a, *Symbolic Misery, Volume 2: The Katastrophé of the sensible*, Polity, Cambridge.

Stiegler, Bernard, 2015b. *States of Shock: Stupidity and knowledge in the 21ˢᵗCentury*, Translated by Daniel Ross, Polity, Cambridge.

Stoker, Wessel, 2000, Are Human Beings Religious by Nature?, *Bijdragen, 61:1*, 51–75, DOI: 10.1080/00062278.2000.10739746

Taylor, Mark, 2007, *After God*, University of Chicago Press, Chicago.

Van Huyssteen, Wentzel, 2006, *Alone in the World? Human Uniqueness in Science and Theology*, Eerdmans, Grand Rapids…

Verhaeghe, Paul & Declercq, Frédéric, 2002, Lacan's analytical goal: "Le Sinthome" or the feminine way. In: L.Thurston (ed.), *Essays on the final Lacan. Re-inventing the symptom*, New York, The Other Press, pp. 59–83.

Virno, Paolo, 2004, *A Grammar of the Multitude*, Semiotex(e), Los Angeles.

White, Michael & Epston, David, 1990, *Narrative Means to Therapeutic Ends*, W.W. Norton & Company, London.

White, Michael, 2011, *Narrative Practice: Continuing the Conversation*, W.W. Norton & Company, London.

Wilson, Jonathan R. 1997, *Living Faithfully in a Fragmented World Lessons for the Church from MacIntyre's After Virtue*, Trinity Press International, Harrisburg, Pennsylvania

Žižek, Slavoj, 2008, *The Sublime object of ideology*, Verso, London.

Žižek, Slavoj, 2009, 'Dialectical Clarity versus the Misty Conceit of Paradox', in C. Davis (ed.), *The monstrosity of Christ: Paradox or dialectic?*, The MIT Press, Cambridge, MA.

Žižek, Slavoj, 2017, *The courage of hopelessness*, Penguin Random House Publishers, London.

Studien zu Religion und Kultur / Studies of Religion and Culture

hrsg. vom / edited by the Institut für Religionssoziologie der Humboldt-Universität zu Berlin

vertreten durch Prof. Dr. Wilhelm Gräb

Wilhelm Gräb; Lars Charbonnier (Eds.)
The Impact of Religion on Social Cohesion, Social Capital Formation and Social Development in Different Cultural Contexts
Entering the Field in International and Interdisciplinary Perspectives
What is the glue of society? Which forms of sociality help to overcome social needs and poverty? The role of religion and religious institutions is often expected to be relevant with regard to questions like these. But until today, these issues were seldom raised from a theological perspective. This volume wants to open the discourses on social cohesion, social capital formation and social development for the theological debate, presenting theoretical reflections and empirical research by scholars from different religion-related disciplines from the Netherlands, South Africa and Germany.
vol. 4, 2014, 176 pp., 29,90 €, pb., ISBN 978-3-643-90464-5

Kristin Merle (Hg.)
Kulturwelten
Zum Problem des Fremdverstehens in der Seelsorge
Dieser Aufsatzband zur Seelsorge nimmt die Frage von lebensweltlicher Fremdheit und kommunikativer Annäherung, wie sie in der interkulturellen und interreligiösen Seelsorge seit einiger Zeit diskutiert wird, konzeptionell in neuer Weise für die allgemeine Seelsorge auf. Das Problem des Fremdverstehens zeigt sich dabei als grundsätzliches Problem der Sozialwelt überhaupt, denn zwischenmenschliches Verstehen stellt sich als komplexer und prinzipiell unabgeschlossener Prozess dar, der auf der situativ-biografischen wie kulturell bedingten Kontextgebundenheit von Deutungsprozessen aufruht.
Bd. 3, 2013, 344 S., 34,90 €, br., ISBN 978-3-643-11629-1

Karsten Jung
Die Mythos-Falle
Religion (ver)lernen im mehrheitlich konfessionslosen Kontext
Kann der Religionsunterricht Kinder Religion verlernen lassen? Kann der Religionsunterricht Kinder sogar zu Atheisten erziehen? Karsten Jung geht diesen Fragen in einer empirischen Studie nach. Den Ausgangspunkt bilden zwei Gruppen von Grundschülern im mehrheitlich konfessionslosen Kontext Mecklenburgs. Seine Perspektive weist mit der Untersuchung einer Lerngruppe in Hessen über Ostdeutschland hinaus. Seine These: Ein mythologischer Religionsunterricht, der Gott unnötig in direkte Konkurrenz zu naturwissenschaftlichen Erkenntnissen stellt, kann bereits Grundschüler nicht mehr überzeugen.
Bd. 2, 2009, 176 S., 19,90 €, br., ISBN 978-3-643-10173-0

Wilhelm Gräb; Lars Charbonnier (Hg.)
Individualisierung – Spiritualität – Religion
Transformationsprozesse auf dem religiösen Feld in interdisziplinärer Perspektive
Individualisierung im Allgemeinen und die Individualisierung der Religion im Besonderen haben oftmals keinen guten Klang. An den negativen Konnotationen, die mit diesem zeitdiagnostischen Begriff gemeinhin verbunden werden, ist allerdings so gut wie alles falsch. Dieser erste Band der neuen Reihe „Studien zu Religion und Kultur" liefert einen Einblick und in verschiedener Hinsicht auch Überblick über die verschiedenen Phänomene, Konzepte und Zugangsweisen zum Themenfeld von „Religion und Individualität". Er vereint dazu die Perspektiven aus Psychologie, Soziologie, Religionswissenschaften und der Theologie zu einem anregenden Diskurs.
Bd. 1, 2008, 312 S., 19,90 €, br., ISBN 978-3-8258-1817-3

LIT Verlag Berlin – Münster – Wien – Zürich – London
Auslieferung Deutschland / Österreich / Schweiz: siehe Impressumsseite

Theology in the Public Square
Theologie in der Öffentlichkeit
edited by/hrsg. von Prof. Dr. Heinrich Bedford-Strohm (Universität Bamberg, Germany), Prof. Dr. James Haire (Charles Sturt University, Canberra, Australia), Prof. Dr. Helga Kuhlmann (Universität Paderborn, Germany), Prof. Dr. Rudolf von Sinner (Lutheran School of Theology, Sao Leopoldo, Brasil) und Prof. Dr. Dirkie Smit (University of Stellenbosch, South Africa)

Heinrich Bedford-Strohm; Tharcisse Gatwa; Traugott Jähnichen;, Elisée Musemakweli (Eds.)
African Christian Theologies and the Impact of the Reformation
Symposium Plass Ruanda February 18 – 23, 2016
vol. 10, 2017, 460 pp., 39,90 €, pb., ISBN 978-3-643-90820-9

Heinrich Bedford-Strohm; Pasal Bataringaya; Traugott Jähnichen (Eds.)
Reconciliation and Just Peace
Impulses of the Theology of Dietrich Bonhoeffer for the European and African Context
vol. 9, 2016, 242 pp., 29,90 €, pb., ISBN 978-3-643-90557-4

Katrin Kusmierz
Theology in Transition
Public Theologies in Post-Apartheid South Africa
vol. 8, 2016, 360 pp., 54,90 €, pb., ISBN 978-3-643-80101-2

Heinrich Bedford-Strohm
Liberation Theology for a Democratic Society
Essays in Public Theology. Collected by Michael Mädler and Andrea Wagner-Pinggéra
vol. 7, 2018, 344 pp., 39,90 €, pb., ISBN 978-3-643-90458-4

Eneida Jacobsen; Rudolf von Sinner; Roberto E. Zwetsch (Eds.)
Public Theology in Brazil
Social and Cultural Challenges
vol. 6, 2013, 160 pp., 29,90 €, pb., ISBN 978-3-643-90409-6

Wolfgang Huber
Christian Responsibility and Communicative Freedom
A challenge for the future of pluralistic societies. Collected essays, edited by Willem Fourie
vol. 5, 2012, 216 pp., 29,90 €, pb., ISBN 978-3-643-90239-9

Heinrich Bedford-Strohm; Florian Höhne; Tobias Reitmeier (Eds.)
Contextuality and Intercontextuality in Public Theology
(Proceedings from the Bamberg Conference 23. – 25. 06. 2011)
vol. 4, 2013, 368 pp., 39,90 €, pb., ISBN 978-3-643-90189-7

Willem Fourie
Communicative Freedom
Wolfgang Huber's Theological Proposal
vol. 3, 2012, 240 pp., 24,90 €, pb., ISBN 978-3-643-90145-3

Helga Kuhlmann (Hg.)
Fehlbare Vorbilder in Bibel, Christentum und Kirche
Von Engeln und Propheten bis zu Heiligen, Päpsten und Bischöfinnen
Bd. 2, 2010, 240 S., 24,90 €, br., ISBN 978-3-643-10749-7

Heinrich Bedford-Strohm; Etienne de Villiers (Eds.)
Prophetic Witness
An Appropriate Contemporary Mode of Public Discourse?
vol. 1, 2012, 200 pp., 19,90 €, pb., ISBN 978-3-643-90044-9

LIT Verlag Berlin – Münster – Wien – Zürich – London
Auslieferung Deutschland / Österreich / Schweiz: siehe Impressumsseite